EXAM✓CRAM

CompTIA®
Security+™

SYO-401
Fourth Edition

**Diane Barrett,
Kalani K. Hausman,
Martin Weiss**

800 East 96th Street, Indianapolis, Indiana 46240 USA

CompTIA® Security+™ SY0-401 Exam Cram, Fourth Edition

ISBN-13: 978-0-7897-5334-2
ISBN-10: 0-7897-5334-0

Library of Congress Control Number: 2015930248

Printed in the United States of America

3 16

Trademarks

Warning and Disclaimer

Special Sales

For information about buying this title in bulk quantities, or for special sales opportunities (which may include electronic versions; custom cover designs; and content particular to your business, training goals, marketing focus, or branding interests), please contact our corporate sales department at corpsales@pearsoned.com or (800) 382-3419.

For government sales inquiries, please contact governmentsales@pearsoned.com.

For questions about sales outside the U.S., please contact international@pearsoned.com.

Editor-in-Chief
Dave Dusthimer

Acquisitions Editor
Betsy Brown

Development Editor
Ellie Bru

Managing Editor
Sandra Schroeder

Senior Project Editor
Tonya Simpson

Copy Editor
Keith Cline

Indexer
Erika Millen

Proofreader
Megan Wade-Taxter

Technical Editor
Chris Crayton

Publishing Coordinator
Vanessa Evans

Media Producer
Lisa Matthews

Cover Designer
Alan Clements

Compositor
Studio Galou

Contents at a Glance

Contents

Part II: Compliance and Operational Security

Part III: Threats and Vulnerabilities

On the CD:

Practice Exam 2

Glossary

About the Authors

Diane Barrett is the president of NextGard Technology and a professor for Bloomsburg University. She has done contract forensic and security assessment work for several years and has authored several other security and forensic books. She is a program director for ADFSL's Conference on Digital Forensics, Security, and Law; the DFCP certification chair for the Digital Forensic Certification Board; and a volunteer for the NIST Cloud Computing Forensic Science Challenges working group. She holds many industry certifications, including CISSP, ISSMP, DFCP, and PCME, along with several from CompTIA, including Security+. Diane's education includes a Ph.D. in business administration with a specialization in information security and a master of science degree in information technology with a specialization in information security.

Kalani Kirk Hausman is an author, GRC professional, enterprise and security architect, ISO, and consultant with experience that includes medium-to large-scale globally deployed networks in governmental, higher education, healthcare, and corporate settings. Kalani's professional certifications include the CISSP, CGEIT, CRISC, CISA, CISM, GIAC-GHSC, PMP, ITIL, and CCP. He is active within the InfraGard; Information Systems Audit and Control Association (ISACA); ISSA; and High Technology Crime Investigation Association (HTCIA). Kalani is currently employed at Texas A&M University and as an adjunct professor of InfoSec at UMUC and APU/AMU. Kalani can be reached at kkhausman@hotmail.com or followed on Twitter at @kkhausman.

Martin M. Weiss has years of experience in information security, risk management, and compliance. Marty holds a bachelor of science degree in computer studies from the University of Maryland University College and an MBA from the Isenberg School of Management at the University of Massachusetts Amherst. He holds several certifications, including CISSP, CISA, and Security+. Marty has authored and co-authored more than a half dozen books on information technology. Occasionally, he molds minds as an adjunct professor with the University of Maryland University College. A Florida native, he now lives in New England somewhere between Boston and New York City.

Dedication

To my husband, Bill, for his patience and understanding.

—Diane Barrett

To Susan and our wonderful children, Jonathan and Cassandra, who remind me of the joy present in the world.

—Kalani K. Hausman

This is for you Annie! Welcome!

From the 3rd edition: Vp,lyos drvitoyu l;id rcs, vts, drvpmf rfoyopm eo;; ntsrl yir vpfr 2521202 0861704 3330307 3251403

Solution: CompTIA Security+ Exam Cram second edition will break the code (keyboard shift cipher) To my future daughter (page;line;word).

—Martin Weiss

Acknowledgments

Publishing a book takes the collaboration and teamwork of many individuals. Thanks to everyone involved in this process from Waterside Productions and Pearson Education (and thanks to those who purchase this book in their quest for certification). Betsy, thanks for keeping us all on track. To our editorial and technical reviewers, especially Chris, thank you for making sure that our work was sound and on target. Special thanks to my coauthors, Marty and Kirk.

—Diane Barrett

Thanks to my agent Carole McClendon, to Betsy Brown, Ellie Bru, and the excellent editorial staff at Pearson. Special thanks go to my coauthors Martin Weiss and Diane Barrett, whose knowledge and dedication produced this remarkable text.

—Kalani K. Hausman

Once again, thank you to the entire team that worked together to get this book updated and published. Special thanks to the work and for the support from Ellie, Betsy, Chris, Tonya, and of course Kirk and Diane. Thank you to you, the reader, for your trust and for looking to us to help you pursue your security knowledge and quest for certification. Finally, I'd like to acknowledge my incredible friends and family.

—Martin Weiss

We Want to Hear from You!

As the reader of this book, *you* are our most important critic and commentator. We value your opinion and want to know what we're doing right, what we could do better, what areas you'd like to see us publish in, and any other words of wisdom you're willing to pass our way.

We welcome your comments. You can email or write to let us know what you did or didn't like about this book—as well as what we can do to make our books better.

Please note that we cannot help you with technical problems related to the topic of this book.

When you write, please be sure to include this book's title and author as well as your name and email address. We will carefully review your comments and share them with the author and editors who worked on the book.

Email: feedback@pearsonitcertification.com

Mail: ATTN: Reader Feedback
800 East 96th Street
Indianapolis, IN 46240 USA

Reader Services

Visit our website and register this book at pearsonitcertification.com/register for convenient access to any updates, downloads, or errata that might be available for this book.

CompTIA.

It Pays to Get Certified

In a digital world, digital literacy is an essential survival skill.

Certification demonstrates that you have the knowledge and skill to solve technical or business problems in virtually any business environment. CompTIA certifications are highly-valued credentials that qualify you for jobs, increased compensation, and promotion.

LEARN > **CERTIFY** > **WORK**

IT is Everywhere	IT Knowledge and Skills Get Jobs	Job Retention	New Opportunities	High Pay-High Growth Jobs
IT is mission critical to almost all organizations and its importance is increasing.	Certifications verify your knowledge and skills that qualifies you for:	Competence is noticed and valued in organizations.	Certifications qualify you for new opportunities in your current job or when you want to change careers.	Hiring managers demand the strongest skill set.
• 79% of U.S. businesses report IT is either important or very important to the success of their company	• Jobs in the high growth IT career field • Increased compensation • Challenging assignments and promotions • 60% report that being certified is an employer or job requirement	• Increased knowledge of new or complex technologies • Enhanced productivity • More insightful problem solving • Better project management and communication skills • 47% report being certified helped improve their problem solving skills	• 31% report certification improved their career advancement opportunities	• There is a widening IT skills gap with over 300,000 jobs open • 88% report being certified enhanced their resume

Certification Helps Your Career

- **Security is one of the highest demand job categories**—growing in importance as the frequency and severity of security threats continues to be a major concern for organizations around the world.
- **Jobs for security administrators are expected to increase by 18%**—the skill set required for these types of jobs maps to the CompTIA Security+ certification.
- **Network Security Administrators**—can earn as much as $106,000 per year.
- **CompTIA Security+ is the first step**—in starting your career as a Network Security Administrator or Systems Security Administrator.
- **More than ¼ million**—individuals worldwide are CompTIA Security+ certified.
- **CompTIA Security+ is regularly used in organizations**—such as Hitachi Systems, Fuji Xerox, HP, Dell, and a variety of major U.S. government contractors.
- **Approved by the U.S. Department of Defense (DoD)**—as one of the required certification options in the DoD 8570.01-M directive, for Information Assurance Technical Level II and Management Level I job roles.

Steps to Getting Certified and Staying Certified

Review Exam Objectives	Review the Certification objectives to make sure you know what is covered in the exam.http://certification.comptia.org/examobjectives.aspx
Practice for the Exam	After you have studied for the certification, review and answer the sample questions to get an idea what type of questions might be on the exam. http://certification.comptia.org/samplequestions.aspx
Purchase an Exam Voucher	Purchase exam vouchers on the CompTIA Marketplace. www.comptiastore.com
Take the Test!	Go to the Pearson VUE website and schedule a time to take your exam. http://www.pearsonvue.com/comptia/
Stay Certified! Continuing Education	Effective January 1, 2011, new CompTIA Security+ certifications are valid for three years from the date of certification. There are a number of ways the certification can be renewed. For more information go to: http://certification.comptia.org/ce

How to obtain more information

- **Visit CompTIA online**—http://certification.comptia.org/home.aspx to learn more about getting CompTIA certified.
- **Contact CompTIA**—call 866-835-8020 and choose Option 2 or email questions@comptia.org.
- **Connect with us**—

To receive your 10% off Exam Voucher, register your product at:

www.pearsonitcertification.com/register

and follow the instructions.

Introduction

Welcome to *CompTIA Security+ SY0-401 Exam Cram*, Fourth Edition. This book aims to help you get ready to take and pass the CompTIA Security+ exam, number SY0-401.

Chapters 1–13 are designed to remind you of everything you need to know to pass the SY0-401 certification exam. The two practice exams at the end of this book should give you a reasonably accurate assessment of your knowledge, and, yes, we've provided the answers and their explanations for these practice exams. Read this book, understand the material, and you'll stand a very good chance of passing the real test.

Exam Cram books help you understand and appreciate the subjects and materials you need to know to pass CompTIA certification exams. Exam Cram books are aimed strictly at test preparation and review. They do not teach you everything you need to know about a subject. Instead, the authors streamline and highlight the pertinent information by presenting and dissecting the questions and problems they've discovered that you're likely to encounter on a CompTIA test.

We strongly recommend that you spend some time installing, configuring, and working with the latest operating systems to patch and maintain them for the best and most current security possible because the Security+ exam focuses on such activities and the knowledge and skills they can provide for you. Nothing beats hands-on experience and familiarity when it comes to understanding the questions you're likely to encounter on a certification test. Book learning is essential, but, without doubt, hands-on experience is the best teacher of all!

Taking a Certification Exam

After you prepare for your exam, you need to register with a testing center. At the time of this writing, the cost to take the Security+ exam is $293 USD for individuals ($226 for CompTIA members). CompTIA corporate members receive discounts on nonmember pricing. For more information about these discounts, a local CompTIA sales representative can provide answers to any questions you might have. If you don't pass, you can take the exam again for the same cost as the first attempt, for each attempt until you pass. In the United States and Canada, tests are administered by Prometric or VUE.

After you sign up for a test, you are told when and where the test is scheduled. You should arrive at least 15 minutes early. To be admitted into the testing room, you must supply two forms of identification, one of which must be a photo ID.

About This Book

We've structured the topics in this book to build on one another. Therefore, some topics in later chapters make the most sense after you've read earlier chapters. That's why we suggest that you read this book from front to back for your initial test preparation. If you need to brush up on a topic or if you have to bone up for a second try, you can use the index, table of contents, or Table I-1 to go straight to the topics and questions that you need to study. Beyond helping you prepare for the test, we think you'll find this book useful as a tightly focused reference to some of the most important aspects of the Security+ certification.

Chapter Format and Conventions

Every Exam Cram chapter follows a standard structure and contains graphical clues about important information. The structure of each chapter includes the following:

▶ **Opening objectives list:** This defines the official CompTIA Security+ exam objectives covered in the chapter.

▶ **Cram Saver questions:** Each major section begins with a Cram Saver to help you determine your current level of knowledge of the topics in that section.

▶ **Topical coverage:** The heart of the chapter. Explains the topics from a hands-on and a theory-based standpoint. This includes in-depth descriptions geared to build your knowledge so that you can pass the exam.

▶ **Exam Alerts:** These are interspersed throughout the book. They include important information on test topics. Watch out for them!

> **ExamAlert**
>
> This is what an Exam Alert looks like. Normally, an alert stresses concepts, terms, hardware, software, or activities that are likely to relate to one or more certification test questions.

▶ **Cram Quiz questions:** At the end of each topic is a quiz. The quizzes, and their explanations, are meant to gauge your knowledge of the subjects. If the answers to the questions don't come readily to you, consider reviewing the section.

Additional Elements

Beyond the chapters there are a few more elements:

▶ **Practice exams:** There are two practice exams. They are printed in the book and included with the Pearson IT Certification Practice Test Engine on the CD.

▶ **Cram Sheet:** The tear-out Cram Sheet is located right in the beginning of the book. This is designed to jam some of the most important facts you need to know for the exam into one small sheet, allowing for easy memorization.

▶ **Glossary:** Definitions of key CompTIA Security+ exam terms.

Exam Objectives

Table I-1 lists the skills measured by the SY0-401 exam and the chapter in which the objective is discussed. Some objectives are covered in other chapters, too.

TABLE I.1 **CompTIA SY0-401 Exam Objectives**

Exam Objective	Chapter
Domain 1: Network Security	
Implement security configuration parameters on network devices and other technologies	1
Given a scenario, use secure network administration principles	1
Explain network design elements and components	1

Exam Objective	Chapter
Domain 6: Cryptography	
Given a scenario, utilize general cryptography concepts	12
Given a scenario, use appropriate cryptographic methods	12
Given a scenario, use appropriate PKI, certificate management and associated components	13

Pearson IT Certification Practice Test Engine and Questions on the CD

The CD in the back of the book includes the Pearson IT Certification Practice Test engine—software that displays and grades a set of exam-realistic multiple-choice questions. Using the Pearson IT Certification Practice Test engine, you can either study by going through the questions in Study Mode or take a simulated exam that mimics real exam conditions.

The installation process requires two major steps: installing the software and then activating the exam. The CD in the back of this book has a recent copy of the Pearson IT Certification Practice Test engine. The practice exam—the database of exam questions—is not on the CD.

> **Note**
>
> The cardboard CD case in the back of this book includes the CD and a piece of paper. The paper lists the activation code for the practice exam associated with this book. Do not lose the activation code. On the opposite side of the paper from the activation code is a unique, one-time-use coupon code for the purchase of the Premium Edition eBook and Practice Test.

Install the Software from the CD

The Pearson IT Certification Practice Test is a Windows-only desktop application. You can run it on a Mac using a Windows Virtual Machine, but it was built specifically for the PC platform. The minimum system requirements are the following:

- ▶ Windows XP (SP3), Windows Vista (SP2), or Windows 7
- ▶ Microsoft .NET Framework 4.0 Client
- ▶ Microsoft SQL Server Compact 4.0
- ▶ Pentium class 1GHz processor (or equivalent)

▶ 512MB RAM

▶ 650MB disc space plus 50MB for each downloaded practice exam

The software installation process is routine compared to other software installation processes. If you have already installed the Pearson IT Certification Practice Test software from another Pearson product, there is no need for you to reinstall the software. Simply launch the software on your desktop and proceed to activate the practice exam from this book by using the activation code included in the CD sleeve.

The following steps outline the installation process:

1. Insert the CD into your PC.

2. The software that automatically runs is the Pearson software to access and use all CD-based features. From the main menu, click the option to **Install the Exam Engine**.

3. Respond to windows prompts as with any typical software installation process.

The installation process gives you the option to activate your exam with the activation code supplied on the paper in the CD sleeve. This process requires that you establish a Pearson website login. You need this login to activate the exam, so please do register when prompted. If you already have a Pearson website login, there is no need to register again. Just use your existing login.

Activate and Download the Practice Exam

After the exam engine is installed, you should then activate the exam associated with this book (if you did not do so during the installation process) as follows:

1. Start the Pearson IT Certification Practice Test software from the Windows Start menu or from your desktop shortcut icon.

2. To activate and download the exam associated with this book, from the My Products or Tools tab, click the **Activate** button.

3. At the next screen, enter the activation key from the paper inside the cardboard CD holder in the back of the book. Once entered, click the **Activate** button.

4. The activation process will download the practice exam. Click **Next**, and then click **Finish**.

After you've completed the activation process, the My Products tab should list your new exam. If you do not see the exam, make sure you have selected the **My Products** tab on the menu. At this point, the software and practice exam are ready to use. Simply select the exam and click the **Open Exam** button.

To update a particular exam you have already activated and downloaded, simply select the **Tools** tab and click the **Update Products** button. Updating your exams ensures you have the latest changes and updates to the exam data.

If you want to check for updates to the Pearson Cert Practice Test exam engine software, simply select the **Tools** tab and click the **Update Application** button. This ensures you are running the latest version of the software engine.

Activating Other Exams

The exam software installation process and the registration process only has to happen once. Then, for each new exam, only a few steps are required. For instance, if you buy another new Pearson IT Certification Cert Guide or Cisco Press Official Cert Guide, extract the activation code from the CD sleeve in the back of that book; you don't even need the CD at this point. From there, all you have to do is start the exam engine (if it is not still up and running) and perform steps 2–4 from the previous list.

Premium Edition

In addition to the free practice exams provided with your purchase, you can purchase one additional exam with expanded functionality directly from Pearson IT Certification. The Premium Edition eBook and Practice Test for this title contains an additional full practice exam as well as an eBook (in both PDF and ePub format). In addition, the Premium Edition title also has remediation for each question to the specific part of the eBook that relates to that question.

If you have purchased the print version of this title, you can purchase the Premium Edition at a deep discount. There is a coupon code in the CD sleeve that contains a one-time-use code as well as instructions for where you can purchase the Premium Edition.

To view the premium edition product page, go to http://www.pearsonitcertification.com/store/product.aspx?isbn=0132939592.

CHAPTER 1

Secure Network Design

This chapter covers the following official CompTIA Security+ SY0-401 exam objectives:

▶ Implement security configuration parameters on network devices and other technologies

▶ Given a scenario, use secure network administration principles

▶ Explain network design elements and components

(For more information on the official CompTIA Security+ SY0-401 exam topics, see the "About the CompTIA Security+ SY0-401 Exam" section in the Introduction.)

The easiest way to keep a computer safe is by physically isolating it from outside contact. Because of how organizations do business today, this is nearly impossible. We have a global economy, and our networks are increasingly more complex. Securing the devices on the network is imperative to protecting the environment. To secure those devices, you must know the different functions of each device and how each device is used in different network scenarios. To secure devices, you must also understand the basic security concepts of network design.

This chapter covers the design elements and components such as firewalls; virtual local-area networks (VLAN); and perimeter network boundaries that distinguish between private networks, intranets, and the Internet, but you also need to know how and when to use these components. Network compromises carry an increased threat with the spread of stealthy botnets and web-based malware. This means that an entire corporate network can be used for spam relay, phishing attacks, and launching distributed denial-of-service (DDoS) attacks. It is important to not only know how to use the proper elements in design, but also how to position and apply these tools to facilitate layered or defense-in-depth security. This chapter discusses just that.

Implement Security Configuration Parameters on Network Devices and Other Technologies

▶ **Firewalls**

▶ **Routers**

▶ **Switches**

▶ **Load balancers**

▶ **Proxies**

▶ **Web security gateways**

▶ **VPN concentrators**

▶ **NIDS and NIPS**

▶ **Protocol analyzers**

▶ **Spam filter**

▶ **UTM appliances**

▶ **Web application firewall versus network firewall**

▶ **Application-aware devices**

CramSaver

If you can correctly answer these questions before going through this section, save time by skimming the Exam Alerts in this section and then completing the Cram Quiz at the end of the section.

1. What purpose does an application-level gateway serve?

2. When an insider threat is detected and you want to implement a solution that monitors the internal network activity as well as incoming external traffic, what two types of devices could you use?

3. Explain the most effective placement of a proxy server.

Answers

1. An application-level gateway understands services and protocols. All traffic is examined to check for Open Systems Interconnection (OSI) application layer (Layer 7) protocols that are allowed. Examples of this type of traffic are File Transfer Protocol (FTP), Simple Mail Transfer Protocol (SMTP), and Hypertext Transfer Protocol (HTTP). Because the filtering is application specific, it adds overhead to the transmissions but is more secure than packet filtering.

2. Network-based intrusion-detection systems (IDS) monitor the packet flow and try to locate packets that are not allowed for one reason or another and might have gotten through the firewall. Host-based IDSs monitor communications on a host-by-host basis and try to filter malicious data. These types of IDSs are good at detecting unauthorized file modifications and user activity.

3. Proxy servers can be placed between the private network and the Internet for Internet connectivity or internally for web content caching. If the organization is using the proxy server for both Internet connectivity and web content caching, the proxy server should be placed between the internal network and the Internet, with access for users who are requesting the web content. In some proxy server designs, the proxy server is placed in parallel with IP routers. This allows for network load balancing by forwarding of all HTTP and FTP traffic through the proxy server and all other IP traffic through the router.

Before you can properly secure a network, you must understand the security function, purpose of network devices, and technologies used to secure the network. This section introduces the implementation of security configuration parameters as they apply to network devices and other technologies that are used to form the protection found on most networks.

Firewalls

A *firewall* is a component placed on computers and networks to help eliminate undesired access by the outside world. It can be composed of hardware, software, or a combination of both. A firewall is the first line of defense for the network. The primary function of a firewall is to mitigate threats by monitoring all traffic entering or leaving a network. How firewalls are configured is important, especially for large companies where a compromised firewall might spell disaster in the form of bad publicity or a lawsuit, not only for the company, but also for the companies it does business with. For smaller companies, a firewall is an excellent investment because most small companies do not have a full-time technology staff and an intrusion could easily put them out of business. All things considered, a firewall is an important part of your defense, but you should not rely on it exclusively for network protection. Figure 1.1 shows the firewall placement in a small network.

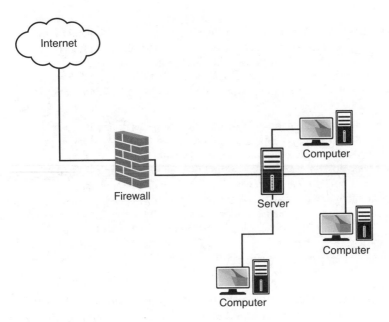

FIGURE 1.1 **A small network firewall placement**

Routers

Routers operate at the network layer of the OSI model. They are the items that receive information from a host and forward that information to its destination on the network or the Internet. Routers maintain tables that are checked each time a packet needs to be redirected from one interface to another. The tables inside the router help speed up request resolution so that packets can reach their destinations quicker. The routes may be added manually to the routing table or may be updated automatically using the following protocols:

- ▶ Routing Information Protocol (RIP/RIPv2)
- ▶ Interior Gateway Routing Protocol (IGRP)
- ▶ Enhanced Interior Gateway Routing Protocol (EIGRP)
- ▶ Open Shortest Path First (OSPF)
- ▶ Border Gateway Protocol (BGP)
- ▶ Exterior Gateway Protocol (EGP)
- ▶ Intermediate System-to-Intermediate System (IS-IS)

Although router placement is primarily determined by the need to segment different networks or subnets, routers also have some good security features. One of the best features of a router is its ability to filter packets by source address, destination address, protocol, or port. These filters are referred to as *access control lists* (ACL). Routers can also be configured to help prevent IP spoofing by using strong protocol authentication. In IP spoofing, an attacker gains unauthorized access to a network by making it appear (by faking the IP address) that traffic has come from a trusted source. Keep in mind that no matter how secure the routing protocol of choice is, if you never change the default password on the router, you have left yourself wide open to attacks.

Switches

Switches are the most common choice when it comes to connecting desktops to the wiring closet. Switches operate at the data link layer (Layer 2) of the OSI model. Their packet-forwarding decisions are based on Media Access Control (MAC) addresses. They allow LANs to be segmented, thus increasing the amount of bandwidth that goes to each device. Each segment is a separate collision domain, but all segments are in the same broadcast domain. Here are the basic functions of a switch:

▶ Filtering and forwarding frames

▶ Learning MAC addresses

▶ Preventing loops

Managed switches are configurable. You can implement sound security with your switches very similarly to configuring security on a firewall or a router. Managed switches allow control over network traffic and who has access to the network. In general, you do not want to deploy managed switches using their default configuration. Often, the default configuration does not provide the most secure network design. A design that properly segments the network can be accomplished using VLANs. Segmentation using VLANs is discussed later in this chapter. Designing the network the proper way from the start is important to ensure that the network is stable, reliable, and scalable. Physical and virtual security controls must be in place. Place switches in a physically secured area if possible. Be sure that strong authentication and password policies are in place to secure access to the operating system and configuration files.

Load Balancers

Network *load balancers* are servers configured in a cluster to provide scalability and high availability. Load balancing distributes IP traffic to multiple copies of a TCP/IP service, such as a web server, each running on a host within the cluster. This is used for enterprise-wide services, such as Internet sites with high traffic requirements, web, FTP, media streaming, and content delivery networks or hosted applications using thin-client architectures such as Windows Terminal Services or Remote Desktop Services. Network load balancing distributes the workload among multiple servers while providing a mechanism for server availability. From the client's point of view, the cluster appears to be a single server. As enterprise traffic increases, network administrators can simply plug another server into the cluster. In the event of server or application failure, a load balancer can provide automatic failover to ensure continuous availability.

Some load balancers integrate IP load balancing and network intrusion prevention into one appliance. This provides failover capabilities in case of server failure, distribution of traffic across multiple servers, and integrated protection from network intrusions, along with optimizing performance for other IP services such as Simple Mail Transfer Protocol (SMTP), Domain Name Service (DNS), Remote Authentication Dial-In User Service (RADIUS), and Trivial File Transfer Protocol (TFTP). To mitigate risks associated with failures of the load balancers themselves, you can deploy two appliances in what is called an *active/passive configuration*. In this type of configuration, all traffic is sent to the active server. The passive server is promoted to active if the active server fails or is taken down for maintenance.

Proxies

A *proxy server* operates on the same principle as a proxy-level firewall in that it is a go-between for the network and the Internet. Proxy servers are used for security, logging, and caching. When the proxy server receives a request for an Internet service, it passes through filtering requirements and checks its local cache for previously downloaded web pages. Because web pages are stored locally, response times for web pages are faster and traffic to the Internet is substantially reduced. The web cache can also be used to block content from websites that you do not want employees to access, such as pornography, social, or peer-to-peer networks. You can use this type of server to rearrange web content to work for mobile devices. It also provides better utilization of bandwidth because it stores all your results from requests for a period of time.

ExamAlert

An exposed server that provides public access to a critical service, such as a proxy, web, or email server, may be configured to isolate it from an organization's internal network and to report attack attempts to the network administrator. Such an isolated server is referred to as a *bastion host*, named for the isolated towers that were used to provide castles advanced notice of a pending assault.

Proxy servers are used for a variety of reasons, so the placement depends on the usage. You can place proxy servers between the private network and the Internet for Internet connectivity or internally for web content caching. If the organization is using the proxy server for both Internet connectivity and web content caching, you should place the proxy server between the internal network and the Internet with access for users who are requesting the web content. In some proxy server designs, the proxy server is placed in parallel with IP routers. This design allows for network load balancing by forwarding of all HTTP and FTP traffic through the proxy server and all other IP traffic through the router.

Every proxy server in your network must have at least one network interface. Proxy servers with a single network interface can provide web content caching and IP gateway services. To provide Internet connectivity, you must specify two or more network interfaces for the proxy server.

Web Security Gateways

With the advent of Web 2.0, social-networking sites, video-sharing sites, wikis, and blogs became popular. Web 2.0 enables users to interact with other users. Although this interactivity might have increased collaboration, it can cause losses in productivity, vulnerabilities to data leaks, and inherent increased security risks.

A *web security gateway* offers a single point of policy control and management for web-based content access. A web security gateway can be either software or hardware and is most often marketed as an appliance. Web security gateways can provide URL filtering, web traffic malware detection, and application control. Managed web security gateway services are another option. Gateways can offer a scalable platform that enables organizations to maintain critical uptime when an attack happens. The advantages of using a web security gateway include protection across multiple protocols for inbound and outbound web traffic, the ability to detect botnets, broad web reporting and alerting, and the ability to monitor and control web application usage by end users.

VPN Concentrators

In the world of a mobile workforce, employers require a secure method for employees to access corporate resources while on the road or working from home. One of the most common methods implemented for this type of access is a virtual private network (VPN). A *VPN concentrator* is used to allow multiple external users to access internal network resources using secure features that are built in to the device and are deployed where the requirement is for a single device to handle a very large number of VPN tunnels. Remote-access VPN connectivity is provided using either Internet Protocol Security (IPsec) or Secure Sockets Layer (SSL) for the VPN. User authentication can be via RADIUS, Kerberos, Microsoft Active Directory, RSA SDI, digital certificates, or the built-in authentication server. The function and purpose of authentication services is covered in detail in Chapter 10, "Authentication, Authorization, and Access Control."

A typical scenario is where the VPN concentrator allows users to utilize an encrypted tunnel to securely access a corporate or other network via the Internet. Another use is internally, to encrypt WLAN or wired traffic, where there is concern about protecting the security of login and password information for high-level users and sensitive information. You can implement a VPN concentrator to prevent login and password information from being captured. It also allows ACLs to be applied to remote user sessions.

VPN concentrators come in various models that you can use, for example, for the numbers of simultaneous users, amount of throughput needed, and amount of protection required. For example, Cisco VPN concentrators include components, called *Scalable Encryption Processing* (SEP) *modules*, that allow for increased capacity and throughput.

NIDS and NIPS

IDS stands for *intrusion-detection system*. Intrusion-detection systems are designed to analyze data, identify attacks, and respond to the intrusion. They differ from firewalls in that firewalls control the information that gets in and out of the network, whereas IDSs can identify unauthorized activity. IDSs are also designed to catch attacks in progress within the network, not just on the boundary between private and public networks. Intrusion detection may be managed by two basic methods: knowledge-based and behavior-based detection.

NIDS and HIDS

The two basic types of IDSs are *network-based* and *host-based*. As the names
suggest, network-based IDSs (NIDS) look at the information exchanged
between machines, and host-based IDSs (HIDS) look at information that
originates on the individual machines.

Here are some basics:

▶ NIDSs monitor the packet flow and try to locate packets that might
have gotten through the firewall and are not allowed for one reason or
another. They are best at detecting DoS attacks and unauthorized user
access.

▶ HIDSs monitor communications on a host-by-host basis and try to filter
malicious data. These types of IDSs are good at detecting unauthorized
file modifications and user activity.

> **ExamAlert**
>
> NIDSs try to locate packets not allowed on the network that the firewall missed.
> HIDSs collect and analyze data that originates on the local machine or a computer
> hosting a service. NIDSs tend to be more distributed.

You should use NIDSs and HIDSs together to ensure a truly secure
environment. IDSs can be located anywhere on the network. You can place
them internally or between firewalls. Many different types of IDSs are
available, all with different capabilities, so make sure they meet the needs of
your company before committing to using them.

NIPS

Network intrusion-prevention systems (NIPS) are sometimes considered to be an
extension of IDSs. NIPSs can be either hardware or software based, like many
other network-protection devices. Intrusion prevention differs from intrusion
detection in that it actually prevents attacks instead of only detecting the
occurrence of an attack. Intrusion-detection software is reactive—scanning for
configuration weaknesses and detecting attacks after they occur. By the time
an alert has been issued, the attack has usually occurred and has damaged the
network or desktop. NIPSs are designed to sit inline with traffic flows and
prevent attacks in real time. An inline NIPS sits between the systems that need
to be protected and the rest of the network. They proactively protect machines

against damage from attacks that signature-based technologies cannot detect because most NIPS solutions can look at application layer protocols such HTTP, FTP, and SMTP.

When implementing a NIPS, keep in mind that the sensors must be physically inline to function properly. This adds single points of failure to the network. A good way to prevent this issue is to use fail-open technology. This means that if the device fails, it does not cause a complete network outage; instead, it acts like a patch cable.

Behavior Based

Behavior-based intrusion detection methods are rooted in the premise that an intrusion can be detected by comparing the normal activity of a network to current activity. Any abnormalities from normal or expected behavior of the network are reported via an alarm. Behavior-based methods can identify attempts to exploit new or undocumented vulnerabilities, can alert to elevation or abuse of privileges, and tend to be independent of operating system-specific processes. Behavior-based methods consider intrusive any activity that does not match a learned behavior; there is a high false alarm rate. If a network is compromised prior to the learned behavior period, any malicious activity related to the compromise will not be reported.

Signature Based

Signature-based detection methods are considered knowledge based because the underlying mechanism is a database of known vulnerabilities. Signature-based methods monitor a network to find a pattern or signature match. When a match is found, an alert is generated. Vendors provide signature updates, similar to antivirus software updates, but generally signatures can be created anytime a particular behavior needs to be identified. Because pattern matching can be done quickly when the rule set is not extensive, there is very little intrusiveness or performance reduction noticed by the system or user. Signature-based methods provide lower false alarms compared to behavior-based methods because all suspect activity is in a known database. Signature-based methods only detect known signatures or patterns, so these events must be created for every suspect activity. They are more reactive because an attack must be known before it can be added to the database.

Anomaly Based

Anomaly-based detection methods are similar to behavior-based intrusion detection methods. Both are based on the concept of using a baseline for network behavior. But, a slight variation exists between the two. In anomaly-based detection methods, after the application is trained, the established profile is used on real data to detect deviations. Training an application entails inputting and defining data criteria in a database. In a behavior-based intrusion detection method, the established profile is used as a comparison to current activity, monitoring for evidence of a compromise rather than the attack itself. Anomaly-based detection methods require the ability of the application engine to decode and process all monitored protocols, causing a high initial overhead. After the initial protocol behavior has been defined, scalability becomes more rapid and straightforward. The rule development process for anomaly-based methods can become complicated due to the differences in vendor protocol implementations.

Heuristic

Heuristic intrusion detection methods are commonly known as anomaly-based methods because heuristic algorithms are used to identity anomalies. Similar to anomaly-based methods, heuristic based methods are typically rule based and look for abnormal behavior. Heuristic rules tend to categorize activity into one of the following types: benign, suspicious, or unknown. As the IDS learns network behavior, the activity category can change. The slight difference between heuristic and anomaly-based methods is that anomaly-based methods are less specific. They target behavior that is out of the ordinary as opposed to classifying all behavior.

Protocol Analyzers

Protocol analyzers help you troubleshoot network issues by gathering packet-level information across the network. These applications capture packets and can conduct protocol decoding, putting the information into readable data for analysis. Protocol analyzers can do more than just look at packets. They prove useful in many other areas of network management, such as monitoring the network for unexpected, unwanted, and unnecessary traffic. For example, if the network is running slowly, a protocol analyzer can tell you whether unnecessary protocols are running on the network. You can also filter specific port numbers and types of traffic so that you can keep an eye on indicators that might cause you problems. Many protocol analyzers can be run on multiple platforms and do live traffic captures and offline analysis. Software USB protocol analyzers are also available for the development of USB devices and analysis of USB traffic.

You can place protocol analyzers inline or in between the devices from which you want to capture the traffic. If you are analyzing storage-area network (SAN) traffic, you can place the analyzer outside the direct link with the use of an optical splitter. The analyzer is placed to capture traffic between the host and the monitored device.

Spam Filter

According to an Internet Threats Trend Report by CYREN, during the first quarter of 2013, an average of 97.4 billion spam emails and 973 million malware emails were sent worldwide daily. Although the percentage of spam has been steadily decreasing in the past few years because of better legislative enforcement and improved products, spam is still an enormous problem for corporations. Spam filters can consist of various filtering technologies, including content, header, blacklist, rule-based, permission, and challenge-response filters. Spam-filtering solutions can be deployed in a number of ways. The most common implementations include using an onsite appliance, installing software on each individual device, and hosted or cloud-based vendor solutions. Spam-filtering products work by checking email messages when they arrive. The messages are then either directed to the user's mailbox or quarantined based on a score value. When the spam score exceeds a certain threshold, the email is sent to the junk folder. In addition to the keyword-scanning methods, which include scoring systems for emails based on multiple criteria, spam filter appliances allow for checksum technology that tracks the number of times a particular message has appeared, and message authenticity checking, which uses multiple algorithms to verify authenticity of a message. In addition, the appliance may perform file-type attachment blocking and scanning using the built-in antivirus protection.

UTM Security Appliances

Spyware, malware, worms, and viruses pose a serious threat to both system integrity and user privacy. The prevalence of such malicious programs could also threaten the stability of critical systems and networks. Vendors have responded by offering unified threat management (UTM) security appliances that contain spam-filtering functions and can also provide antivirus protection. For example, the Barracuda Spam & Virus Firewall has antivirus protection as a built-in feature along with spam filtering. Another example is the Cisco Web Security appliance. In these devices, updates are posted hourly to ensure that the latest definitions are in place. As with any appliance that provides multiple functions, it is a single point of failure. To maintain availability, organizations might need to have two units deployed in automatic failover mode.

URL Filter

Internet content filters use a collection of terms, words, and phrases that are compared to content from browsers and applications. This type of software can filter content from various types of Internet activity and applications, such as instant messaging, email, and Microsoft Office documents. Content filtering will report only on violations identified in the specified applications listed for the filtering application. In other words, if the application filters only Microsoft Office documents and a user chooses to use Office, the content is filtered. If the user chooses to use something other than Office, that content is not filtered. Internet content filtering works by analyzing data against a database contained in the software. If a match occurs, the data can be addressed in one of several ways, including filtering, capturing, or blocking the content and closing the application. An example of such software is the Windows Parental Controls.

Content Inspection

Content filters can be hardware or software. Many network solutions combine both. Hardware appliances are usually connected to the same network segment as the users they monitor. Other configurations include being deployed behind a firewall or in a demilitarized zone (DMZ), with public addresses behind a packet-filtering router. These appliances use access control filtering software on the dedicated filtering appliance. The device monitors every packet of traffic that passes over a network. Unlike antivirus and antispyware applications, content monitoring does not require daily updates to keep the database effective and current. On the downside, content filtering needs to be "trained." For example, to filter pornographic material, the terminology must be input and defined in the database.

Malware Inspection

A malware inspection filter is basically a web filter applied to traffic that uses HTTP. The body of all HTTP requests and responses is inspected. Malicious content is blocked, and legitimate content passes through unaltered. Passing files may be hashed and matched against the signatures stored in a malware signature database. Other approaches include caching files for running a heuristic scan later within the file cache. If a file within the file cache is found to be malicious by the heuristic scan, the signature is inserted in the malware signature database so that it can be blocked in the future. The context for malware inspection is scanning downloaded content allowed by web access rules to inspect web pages and files downloaded over HTTP from external websites.

Web Application Firewall Versus Network Firewall

The main objective for the placement of network firewalls is to allow only traffic that the organization deems necessary and provide notification of suspicious behavior. Most organizations deploy, at a minimum, two firewalls. The first firewall is placed in front of the DMZ to allow requests destined for servers in the DMZ or to route requests to an authentication proxy. The second firewall is placed between the DMZ and the internal network to allow outbound requests. All initial necessary connections are located on the DMZ machines. For example, a RADIUS server might be running in the DMZ for improved performance and enhanced security, even though its database resides inside the company intranet. DMZ is covered in more detail later in this chapter, and RADIUS is covered in Chapter 10. Most organizations have many firewalls with the level of protection at its strongest where it is closest to the outside edge of the environment. Figure 1.2 shows an example.

ExamAlert

Watch for scenarios that ask you to select the proper firewall placement based on organizational need.

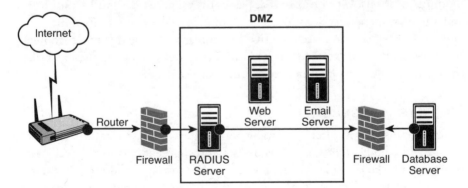

FIGURE 1.2 **A network with two firewalls**

When deploying multiple firewalls, you might experience network latency. If you do, check the placement of the firewalls and possibly reconsider the topology to ensure that you get the most out of the firewalls. Another factor to think about is the use of a SAN or network-area storage (NAS) behind a firewall. Because most storage environments span multiple networks, this creates a virtual bridge that can counteract a firewall, providing a channel into the storage environment if a system is compromised in the DMZ.

In response to the onslaught of web-based attacks, many organizations have implemented a web application firewall in addition to network firewalls. Put simply, a *web application firewall* is software or a hardware appliance used to protect the organization's web server from attack. A web application firewall can be an appliance, server plug-in, or filter that is used specifically for preventing execution of common web-based attacks such as Cross-Site Scripting (XSS) and SQL Injection on a web server. These and other attack methods are covered in Chapter 5, "Attacks." Web application firewalls can be either signature based or anomaly based. So, some look for particular attack signatures to try to identify an attack, whereas others look for abnormal behavior outside the website's normal traffic patterns. The device sits between a web client and a web server and analyzes communication at the application layer, much like a network stateful-inspection firewall. Web application firewalls are placed in front of a web server in an effort to try to shield it from incoming attacks. Web application firewalls are sometimes referred to as *deep packet inspection* (DPI) *firewalls* because they can look at every request and response within web service layers.

Application-Aware Devices

Application awareness refers to the ability of a device to retain information about applications such as application state and resource use to optimize operation. Often, we do not think in terms of application-level security when discussing devices such as firewalls, IPSs, IDSs, and proxies. Yet most next-generation devices are capable of being application aware.

More applications are being offered as a service, and most enterprise applications use some type of cloud service. Using applications in this manner subjects the organization to attacks on several different fronts, including direct attacks on the application and multitenant environment hosting attacks. To meet the changing ways organizations do business, next-generation firewalls (NGFW) have been developed. NGFWs are considered application aware. This means that they go beyond the traditional port and IP address examination to inspect traffic at a deeper level. Application-aware firewalls integrate the functions of other network devices such as proxies, IDSs, and IPSs. Many application-aware firewalls use an IPS engine to provide application support. As a result, various blended techniques are used to identify applications and formulate policies based on business rules. Application-aware firewalls can examine application traffic and identify threats through DPI techniques.

In addition to application-aware firewalls, vendors such as McAfee provide security platforms that are based on next-generation inspection architecture designed specifically for Layer 7 detection and identification. This type of platform includes the capability for generating analytics, risk ratings, and enhanced rule definitions. Many organizations have begun to embrace next-generation devices to reduce network costs and complexity.

Cram Quiz

Answer these questions. The answers follow the last question. If you cannot answer these questions correctly, consider reading this section again until you can.

1. You want to implement a solution that offers a single point of policy control and management for web-based content access. Which of the following devices would best fit this requirement?

   ○ **A.** Proxy gateway

   ○ **B.** Web security gateway

   ○ **C.** Application-level gateway

   ○ **D.** URL filtering

2. You have recently had some security breaches in the network. You suspect the cause might be a small group of employees. You want to implement a solution that monitors the internal network activity and incoming external traffic. Which of the following devices would you use? (Choose two correct answers.)

   ○ **A.** A router

   ○ **B.** A network-based IDS

   ○ **C.** A firewall

   ○ **D.** A host-based IDS

3. Which of the following are uses for proxy servers? (Choose all correct answers.)

   ○ **A.** Intrusion detection

   ○ **B.** Internet connectivity

   ○ **C.** Load balancing

   ○ **D.** Web content caching

Cram Quiz Answers

1. **B.** A web security gateway offers a single point of policy control and management for web-based content access. Answer A is too generic to be a proper answer. Answer C is incorrect because, although an application-level gateway understands services and protocols, the requirement is specifically for web-based content. Answer D is incorrect because content filtering reports only on violations identified in the specified applications listed for the filtering application.

2. **B, D**. Because you want to monitor both types of traffic, the IDSs should be used together. Network-based IDSs monitor the packet flow and try to locate packets that are not allowed for one reason or another and might have gotten through the firewall. Host-based IDSs monitor communications on a host-by-host basis and try to filter malicious data. These types of IDSs are good at detecting unauthorized file modifications and user activity. Answer A is incorrect because a router forwards information to its destination on the network or the Internet. A firewall protects computers and networks from undesired access by the outside world; therefore, Answer C is incorrect.

3. **B, C**, and **D**. You can place proxy servers between the private network and the Internet for Internet connectivity or internally for web content caching. If the organization is using the proxy server for both Internet connectivity and web content caching, you should place the proxy server between the internal network and the Internet, with access for users who are requesting the web content. In some proxy server designs, the proxy server is placed in parallel with IP routers. This allows for network load balancing by forwarding of all HTTP and FTP traffic through the proxy server and all other IP traffic through the router. Answer A is incorrect because proxy servers are not used for intrusion detection.

Given a Scenario, Use Secure Network Administration Principles

▶ **Rule-based management**

▶ **Firewall rules**

▶ **VLAN management**

▶ **Secure router configuration**

▶ **Access control lists**

▶ **Port security**

▶ **802.1X**

▶ **Flood guards**

▶ **Loop protection**

▶ **Implicit deny**

▶ **Network separation**

▶ **Log analysis**

▶ **Unified threat management**

If you can correctly answer these questions before going through this section, save time by skimming the Exam Alerts in this section and then completing the Cram Quiz at the end of the section.

CramSaver

1. What is the purpose of loop protection?

2. Explain implicit deny.

3. Explain the principle behind network separation.

Answers

1. The loop guard feature makes additional checks in Layer 2 switched networks. If bridge protocol data units (BPDU) are not received on a nondesignated port and loop guard is enabled, that port is moved into the STP loop-inconsistent blocking state, instead of the listening/learning/ forwarding state. Without the loop guard feature, the port assumes the designated port role.

2. Implicit deny is an access control practice wherein resource availability is restricted to only those logins explicitly granted access, remaining unavailable even when not explicitly denied access.

3. With interconnected networks, the potential for damage greatly increases because one compromised system on one network can easily spread to other networks. Networks that are shared by partners, vendors, or departments should have clear separation boundaries.

Network security goes beyond just knowing the risks and vulnerabilities. To mitigate threats and risks, you must also know how to assess your environment and protect it. This section discusses how to implement security applications to help mitigate risk and how to use security groups, roles, rights, and permissions in accordance with industry best practices.

Rule-Based Management

Rule-based access control (RBAC) is based on ACLs. The basis of this type of access is to determine what can happen to an object based on a set of rules. The most common use of this is on routers and firewalls. Access is determined by looking at a request to see whether it matches a predefined set of conditions. Suppose, for example, that you configure your router to deny any IP addresses from the 10.10.0.0 subnet and allow addresses from the 192.168.10.0 network. When a machine with an address of 192.168.10.15 requests access, the router looks at the rules and accepts the request. In RBAC, the administrator sets the rules. This is considered a type of mandatory control because the users cannot change these rules. In other words, if the administrator sets the aforementioned router conditions, you, as a user, cannot have the router accept requests from a 10.10.0.25 address.

> **ExamAlert**
>
> RBAC is based on a predefined set of rules that determines the object's access.

In an RBAC solution, accounts may be granted varying levels of access, such as read, write, or execute. An example of this would be setting the filtering of IP packets on a proxy server or firewall. Suppose that you want to keep the production staff from downloading bitmap (BMP) files, but you want to allow the development staff to do so. Before you allow any file to be downloaded, you check conditions such as the file type and the access list configuration. Remember that the most common form of RBAC involves testing against an ACL that details systems and accounts with access rights and the limits of their access for the resources. In addition to firewalls and routers, ACLs are used in operating is based on ACLs. The basis of this type osystems.

Firewall Rules

Firewall rules are configured to allow traffic associated with programs or services to be sent or received. A firewall rule set is similar to an ACL in that the rules determine parameters for each connection based on a set of conditions. Firewall rules specify what services are allowed or not allowed through the firewall. Rules consist of a source address, a destination address, a service, and an associated action. For example, a firewall rule to allow FTP traffic might look like this:

```
ipfw add allow tcp from any to any 21 keep-state
```

You can also specify the type of network adapter the rule is applied to, such as LAN, wireless, or remote access.

Generally speaking, you can create firewall rules to take one of three actions for all connections that match the rule's criteria. These actions are allow the connection, allow the connection if it is secured, or block the connection. Rules can be created for either inbound traffic or outbound traffic. Inbound rules explicitly allow, or explicitly block, inbound network traffic that matches the criteria in the rule. Outbound rules explicitly allow, or explicitly block, network traffic originating from the computer that matches the criteria in the rule.

In many firewalls, the rules can be granulized and configured to specify the computers or users, program, service, or port and protocol. Rules can be configured to be applied when profiles are used. As soon as a network packet matches a rule, that rule is applied and processing stops. The more restrictive rules should be listed first, and the least restrictive rules should follow. Otherwise, if a less-restrictive rule is placed before a more-restrictive rule, the checking is stopped at the first rule.

ExamAlert

Order of firewall rules affects application. When a less-restrictive rule is placed before a more-restrictive rule, the checking is stopped at the first rule.

VLAN Management

VLANs provide a way to limit broadcast traffic in a switched network. This creates a boundary and, in essence, creates multiple, isolated LANs on one switch. VLANs are a logical separation of a physical network. Ideally, limit a VLAN to one access switch or switch stack. However, it might be necessary to extend a VLAN across multiple access switches within a switch block to support a capability such as wireless mobility. In this situation, if you are using multiple switches from various vendors to be connected, some switch features might be supported on only one vendor's switches (but not on other vendors' switches). You need to consider things such as VLAN Trunking Protocol (VTP) domain management and inter-VLAN routing when you have two or more switches in the network.

When working with VLANs, you have various configurations and considerations. For example, when mapping VLANs onto a new hierarchical network design, check the subnetting scheme that has been applied to the network and associate a VLAN to each subnet. By allocating IP address spaces in contiguous blocks, it allows each switch block to be summarized into one large address block. In addition, different types of traffic may exist on the network, and that should be considered before device placement and VLAN configuration.

VTP reduces administration in a switched network. One way of setting up the network is to have all switches in the same VTP domain. This reduces the need to configure the same VLAN everywhere. VTP is a Cisco proprietary protocol. Another option for VLAN management in a Cisco environment is the use of a VLAN Management Policy Server (VMPS). This is a network switch that contains a mapping of device information to VLAN.

Secure Router Configuration

Because routers are the lifeblood of the network, it is important that they are properly secured. The security that is configured when setting up and managing routers can make the difference between keeping data secure and providing an open invitation to hackers. You can find what is perhaps the most useful information on router security in the NSA/SNAC Router Security Configuration Guide Version 1.1 located at http://www.nsa.gov/ia/_files/routers/C4-040R-02.pdf. The following are general recommendations for router security:

▶ Create and maintain a written router security policy. The policy should identify who is allowed to log in to the router, who is allowed to configure and update it, and outline the logging and management practices for it.

▶ Comment and organize offline master editions of your router configuration files. Keep the offline copies of all router configurations in sync with the actual configurations running on the routers.

▶ Implement access lists that allow only those protocols, ports, and IP addresses that are required by network users and services and that deny everything else.

▶ Test the security of your routers regularly, especially after any major configuration changes.

A router that is too tightly locked down can turn a functional network into a completely isolated network that does not allow access to anyone.

Access Control Lists

Access control generally refers to the process of making resources available to accounts that should have access, while limiting that access to only what is required. In its broadest sense, an ACL is the underlying data associated with a network resource that defines the access permissions. The most common privileges are read, write to, delete, and execute a file. ACLs can apply to routers and other devices. In Microsoft operating systems, each ACL has one or more access control entries (ACE). The access privileges are stated in a string of bits called an *access mask*. Generally, the object owner or the system administrator creates the ACL for an object.

Port Security

Port security is a Layer 2 traffic control feature on Cisco Catalyst switches. It enables individual switch ports to be configured to allow only a specified number of source MAC addresses coming in through the port. Its primary use is to keep two or three users from sharing a single access port. You can use the port security feature to restrict input to an interface by limiting and identifying MAC addresses of the workstations that are allowed to access the port. When you assign secure MAC addresses to a secure port, the port does not forward packets with source addresses outside the group of defined addresses. If you limit the number of secure MAC addresses to one and assign a single secure MAC address, the workstation attached to that port is ensured the full bandwidth of the port. By default, a port security violation forces the interface into the error-disabled state. Port security can be configured to take one of three actions upon detecting a violation. In addition to the default shutdown, protect and restrict modes can be set. In protect mode, frames from MAC addresses other than the allowed addresses are dropped, and restrict mode is similar to protect mode but generates a syslog message and increases the violation counter.

> **ExamAlert**
>
> Although a deterrent, port security is not a reliable security feature. MAC addresses can be spoofed, and multiple hosts can still easily be hidden behind a small router.

802.1X

The IEEE 802.1X standard passes Extensible Authentication Protocol (EAP) over a wired or wireless LAN. It is used for access control, providing the capability to permit or deny network connectivity, control VLAN access and apply traffic policy, based on user or machine identity. 802.1X, ideal for wireless access points and the authentication process, helps mitigate many of the risks involved in using WEP. 802.1X and keeps the network port disconnected until authentication is completed. If authentication is successful, the port is made available to the user; otherwise, the user is denied access to the network. The communication process is as follows:

▶ The authenticator sends an EAP-Request/Identity packet to the supplicant when it detects the active link.

▶ The supplicant sends an EAP-Response/Identity packet to the authenticator, which is then passed on to the authentication (RADIUS) server.

▶ The authenticator sends an EAP-Request/EAP-Packet packet of the desired authentication type.

▶ The supplicant responds to the challenge via the authenticator and passes the response on to the authentication server.

Flood Guards

Flood guard is most commonly associated with the Cisco PIX Firewall. It is an advanced firewall guard feature used to control network activity associated with DoS attacks. Flood guard controls how the authentication, accounting, and authorization (AAA) service handles bad login attempts that are tying up connections. It allows the PIX Firewall resources to automatically be reclaimed if the authentication subsystem runs out of resources, thereby defeating DoS attacks. The PIX actively reclaims TCP user resources when an inbound or outbound authorization connection is being attacked. The **floodguard** command is enabled by default.

In addition to the flood guard feature in PIX firewalls, there is a name brand device called *FloodGuard*. This is a distributed software application combined with a network appliance used for detecting and blocking DDoS attacks in an enterprise data center or a service provider's network.

Loop Protection

A major feature in Layer 2 managed switches is the Spanning Tree Protocol (STP). STP is a link management protocol that provides path redundancy while preventing undesirable loops in the network. Multiple active paths between stations cause loops in the network. When loops occur, some switches see stations that appear on both sides of the switch. This condition confuses the forwarding algorithm and allows duplicate frames to be forwarded.

A bridge loop occurs when data units can travel from a first LAN segment to a second LAN segment through more than one path. To eliminate bridge loops, existing bridge devices typically employ a technique referred to as the *spanning-tree algorithm*. The spanning tree algorithm is implemented by bridges interchanging special messages known as *bridge protocol data units* (BPDU). The STP loop guard feature provides additional protection against STP loops. An STP loop is created when an STP blocking port in a redundant topology erroneously transitions to the forwarding state. This usually happens because one of the ports of a physically redundant topology no longer receives STP BPDUs. In its operation, STP relies on continuous reception or transmission of BPDUs based on the port role. The loop guard feature makes additional checks. If BPDUs are not received on a nondesignated port and loop guard is enabled, that port is moved into the STP loop-inconsistent blocking state, instead of the listening/learning/forwarding state. Without the loop guard feature, the port assumes the designated port role. The port moves to the STP forwarding state and creates a loop.

Implicit Deny

Implicit deny is an access control practice wherein resource availability is restricted to only those logins explicitly granted access, remaining unavailable even when not explicitly denied access. This practice is used commonly in Cisco networks, where most ACLs have a default setting of implicit deny. By default, an implicit deny all clause appears at the end of every ACL. Anything that is not explicitly permitted is denied. Essentially, an implicit deny is the same as finishing the ACL with **deny ip any any**. This ensures that when access is not explicitly granted, it is automatically denied by default.

> **ExamAlert**
>
> The implicit deny is generally used by default in firewall configurations. Access lists have an implicit deny at the end of the list; so unless you explicitly permit it, traffic cannot pass.

Network Separation

Besides securing ports and protocols from outside attacks, you should secure connections between interconnecting networks. This situation might come into play when an organization establishes network interconnections with partners as in an extranet or an actual connection between the involved organizations because of a merger, acquisition, or joint project. Business partners can include government agencies and commercial organizations. Although this type of interconnection increases functionality and reduces costs, it can result in security risks. These risks include compromise of all connected systems and any network connected to those systems, along with exposure of data the systems handle. With interconnected networks, the potential for damage greatly increases because one compromised system on one network can easily spread to other networks. Networks that are shared by partners, vendors, or departments should have clear separation boundaries.

Log Analysis

Logging is the process of collecting data to be used for monitoring and auditing purposes. The log files themselves are documentation, but how do you set up a log properly? You should develop standards for each platform, application, and server type to make this a checklist or monitoring function. When choosing what to log, be sure you choose carefully. Logs take up disk space and use system resources. They also have to be read; if you log too much, the system bogs down, and it takes a long time to weed through the log files to determine what is important. You should mandate a common storage location for all logs, and documentation should state proper methods for archiving and reviewing logs.

All devices, operating systems, and applications have log files. For example, application log files contain error messages, operational data, and usage information that can help manage applications and servers. Analysis of web application logs enables you to understand who visited the application, on what pages, and how often, and it also provides information on errors and performance problems of the web application. Analyzing logs from web servers such as Apache, Internet Information Services (IIS), Internet Security and Acceleration Server (ISA), Tomcat, and others is automatic and can contribute important insight into website and web application quality and availability. Web server logs are usually access logs, common error logs, custom logs, and World Wide Web Consortium (W3C) logs. W3C logs are used mainly by web servers to log web-related events, including web logs.

Unified Threat Management

Similar to other all-in-one devices, the intent of unified threat management (UTM) is to safeguard users from blended threats and to reduce complexity. UTM security appliances integrate a wide range of security features into one appliance. UTM appliances are a combination of firewall, gateway antivirus, IDS/IPS, VPN, and endpoint control. Because a UTM appliance can provide multiple functions, it also provides better incident awareness, security control, network traffic notification, and monitoring of user behavior and application content than individual devices.

Organizations choose to implement UTM appliances for reduced administration time and costs, realized because the organization no longer has to support multiple vendors, contracts, or licensing. UTM appliances can be hardware, software, virtual, or cloud based. When a UTM appliance is used in a multitenant network or multiple networks, it is important to verify that the specifications include virtual network segmentation.

Cram Quiz

Answer these questions. The answers follow the last question. If you cannot answer these questions correctly, consider reading this section again until you can.

1. If the organization requires a switch feature that makes additional checks in Layer 2 networks to prevent STP issues, which of the following safeguards should you implement?

   ○ **A.** Loop protection

   ○ **B.** Flood guard

   ○ **C.** Implicit deny

   ○ **D.** Port security

2. An organization would limit resource availability to only specific traffic through the use of which of the following access control practices?

   ○ **A.** Loop protection

   ○ **B.** Flood guard

   ○ **C.** Implicit deny

   ○ **D.** Port security

3. You are implementing network access to a new business partner that will work with the development team on a new product. Which of the following would best mitigate risk associated with allowing this new partner access to the network?

   ○ **A.** Log analysis

   ○ **B.** ACLs

   ○ **C.** Network segmentation

   ○ **D.** VPN implementation

Cram Quiz Answers

1. **A.** The loop guard feature makes additional checks in Layer 2 switched networks. Answer B is incorrect because a flood guard is a firewall feature to control network activity associated with DoS attacks. Answer C is incorrect because implicit deny is an access control practice wherein resource availability is restricted to only those logins explicitly granted access. Answer D is incorrect because port security is a Layer 2 traffic control feature on Cisco Catalyst switches. It enables individual switch ports to be configured to allow only a specified number of source MAC addresses coming in through the port.

2. **C**. Implicit deny is an access control practice wherein resource availability is restricted to only those logins explicitly granted access. Answer A is incorrect because the loop guard feature makes additional checks in Layer 2 switched networks. Answer B is incorrect because a flood guard is a firewall feature to control network activity associated with DoS attacks. Answer D is incorrect because port security is a Layer 2 traffic control feature on Cisco Catalyst switches. It enables individual switch ports to be configured to allow only a specified number of source MAC addresses coming in through the port.

3. **C**. With interconnected networks, the potential for damage greatly increases because one compromised system on one network can easily spread to other networks. Networks that are shared by partners, vendors, or departments should have clear separation boundaries. Answer A is incorrect because logging is the process of collecting data to be used for monitoring and auditing purposes. Answer B is incorrect because access control generally refers to the process of making resources available to accounts that should have access, while limiting that access to only what is required. Answer D is incorrect because implementing a VPN does not separate the networks.

Explain Network Design Elements and Components

▶ **DMZ**

▶ **Subnetting**

▶ **VLAN**

▶ **NAT**

▶ **Remote access**

▶ **Telephony**

▶ **NAC**

▶ **Virtualization**

▶ **Cloud computing**

▶ **Layered security/defense in depth**

If you can correctly answer these questions before going through this section, save time by skimming the Exam Alerts in this section and then completing the Cram Quiz at the end of the section.

CramSaver

1. You are setting up a switched network and want to group users by department. Which network design element would you implement?

2. You are setting up a web server that needs to be accessed by both the internal employees and by external customers. What type of architecture should you implement?

3. You are the administrator of a small organization with 50 users. Which internal address range and subnet mask should you use on the network?

Answers

1. The purpose of a VLAN is to unite network nodes logically into the same broadcast domain regardless of their physical attachment to the network. VLANs provide a way to limit broadcast traffic in a switched network. This creates a boundary and, in essence, creates multiple, isolated LANs on one switch, allowing the users to be grouped by department.

2. The DMZ is an area that allows external users to access information that the organization deems necessary but will not compromise any internal organizational information. This configuration allows outside access yet prevents external users from directly accessing a server that holds internal organizational data.

> **3.** Class C addresses are network addresses with the first byte between 192 and 223 and can have about 250 hosts. The nonroutable internal address range for a Class C network is from 192.168.1.1 to 192.168.1.254. The default subnet mask for a Class C address is 255.255.255.0.

As you create a network security policy, you must define procedures to defend your network and users against harm and loss. With this objective in mind, a network design and the included components play an important role in implementing the overall security of the organization.

An overall security solution includes design elements and components such as firewalls, VLANs, and perimeter network boundaries that distinguish between private networks, intranets, and the Internet. This section discusses these elements and helps you tell them apart and understand their function in the security of the network.

DMZ

A *demilitarized zone* (DMZ) is a small network between the internal network and the Internet that provides a layer of security and privacy. Both internal and external users may have limited access to the servers in the DMZ. Figure 1.3 depicts a DMZ.

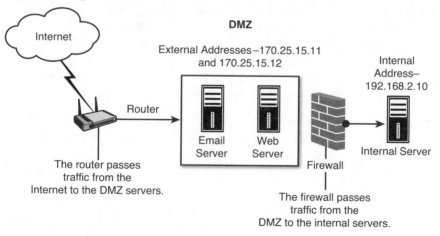

FIGURE 1.3 **A DMZ**

Often, web and mail servers are placed in the DMZ. Because these devices are exposed to the Internet, it is important that they are hardened and patches are kept current. Table 1.1 lists the most common services and ports that are run on servers inside the DMZ. Services and ports are explained in greater detail in Chapter 2, "Network Implementation."

The DMZ is an area that allows external users to access information that the organization deems necessary but will not compromise any internal organizational information. This configuration allows outside access, yet prevents external users from directly accessing a server that holds internal organizational data.

Subnetting

Subnetting can be done for several reasons. If you have an IPv4 Class C address and 1,000 clients, you will have to subnet the network or use a custom subnet mask to accommodate all the hosts. The most common reason networks are subnetted is to control network traffic. Splitting one network into two or more and using routers to connect each subnet together means that broadcasts can be limited to each subnet. However, often networks are subnetted to improve network security, not just performance. Subnetting allows you to arrange hosts into the different logical groups that isolate each subnet into its own mini network. Subnet divisions can be based on business goals and security policy objectives. For example, perhaps you use contract workers and want to keep them separated from the organizational employees. Often, organizations with branches use subnets to keep each branch separate. When your computers are on separate physical networks, you can divide your network into subnets that enable you to use one block of addresses on multiple physical networks. If an incident happens and you notice it quickly, you can usually contain the issue to that particular subnet. Other instances where subnetting would be used are for intranets and extranets.

An *intranet* is a subnet portion of the internal network that uses web-based technologies. The information is stored on web servers and accessed using browsers. Although web servers are used, they do not necessarily have to be accessible to the outside world. This is possible because the IP addresses of the servers are reserved for private, internal use. If the intranet can be accessed from public networks, it should be through a VPN for security reasons. VPNs and VPN concentrators were discussed earlier in this chapter.

An *extranet* is a subnet of the public portion of the company's IT infrastructure that allows resources to be used by authorized partners and resellers that have proper authorization and authentication. This type of arrangement is commonly used for business-to-business relationships. Because an extranet can provide liability for a company, care must be taken to ensure that VPNs and firewalls are configured properly and that security policies are strictly enforced.

When subnetting for IPv4 is done, an IP address usually originates from one of the IP address classes and default subnet masks listed in Table 1.2.

TABLE 1.2   **IPv4 Address Class, IP Range, and Default Subnet Mask**

Address Class	IP Address Range	Default Subnet Mask
Class A	0.0.0.0 to 126.255.255.255	255.0.0.0
Class B	128.0.0.0 to 191.255.255.255	255.255.0.0
Class C	192.0.0.0 to 223.255.255.255	255.255.255.0

Notice that the 127 network address is missing. Although the 127.0.0.0 network is in technically in the Class A area, using addresses in this range causes the protocol software to return data without sending traffic across a network. For example, the address 127.0.0.1 is used for TCP/IPv4 loopback testing, and the address 127.0.0.2 is used by most DNS blacklists for testing purposes. A blacklist is a list of IP addresses that are identified addresses used by spammers and other abusive email senders. Blacklisting is discussed in further detail in Chapter 8, "Host Security."

To denote the network prefix for the subnet mask, the number of bits in the prefix is appended to the address with a slash (/) separator. This type of notation is called *classless interdomain routing* (CIDR). Here is an example: A Class C internal address of 192.168.0.0 with a subnet mask of 255.255.255.0 is written as 192.168.0.0/24.

IPv6 is designed to replace IPv4. Addresses are 128 bits rather than the 32 bits used in IPv4. IPv6 addresses are represented in hexadecimal. In IPv6, subnets use IPv6 addresses with 64 bits for the host portion. These addresses can be further subnetted just as in IPv4. IPv6 is based on the concepts of variable-length subnet masking (VLSM) and CIDR. A VLSM allocates IP addresses to subnets based on individual need rather than a general network-wide rule. An example of CIDR notation for IPv6 is 2001:db8::/32 designating the address 2001:db8:: with a network prefix consisting of the most significant 32 bits. For more information about IPv6, visit http://ipv6.com/.

Should you need additional review on IP addressing and subnetting, a wide variety of information is available. One such website is IP Addressing and Subnetting for New Users, which hosted by Cisco and available at http://www.cisco.com/c/en/us/support/docs/ip/routing-information-protocol-rip/13788-3.html. Figure 1.4 shows an internal network with two different subnets. Notice the IP addresses, subnet masks, and default gateway.

IP address: 192.168.1.15
Subnet mask: 255.255.255.0
Default Gateway: 192.168.1.1

IP address: 192.168.2.15
Subnet mask: 255.255.255.0
Default Gateway: 192.168.2.1

Subnet
192.168.1.0

Subnet
192.168.2.0

IP address: 192.168.1.25
Subnet mask: 255.255.255.0
Default Gateway: 192.168.1.1

IP address: 192.168.2.25
Subnet mask: 255.255.255.0
Default Gateway: 192.168.2.1

FIGURE 1.4 **A segmented network**

Notice in Figure 1.4 the subnets 192.168.1.0 and 192.168.2.0 identified next to the router. These are not valid IP addresses for a network router and are used to identify the 192.168.1.x and 192.168.2.x networks in routing tables.

VLAN

As you create a network security policy, you must define procedures to defend your network and users against harm and loss. With this objective in mind, a network design and the included components play an important role in implementing the overall security of the organization.

An overall security solution includes design elements and components such as firewalls, VLANs, and perimeter network boundaries that distinguish between private networks, intranets, and the Internet. This section discusses these elements and helps you tell them apart and understand their function in the security of the network.

The purpose of a *virtual local-area network* (VLAN) is to unite network nodes logically into the same broadcast domain regardless of their physical attachment to the network. VLANs provide a way to limit broadcast traffic in a switched network. This creates a boundary and, in essence, creates multiple, isolated LANs on one switch. Because switches operate on Layer 2 (data link layer) of the OSI model, a router is required if data is to be passed from one VLAN to another.

> **ExamAlert**
>
> The purpose of a VLAN is to logically group network nodes regardless of their physical location.

Frame tagging is the technology used for VLANs. The IEEE 802.1Q standard defines a mechanism that encapsulates the frames with headers, which then tags them with a VLAN ID. VLAN-aware network devices look for these tags in frames and make appropriate forwarding decisions. A VLAN is basically a software solution that allows creating unique tag identifiers to be assigned to different ports on the switch.

The most notable benefit of using a VLAN is that it can span multiple switches. Because users on the same VLAN do not have to be associated by physical location, they can be grouped by department or function. Here are the benefits that VLANs provide:

▶ Users can be grouped by department rather than physical location.

▶ Moving and adding users is simplified. No matter where a user physically moves, changes are made to the software configuration in the switch.

▶ Because VLANs allow users to be grouped, applying security policies becomes easier.

Keep in mind that use of a VLAN is not an absolute safeguard against security infringements. It does not provide the same level of security as a router. A VLAN is a software solution and cannot take the place of a well-subnetted or well-routed network. It is possible to make frames hop from one VLAN to another. This takes skill and knowledge on the part of an attacker, but it is possible. For more information about frame tagging and VLANs, refer to IEEE standard 802.1Q.

NAT

Network Address Translation (NAT) acts as a liaison between an internal network and the Internet. It allows multiple computers to connect to the Internet using one IP address. An important security aspect of NAT is that it hides the internal network from the outside world. In this situation, the internal network uses a private IP address. Special ranges in each IP address class are used specifically for private addressing. These addresses are considered nonroutable on the Internet.

Here are the private address ranges:

- ▶ **Class A:** 10.0.0.0 network. Valid host IDs are from 10.0.0.1 to 10.255.255.254.

- ▶ **Class B:** 172.16.0.0 through 172.31.0.0 networks. Valid host IDs are from 172.16.0.1 through 172.31.255.254.

- ▶ **Class C:** 192.168.0.0 network. Valid host IDs are from 192.168.0.1 to 192.168.255.254.

Just as in IPv4, blocks of addresses are set aside in IPv6 for private addresses. In IPv6, internal addresses are called *unique local addresses* (ULA). Addresses starting with fe80: are called *link-local addresses* and are routable only in the local link area.

For smaller companies, NAT can be used in the form of Windows Internet Connection Sharing (ICS), where all machines share one Internet connection, such as a broadband modem. NAT can also be used for address translation between multiple protocols, which improves security and provides for more interoperability in heterogeneous networks.

NAT and IPsec may not work well together. IPsec uses cryptography to protect communications. NAT has to replace the headers of the incoming packet with its own headers before sending the packet. This might not be possible because IPsec information is encrypted.

IPv6 was developed before NAT was in general use. Because IPv6 has an almost infinite number of addresses, having to provide renumbering makes NAT unnecessary. However Network Address Translation - Protocol Translation (NAT-PT, RFC 2766) was developed as a means for hosts that run IPv6 to communicate with hosts that run IPv4. For more information on how NAT works, go to http://www.cisco.com/c/en/us/support/docs/ip/network-address-translation-nat/4606-8.html.

> **ExamAlert**
>
> Another address range to keep in mind when designing IP address space is Automatic Private IP Addressing (APIPA). If no Dynamic Host Configuration Protocol (DHCP) server is available at the time that the client issues a DHCP lease request, the client is automatically configured with an address from the 169.254.0.1 through 169.254.255.254 range.

Remote Access

Broadband solutions such as cable modems and digital subscriber line (DSL) connections are readily available. Most Internet service providers (ISP) offer this type of network connectivity for their users. Remote Access Services (RAS) lets you connect your computer from a remote location, such as your home or any on-the-road location, to a corporate network. Many organizations maintain the use of RAS servers to provide direct connectivity for remote users or administrators. Due to concerns about "always-on" connections, RAS is achieved primarily through VPNs using IPsec or SSL or other remote-access software. By using a remote-access VPN, secure access to corporate resources can be provided using an encrypted tunnel over the Internet. In addition to using hardware such as VPN concentrators discussed earlier in the chapter, you can establish remote access with Routing and Remote Access (RRAS). RRAS is a network service available on Microsoft server installations that allows the deployment of VPNs and dialup remote-access services. The type of service you choose depends on many factors, such as cost, connect and transfer speeds, reliability, availability, and so on.

Telephony

The transmission of data through equipment in a telecommunications environment is known as *telephony*. Telephony includes transmission of voice, fax, or other data. This section describes the components that need to be considered when securing the environment. Often, these components are neglected because they are not really network components. However, they use communications equipment that is susceptible to attack and therefore must be secured.

The telecommunications (telecom) system and private branch exchange (PBX) are a vital part of an organization's infrastructure. Besides the standard block, there are also PBX servers, where the PBX board plugs into the server and is configured through software on the computer. Many companies have moved to Voice over IP (VoIP) to integrate computer telephony, videoconferencing, and document sharing.

For years, PBX-type systems have been targeted by hackers, mainly to get free long-distance service. The vulnerabilities that phone networks are subject to include social engineering, long-distance toll fraud, and breach of data privacy.

To protect your network, make sure that the PBX is in a secure area, any default passwords have been changed, and only authorized maintenance is done. Many times, hackers gain access to the phone system via social engineering because this device is usually serviced through a remote maintenance port.

VoIP uses the Internet to transmit voice data. A VoIP system might be composed of many different components, including VoIP phones, desktop systems, PBX servers, and gateways. VoIP PBX servers are susceptible to the same type of exploits as other network servers. These attacks include DoS and buffer overflows, with DoS being the most prevalent. In addition, there are voice-specific attacks and threats. H.323 and Inter Asterisk eXchange (IAX) are specifications and protocols for audio/video. They enable VoIP connections between servers and enable client/server communication. H.323 and IAX protocols can be vulnerable to sniffing during authentication. This allows an attacker to obtain passwords that might be used to compromise the voice network. Session Initiation Protocol (SIP) is commonly used in instant messaging, but it can also be used as an alternative for VoIP. Using SIP can leave VoIP networks open to unauthorized transport of data. Man-in-the-middle attacks between the SIP phone and SIP proxy allow the audio to be manipulated, causing dropped, rerouted, or playback calls. In a man-in-the-middle attack, the attacker intercepts and relays communications between two entities, making the entities believe that they are talking directly to each other when, in fact, the entire conversation is controlled by the attacker. Many components comprise a VoIP network, and VoIP security is built upon many layers of traditional data security. Therefore, access can be gained in a lot of areas.

Modems are used via the phone line to dial in to a server or computer. They are gradually being replaced by high-speed cable and DSL solutions, which are faster than dialup access. However, some companies still use modems for employees to dial in to the network and work from home. The modems on network computers or servers are usually configured to take incoming calls. Leaving modems open for incoming calls with little to no authentication for users who are dialing in can be a clear security vulnerability in the network. For example, war-dialing attacks take advantage of this situation. War dialing is the process by which an automated software application is used to dial numbers in a given range to determine whether any of the numbers are serviced by modems that accept dial-in requests. This attack can be set to target connected modems that are set to receive calls without any authentication, thus allowing attackers an easy path into the network. You can resolve this problem area in several ways:

▶ Set the callback features to have the modem call the user back at a preset number.

▶ Make sure that authentication is required using strong passwords.

▶ Ensure that employees have not set up modems at their workstations with remote-control software installed.

NAC

One the most effective ways to protect the network from malicious hosts is to use *network access control* (NAC). NAC offers a method of enforcement that helps ensure computers are properly configured. The premise behind NAC is to secure the environment by examining the user's machine and based on the results grant (or not grant) access accordingly. It is based on assessment and enforcement. For example, if the user's computer patches are not up to date, and no desktop firewall software is installed, you can decide whether to limit access to network resources. Any host machine that does not comply with your defined policy could be relegated to a remediation server or put on a guest VLAN. The basic components of NAC products are as follows

▶ **Access requestor (AR):** This is the device that requests access. The assessment of the device can be self-performed or delegated to another system.

▶ **Policy decision point (PDP):** This is the system that assigns a policy based on the assessment. The PDP determines what access should be granted and may be the NAC's product-management system.

▶ **Policy enforcement point (PEP):** This is the device that enforces the policy. This device may be a switch, firewall, or router.

The four ways NAC systems can be integrated into the network are the following:

▶ **Inline:** An appliance in the line, usually between the access and the distribution switches

▶ **Out of band:** Intervenes and performs an assessment as hosts come online and then grants appropriate access

▶ **Switch based:** Similar to inline NAC except enforcement occurs on the switch itself

▶ **Host based:** Relies on an installed host agent to assess and enforce access policy

In addition to providing the ability to enforce security policy, contain noncompliant users, and mitigate threats, NAC offers a number of business benefits. The business benefits include compliance, a better security posture, and operational cost management.

Virtualization

With more emphasis being placed on going green and power becoming more expensive, virtualization offers cost benefits by decreasing the number of physical machines required within an environment. This applies to both servers and desktops. On the client side, the ability to run multiple operating environments allows a machine to support applications and services for an operating environment other than the primary environment. Currently, many implementations of virtual environments are available to run on just about everything from servers and routers to USB thumb drives.

The security concerns of virtual environments begin with the guest operating system. If a virtual machine is compromised, an intruder can gain control of all the guest operating systems. In addition, because hardware is shared, most virtual machines run with very high privileges. This can allow an intruder who compromises a virtual machine to compromise the host machine, too. Vulnerabilities also come into play. For example, a few years ago, VMware's NAT service had a buffer-overflow vulnerability that allowed remote attackers to execute malicious code by exploiting the virtual machine itself. Virtual machine environments need to be patched just like host environments and are susceptible to the same issues as a host operating system. You should be cognizant of share files among guest and host operating systems.

ExamAlert

Virtualized environments, if compromised, can provide access to not only the network, but also any virtualization infrastructure. This puts a lot of data at risk.

Security policy should address virtual environments. Any technology software without a defined business need should not be allowed on systems.

This applies to all systems, including virtual environments. To secure a virtualized environment, machines should be segmented by the sensitivity of the information they contain. A policy should be in place that specifies that hardware is not shared for test environments and sensitive data. Another way to secure a virtualized environment is to use standard locked-down images. Other areas that present issues for a virtualized environment and need special consideration are deploying financial applications on virtualized shared hosting and secure storage on SAN technologies.

Cloud Computing

Cloud computing, as it is used today, is a very general term that basically describes anything that involves delivering hosted computing services over the Internet. The term came from the cloud symbol that is commonly used to represent the Internet in network diagrams. Although cloud computing has come to the forefront over the past couple of years, the concepts of cloud computing can be traced back to mainframe computing, where multiple users were given small slices of the computer's time to run whatever program they needed at that time. Today, the typical cloud computing provider delivers computing power, storage, and common applications online to users who access them from a web browser or portal. In essence, cloud computing is the blending of virtualization, distributed computing, and prevalent high-speed bandwidth. Cloud computing falls into a variety of categories and models which are discussed in the following sections.

Platform-as-a-Service

Platform-as-a-service (PaaS) is the delivery of a computing platform, often an operating system with associated services, that is delivered over the Internet without downloads or installation. PaaS systems are often development platforms designed to operate specifically in the cloud environment. Google Apps are examples of PaaS. PaaS implementations typically have integrated development environment services, interface-creation tools, and web and database integration.

Software-as-a-Service

Software-as-a-service (SaaS) is the delivery of a licensed application to customers over the Internet for use as a service on demand. A SaaS vendor hosts an application and allows the customer to download the application for a set period of time, after which the application becomes inactive. This model is useful for individuals and businesses to have the right to access a certain application without having to purchase a full license. This creates an on-demand licensing environment that allows for all the benefits of the full application without the up-front costs and maintenance associated with traditional software purchases.

Infrastructure-as-a-Service

Infrastructure-as-a-service (IaaS) is the delivery of computer infrastructure in a hosted service model over the Internet. This method of cloud computing allows the client to literally outsource everything that would normally be in a typical IT department. Data center space, servers, networking equipment, and software can all be purchased as a service. IaaS follows the same model as power and water; you're billed for how much you use, so it falls under the category of "utility computing." IaaS implementations typically have Internet connectivity, computer networking, servers or grid computing, and hardware virtualization.

> **ExamAlert**
>
> Watch for scenarios or examples asking you to identify a correct/incorrect cloud service type or service implementation choice.

Private

A *private cloud* is a hosted infrastructure on a private platform and can sometimes be referred to as an *internal*, *corporate*, or *enterprise cloud*. Because it is hosted on a private platform, this type of cloud affords organizations more control over the infrastructure and is usually restricted to organizational employees and business partners. A private cloud offers the ability to add applications and services on-demand similar to a public cloud. The advantages of using a private cloud design include better control over organizational data, higher levels of security and customization due to flexibility in design specifications, better performance because the private cloud is deployed separately, and easier access to compliance data because the information is readily available. The disadvantages of a private cloud include building-capacity limitations, along with higher costs for infrastructure, maintenance, and administration. A private cloud is the best choice for an organization that needs strict control of business-critical data or highly regulated businesses such as financial institutions.

Public

A *public cloud* is an environment where the services and infrastructure are hosted at a service provider's offsite facility and accessed over the Internet based on a monthly or yearly usage fee. The main infrastructure is shared among many organizations but each organization's data is logically separated. This is referred to as multitenancy. The advantages of using a public cloud include lower infrastructure, maintenance, and administrative costs, greater level of hardware efficiency, reduced implementation time, and availability of short-term usage. The disadvantages of a public cloud are greater vulnerable risk due to multitenancy, diminished control of organizational data and the environment because it is hosted at a service provider's facility, and reduced bandwidth because data transfer capability is limited to that of the ISP. A public cloud is the best choice when an organization requires scalability, wants reduced costs, lacks in-house administrative personnel, or has a high-maintenance distributed network.

Hybrid

A *hybrid cloud* is a combination of public and private clouds where control of data is kept using a private cloud, while other functions are hosted using a public cloud. This approach allows the organization to utilize the advantages of both environment types. A hybrid cloud environment is the best choice when an organization offers services that need to be configured for diverse vertical markets or wants to use a SaaS application but is concerned about security.

Community

Community clouds are designed to accommodate the mutual needs of a particular business community. This is generally industry specific, such as healthcare, public sector, or energy. Community clouds provide collaborative business processes in a cloud environment while maintaining a higher level of security level using a hybrid cloud. A community cloud is best suited for organizations that want to increase cross-organizational or collaborative processes when in-house implementation is not possible due to conditions such as geographically distributed participants, fluctuating resource requirements, or resource limitations. An example of a community cloud is Google's implementation of Google Apps for U.S. government agencies.

ExamAlert

Watch for scenarios or examples asking you to identify the best cloud choice based on public, private, hybrid, or community features.

Layered Security/Defense in Depth

Layered security is based on the premise that by implementing security at different levels or layers to form a complete security strategy, better protection is provided than by implementing an individual security defense. A layered security approach includes using firewalls, IDSs, content filters, encryption, and auditing procedures. Each of these provides a different type of security protection individually; when implemented together, however, they help to improve the overall security posture of the organization.

Defense in depth is a comprehensive security approach for protecting the integrity of organizational information assets. Defense in depth is rooted in military strategy and requires a balanced emphasis on people, technology, and operations to maintain information assurance (IA). Defense in depth stems from a philosophy that complete security against threats can never be achieved and that the components that comprise a layered security strategy impede threat progress until the attacker either gives up or the organization can respond to the threat.

Although closely related, layered security and defense in depth are two different concepts. Layered security can be considered a subset of defense in depth. Layered security focuses on protecting IT resources. Defense in depth focuses on a wider, holistic approach that includes components such as disaster recovery and forensic analysis.

Cram Quiz

Answer these questions. The answers follow the last question. If you cannot answer
these questions correctly, consider reading this section again until you can.

1. You are the administrator of a small organization with 50 users. Which IPv4
   internal address range should you use on the network?

   ○ **A.** 10.x.x.x

   ○ **B.** 172.16.x.x

   ○ **C.** 172.31.x.x

   ◉ **D.** 192.168.x.x

2. You are setting up a switched network and want to group users by department.
   Which technology would you implement?

   ○ **A.** DMZ

   ○ **B.** VPN

   ◉ **C.** VLAN

   ○ **D.** NAT

3. You are setting up a web server that needs to be accessed by both the
   employees and external customers. What type of architecture should you
   implement?

   ○ **A.** VLAN

   ◉ **B.** DMZ

   ○ **C.** NAT

   ○ **D.** VPN

4. The organization is interested in using a vendor SaaS application but is
   concerned about the lack of cloud security. What type of cloud architecture
   would be the most appropriate?

   ○ **A.** Public

   ◉ **B.** Private

   ○ **C.** Hybrid

   ○ **D.** Community

5. Using a combination of firewalls, intrusion detection systems, content filters,
   encryption, and auditing procedures in the organization for protection against
   intrusions is an example of which of the following?

   ○ **A.** Defense in depth

   ○ **B.** Infrastructure-as-a-service

   ○ **C.** Community cloud

   ◉ **D.** Layered security

Cram Quiz Answers

1. **D**. In a Class C network, valid host IDs are from 192.168.0.1 to 192.168.255.254, allowing for a maximum of 254 hosts on the network. Answer A is incorrect because it is a Class A address. Valid host IDs are from 10.0.0.1 to 10.255.255.254, which allows a much higher number of IP addresses than are possibly needed. Answers B and C are incorrect because they are both Class B addresses; valid host IDs are from 172.16.0.1 through 172.31.255.254, which allows a much higher number of IP addresses than are possibly needed.

2. **C**. The purpose of a VLAN is to unite network nodes logically into the same broadcast domain regardless of their physical attachment to the network. Answer A is incorrect because a DMZ is a small network between the internal network and the Internet that provides a layer of security and privacy. Answer B is incorrect because a VPN is a network connection that allows you access via a secure tunnel created through an Internet connection. Answer D is incorrect because NAT acts as a liaison between an internal network and the Internet.

3. **B**. A DMZ is a small network between the internal network and the Internet that provides a layer of security and privacy. Answer A is incorrect. The purpose of a VLAN is to unite network nodes logically into the same broadcast domain regardless of their physical attachment to the network. Answer C is incorrect because NAT acts as a liaison between an internal network and the Internet. Answer D is incorrect because a VPN is a network connection that allows you access via a secure tunnel created through an Internet connection.

4. **C**. A hybrid cloud environment is the best choice when an organization offers services that need to be configured for diverse vertical markets or wants to use a SaaS application but is concerned about security. Answer A is incorrect because using a public cloud increases the concern about security. Answer B is incorrect because a private cloud would not allow the public vendor SaaS implementation. Answer D is incorrect because a community cloud provides collaborative business processes in a cloud environment.

5. **D**. Layered security is based on the premise that by implementing security at different levels or layers to form a complete security strategy, better protection is provided than by implementing an individual security defense. Answer A is incorrect. Defense in depth is rooted in military strategy and requires a balanced emphasis on people, technology, and operations to maintain information assurance (IA). Answer B is incorrect because infrastructure-as-a-service is the delivery of computer infrastructure in a hosted service model over the Internet. Answer C is incorrect because a community cloud provides collaborative business processes in a cloud environment.

What Next?

If you want more practice on this chapter's exam objectives before you move on, remember that you can access all the Cram Quiz questions on the CD. You can also create a custom exam by objective with the practice exam software. Note any objective that you struggle with and go to the material that covers that objective in this chapter.

CHAPTER 2

Network Implementation

> **This chapter covers the following official CompTIA Security+ SY0-401 exam objectives:**
>
> ▶ Given a scenario, implement common protocols and services
>
> ▶ Given a scenario, troubleshoot security issues related to wireless networking
>
> (For more information on the official CompTIA Security+ SY0-401 exam topics, see the "About the CompTIA Security+ SY0-401 Exam" section in the Introduction.)

The network infrastructure is subject to myriad internal and external attacks through services, protocols, and open ports. It is imperative that you understand how to properly implement services and protocols, especially if the network has been in existence for some period of time and some services are no longer needed or have been forgotten. To stop many would-be attackers, you must understand how protocols are used on the network, what common ports are used by network protocols, and how to securely implement a wireless network.

This chapter discusses these concepts to help you understand how to use the proper network implementation of protocols and services as a tool to protect and mitigate threats against network infrastructure based on organizational needs. It also has a section specifically dedicated to wireless security implementation based on organization requirements.

Given a Scenario, Implement Common Protocols and Services

▶ Protocols

▶ Ports

▶ OSI relevance

CramSaver

If you can correctly answer these questions before going through this section, save time by skimming the Exam Alerts in this section and then completing the Cram Quiz at the end of the section.

1. Explain how IPsec is used, including the OSI model layer it operates on.

2. Explain what ICMP is and how it is used in a networking environment.

3. What are the major differences between IPv4 and IPv6?

4. Explain the purpose of ports 137, 138, and 139.

5. Explain what services/protocols operate on port 22.

Answers

1. The Internet Protocol Security (IPsec) authentication and encapsulation standard is widely used to establish secure VPN communications. The use of IPsec can secure transmissions between critical servers and clients. This helps prevent attacks from taking place. Unlike most security systems that function within the application layer of the Open Systems Interconnection (OSI) model, IPsec functions within the network layer.

2. Internet Control Message Protocol (ICMP) is a protocol meant to be used as an aid for other protocols and system administrators to test for connectivity and search for configuration errors in a network. Ping uses the ICMP echo function and is the lowest-level test of whether a remote host is alive. A small packet containing an ICMP echo message is sent through the network to a particular IP address. The computer that sent the packet then waits for a return packet. If the connections are good and the target computer is up, the echo message return packet will be received.

3. The differences between IPv4 and IPv6 are in five major areas: addressing and routing, security, network address translation, administrative workload, and support for mobile devices.

4. These are NetBIOS ports that are required for certain Windows network functions such as file sharing. But these ports also provide information about your computer that can be exploited by attackers. They also contain vulnerabilities that are widely used to break into systems and exploit them in various ways.

5. Secure Shell (SSH), Secure File Transfer Protocol (SFTP), and Secure
   Copy Protocol (SCP) are all protocols that operate on port 22. SSH is
   used to securely access a remote computer. SFTP is used for FTP access
   and encrypts both commands and data. SCP is used to securely transfer
   files to a remote host.

Protocols

Internet Protocol Security

The *Internet Protocol Security* (IPsec) authentication and encapsulation standard
is widely used to establish secure VPN communications. The use of IPsec can
secure transmissions between critical servers and clients. This helps prevent
network-based attacks from taking place. Unlike most security systems that
function within the application layer of the OSI model, IPsec functions within
the network layer. IPsec provides authentication services and encapsulation of
data through support of the Internet Key Exchange (IKE) protocol.

The asymmetric key standard defining IPsec provides two primary security
services:

▶ **Authentication Header (AH):** This provides authentication of the
data's sender, along with integrity and nonrepudiation. RFC 2402 states
that AH provides authentication for as much of the IP header as possible,
as well as for upper-level protocol data. However, some IP header fields
might change in transit, and when the packet arrives at the receiver, the
value of these fields might not be predictable by the sender. The values
of such fields cannot be protected by AH. So, the protection provided to
the IP header by AH is somewhat piecemeal.

▶ **Encapsulating Security Payload (ESP):** This supports authentication
of the data's sender and encryption of the data being transferred along
with confidentiality and integrity protection. ESP is used to provide
confidentiality, data origin authentication, connectionless integrity, an
antireplay service (a form of partial sequence integrity), and limited
traffic-flow confidentiality. The set of services provided depends on
options selected at the time of security association establishment and on
the placement of the implementation. Confidentiality may be selected
independently of all other services. However, the use of confidentiality without integrity/authentication (either in ESP or separately in AH)
might subject traffic to certain forms of active attacks that could undermine the confidentiality service.

Protocols 51 and 50 are the AH and ESP components of the IPsec protocol. IPsec inserts ESP or AH (or both) as protocol headers into an IP datagram that immediately follows an IP header.

The protocol field of the IP header will be 50 for ESP or 51 for AH. If IPsec is configured to do authentication rather than encryption, you must configure an IP filter to let protocol 51 traffic pass. If IPsec uses nested AH and ESP, you can configure an IP filter to let only protocol 51 (AH) traffic pass.

IPsec supports the IKE protocol, which is a key management standard used to allow specification of separate key protocols to be used during data encryption. IKE functions within the Internet Security Association and Key Management Protocol (ISAKMP), which defines the payloads used to exchange key and authentication data appended to each packet.

The common key exchange protocols and standard encryption algorithms—including asymmetric key solutions such as the Diffie-Hellman Key Agreement and Rivest-Shamir-Adleman (RSA) standards; symmetric key solutions such as the International Data Encryption Algorithm (IDEA) and Digital Encryption Standard (DES); Triple DES (3DES) and hashing algorithms, such as the message digest 5 (MD5) and Secure Hash Algorithm (SHA)—are covered in detail in Chapter 12, "Cryptography Tools and Techniques."

Although IPsec by itself does not control access to the wireless local-area network (WAN), it can be used in conjunction with 802.1X to provide security for data being sent to client computers that are roaming between access points (AP) on the same network. For better security, segment the wireless network by placing a firewall between the WLAN and the remainder of the network. Because IPsec is a solution to securely authenticate and encrypt network IP packets, you can use IPsec to provide strong security between a Remote Authentication Dial-In User Service (RADIUS) server and a domain controller, or to secure traffic to a partner organization's RADIUS servers. RADIUS provides authentication and access control within an enterprise network and is explained in greater detail in Chapter 10, "Authentication, Authorization, and Access Control." Many of the VPN solutions use IPsec, and, like a virtual private network (VPN), IPsec is an excellent solution in many circumstances. However, it should not be a direct alternative for WLAN protection implemented at the network hardware layer.

Simple Network Management Protocol

Older protocols that are still in use might leave the network vulnerable. Protocols such as Simple Network Management Protocol (SNMP) and Domain Name Service (DNS) that were developed a long time ago and have been widely deployed can pose security risks, too. *SNMP* is an application layer protocol whose purpose is to collect statistics from TCP/IP devices. SNMP is used for monitoring the health of network equipment, computer equipment, and devices such as uninterruptible power supplies (UPS). Many of the vulnerabilities associated with SNMP stem from using SNMPv1. Although these vulnerabilities were discovered in 2002, vulnerabilities are still being reported with current SNMP components. A recent Ubuntu Linux Security Advisory noted that vulnerabilities in Net-SNMP allow remote attackers to cause a denial of service.

The SNMP management infrastructure consists of three components:

▶ SNMP managed node

▶ SNMP agent

▶ SNMP network management station

The device loads the agent, which in turn collects the information and forwards it to the management station. Network management stations collect a massive amount of critical network information and are likely targets of intruders because SNMPv1 is not secure. The only security measure it has in place is its community name, which is similar to a password. By default, this is "public," and many times is not changed, thus leaving the information wide open to intruders. SNMPv2 uses message digest 5 (MD5) for authentication. The transmissions can also be encrypted. SNMPv3 is the current standard, but some devices are likely to still be using SNMPv1 or SNMPv2.

SNMP can help malicious users learn a lot about your system, making password-guessing attacks a bit easier than brute-force attacks. SNMP is often overlooked when checking for vulnerabilities because it uses User Datagram Protocol (UDP) ports 161 and 162. Make sure that network management stations are secure physically and secure on the network. You might even consider using a separate management subnet and protecting it using a router with an access list. Unless this service is required, you should turn it off.

Secure Shell

As a more secure replacement for the common command-line terminal utility Telnet, the *Secure Shell* (SSH) utility establishes a session between the client and host computers using an authenticated and encrypted connection. SSH requires encryption of all data, including the login portion. SSH uses the asymmetric (public key) RSA cryptography method to provide both connection and authentication.

Data encryption is accomplished using one of the following algorithms:

▶ **Encryption Algorithm (IDEA):** The default encryption algorithm used by SSH, which uses a 128-bit symmetric key block cipher.

▶ **Blowfish:** A symmetric (private key) encryption algorithm using a variable 32- to 448-bit secret key.

▶ **Data Encryption Standard (DES):** A symmetric key encryption algorithm using a random key selected from a large number of shared keys. Most forms of this algorithm cannot be used in products meant for export from the United States.

▶ **Triple Data Encryption Standard (#DES):** A symmetric key encryption algorithm that dramatically improves upon the DES by using the DES algorithm three times with three distinct keys.

Using SSH helps guard against attacks such as eavesdropping, man-in-the-middle attacks, and spoofing. Attempts to spoof the identity of either side of a communication can be thwarted because each packet is encrypted using a key known only by the local and remote systems.

ExamAlert

Some versions of SSH, including the Secure Shell for Windows Server, provide a secure version of the File Transfer Protocol (SFTP) along with the other common SSH utilities.

Domain Name Service

Domain Name Service (DNS) was originally designed as an open protocol. DNS servers are organized in a hierarchy. At the top level of the hierarchy, root servers store the complete database of Internet domain names and their corresponding IP addresses. There are different types of DNS servers. The most common types are the following:

▶ **Authoritative servers:** Definitive for particular domains providing information about only those domains. An authoritative-only name server only returns answers to queries about domain names that have been specifically configured.

▶ **Caching servers:** Uses recursion to resolve a given name starting with the DNS root through to the authoritative name servers of the queried domain.

Internal DNS servers can be less susceptible to attacks than external DNS servers, but they still need to be secured. To stop outside intruders from accessing the internal network of your company, use separate DNS servers for internal and Internet name resolution. To provide Internet name resolution for internal hosts, you can have your internal DNS servers use a forwarder.

The following are some considerations for internal DNS servers:

▶ Eliminate any single point of failure by making sure that the structure is planned properly. Analyze where the clients of each DNS zone are located and how they will resolve names if the DNS server is unavailable.

▶ Prevent unauthorized access to your servers by implementing integrated zones with secure dynamic updates. Keep the list of DNS servers that are allowed to obtain a zone transfer small.

▶ Monitor the server events and DNS logs. Proper monitoring of logs and server events can help prevent unauthorized access as well as diagnose problems.

Transport Layer Security

Another asymmetric key encapsulation currently considered the successor to SSL is the Transport Layer Security (TLS) protocol, based on Netscape's Secure Sockets Layer 3.0 (SSL3) transport protocol, which provides encryption using stronger encryption methods, such as DES, or without encryption altogether if desired for authentication only. SSL and TLS transport are similar but not entirely interoperable. TLS also provides confidentiality and data integrity.

TLS has two layers of operation:

▶ **TLS Record Protocol:** This protocol allows the client and server to communicate using some form of encryption algorithm (or without encryption if desired).

▶ **TLS Handshake Protocol:** This protocol allows the client and server to authenticate one another and exchange encryption keys to be used during the session.

Secure Sockets Layer

Secure Sockets Layer (SSL) protocol communications occur between the HTTP (application) and TCP (transport) layers of Internet communications. SSL is used by millions of websites in the protection of their online transactions with their customers. SSL is a public key-based security protocol that is used by Internet services and clients for authentication, message integrity, and confidentiality. The SSL process uses certificates for authentication and encryption for message integrity and confidentiality. SSL establishes what is called a *stateful connection*. In a stateful connection, both ends set up and maintain information about the session itself during its life. This is different from a stateless connection, where there is no prior connection setup. The SSL stateful connection is negotiated by a handshaking procedure between client and server. During this handshake, the client and server exchange the specifications for the cipher that will be used for that session. SSL communicates using an asymmetric key with cipher strength of 40 or 128 bits.

SSL works by establishing a secure channel using public key infrastructure (PKI). This can eliminate a vast majority of attacks, such as session hijackings and information theft.

You can secure communications when performing administration on wireless access points (WAP) by leveraging protocols such as SSH or HTTP with SSL or TLS. A WAP can implement access control functions to allow or deny access to the network and provides the capability of encrypting wireless traffic. It also has the means to query an authentication and authorization service for authorization decisions and securely exchange encryption keys with the client to secure the network traffic.

As a general rule, SSL is not as flexible as IPsec from an application perspective but is more flexible for access from any location. One must determine the usage requirements for each class of user and determine the best approach.

Transmission Control Protocol/Internet Protocol

The core of TCP/IP consists of four main protocols: the Internet Protocol (IP), the Transmission Control Protocol (TCP), the User Datagram Protocol (UDP), and the Internet Control Message Protocol (ICMP). IP is responsible for providing essential routing functions for all traffic on a TCP/IP network. TCP provides connection-oriented communication. UDP provides connectionless communications. TCP connections are initiated and terminated with a three-way handshake process. ICMP provides administrative services to TCP/IP networks.

TCP/IP's implementation of the OSI model makes functionality simpler by mapping the same seven layers of the OSI model to a four-layer model instead. Unlike the OSI reference model, the TCP/IP model focuses more on delivering interconnectivity than on functional layers. It does this by acknowledging the importance of a structured hierarchical sequence of functions, yet leaves protocol designers flexibility for implementation. Table 2.1 compares the OSI and TCP/IP models.

TABLE 2.1 **OSI and TCP/IP Model Comparison**

OSI Reference Model	TCP/IP Reference Model
Application Presentation Session	Application
Transport	Transport
Network	Internet
Data link	Network access Physical

File Transfer Protocol Secure

FTP passes the username and password in a plain-text form, allowing packet sniffing of the network traffic to read these values, which may then be used for unauthorized access to the server. *FTPS*, also known as *FTP Secure* and *FTP-SSL*, is an FTP extension that adds support for TLS and SSL. FTPS supports channel encryption as defined in RFC 2228.

With FTPS, data transfers take place in a way designed to allow both parties to authenticate each other and to prevent eavesdropping, tampering, and forgery on the messages exchanged. FTPS includes full support for the TLS and SSL cryptographic protocols, including the use of server-side public key authentication certificates and client-side authorization certificates. It also supports compatible ciphers, including AES, RC4, RC2, Triple DES and DES, as well as hash functions SHA1, MD5, MD4, and MD2.

You should use FTPS when you need to transfer sensitive or confidential data between a client and a server that is configured to use SSL for secure transactions.

Secure variations of FTP ensure that data cannot be intercepted during transfer and allow the use of more secure transfer of user access credentials during FTP login. However, the same certificate vulnerabilities discussed earlier in this chapter apply here, too.

Hypertext Transport Protocol over Secure Sockets Layer

Basic web connectivity using Hypertext Transport Protocol (HTTP) occurs over TCP port 80, providing no security against interception of transacted data sent in clear text. An alternative to this involves the use of SSL transport protocols operating on port 443, which creates an encrypted pipe through which HTTP traffic can be conducted securely. To differentiate a call to port 80 (http://servername/), HTTP over SSL calls on port 443 using HTTPS as the URL port designator (https://servername/).

HTTP Secure (HTTPS) was originally created by the Netscape Corporation and used a 40-bit RC4 stream encryption algorithm to establish a secured connection encapsulating data transferred between the client and web server, although it can also support the use of X.509 digital certificates to allow the user to authenticate the sender. Now, 256-bit encryption keys have become the accepted level of secure connectivity for online banking and electronic commerce transactions.

ExamAlert

An alternative to HTTPS is the Secure Hypertext Transport Protocol (S-HTTP), which was developed to support connectivity for banking transactions and other secure web communications. S-HTTP supports DES, 3DES, RC2, and RSA2 encryption, along with Challenge Handshake Authentication Protocol (CHAP) authentication but was not adopted by the early web browser developers (for example, Netscape and Microsoft) and so remains less common than the HTTPS standard.

Although HTTPS encrypts communication between the client and server, it does not guarantee that the merchant is trustworthy or that the merchant's server is secure. SSL/TLS is designed to positively identify the merchant's server and encrypt communication between the client and server.

Secure Copy Protocol

The *Secure Copy Protocol* (SCP) is a network protocol that supports file transfers. SCP is a combination of RCP and SSH. It uses the BSD RCP protocol tunneled through the SSH protocol to provide encryption and authentication. The RCP performs the file transfer, and the SSH protocol performs authentication and encryption. SCP runs on port 22 and protects the authenticity and confidentiality of the data in transit. It thwarts the ability for packet sniffers to extract information from data packets.

An SCP download request is server driven, which imposes a security risk when connected to a malicious server. SCP has been mostly superseded by the more comprehensive SFTP, and some implementations of the SCP utility actually use SFTP instead.

Internet Control Message Protocol

Internet Control Message Protocol (ICMP) is a protocol meant to be used as an aid for other protocols and system administrators to test for connectivity and search for configuration errors in a network. Ping uses the ICMP echo function and is the lowest-level test of whether a remote host is alive. A small packet containing an ICMP echo message is sent through the network to a particular IP address. The computer that sent the packet then waits for a return packet. If the connections are good and the target computer is up, the echo message return packet will be received. It is one of the most useful network tools available because it tests the most basic function of an IP network. It also shows the Time To Live (TTL) value and the amount of time it takes for a packet to make the complete trip, also known as *round-trip time* (RTT), in milliseconds (ms). One caveat with using ICMP: It can be manipulated by malicious users, so some administrators block ICMP traffic. If that is the case, you will receive a request timeout even though the host is available.

Traceroute is a computer network diagnostic tool for displaying the route (path) and measuring transit delays of packets across an IP network. Traceroute outputs the list of traversed routers in simple text format, together with timing information. Traceroute is available on most operating systems. On Microsoft Windows operating systems, it is named tracert. Traceroute uses an ICMP echo request packet to find the path. It sends an echo reply with the TTL value set to 1. When the first router sees the packet with TTL 1, it decreases it by 1 to 0 and discards the packet. As a result, it sends an ICMP Time Exceeded message back to the source address. The source address of the ICMP error message is the first router address. Now the source knows the address of the first router. Generally, three packets are sent at each TTL, and the RTT is measured for each one. Most implementations of traceroute keep working until they have gone 30 hops, but this can be extended up to 254 routers.

Pathping is a Windows route-tracing tool that combines features of the ping and tracert commands with additional information. The command uses traceroute to identify which routers are on the path. When the traceroute is complete, pathping sends pings periodically to all the routers over a given time period and computes statistics based on the number of packets returned from each hop. By default, pathping pings each router 100 times, with a single ping every 0.25 seconds. Consequently, a default query requires 25 seconds per router hop. This is especially helpful in identifying routers that cause delays or other latency problems on a connection between two IP hosts.

IPv4

IPv4 is a connectionless protocol for use on packet-switched networks. It operates on a best effort delivery model, in that it does not guarantee delivery, nor does it ensure proper sequencing or avoidance of duplicate delivery. These aspects, including data integrity, are addressed by an upper-layer transport protocol, such as TCP. IPv4 currently routes the majority of Internet traffic. IPv4 is widely used in both internal and external networks throughout the world.

IPv4 is susceptible to ping sweeps, port scans, and application and vulnerability scans. To mitigate sweeps and scans, filtering messages or traffic types is an acceptable solution because it is impossible to eliminate reconnaissance activity.

IPv6

Because of the increased demand of devices requiring IP addresses, IPv4 could not keep up with such an expansive demand. As a result, a new method was needed to address all the new devices requiring IP addresses. The Internet Engineering Task Force (IETF) published a new standard for IP addresses in RFC 2460. The new standard, *IPv6*, makes several changes to the older IPv4 standard. IPv6 increases the address size from IPv4 32 bits to 128 bits.

The differences between IPv6 and IPv4 are in five major areas: addressing and routing, security, network address translation, administrative workload, and support for mobile devices. Table 2.2 provides a comparison of some of the differences between IPv4 and IPv6.

TABLE 2.2 **IPv4 and IPv6 Comparison**

IPv4	IPv6
Addresses are 32 bits (4 bytes) in length.	Addresses are 128 bits (16 bytes) in length.
Header includes a checksum and options.	Header does not include a checksum, and all optional data is moved to IPv6 extension headers.
ARP uses broadcast request frames to resolve an IP address to a link-layer address.	Multicast Neighbor Solicitation messages are used to resolve IP addresses to link-layer addresses.
IPv4 header does not identify packet flow for quality of service (QoS).	IPv6 header identifies packet flow for QoS.

IPv4	IPv6
IPsec support is optional.	IPsec support is required.
IPv4 limits packets to 64 KB of payload.	IPv6 has optional support for jumbograms, which can be as large as 4 GB.
Must be configured either manually or through Dynamic Host Configuration Protocol (DHCP).	Does not require manual configuration or DHCP.

In addition to the difference in the address structure in IPv6, there are IPv6 versions of protocols and commands. The following are some of the more prevalent ones:

▶ **DHCPv6:** Provides stateful address configuration or stateless configuration settings to IPv6 hosts.

▶ **EIGRPv6:** Enhanced Interior Gateway Routing Protocol (EIGRP) is a routing protocol that was developed by Cisco. EIGRPv6 runs on IPv6 networks. It operates in the same manner as the IPv4 version, except that is routes IPv6 addresses.

▶ **ICMPv6:** Used by IPv6 nodes to report packet processing errors and diagnostics.

▶ **Pingv6:** Used in the same capacity as Ping except for IPv6 addresses. On Windows-based machines, is used, and on Linux/UNIX-based machines is used.

Internet Small Computer System Interface

Internet Small Computer System Interface (iSCSI) is an IP-based storage networking standard for linking data storage facilities. iSCSI is used for faster data transfers over intranets and handling remote storage access mainly in local-area networks (LAN) and WANs. It can be used in cloud environments as well, allowing remote resources to appear as local.

Businesses choose iSCSI because of ease of installation, cost, and utilization of current Ethernet networks. iSCSI clients or initiators send SCSI commands to SCSI targets on remote servers to communicate. iSCSI typically uses TCP port 860, with the target service using port 3260. iSCSI uses IPsec for protection. IPsec provides greater levels of security and integrity, as mentioned earlier in this section.

Fibre Channel

Fibre Channel (FC) is a gigabit network technology predominantly used to link data storage facilities or a storage-area network (SAN). FC is similar to iSCSI, but requires a Fibre Channel infrastructure. An FC infrastructure generally is more costly and complex to manage due to the separate network switching infrastructure. FC uses the Fibre Channel Protocol (FCP) to transport SCSI commands over the network consisting of ports and fabric. FC allows devices to attach through an interconnected switching system called a *fabric*. An FC port is not the same thing as computer port or network port. It is the node path performing data communications over the channel. The fiber may attach to a node port (N_Port) and to a port of the fabric (F_Port). The FC port manages a point-to-point connection between itself and the fabric.

FC network protection is primarily security through obscurity because direct access to the FC network is not available to most users, but this does not eliminate the need for security. Approved in 2004, the Fibre Channel Security Protocols standard (FC-SP) specifies how to protect against security breaches. This standard defines protocols for authentication, session keys, integrity and confidentiality, and policy implementation across an FC fabric. Basic FC security occurs through authentication and access control. To secure FC, authentication between FC devices and other devices with whom they communicate can be established using mutual authentication. Proper access control can be achieved through port locking, hard zoning, logical unit number (LUN) masking, and using secure management interfaces and protocols.

Fiber Channel over Ethernet

Fiber Channel over Ethernet (FCoE) is similar in concept to FC except that it allows Ethernet as a method of linking devices to storage. FC traffic runs over an Ethernet infrastructure by encapsulating FC over the Ethernet portions of the connectivity, allowing FC to run alongside IP traffic. FC traffic is used for the server applications, FC SAN, and FC storage. Because FCoE allows FC to be carried over Ethernet, the amount of equipment required in the data center can be reduced. FCoE uses a converged network adapter (CNA), lossless Ethernet links, and an FCoE switch.

Organizations often choose FCoE to maintain or evolve their existing FC network. SAN basic security flaws include weaknesses with authentication and authorization. FCoE can be secured in the manners suggested for FC but also includes control-plane protection and data-plane protection. Control-plane protection is access protection for the switches. Data-plane protection is security for traffic passing through the switches.

File Transfer Protocol

File Transfer Protocol (FTP) servers provide user access to upload or download files between client systems and a networked FTP server. FTP servers include many potential security issues, including anonymous file access and unencrypted authentication. Many FTP servers include the ability for anonymous access in their default installation configuration. Anonymous access is a popular method to provide general access to publicly available information. The problem with this form of access is that any user may download (and potentially upload) any file desired. This might result in a server's available file storage and network access bandwidth being rapidly consumed for purposes other than those intended by the server's administrator. If unauthorized file upload is allowed along with download, illegal file content could be placed on the server for download, without the knowledge of the system's administrator.

Even when user authentication is required, FTP passes the username and password in an unencrypted (plain-text) form, allowing packet sniffing of the network traffic to read these values, which may then be used for unauthorized access. To mitigate FTP vulnerabilities, actions such as disabling anonymous access, hardening access control lists (ACL), enabling logging and disk quotas, setting access restrictions by IP, and enabling "blind" puts can be implemented. Using more secure variations of FTP ensures that data cannot be intercepted during transfer and allows the use of more secure transfer of user access credentials during FTP login.

Secure File Transfer Protocol

Secure File Transfer Protocol (SFTP), or Secure FTP, is a program that uses SSH to transfer files. Unlike standard FTP, it encrypts both commands and data, preventing passwords and sensitive information from being transmitted in the clear over the network. It is functionally similar to FTP, but because it uses a different protocol, you cannot use a standard FTP client to talk to an SFTP server, nor can you connect to an FTP server with a client that supports only SFTP.

ExamAlert

A more secure version of FTP (SFTP) has been developed that includes SSL encapsulation. This version is referred to as FTP over SSH and uses the SSH TCP port 22. Do not confuse it with FTPS (FTP over SSL), which uses TCP ports 989 and 990. Either may be used within a modern enterprise network.

Trivial File Transfer Protocol

Trivial File Transfer Protocol (TFTP) is a simple version of FTP used for transferring files between network devices. TFTP uses UDP port 69, has no login feature, and because it is implemented using UDP generally works only on LANs. TFTP works with either Bootstrap Protocol (BOOTP) or DHCP.

Because of the lack of security in TFTP, it is a good idea to place the TFTP server behind a firewall on an isolated LAN that only the essential equipment can reach.

Telnet

Telnet is a terminal emulation program used to access remote routers and UNIX systems. Telnet can be used as a tool to determine whether the port on a host computer is working properly. Telnet passes the username, password, and even transacted data in an unencrypted form (clear text), allowing packet sniffing of the network traffic to read these values, which may then be used for unauthorized access to the server. Telnet-type clear-text connections create the ideal situation for TCP hijacking and man-in-the-middle attacks. Methods for mitigating Telnet vulnerabilities include using enhanced encryption or authentication security such as Kerberos, IPsec, SSH, SSL, or Cisco Secure Telnet.

Hypertext Transport Protocol

Hypertext Transfer Protocol (HTTP) allows users to connect to sources of information, services, products, and other functionality through the Internet. Business transactions, membership information, vendor/client communications, and even distributed business logic transactions can all occur though HTTP using basic Internet connectivity on TCP port 80.

An HTTP message contains a header and a body. The message header of an HTTP request has a request line and a collection of header fields. All HTTP messages must include the protocol version. Some HTTP messages can contain a content body, which is optional. The original HTTP specification has little support for the security mechanisms appropriate for today's Internet transactions. Methods for mitigating HTTP vulnerabilities include using enhanced encryption or authentication security HTTPS or SSL.

NetBIOS

Network Basic Input/Output System (NetBIOS) is an application programming interface (API) providing various networking services. NetBIOS provides name, datagram, and session services, allowing applications on different computers to communicate within a LAN. The session mode establishes a connection and provides error detection. The datagram mode is connectionless and supports LAN broadcast. NetBIOS is most commonly found in use with Microsoft Windows operating systems. Because it does not support routing, NetBIOS must be used with another transport mechanism such as TCP when it is implemented in an organization that has a WAN.

Ports

There are 65,535 TCP and UDP ports on which a computer can communicate. The port numbers are divided into three ranges:

▶ **Well-known ports:** The well-known ports are those from 0 through 1,023.

▶ **Registered ports:** The registered ports are those from 1,024 through 49,151.

▶ **Dynamic/private ports:** The dynamic/private ports are those from 49,152 through 65,535.

Often, many of these ports are not secured and, as a result, are used for exploitation. Table 2.3 lists some of the most commonly used ports and the services and protocols that use them. Many of these ports and services have vulnerabilities associated with them. It is important that you know what common ports are used by network protocols and how to securely implement services on these ports.

ExamAlert

Know the difference between the various ports that are used for network services and protocols.

TABLE 2.3 **Commonly Used Ports**

Port	Service/Protocol
15	Netstat
20	FTP-Data transfer
21	FTP-Control (command)
22	SSH/SFTP/SCP

Port	Service/Protocol
23	Telnet
25	SMTP
53	DNS
69	TFTP
80	HTTP
110	POP3
137, 138, 139	NetBIOS
143	IMAP
161/162	SNMP
443	HTTPS
445	SMB
989/990	FTPS
1,812	RADIUS
3389	RDP

Table 2.3 includes a list of protocols that may be currently in use on a network. These protocols, along with some older or antiquated protocols, may be configured open by default by the machine manufacturer or when an operating system is installed. Every operating system requires different services for it to operate properly. If ports are open for manufacturer-installed tools, the manufacturer should have the services listed in the documentation. Ports for older protocols such as Chargen (port 19) and Telnet (port 23) may still be accessible. For example, Finger, which uses port 79, was widely used during the early days of Internet, and today's sites no longer offer the service. However, you might still find some old implementations of Eudora mail that use the Finger protocol, or worse, the mail clients have long since been upgraded, but the port used 10 years ago was somehow left open. The quickest way to tell which ports are open and which services are running is to do a Netstat on the machine. You can also run local or online port scans.

The best way to protect the network infrastructure from attacks aimed at antiquated or unused ports and protocols is to remove any unnecessary protocols and create access control lists to allow traffic on necessary ports only. By doing so, you eliminate the possibility of unused and antiquated protocols being exploited and minimize the threat of an attack.

OSI Relevance

You should be very familiar with the OSI model as well as the common protocols and network hardware that function within each level. For example, you should know that hubs operate at the physical layer of the OSI model. Intelligent hubs, bridges, and network switches operate at the data link layer, and Layer 3 switches and routers operate at the network layer. The Network+ Exam Cram and Exam Prep books cover the OSI model in much more detail. If you will be working extensively with network protocols and hardware, you should also look at these texts.

The layers of the OSI model are as follows:

7. Application layer

6. Presentation layer

5. Session layer

4. Transport layer

3. Network layer

2. Data link layer (subdivided into the Logical-Link Control [LLC] and Media Access Control [MAC] sublayers)

1. Physical layer

Most applications, like web browsers or email clients, incorporate functionality of the OSI layers 5, 6, and 7.

Cram Quiz

Answer these questions. The answers follow the last question. If you cannot answer these questions correctly, consider reading this section again until you can.

1. Which of the following is the correct address size for IPv6 addresses?

   ○ **A.** 32 bit

   ○ **B.** 64 bit

   ○ **C.** 128 bit

   ○ **D.** 256 bit

2. Which of the following protocols runs on port 22 and protects the authenticity and confidentiality of file transfer data in transit?

   ○ **A.** DHCP

   ○ **B.** SSL

   ○ **C.** FTP

   ○ **D.** SCP

3. You are troubleshooting connectivity issues on the network. Which of the following would be most helpful in determining where the connectivity issues lie?

   ○ **A.** SNMP

   ○ **B.** ICMP

   ○ **C.** SSL

   ○ **D.** IPsec

4. You want to be sure that the NetBIOS ports that are required for certain Windows network functions have been secured. Which of the following ports would you check?

   ○ **A.** 25/110/143

   ○ **B.** 161/162

   ○ **C.** 137/138/139

   ○ **D.** 20/21

5. Your company is in the process of setting up a management system on your network, and you want to use SNMP. You have to allow this traffic through the router. Which UDP ports do you have to open? (Choose two correct answers.)

   ○ **A.** 161

   ○ **B.** 139

   ○ **C.** 138

   ○ **D.** 162

6. Which standard port is used to establish a web connection using the 40-bit RC4 encryption protocol?

   ○ **A.** 21

   ○ **B.** 80

   ○ **C.** 443

   ○ **D.** 8,250

Cram Quiz Answers

1. **C**. IPv6 increases the address size from IPv4 32 bits to 128 bits. Answers A, B, and D are incorrect because IPv6 addresses sizes are 128 bit.

2. **D**. SCP runs on port 22 and protects the authenticity and confidentiality of the data in transit. Answer A is incorrect because DHCP is used to automatically assign IP addresses. Answer B is incorrect because SSL is a public key-based security protocol that is used by Internet services and clients for authentication, message integrity, and confidentiality. The standard port for SSL is port 443. Answer C is incorrect because in FTP the data is not protected.

3. **B**. Traceroute uses an ICMP echo request packet to find the path between two addresses. Answer A is incorrect because SNMP is an application layer protocol whose purpose is to collect statistics from TCP/IP devices. SNMP is used for monitoring the health of network equipment, computer equipment, and devices such as uninterruptible power supplies (UPS). Answer C is incorrect because SSL is a public key-based security protocol that is used by Internet services and clients for authentication, message integrity, and confidentiality. Answer D is incorrect because IPsec authentication and encapsulation standard is widely used to establish secure VPN communications.

4. **C**. There are NetBIOS ports that are required for certain Windows network functions, such as file sharing, which are 137, 138, and 139. Answer A is incorrect because these ports are used for email. Answer B is incorrect because these ports are used for SNMP. Answer D is incorrect because these ports are used for FTP.

5. **A** and **D**. UDP ports 161 and 162 are used by SNMP. Answer B is incorrect because UDP port 139 is used by the NetBIOS session service. Answer C is incorrect because port 138 is used to allow NetBIOS traffic for name resolution.

6. **C**. A connection using HTTPS is made using the RC4 cipher and port 443. Answer A is incorrect because port 21 is used for FTP connections. Answer B is incorrect because port 80 is used for unsecure plain-text HTTP communications. Answer D is incorrect because port 8,250 is not designated to a particular TCP/IP protocol.

Given a Scenario, Troubleshoot Security Issues Related to Wireless Networking

▶ **WPA**

▶ **WPA2**

▶ **WEP**

▶ **EAP**

▶ **PEAP**

▶ **LEAP**

▶ **MAC filter**

▶ **Disable SSID broadcast**

▶ **TKIP**

▶ **CCMP**

▶ **Antenna placement**

▶ **Power-level controls**

▶ **Captive portals**

▶ **Antenna types**

▶ **Site surveys**

▶ **VPN (over open wireless)**

CramSaver

If you can correctly answer these questions before going through this section, save time by skimming the Exam Alerts in this section and then completing the Cram Quiz at the end of the section.

1. Explain the difference between PEAP and LEAP.

2. Explain how to improve the security of wireless networks with regard to SSIDs.

3. Explain what CCMP is.

Answers

1. PEAP provides several benefits within TLS, including an encrypted authentication channel, dynamic keying material from TLS, fast reconnect using cached session keys, and server authentication that protects against the setting up of unauthorized access points. LEAP is a proprietary EAP method because it requires the use of a Cisco AP. It features mutual authentication, secure session key derivation, and dynamic per-user, per-session WEP keys.

2. To improve the security of your network, change the SSID. Using the default SSID poses a security risk even if the AP is not broadcasting it. When changing default SSIDs, do not change the SSID to reflect your company's main names, divisions, products, or address. Turning off SSID broadcast does not effectively protect the network from attacks.

3. Counter Mode with Cipher Block Chaining Message Authentication Code Protocol (CCMP) is an encryption protocol that forms part of the 802.11i standard for wireless local-area networks (WLAN). CCMP uses 128-bit keys with a 48-bit initialization vector (IV) that reduces vulnerability to replay attacks.

WPA

Wireless security comes in two major varieties: Wired Equivalent Privacy (WEP) and Wi-Fi Protected Access (WPA). Both include methods to encrypt wireless traffic between wireless clients and WAPs. WEP has been included in 802.11–based products for some time and includes a strategy for restricting network access and encrypting network traffic based upon a shared key. The Wi-Fi Protected Access (WPA and WPA2) standards were developed by the Wi-Fi Alliance to replace the WEP protocol. WPA was developed after security flaws were found in WEP. WPA protects networks by incorporating a set of enhanced security features. WPA-protected networks require users to enter a passkey to access a wireless network. There are two different modes of WPA: WPA-PSK (Personal Shared Key) mode and WPA-802.1X mode, which is more often referred to as WPA-RADIUS or WPA-Enterprise. For the PSK mode, a passphrase consisting of 8 to 63 ASCII characters is all that is required. The Enterprise mode requires the use of security certificates. WPA includes many of the functions of the 802.11i protocol but relies on Rivest Cipher 4 (RC4), which is considered vulnerable to keystream attacks.

WPA2

WPA2 is based on the IEEE 802.11i standard and provides government-grade security by implementing the AES encryption algorithm and 802.1X-based authentication. AES is a block cipher that encrypts 128-bit blocks of data at a time with a 128-bit encryption key. WPA2 incorporates stricter security standards and is configurable in either the PSK or Enterprise mode. There are two versions of WPA2: WPA2-Personal and WPA2-Enterprise. WPA2-Personal protects unauthorized network access via a password. WPA2-Enterprise verifies network users through a server.

WPA2 is backward compatible with WPA and supports strong encryption and authentication for both infrastructure and ad hoc networks. In addition, it has support for the CCMP (Counter Mode with Cipher Block Chaining Message Authentication Code Protocol) encryption mechanism based on the Advanced Encryption Standard (AES) cipher as an alternative to the Temporal Key Integrity Protocol (TKIP). TKIP is an encryption protocol included as part of the IEEE 802.11i standard for WLANs. An AES-based encryption mechanism that is stronger than TKIP.

WEP

Wired Equivalent Privacy (WEP) is the most basic form of encryption that can be used on 802.11-based wireless networks to provide privacy of data sent between a wireless client and its AP. Originally, many wireless networks were based on the IEEE 802.11 standard, which had serious data transmission security shortcomings. When this standard was put into place, the 802.11 committee adopted an encryption protocol called *WEP*. To discuss WEP's shortcomings, we have to understand how it operates. WEP uses a stream cipher for encryption called *RC4*. RC4 uses a shared secret key to generate a long sequence of bytes from what is called a *generator*. This stream is then used to produce the encrypted ciphertext. Early 802.11b networks used 40-bit encryption because of government restrictions. Hackers can crack a 40-bit key in a few hours. It is much easier to break RC4 encryption if a second instance of encryption with a single key can be isolated. In other words, the weakness is that the same keys are used repeatedly. Specifications for the WEP standard are detailed within the 802.11b (Wi-Fi) specification. This specification details a method of data encryption and authentication that may be used to establish a more secured wireless connection.

> **ExamAlert**
>
> Developments in the field of cryptography revealed the WEP encryption method to be less secure than originally intended and vulnerable to cryptographic analysis of network traffic. More advanced protocols such as WPA2 and the 802.11i standard supersede WEP, but recommendations for a more secure wireless network may also include the use of IPsec and VPN connectivity to tunnel data communications through a secured connection.

Although using WEP is much better than no encryption at all, it's important to understand its limitations so that you have an accurate picture of the consequences and what you must do to properly protect your wireless environment.

EAP

The *802.1X standard* is a means of wireless authentication. The 802.1X authentication standard is an extension of point-to-point protocol (PPP) that relies on the Extensible Authentication Protocol (EAP) for its authentication needs. EAP is a challenge-response protocol that can be run over secured transport mechanisms. It is a flexible authentication technology and can be used with smart cards, one-time passwords, and public key encryption. It also allows for support of public certificates deployed using auto enrollment or smart cards. These security improvements enable access control to Ethernet networks in public places such as malls and airports. EAP-Transport Layer Security (EAP-TLS) uses certificate-based mutual authentication, negotiation of the encryption method, and encrypted key determination between the client and the authenticating server.

EAP messages are encapsulated into 802.1X packets and are marked as EAP over LAN (EAPOL). After the client sends a connection request to a wireless AP, the authenticator marks all initial communication with the client as unauthorized, and only EAPOL messages are accepted while in this mode. All other types of communication are blocked until credentials are verified with an authentication server. Upon receiving an EAPOL request from the client, the wireless AP requests login credentials and passes them on to an authentication server. Remote Authentication Dial-In User Service (RADIUS) is usually employed for authentication purposes; however, 802.1X does not make it mandatory.

PEAP

Protected EAP (PEAP) was co-developed by Cisco, Microsoft Corporation, and RSA Security, Inc. PEAP provides several additional benefits within TLS, including an encrypted authentication channel, dynamic keying material from TLS, fast reconnect using cached session keys, and server authentication that protects against the setting up of unauthorized access points. PEAP is a means of protecting another EAP method (such as MS-CHAPv2) within a secure channel. The use of PEAP is essential to prevent attacks on password-based EAP methods. As part of the PEAP negotiation, the client establishes a TLS session with the RADIUS server. Using a TLS session as part of PEAP serves a number of purposes:

▶ It allows the client to authenticate the RADIUS server; this means that the client only establishes the session with a server holding a certificate that is trusted by the client.

▶ It protects the MS-CHAPv2 authentication protocol against packet snooping.

▶ The negotiation of the TLS session generates a key that can be used by the client and RADIUS server to establish common master keys. These keys are used to derive the keys used to encrypt the WLAN traffic.

Secured within the PEAP channel, the client authenticates itself to the RADIUS server using the MS-CHAPv2 EAP protocol. During this exchange, the traffic within the TLS tunnel is visible only to the client and RADIUS server and is never exposed to the WAP.

LEAP

Lightweight Extensible Authentication Protocol (LEAP) combines centralized two-way authentication with dynamically generated wireless equivalent privacy keys or WEP keys. LEAP was developed by Cisco for use on WLANs that use Cisco 802.11 wireless devices. LEAP is a proprietary EAP method because it requires the use of a Cisco AP. It features mutual authentication; secure session key derivation; and dynamic per-user, per-session WEP keys. However, because it uses unencrypted challenges and responses, LEAP is vulnerable to dictionary attacks. Still, when LEAP is combined with a rigorous user password policy, it can offer strong authentication security without the use of certificates. LEAP can only authenticate the user to the WLAN, not the computer. Without computer authentication, machine group policies will not execute correctly.

MAC Filter

Most wireless network routers and access points can filter devices based on their Media Access Control (MAC) address. The MAC address is a unique identifier for network adapters. *MAC filtering* is a security access control method whereby the MAC address is used to determine access to the network. When MAC address filtering is used, only the devices with MAC addresses configured in the wireless router or access point are allowed to connect. MAC filtering permits and denies network access through the use of blacklists and whitelists. A *blacklist* is a list of MAC addresses that are denied access. A *whitelist* is a list of MAC addresses that are allowed access. Blacklisting and whitelisting are discussed in further detail in Chapter 8, "Host Security."

While giving a wireless network some additional protection, it is possible to spoof the MAC address. An attacker could potentially capture details about a MAC address from the network and pretend to be that device in order to connect. MAC filtering can be circumvented by scanning a valid MAC using a tool such as airodumping and then spoofing one's own MAC into a validated MAC address. After an attacker knows a MAC address that is out of the blacklist or within the whitelist, MAC filtering is almost useless.

Disable SSID Broadcast

A *service set identifier* (SSID) is used to identify WAPs on a network. The SSID is transmitted so that wireless stations searching for a network connection can find it. By default, SSID broadcast is enabled. This means that it accepts any SSID. When you disable this feature, the SSID configured in the client must match the SSID of the AP; otherwise, the client does not connect to the AP. Having SSID broadcast enabled essentially makes your AP visible to any device searching for a wireless connection.

To improve the security of your network, change the SSIDs on your APs. Using the default SSID poses a security risk even if the AP is not broadcasting it. When changing default SSIDs, do not change the SSID to reflect your company's main names, divisions, products, or address. This just makes you an easy target for attacks such as war driving and war chalking. *War driving* is the act of searching for Wi-Fi wireless networks by a person in a moving vehicle, using a portable computer or other mobile device. *War chalking* is the drawing of symbols in public places to advertise an open Wi-Fi network. Keep in mind that if an SSID name is enticing enough, it might attract hackers.

Turning off SSID broadcast does not effectively protect the network from attacks. Tools such as Kismet enable nonbroadcasting networks to be discovered almost as easily as broadcasting networks. From a security standpoint, it is much better to secure a wireless network using protocols that are designed specifically to address wireless network threats than to disable SSID broadcast.

> **ExamAlert**
>
> Turning off SSID broadcast does not effectively protect the network from attacks. It is much better to secure a wireless network using protocols that are designed specifically to address wireless network threats than to disable SSID broadcast.

TKIP

Temporal Key Integrity Protocol (TKIP) is the security protocol designed to replace WEP and is also known by its later iterations of *Wi-Fi Protected Access*

(WPA) or *WPA2*. Similar to WEP, TKIP uses the RC4 algorithm and does not require an upgrade to existing hardware, whereas more recent protocols, such as CCMP, which use the AES algorithm, do require an upgrade. TKIP was designed to provide more secure encryption than WEP by using the original WEP programming, but it wraps additional code at the beginning and end to encapsulate and modify it. To increase key strength, TKIP includes four additional algorithms: a cryptographic message integrity check, an IV sequencing mechanism, a per-packet key-mixing function, and a rekeying mechanism.

TKIP is useful for upgrading security on devices originally equipped with WEP, but does not address all security issues and might not be reliable enough for sensitive transmission. AES is a better choice and has become the accepted encryption standard for WLAN security.

CCMP

Counter Mode with Cipher Block Chaining Message Authentication Code Protocol (CCMP) is an encryption protocol that forms part of the 802.11i standard for WLANs. CCMP offers enhanced security compared with similar technologies such as TKIP. AES is a block cipher that encrypts 128-bit blocks of data at a time with a 128-bit encryption key. The AES cipher suite uses the Counter-Mode Cipher Block Chaining (CBC) Message Authentication Code (MAC) Protocol (CCMP) as defined in RFC 3610. CCMP uses 128-bit keys with a 48-bit IV that reduces vulnerability to replay attacks. To provide for replay protection, a packet number (PN) field is used. CCMP produces a message integrity code (MIC) that provides data origin authentication and data integrity for the packet payload data. The PN is included in the CCMP header and incorporated into the encryption and MIC calculations. Counter mode makes it difficult for an eavesdropper to spot patterns, and the CBC-MAC message integrity method ensures that messages have not been tampered with.

Antenna Placement

When designing wireless networks, antenna placement and power output should be configured for maximum coverage and minimum interference. Four basic types of antennas are commonly used in 802.11 wireless networking applications: parabolic grid, yagi, dipole, and vertical. APs with factory-default omni antennas cover an area that is roughly circular and are affected by RF obstacles such as walls. When using this type of antenna, it is common to place APs in central locations or divide an office into quadrants. Many APs use multiple-input, multiple-output (MIMO) antennas. This type of antenna takes advantage of multipath signal reflections. Ideally, locate the AP as close as possible to the antennas. The farther the signal has to travel across the cabling between the AP and the antenna, the more signal loss that occurs. Loss is an important factor when deploying a wireless network, especially at higher power levels. Loss occurs as a result of the signal traveling between the wireless base unit and the antenna.

APs that require external antennas need additional consideration. You need to configure the antennas properly, consider what role the AP serves (AP or bridge), and consider where the antennas are placed. When the antenna is mounted on the outside of the building or the interface between the wired network and the transceiver is placed in a corner, it puts the network signal in an area where it is easy to intercept. Antenna placement should not be used as a security mechanism.

Professional site surveys for wireless network installations and proper AP placement are sometimes used to ensure coverage area and security concerns. Up-front planning takes more time and effort but can pay off in the long run, especially for large WLANs.

> **ExamAlert**
>
> Physical placement and transmit power adjustments can make it harder for intruders to stay connected to your APs. But never count on physical placement alone to stop attackers.

Power-Level Controls

One of the principle requirements for wireless communication is that the transmitted wave must reach the receiver with ample power to allow the receiver to distinguish the wave from the background noise. An antenna that is too strong raises security concerns. Strong omnidirectional Wi-Fi signals are radiated to a greater distance into neighboring areas, where the signals can be readily detected and viewed. Minimizing transmission power reduces the chances your data will leak out. Companies such as Cisco and Nortel have implemented dynamic power controls in their products. The system dynamically adjusts the power output of individual access points to accommodate changing network conditions, helping ensure predictable wireless performance and availability.

> **ExamAlert**
>
> Reducing the energy consumption by wireless communication devices is an important issue in WLANs. Know the mechanisms that prevent interference and increase capacity.

Transmit power control is a mechanism used to prevent too much unwanted interference between different wireless networks. Adaptive transmit power control in 802.11 WLANs on a per-link basis helps increase network capacity and improves battery life of Wi-Fi-enabled mobile devices.

Captive Portals

The *captive portal* technique enables administrators to block Internet access for users until some action is taken. When a user attempts to access the Internet, the HTTP client is directed to a special web page that usually requires the user to read and accept an acceptable use policy (AUP). By using a captive portal, the web browser is used to provide authentication. Captive portals are widely used in businesses such as hotels and restaurants that offer free Wi-Fi hotspots to Internet users. A captive portal web page can be used to require authentication, require payment for usage, or display some type of policy or agreement. Although captive portals are mainly for Wi-Fi hotspots, you can also use them to control wired access.

Antenna Types

Wireless antenna types are either omnidirectional or directional. *Omni-directional* antennas provide a 360-degree radial pattern to provide the widest possible signal coverage. An example of omnidirectional antennas are the antennas commonly found on APs. *Directional* antennas concentrate the wireless signal in a specific direction, limiting the coverage area. An example of a directional antenna is a yagi antenna.

The need or use determines the type of antenna required. When an organization wants to connect one building to another building, a directional antenna is used. If an organization is adding Wi-Fi internally to an office building or a warehouse, an omnidirectional antenna is used. If the desire is to install Wi-Fi in an outdoor campus environment, a combination of both antennas would be used.

Site Surveys

A *site survey* is necessary before implementing any WLAN solution, to optimize network layout within each unique location. This is particularly important in distributed wireless network configurations spanning multiple buildings or open natural areas, where imposing structures and tree growth may affect network access in key areas.

A site survey should include a review of the desired physical and logical structure of the network, selection of possible technologies, and several other factors, including the following:

▶ Federal, state, and local laws and regulations relating to the proposed network solution.

▶ Potential sources of radio frequency (RF) interference, including local broadcast systems as well as motors, fans, and other types of equipment that generate RF interference. This includes an analysis of potential channel overlap between WAP hardware.

▶ Available locations for WAP hardware installation and physical network integration connectivity.

▶ Any special requirements of users, applications, and network equipment that must function over the proposed wireless network solution.

▶ Whether a point-to-point (ad hoc or wireless bridge) or multipoint wireless solution is required. In most solutions, point-to-multipoint connectivity will be required to support multiple wireless clients from each WAP connected to the physical network.

ExamAlert

All wireless networks share several common security vulnerabilities related to their use of RF broadcasts, which may potentially be detected and compromised without the knowledge of the network administrator.

Data transported over this medium is available to anyone with the proper equipment, and so must be secured through encryption and encapsulation mechanisms no subject to public compromise.

VPN (Over Open Wireless)

VPNs are commonly used to securely connect employees to corporate networks when they are not in the office by using an Internet connection. More organizations are requiring hotspot visitors to VPN into the organizational network because they have no control over the security used in public Wi-Fi hotspots. The same principles that apply to wired VPNs can be applied to VPNs over open wireless networks. The use of a VPN over public Wi-Fi hotspots can increase privacy and provide data protection. VPNs over open wireless are not always immune to man-in-the-middle attacks. They can be susceptible to Wi-Fi-based attacks and VPN-based attacks.

Cram Quiz

Answer these questions. The answers follow the last question. If you cannot answer
these questions correctly, consider reading this section again until you can.

1. You want to implement non-vendor-specific strong authentication protocols for
   wireless communications. Which of the following would best meet your requirements? (Select two correct answers.)

   ○ **A.** EAP

   ○ **B.** PEAP

   ○ **C.** LEAP

   ○ **D.** WEP

2. Which of the following technologies would be selected when looking to reduce
   a vulnerability to replay attacks by using 128-bit keys with a 48-bit initialization
   vector (IV)?

   ○ **A.** ICMP

   ○ **B.** WEP

   ○ **C.** WPA

   ○ **D.** CCMP

3. Which of the following technologies would be used by a hotel for guest
   acceptance of an acceptable use policy?

   ○ **A.** Site survey

   ○ **B.** MAC filtering

   ○ **C.** VPN over wireless

   ○ **D.** Captive portal

Cram Quiz Answers

1. **A** and **B**. The IEEE specifies 802.1X and EAP as the standard for secure wireless
   networking, and PEAP is standards based. PEAP provides mutual authentication
   and uses a certificate for server authentication by the client, while users have
   the convenience of entering password-based credentials. Answer C is incorrect
   because LEAP is a Cisco proprietary protocol. Answer D is incorrect because
   WEP is the most basic form of encryption that can be used on 802.11-based
   wireless networks to provide privacy of data sent between a wireless client and
   its access point.

2. **D**. CCMP uses 128-bit keys with a 48-bit IV that reduces vulnerability to replay
   attacks. Answer A is incorrect because ICMP is a network troubleshooting
   protocol. Answer B is incorrect because WEP is the most basic form of
   encryption that can be used on 802.11-based wireless networks. Answer C is
   incorrect because WPA protects networks by incorporating a set of enhanced
   security features. WPA-protected networks require users to enter a passkey in
   order to access a wireless network.

3. **D**. A captive portal web page can be used to require authentication, require payment for usage, or display some type of policy or agreement. Answer A is incorrect because a site survey is used to optimize network layout within each unique wireless location. Answer B is incorrect because MAC filtering is a security access control method whereby the MAC address is used to determine access to the network. Answer C is incorrect because the use of a VPN over public Wi-Fi hotspots can increase privacy and provide data protection, but is not used to force acceptance of an acceptable use policy.

What Next?

If you want more practice on this chapter's exam objectives before you move on, remember that you can access all the Cram Quiz questions on the CD. You can also create a custom exam by objective with the practice exam software. Note any objective that you struggle with and go to the material that covers that objective in this chapter.

CHAPTER 3
Risk Management

This chapter covers the following official CompTIA Security+ SY0-401 exam objectives:

▶ Explain the importance of risk-related concepts

▶ Summarize the security implications of integrating systems and data with third parties

▶ Given a scenario, implement appropriate risk mitigation strategies

▶ Given a scenario, implement basic forensic procedures

▶ Summarize common incident response procedures

(For more information on the official CompTIA Security+ SY0-401 exam topics, see the "About the CompTIA Security+ SY0-401 Exam" section in the Introduction.)

Risk is impossible to utterly avoid, so effective management strategies must be applied to mitigate (reduce) the likelihood and impact of "bad risks" or enhance (improve) the likelihood and results of "good risks." A "good risk" would be the chance of a windfall profit or other beneficial outcome, while most risks addressed by the exam will be of the "bad risk" type where an attacker seeks unauthorized access to data or services denied to them. This chapter covers important concepts related to risk and how to recognize areas that may open the organization to additional risk such as integrating systems and data with third parties. It also contains information on the implementation of appropriate risk mitigation strategies, basic forensic procedures, and incident response procedures.

Explain the Importance of Risk-Related Concepts

▶ **Control types**

▶ **False positives**

▶ **False negatives**

▶ **Importance of policies in reducing risks**

▶ **Risk calculation**

▶ **Quantitative vs. qualitative**

▶ **Vulnerabilities**

▶ **Threat vectors**

▶ **Probability/threat likelihood**

▶ **Risk avoidance, transference, acceptance, mitigation, deterrence**

▶ **Risks associated with cloud computing and virtualization**

▶ **Recovery time objective and recovery point objective**

CramSaver

If you can correctly answer these questions before going through this section, save time by skimming the Exam Alerts in this section and then completing the Cram Quiz at the end of the section.

1. Purchasing an insurance plan to cover the costs of a stolen computer is an example of which risk management strategy?

2. If an event occurs about once every 4 years and has an asset value of $100,000, assuming the asset would have to be fully replaced after the event, explain how to calculate the ARO, SLE, and ALE.

3. What three categories are commonly used to identify the likelihood of a risk?

Answers

1. Transference. The cost of the risk is actualized and transferred to the insurance company. The risk, however, is not reduced; only its cost effect has been transferred, and other issues, such as client loss of trust, might produce second-order effects.

2. Annualized rate of occurrence (ARO) identifies how often in a single year the successful threat attack will occur. With an ARO of 25%, this risk is expected to occur once every 4 years on average. The single loss expectancy (SLE) is $100,000 per event because the asset would require full replacement. SLE is the amount of loss expected for any single successful threat attack on any given asset. With an ARO of 25%, the annualized loss expectancy (ALE) is equal to the SLE ($100,000) times the ARO (.25), or $25,000.

3. Likelihood is commonly assigned as high (1.0), medium (0.5), or low (0.1) values for risk comparison.

Control Types

You can apply three general types of controls to mitigate risks, typically by layering defensive controls to protect data with multiple control types when possible. This technique is called a layered defensive strategy or *defense in depth*. The three types of controls are technical, management, and operational:

▶ **Technical:** Technical controls are security controls put in place that are executed by system. Technical controls include logical access control systems, security systems, encryption, and data classification solutions.

▶ **Management:** Management or administrative controls include business and organizational processes and procedures, such as security policies and procedures, personnel background checks, security awareness training, and formal change-management procedures.

▶ **Operational:** Operational controls include organizational culture as well as physical controls that form the outer line of defense against direct access to data, such as protection of backup media; securing output and mobile file storage devices; and facility design details, including layout, doors, guards, locks, and surveillance systems.

False Positives

False positives occur when any normal or expected behavior is identified as anomalous or malicious. False positives generally occur when an intrusion detection system (IDS) detects the presence of a newly installed application and the IDS has not yet been trained for this new behavior. Sometimes anomalous behavior in one area of an organization may be acceptable but highly suspect in another. False positives are one of the largest problems encountered in IDS management. False positives can easily prevent legitimate IDS alerts from quickly being identified. A single rule that generates false positives may create thousands of alerts in a short period of time. The alerts for rules that are causing repeated false positives are often ignored or disabled. This increases risk to the organization because legitimate attacks can be ignored and increases the probability of an effective compromise from the type of attack the disabled or ignored rule was looking for.

False Negatives

False negatives occur when an alert that should have been generated did not occur. False negatives most often happen because the IDS is reactive and signature-based systems do not recognize new attacks. Sometimes in a signature-based system a rule can be written such that it will catch only a subset of an attack vector. Several risks are associated with false negatives. When false negatives occur, missed attacks will not be mitigated and the organization will have a false sense of security. One more item to note about false negatives is that in an environment relying on anomaly detection or a host-based intrusion detection system (HIDS) relying on file changes, if a system was compromised at the time of IDS training, there will be false negatives for any already exploited conditions.

ExamAlert

Controls are intended to mitigate risk in some manner, but at times they might fail in operation. You should be familiar with the following terms for the exam:

▶ **False Negative:** A control that allows unauthorized access, falsely identifying the access as valid

▶ **False Positive:** A control that refuses authorized access, falsely identifying the access as invalid

Importance of Policies in Reducing Risk

To ensure that proper risk management and incident response planning is coordinated, updated, communicated, and maintained, it is important to establish clear and detailed security policies that are ratified by an organization's management and brought to the attention of its users through regular security-awareness training. Policies of which the users have no knowledge are rarely effective, and those that lack management support can prove to be unenforceable. A number of policies can support risk-management within the organization, as described in the sections that follow.

Privacy Policy

Certain federal and state legislation requires owners of commercial websites or online services to post a privacy policy. For example, the Children's Online Privacy Protection Act (COPPA) applies to the online collection of personal information from children under the age of 13. This type of legislation requires that each operator of a commercial website conspicuously post a privacy policy on its website. The privacy policy itself must contain the following features:

▶ A list of the categories of personally identifiable information (PII) the operator collects

▶ A list of the categories of third parties with whom the operator might share such PII

▶ A description of the process by which the consumer can review and request changes to his or her PII collected by the operator

▶ A description of the process by which the operator notifies consumers of material changes to the operator's privacy policy

▶ The effective date of the privacy policy

Other federal and state laws might apply to privacy protection. In addition, other countries have laws as to what information can be collected and stored by organizations. As with most of the information in this chapter, it is imperative that you know the regulations that govern the digital terrain in which your organization operates. The organization then has an obligation to put proper policies and procedures in place.

By limiting the collection of personal information to the least amount necessary to conduct business, an organization may limit potential negative consequences in the event of a data breach involving PII. Organizations should consider the types, categories, and total amount of PII used, collected, and maintained. When PII is no longer relevant or necessary, PII should be properly destroyed in accordance with any litigation holds and the Federal Records Act. Organizations should also ensure that retired hardware has been properly sanitized before disposal.

Acceptable Use

An organization's acceptable use policy must provide details that specify what users may do with their network access. This includes email and instant messaging usage for personal purposes, limitations on access times, and the storage space available to each user. It is important to provide users the least possible access rights while allowing them to fulfill legitimate actions.

An acceptable use policy should contain these main components:

▶ Clear, specific language

▶ Detailed standards of behavior

▶ Detailed enforcement guidelines and standards

▶ Outline of acceptable and unacceptable uses

▶ Consent forms

▶ Privacy statement

▶ Disclaimer of liability

The organization should be sure the acceptable use policy complies with current state and federal legislation and does not create unnecessary business risk to the company by employee misuse of resources. Upon logon, show a statement to the effect that network access is granted under certain conditions and that all activities may be monitored. This way you can be sure that any legal ramifications are covered.

Security Policy

Security deals with risk. The goal of security management is to reduce unacceptable risk while keeping the impact on workflow and total cost of ownership (TCO) of the infrastructure to a minimum. Security policies impact both reducing risk and minimizing workflow impact. Security policies should be designed in a multitiered or defense-in-depth approach. When formulating security policies, you must understand how each component protects your infrastructure and how each might be vulnerable. You need to know how best to protect your end users and how to protect your infrastructure from those end users through effective policies that do not impede workflow.

Mandatory Vacations

Users should be required to take mandatory vacations and rotate positions or functional duties as part of the organization's security policy. These policies outline the manner in which a user is associated with necessary information and system resources and that access is rotated between individuals. There must be other employees who can do the job of each employee so that corruption does not occur, cross-checks can be validated, and the effect of personnel loss is minimized. It is imperative that all employees are adequately cross-trained and only have the level of access necessary to perform their normal duties (least privilege).

Job Rotation

As an extension of the separation of duties best practice, rotating administrative users between roles both improves awareness of the mandates of each role while also ensuring that fraudulent activity cannot be sustained. This is also the reason that users with administrative access might be required to take mandatory vacations, allowing other administrators to review standard operating practices and protocols in place. This is easily remembered by the Latin phrase *Quis custodiet ipsos custodies?*, which translates to "Who will guard the guardians themselves?"

Separation of Duties

Too much power can lead to corruption, whether it is in politics or network administration. Most governments and other organizations implement some type of a balance of power through a separation of duties. It is important to include a separation of duties when planning for security policy compliance. Without this separation, all areas of control and compliance may be left in the hands of a single individual. The idea of separation of duties hinges on the concept that multiple people conspiring to corrupt a system is less likely than a single person corrupting it. Often, you will find this in financial institutions, where to violate the security controls all the participants in the process have to agree to compromise the system.

ExamAlert

For physical or operational security questions, avoid having one individual who has complete control of a transaction or process from beginning to end, and implement policies such as job rotation, mandatory vacations, and cross-training. These practices also protect against the loss of a critical skill set due to injury, death, or another form of personnel separation.

Least Privilege

Policies addressing access rights for user accounts must mandate that only the minimum permissions necessary to perform work should be assigned to a user. This protects against unauthorized internal review of information and protects against inadvertently enacted viral agents running with elevated permissions.

Risk Calculation

Risk is the possibility of loss or danger. Risk management is the process of identifying and reducing risk to a level that is comfortable and then implementing controls to maintain that level.

Risk analysis helps align security objectives with business objectives. Here we deal with how to calculate risk and return on investment. Risk comes in a variety of forms. Risk analysis identifies risks, estimates the effect of potential threats, and identifies ways to reduce the risk without the cost of the prevention outweighing the risk. To calculate risk, use this formula:

Risk = Threat × Vulnerability

> **ExamAlert**
>
> Risk management employs several terms that you should familiarize yourself with before taking the exam:
>
> ▶ **Vulnerability:** A vulnerability is a weakness in hardware, software, process, or people that can be employed or engaged to affect enterprise security.
>
> ▶ **Exploit:** An exploit is a mechanism of taking advantage of an identified vulnerability.
>
> ▶ **Threat:** A threat is the potential that a vulnerability will be identified and exploited.
>
> ▶ **Risk:** A risk is the likelihood that a threat will occur and the measure of its effect.
>
> ▶ **Control:** Controls act to close vulnerabilities, prevent exploitation, reduce threat potential, and/or reduce the likelihood of a risk or its impact.

To determine the relative danger of an individual threat, or to measure the relative value across multiple threats to better allocate resources designated for risk mitigation, it is necessary to map the resources, identify threats to each, and establish a metric for comparison. The first step in a risk assessment is the business impact analysis (BIA). The BIA is not only a technical matter to identify services and technology assets, but also a business process by which the relative value of each identified asset can be determined if it fails one or more of the C-I-A requirements (confidentiality, integrity, and availability). The failure to meet one or more of the C-I-A requirements is often a sliding scale, with increased severity as time passes. Recovery point objectives (RPOs) and recovery time objectives (RTOs) in incident handling, business continuity, and disaster recovery are all areas that must be considered when calculating risk.

Likelihood

When examining threat assessment, you have to consider the likelihood that the threats you've identified might actually occur. To gauge the probability of an event occurring as accurately as possible, you can use a combination of estimation and historical data. Most risk analyses use a fiscal year to set a time limit of probability and confine proposed expenditures, budget, and depreciation.

The National Institute of Standards and Technology (NIST) SP 800-30 document suggests measuring likelihood as high, medium, or low based on the motivation and capability of the threat source, the nature of the vulnerability, and the existence and effectiveness of current controls to mitigate the threat. Often the three values are translated into numeric equivalents for use in quantitative analytical processes: high (1.0), medium (0.5), low (0.1).

Responses must be coupled to the likelihood determined in the risk analysis, such as identifying the need to put corrective measures in place as soon as possible for all high-level threats, whereas medium-level threats might only require an action plan for implementation as soon as is reasonable, and low-level threats might be dealt with as possible or simply accepted.

Impact

By nature, risk always has a negative impact. The size of the impact varies in terms of cost and impact on critical factors. Risk impact assessment is the process of assessing the probabilities and consequences of risk events if they are realized. Risks are then prioritized based on the assessment to establish a most-to-least-critical importance ranking. Ranking risks in terms of their criticality or importance is an important business function because it provides insight into where resources may be needed to mitigate the realization of high-probability risk events.

SLE

The single loss expectancy (SLE) is the expected monetary loss every time a risk occurs. The SLE, asset value, and exposure factor are related by the formula used in calculating SLE. SLE equals asset value multiplied by the threat exposure factor. The exposure factor is the percent of the asset lost from a successful attack. The formula looks like this:

Asset value × Exposure factor = SLE

To help you understand this, let's look at an example using denial-of-service (DoS) attacks. Firewall logs indicate that the organization was hit hard one time per month by a DoS attack in each of the past 6 months. You can use this historical data to estimate that it's likely you will be hit 12 times per year. This information helps you calculate the SLE and the ALE. ALE is explained in greater detail after the next section on annual rate of occurrence.

The exposure factor is the percentage of loss that a realized threat could have on a certain asset. In the DoS example, let's say that if a DoS were successful, 25% of business would be lost. The daily sales from the website are $100,000, so the SLE would be $25,000 (SLE = $100,000 × .25). The possibility of certain threats is greater than that of others. Historical data presents the best method of estimating these possibilities.

ARO

The annual rate of occurrence (ARO) is the estimated possibility of a specific threat taking place in a one-year time frame. The possible range of frequency values is from 0.0 (the threat is not expected to occur) to some whole number whose magnitude depends on the type and population of threat sources. When the probability that a DoS attack will occur is 50%, the ARO is 0.5. After you calculate the SLE, you can calculate the ALE. This gives you the probability of an event happening over a single year's time.

ALE

The annualized loss expectancy (ALE) is the expected monetary loss that can be expected for an asset due to a risk over a one-year period. ALE equals the SLE times the ARO:

SLE × ARO = ALE

ALE can be used directly in a cost-benefit analysis. Going back to the example, if the SLE is estimated at $25,000 and the ARO is .5, our ALE is 12,500. ($25,000 × .5 = $12,500). Spending more than $12,500 might not be prudent because the cost would outweigh the risk.

ExamAlert

Calculating risk includes the following formulas:

Risk = Threat × Vulnerability

Asset value × Exposure factor = SLE

SLE × ARO = ALE

MTTR

Other risk calculations involve determining the lifespan and failure rates of components. These calculations help an organization measure the reliability of a product. The mean time to recovery or mean time to repair (MTTR) is the average time required to fix a failed component or device and return it to production status. MTTR is considered to be corrective maintenance, and the calculation includes preparation time, active maintenance time, and delay time. Due to the uncertainty of these factors, MTTR is often difficult to calculate. Often, MTTR is part of a maintenance contract, where the user would pay more for a system MTTR. Some systems have redundancy built in to them so that when one subsystem fails, another takes its place and keeps the whole system running to reduce MTTR.

MTTF

Mean time to failure (MTTF) is the length of time a device or product is expected to last in operation. It represents how long a product can reasonably be expected to perform based on specific testing. MTTF metrics supplied by vendors about their products or components may not have been collected by running one unit continuously until failure. MTTF data is often collected by running many units for a specific number of hours and then calculated as an average based on when the components fail.

MTTF is one of many ways to evaluate the reliability of hardware or other technology and is extremely important as the hardware is used in mission-critical systems. It is vital to know about general reliability of hardware, especially when it is part of a larger system. MTTF is used for nonrepairable products. When MTTF is used as a measure, repair is not an option.

MTBF

Mean time between failures (MTBF) is the average amount of time that passes between hardware component failures, excluding time spent waiting for or being repaired. MTBF is intended to measure only the time a component is available and operating. MTBF is extremely similar to MTTF. The difference between these terms is that MTBF is used for products that can be repaired and returned to use. MTTF is used for nonrepairable products. MTBF is calculated as a ratio of the cumulative operating time to the number of failures for that item.

MTBF ratings can be predicted based on product experience or by analyzing data supplied by the manufacturer. MTBF ratings are measured in hours and are often used to determine the durability of hard drives and printers. For example, typical hard drives for personal computers have MTBF ratings of about 500,000 hours.

Qualitative Versus Quantitative Measures

Quantitative measures allow for the clearest measure of relative risk and expected return on investment or risk reduction on investment. Not all risk can be measured quantitatively, though, requiring qualitative risk assessment strategies. The culture of an organization greatly affects whether its risk assessments can be performed via quantitative (numeric) or qualitative (subjective/relative) measures.

Qualitative risk assessment can involve brainstorming, focus groups, surveys, and other similar processes to determine asset worth and valuation to the organization. Uncertainty is also estimated, allowing for a relative projection of qualitative risk for each threat based on its position in a risk matrix plotting the probability (low to high) and impact (low to high) of each. It is possible to assign numeric values to each state (very low = 1, low = 2, moderate = 3, and so on) so that a quasi-quantitative analysis can be performed, but because the categories are subjectively assigned, the result remains a qualitative measure.

Quantitative measures tend to be more difficult for management to understand, require very intensive labor to gather all related measurements, and are more time-consuming to determine. Qualitative measures tend to be less precise, more subjective, and difficult to assign direct costs for measuring ROI/RROI (return on investment / rate of return on investment).

Vulnerabilities

To conduct a risk assessment, it is important to understand several terms as they relate to calculating risk. Recall in a previous section, the formula used to determine risk is as follows:

Risk = Threat × Vulnerability

Risk is assessed by multiplying threats by exploitable vulnerabilities to obtain the amount of damage to assets. Vulnerability is a weakness in hardware, software, process, or people that can be employed or engaged to affect enterprise security. The Information Technology Security Evaluation Criteria (ITSEC) provides a more formal definition of risk:

The existence of a weakness, design, or implementation error that can lead to an unexpected, undesirable event compromising the security of the computer system, network, application, or protocol involved.

Threats may exist, but if there are no vulnerabilities, there is little or no risk to the environment. Likewise, there is little or no risk to the environment if there is vulnerability without threat.

Threat Vectors

A threat is the potential that a vulnerability will be identified and exploited. A threat vector is the method a threat uses to get to the target. Threat vectors include viruses, botnets, drive-by downloads, malware, phishing attacks, and keyloggers. Analyzing threats can help the organization develop security policies and prioritize securing resources. Threat assessments are performed to determine the best approaches to securing the environment against a particular threat or class of threat. NIST SP800-30 is more specific on the definitions involving threat and divides it into threat source and threat, with threat source being the interaction of an actor and motivation and with threat as the interaction between a threat source and a vulnerability.

Probability/Threat Likelihood

Probability is the likelihood that an event will occur. In assessing risk, it is important to estimate the probability or likelihood that a threat will occur. Assessing the likelihood of some types of threats is easier then assessing other types. For example, you can use the frequency data to estimate the probability of natural disasters. You might also be able to use MTTF and MTBF to estimate the probability of component problems. Determining the probability of attacks by human threat sources is difficult. Threat source likelihood is assessed using skill level, motive, opportunity, and size. Vulnerability likelihood is assessed using ease of discovery, ease of exploit, awareness, and intrusion detection.

Risk-Avoidance, Transference, Acceptance, Mitigation, Deterrence

Risk management involves creation of a risk, detailing all known risks and their related mitigation strategies. Creating this register involves mapping the enterprise's expected services and data sets, as well as vulnerabilities in both implementation and procedures for each. Risk cannot be eliminated outright in all cases, but mitigation strategies can be integrated with policies for user awareness training ahead of an incident. Formal risk management deals with the alignment of five potential responses to each identified risk:

▶ **Avoidance:** Elimination of the vulnerability that gives rise to a particular risk so that it is avoided altogether. This is the most effective solution, but often not possible due to organizational requirements. Eliminating email to avoid the risk of email-borne viruses is an effective solution but not likely to be a realistic approach in the modern enterprise.

▶ **Transference:** A risk or the effect of its exposure may be transferred by moving to hosted providers who assume the responsibility for recovery and restoration or by acquiring insurance to cover the costs emerging from equipment theft or data exposure.

▶ **Acceptance:** Recognizing a risk, identifying it, and then accepting that it is sufficiently unlikely or of such limited impact that corrective controls are not warranted. Risk acceptance must be a conscious choice, documented, approved by senior administration, and regularly reviewed.

▶ **Mitigation/deterrence:** Risk mitigation involves the reduction in likelihood or impact of a risk's exposure. Risk deterrence involves putting into place systems and policies to mitigate a risk by protecting against the exploitation of vulnerabilities that cannot be eliminated. Most risk management decisions focus on mitigation and deterrence, balancing costs and resources against the level of risk and mitigation that will result.

Risks Associated with Cloud Computing and Virtualization

Risks can vary based on the implementation scenario, such as a migration to cloud-based or virtualized services and software applications compared to traditional in-house data center operations.

ExamAlert

Because risks within cloud and virtualized hosting systems require knowledge of location, host system, shared tenancy, and other operational details subject to regular and ongoing change as data is migrated within the hosting environment, risk assessment of these environments depends on subjective assessment and service-level contractual expectations. The subjective and uncertain nature of assessments within these environments falls into the qualitative form of risk assessment.

Cloud computing solutions, except for a private cloud (meaning both public and hybrid clouds), encompass all the normal concerns of enterprise resources, together with those for outsourced resources. And because cloud computing is built atop virtualized computing models, the same factors apply to virtualized and to cloud-based computing systems and services.

These considerations include the following:

▶ **Secure data transfer:** Because data must travel over public Internet connections for both hosted and hybrid clouds, data must be encrypted and authenticated between endpoints.

▶ **Secure application programming interfaces (APIs):** Application interfaces must be protected against unauthorized access as well as flood attacks intended to deny legitimate access to remote resources.

▶ **Secure data storage:** Data must be encrypted at rest and in backup media to protect against unauthorized access even with physical server access.

▶ **User access controls:** Logging and audit provisions for all access should be implemented to ensure that all access, both organizational and host side, is limited to authorized requests.

▶ **Data separation:** Shared hosting creates the potential for resource competition on the host server and its network connections. Compartmentalization of data storage and service function may also be mandated by regulatory directives in some industries.

Recovery Time Objective and Recovery Point Objective

RPO and RTO are crucial in risk mitigation planning. RPO is specifically targeted toward data backup capabilities. RPO is the amount of time that can elapse during a disruption before the quantity of data lost during that period exceeds business continuity planning's maximum allowable threshold. Simply put, RPO specifies the allowable data loss. It determines up to what point in time data recovery could happen before business is disrupted. For example, if an organization does a backup at 10:00 p.m. every day and an incident happens at 7:00 p.m. the following day, everything that was changed since the last backup is lost. The RPO in this particular context is the backup from the previous day. If the organization set the threshold at 24 hours, the RPO is within threshold because it is under 24 hours.

The RTO is the amount of time within which a process must be restored after a disaster to meet business continuity. The RTO is how long the organization can go without a specific application. It defines how much time it takes to recover after notification of process disruption.

The distinction between the two terms is this: RPO designates the amount of data that will be lost or will have to be reentered due to network downtime, and RTO designates the amount of actual time that can pass before the disruption begins to seriously impede normal business operations.

Cram Quiz

Answer these questions. The answers follow the last question. If you cannot answer these questions correctly, consider reading this section again until you can.

1. Which of the following designates the amount of data loss that is sustainable and up to what point in time data recovery could happen before business is disrupted?

   ○ **A.** RTO

   ○ **B.** MTBF

   ○ **C.** RPO

   ○ **D.** MTTF

2. Eliminating email to avoid the risk of email-borne viruses is an effective solution but not likely to be a realistic approach for which of the following?

   ○ **A.** Risk avoidance

   ○ **B.** Risk transference

   ○ **C.** Risk acceptance

   ○ **D.** Risk mitigation

3. Which of the following policies addresses access rights for user accounts mandating that only the minimum permissions necessary to perform work are assigned to a user?

   ○ **A.** Acceptable use

   ○ **B.** Least privilege

   ○ **C.** Job rotation

   ○ **D.** Privacy policy

Cram Quiz Answers

1. **C**. RPO is the amount of time that can elapse during a disruption before the quantity of data lost during that period exceeds business continuity planning's maximum allowable threshold. Simply put, RPO specifies the allowable data loss. It determines up to what point in time data recovery could happen before business is disrupted. Answer A is incorrect because RTO is the amount of time within which a process must be restored after a disaster to meet business continuity. It defines how much time it takes to recover after notification of process disruption. Answer B is incorrect because MTBF is the average amount of time that passes between hardware component failures, excluding time spent waiting for or being repaired. Answer D is incorrect because MTTF is the length of time a device or product is expected to last in operation.

2. **A**. Risk avoidance is the elimination of the vulnerability that gives rise to a particular risk so that it is avoided altogether. This is the most effective solution, but often not possible due to organizational requirements. Answer B is incorrect because risk transference is moving the risk to hosted providers who assume the responsibility for recovery and restoration or by acquiring insurance to cover the costs emerging from a risk. Answer C is incorrect because risk acceptance is recognizing a risk, identifying it, and then accepting that it is sufficiently unlikely or of such limited impact that corrective controls are not warranted. Answer D is incorrect because risk mitigation involves the reduction in likelihood or impact of a risk's exposure by putting systems and policies into place to mitigate a risk by protecting against the exploitation of vulnerabilities.

3. **B**. Least privilege addresses access rights for user accounts mandating that only the minimum permissions necessary to perform work should be assigned to a user. Answer A is incorrect because an organization's acceptable use policy provides details that specify what users may do with their network access. Answer C is incorrect because job rotation requires rotating administrative users between roles to improve awareness of the mandates of each role while also ensuring that fraudulent activity cannot be sustained. Answer D is incorrect because privacy policy describes federal and state legislation requiring owners of commercial websites or online services to post how they collect and protect personal data.

Summarize the Security Implications of Integrating Systems and Data with Third Parties

▶ **On-boarding/off-boarding business partners**

▶ **Social media networks and/or applications**

▶ **Interoperability agreements**

▶ **Privacy considerations**

▶ **Risk awareness**

▶ **Unauthorized data sharing**

▶ **Data ownership**

▶ **Data backups**

▶ **Follow security policy and procedures**

▶ **Review agreement requirements to verify compliance and performance standards**

If you can correctly answer these questions before going through this section, save time by skimming the Exam Alerts in this section and then completing the Cram Quiz at the end of the section.

CramSaver

1. Describe the various interoperability agreements that might be encountered in the normal course of business.

2. Explain some things an organization can do to protect privacy when entering into a business partnership.

3. Identify some ways an organization can verify third-party or partner agreement compliance and performance standards.

Answers

1. A service level agreement (SLA) is a contract between a service provider and a customer that specifies the nature of the service to be provided and the level of service that the provider will offer to the customer. An SLA often contains technical and performance parameters, such as response time and uptime, but generally does not include security measures. A business partner agreement (BPA) is a contract that establishes partner profit percentages, partner responsibilities, and exit strategies for partners. This is strictly a business arrangement specifying partner financial and fiduciary responsibilities. It does not cover any security measures. A memorandum of understanding (MOU) is a document that outlines the

terms and details of an agreement between parties, including each party's requirements and responsibilities. An MOU expressing mutual accord on an issue between two or more organizations does not need to contain legally enforceable promises but may be legally enforceable based on the intent of the parties. An interconnection security agreement (ISA) is an agreement between the organizations that have connected IT systems. The purpose of the ISA is to document the technical requirements of the interconnection, such as identifying the basic components of an interconnection, methods and levels of interconnectivity, and potential security risks associated with an interconnection. The ISA also supports an MOU between the organizations.

2. Both organizations should examine privacy issues related to data that will be exchanged or accessible and determine whether it is restricted under current statutes, regulations, or privacy policies. To protect privacy where business partners are concerned, the following can be used: a map of information flows associated with partner access or interconnected systems to determine privacy vulnerabilities; an analysis of the information flow that examines whether privacy principles, current statutes, and regulations are adhered to and compliance requirements are met; and an analysis of privacy issues identified by the system review, including a risk assessment, and mitigation for any identified risks.

3. An organization can take additional steps to ensure compliance and performance standards are met, such as the following: approve and review third-party arrangements and performance annually, maintain an updated list of all third-party relationships and review the list periodically, take appropriate action with any relationship that presents elevated risk, and review all contracts for compliance with expectations and obligations. The organization might also consider requiring an annual attestation by the partner or third-party stating adherence to the contract and its established controls, policies, and procedures.

On-Boarding/Off-Boarding Business Partners

Part of risk assessment is ensuring that the relationships with business partners are consistent with overall business strategy. The organization has a duty to conduct due diligence in selecting a business partner, structuring and reviewing contracts, and overseeing partners. Failure to manage these risks can expose the organization to regulatory action, financial loss, litigation, and reputation damage and may even hinder the organization's ability to establish new partnerships. As organizations expand their businesses through partnerships, mergers, and acquisitions, on-boarding processes become important. On-boarding is the initial phase of allowing new partners to access a portion of your infrastructure. Effective business process on-boarding clearly articulates how the functions of your organization and your partner's systems connect, interact, and communicate. On-boarding procedures include items such as establishing any communication standard, protocol, data formats, file transfer procedures, data mapping, testing, and multilingual support. All these considerations must be securely integrated and include provisions for data separation, data access, encryption, certificate types, digital signatures, and identity management methods.

When a collaborative project ends or a merger is complete, a similar but opposite process called off-boarding is performed. Off-boarding procedures play an important role in protecting the interests of both the organization and the exiting partner. Off-boarding procedures include securing and protecting both digital and physical assets while technical controls are changed and contractual obligations are terminated. A proper off-boarding process protects physical property and maintains an operating knowledge base, ensures compliance and security related to systems and physical access, assists in the transfer of knowledge, and provides partners with an organized way to wrap up and transfer projects. When the length and nature of the contract is specified during on-boarding, access can be set to expire automatically. On-boarding and off-boarding procedures must be documented to ensure compliance with regulatory requirements.

Social Media Networks and/or Applications

Social media networks provide open platforms that enable the seamless sharing of data, allowing organizations and partners to interface and extend social network services and applications. Organizations use social media to garner opinions about their products and services. Employees use social media either internally or externally. Using social technologies improves collaboration and communication within and across partners and raises the level of productivity and interaction between workers. Although social media networks allow instant collaboration and increase productivity, they pose serious privacy concerns, and organizations must be cautious because of negative impacts such as damage to brand recognition and liability for online defamation and libel claims.

ExamAlert

Organizations must carefully consider risks versus benefits when deciding on a social media strategy. Risks must be evaluated for using social media as a business tool to communicate with affiliates, employee access to social media sites while on the corporate network, and employee use of social media tools from corporate-issued mobile devices.

Strategies to address the risks of social media usage should focus on user behavior by developing policies and supporting user training and awareness programs. Technical controls can assist in policy enforcement and in blocking, preventing, or identifying potential incidents. Examples of technical controls include mobile device management (MDM) and mobile application management (MAM). These are enterprise solutions that you can use in social media application security, protection, and asset management. MDM and MAM are discussed in greater detail in Chapter 8, "Host Security."

Controls should be monitored to ensure that they are effective. In addition, the organization may engage a brand protection firm that can scan the Internet and search out misuse of the organization's brand to maintain awareness of potential fraud and to establish clear guidelines about what information should be posted as part of a social media presence.

Interoperability Agreements

Third-party risk can vary greatly, depending on each individual third-party arrangement. Sometimes the risks are clear-cut. Other times, the risks seem unclear. To establish responsibilities where collaboration or the delivery of services is concerned, interoperability agreements are used. Agreements can be tailored to the circumstances and requirements of the participating parties, the various collaborative arrangements agreed upon, or the complexity of the service relationship. These agreements help to create a common understanding about the agreement and the responsibilities of each party. The following list describes several agreements commonly used in business:

▶ **SLA:** A service level agreement is a contract between a service provider and a customer that specifies the nature of the service to be provided and the level of service that the provider will offer to the customer. An SLA often contains technical and performance parameters, such as response time and uptime, but generally does not include security measures.

▶ **BPA:** A business partner agreement is a contract that establishes partner profit percentages, partner responsibilities, and exit strategies for partners. This is strictly a business arrangement specifying partner financial and fiduciary responsibilities. It does not cover any security measures.

▶ **MOU:** A memorandum of understanding is a document that outlines the terms and details of an agreement between parties, including of each party's requirements and responsibilities. An MOU expressing mutual accord on an issue between two or more organizations does not need to contain legally enforceable promises; it may be legally enforceable based on the intent of the parties.

▶ **ISA:** An interconnection security agreement is an agreement between organizations that have connected IT systems. The purpose of the ISA is to document the technical requirements of the interconnection, such as identifying the basic components of an interconnection, methods and levels of interconnectivity, and potential security risks associated with an interconnection. The ISA also supports an MOU between the organizations.

Another agreement commonly encountered is a Health Insurance Portability and Accountability Act (HIPAA) business associate agreement (BAA). This contract signed between a HIPAA-covered entity and a HIPAA business associate (BA) protects personal health information (PHI) in accordance with HIPAA guidelines.

ExamAlert

Third-party risk includes determining expectations, which can then be spelled out in SLAs, BPAs, MOUs, and ISAs. Depending on the situation, an SLA, MOU, and ISA may be necessary. An ISA is the only one of these documents that specifically outlines any technical solution and addresses security requirements.

Privacy Considerations

Confidentiality is about limiting access to personal information and preventing its disclosure to unauthorized third parties. This extends to third-party providers and business partners. Ongoing privacy policy development and privacy impact assessments are critical to protecting privacy and technology investment. In any business partnership, both organizations should examine privacy issues related to data that will be exchanged or accessible and determine whether it is restricted under current statutes, regulations, or privacy policies.

To protect privacy where business partners are concerned, you can use the following:

▶ A map of information flows associated with partner access or interconnected systems to determine privacy vulnerabilities

▶ An analysis of the information flow that examines whether privacy principles, current statutes, and regulations are adhered to and compliance requirements are met

▶ An analysis of privacy issues identified by the system review, including a risk assessment, and mitigation for any identified risks

The use of third-party sites and tools by employees will also present privacy risks that the organization should take into account before deciding to allow access to a particular site or tool. By design, many online tools such as social networks and sharing platforms are designed to gather and share personal information. Before you allow access to sites, you should review privacy policies of these third-party sites to determine how personal information is collected and used. A concern about not only privacy but also data collection in general is a cause for careful review of third-party application EULAs (end-user license agreements). For example, Twitter has announced it will be collecting a list of user-installed applications on iOS and Android devices as part of its app graph program, and the Federal Trade Commission (FTC) became involved when a popular mobile flashlight application collected and shared geolocation user data.

Risk Awareness

Organizations often fail to properly assess and understand the risks involved in third-party relationships. Third-party risk tends to be a combination of risks ranging from the familiar to the highly complex and can vary greatly, depending on each individual third-party arrangement. Reputation, compliance, and legal risks are all considerations that must be assessed when third-party interactions occur. Careful review of all risks is necessary, and you must consider adequate mitigation measures and address compliance. Risk awareness can help organizations set policies and procedures when conducting business with third parties. Establishing a comprehensive due diligence program to screen partners all the way through the supply chain and providing continuous monitoring throughout the life of the commitment will help mitigate risk. Other avenues the organization can pursue to increase risk awareness include conducting a thorough risk assessment, verifying that the proposed relationship is consistent with the overall business strategy, and reviewing all contracts to confirm that expectations and obligations of both parties are outlined. After due diligence and risk assessment are completed, a comprehensive monitoring program should be developed to periodically verify that the third party is abiding by the terms of the contractual agreement and that identified risks are appropriately addressed. When security risks are high, the security controls are found to be inadequate, or the risks cannot be effectively mitigated, the organization should consider not collaborating with the third party.

Unauthorized Data Sharing

Using unauthorized applications on business networks can place sensitive corporate data and employee personal information at risk. A survey recently conducted by M-Files emphasizes risks associated with unauthorized and unregulated use of file sharing and sync tools by employees in a corporate environment. The study results show that 46% of respondents acknowledged using such applications for work-related activities. More troubling is that 56% of employees said that their company does not have policies in place that prohibit the use of personal file sharing and sync solutions for storing and sharing company documents, and 14% said they did not know whether their company had such policies in place. In addition to data sharing policies for employees, data sharing must be covered in third-party agreements.

ExamAlert

To prevent unauthorized data sharing by third-party applications or partners, organizations should use a layered defense-in-depth approach and include data-loss prevention (DLP) technology.

DLP is discussed later in this chapter. Some protective measures an organization can put in place include implementing tools and processes that track movement of data and how it is accessed, identifying the types of data that require unique protection, and specifically addressing data sharing in contracts and agreements.

Should an organization choose to allow data sharing with a third party, a data sharing agreement can be used. A data sharing agreement is a formal contract that clearly documents the data being shared and how the data can be used, specifically addressing data confidentiality. A data sharing agreement can offer some mitigation by defining how long the third party will be able to use the data; whether the data can be shared, sold, or distributed; and methods that the third party must use to maintain data security.

Data Ownership

All data in your organization should have an owner. The owner is responsible for determining how much risk to accept. On the surface, data ownership may seem to be a simple matter. However, one look at a transaction when third parties are involved proves otherwise. When an employee purchases an airline ticket for business travel, processing intermediaries such as payment systems, ticket processors, and online booking tools assert a right to capture and distribute travel data. These intermediaries also may make data available to third-party aggregators. The question of rightful ownership remains murky. Depending on whom you ask, the data being collected could belong to the organization, the booking agency, or the airline.

The organization must decide who will be permitted to access data and how they will use it. To protect organizational data, when the organization enters any third-party agreement, the topic of data ownership and data aggregation must be addressed.

Some cloud services offer data ownership agreements that specifically identify the data owner and outline ownership of relevant data. When assessing data ownership, especially when the organization is using a cloud provider, consider the following points:

► A determination of what is relevant data

► Provisions for exercising rights of ownership over the data

► Access to the organization's environments

► Costs associated exercising rights of ownership over the data

► Contract term and termination conditions

► Liability of cloud provider

Data classification and appropriate data ownership are key elements in an organization's security policy. These concepts must be extended to third-party entities to properly protect data that belongs to the organization.

Data Backups

In addition to unauthorized data sharing and data ownership, third-party contracts or agreements should address data backups. Items such as identifying the types of data that will be backed up, determining the backup frequency, and whether backups will be performed by one or both parties must be specified. Data backup terms may be detailed and specify how to perform backups and how to link backups to contingency plan procedures. Critical data should be backed up regularly, stored in a secure offsite location to prevent loss or damage, and retained for a period approved by both parties.

When dealing with third-party providers such as cloud services, most providers rely on the customers to back up their own environments. It is important to thoroughly understanding the provider's data protection, encryption, and security strategy.

Too often, organizations rely on the service provider to automatically back up and be able to restore lost data. Transferring risk to the cloud provider is not the same as eliminating it and may prove to be costly. Most cloud providers have methodologies in place to back up and restore data in the event of data loss or a disaster, but these methodologies are only for the provider and are only available to the customer at a high cost. For example, Salesforce.com automatically backs up customer data to a tape library on a nightly basis. Salesforce.com can recover customer data as a last resort. When data has been permanently deleted or corrupted, the data is recovered to a specific point in time. The price for this service is a minimum of $10,000.

Follow Security Policy and Procedures

Integrating systems and data with third parties or partners can combine complexity and inefficiency, leading to increased risk for the organization. Risks in partnerships are usually only analyzed during the on-boarding process, and once the relationship is established, organizations often forget about associated risks. Security policies and procedures need to be followed to identify risks and security controls that will be implemented to protect the confidentiality, integrity, and availability of any connected systems and the data that will pass between them or accessed. Controls should be appropriate for the environment and contain a centralized platform to and monitor the range of assessments, tasks, and responsibilities of all parties. Policies should define ownership and accountability. It is critical that both organizations maintain clear lines of communication and communicate regularly. Regular risk assessments and audits should occur, and a record of compliance should be established so that there is a documentation pertaining to the due diligence performed. In addition, changes in the legal and regulatory environment should be monitored for changes that impact the partnership or third-party agreement.

Review Agreement Requirements to Verify Compliance and Performance Standards

Monitoring risks should be a standard part of program reviews. As part of a comprehensive monitoring program, periodically verify that the third party is abiding by the terms of the contractual agreement and that identified risks are appropriately controlled. The organization should conduct a regular assessment of the business relationship to verify that it conforms to laws, regulations, and established policies and procedures.

Additional steps an organization can take to ensure compliance and performance standards are met include the following:

▶ Approve and review third-party arrangements and performance annually

▶ Maintain an updated list of all third-party relationships and review the list periodically

▶ Take appropriate action with any relationship that presents elevated risk

▶ Review all contracts for compliance with expectations and obligations

The organization might also consider requiring an annual attestation by the partner or third-party stating adherence to the contract and its established controls, policies, and procedures.

Cram Quiz

Answer these questions. The answers follow the last question. If you cannot answer these questions correctly, consider reading this section again until you can.

1. An organization is partnering with another organization that requires shared systems. Which of the following documents would outline how the shared systems interface?

   ○ **A.** SLA

   ○ **B.** BPA

   ○ **C.** MOU

   ○ **D.** ISA

2. Which of the following is the initial phase of allowing new partners to access a portion of your infrastructure?

   ○ **A.** Off-boarding

   ○ **B.** On-boarding

   ○ **C.** Signing a data sharing agreement

   ○ **D.** Signing a business associate agreement

3. Which of the following are steps an organization can take to be sure compliance and performance standards are met in third-party or partner agreements? (Select two correct answers.)

   ○ **A.** Implement an acceptable use policy

   ○ **B.** Take appropriate action if the relationship presents elevated risk

   ○ **C.** Review third-party arrangements and performance annually

   ○ **D.** Sign a data ownership agreement

Cram Quiz Answers

1. **D.** An ISA is an agreement between organizations that have connected IT systems. Answer A is incorrect because an SLA is contract between a service provider and a customer that specifies the nature of the service to be provided and the level of service that the provider will offer to the customer. Answer B is incorrect because a BPA is a contract that establishes partner profit percentages, partner responsibilities, and exit strategies for partners. Answer C is incorrect because an MOU is a document that outlines the terms and details of an agreement between parties, including of each party's requirements and responsibilities.

2. **B**. On-boarding is the initial phase of allowing new partners to access a portion of your infrastructure. Answer A is incorrect because off-boarding is the process used when a collaborative project ends or a merger is complete. Answer C is incorrect because a data sharing agreement is a formal contract that clearly documents the data being shared and how the data can be used, specifically addressing data confidentiality. Answer D is incorrect because a business associate agreement is a contract signed between a HIPAA-covered entity and a HIPAA business associate and protects PHI in accordance with HIPAA guidelines.

3. **B** and **C**. Some additional steps an organization can take to ensure compliance and performance standards are met include approving and reviewing third-party arrangements and performance annually, maintaining an updated list of all third-party relationships and reviewing the list periodically, taking appropriate action with any relationship that presents elevated risk, and reviewing all contracts for compliance with expectations and obligations. Answer A is incorrect because an acceptable use policy is geared toward terms a user must agree to follow in order to be provided with access service. Answer D is incorrect because a data ownership agreement is an agreement offered by some cloud service providers that specifically identifies the data owner and outlines ownership of relevant data.

Given a Scenario, Implement Appropriate Risk Mitigation Strategies

▶ **Change management**

▶ **Incident management**

▶ **User rights and permissions reviews**

▶ **Perform routine audits**

▶ **Enforce policies and procedures to prevent data loss or theft**

▶ **Enforce technology controls**

If you can correctly answer these questions before going through this section, save time by skimming the Exam Alerts in this section and then completing the Cram Quiz at the end of the section.

CramSaver

1. Identify items to consider when implementing an audit policy.

2. Identify items that are included in a change management policy.

3. Explain data-loss prevention (DLP).

Answers

1. You want to consider the following items when you are ready to implement an audit policy: identify potential resources at risk within your networking environment; after the resources are identified, set up the audit policy through the operating system tools; auditing can easily add an additional 25% load or more on a server. If the policy incorporates auditing large amounts of data, be sure that the hardware has the additional space needed and processing power and memory.

2. Change documentation should include specific details such as the files being replaced, the configuration being changed, the machines or operating systems affected, the name of the authority who approved the changes, a list of the departments that are involved in performing the changes and the names of the supervisors in those departments, what the immediate effect of the change will be, what the long-term effect of the change will be, and the date and time the change will occur.

3. DLP is a way of detecting and preventing confidential data from being exfiltrated physically or logically from an organization by accident or on purpose. DLP systems are basically designed to detect and prevent unauthorized use and transmission of confidential information based on one of the three states of data.

Change Management

You should document all configuration changes. Many companies are lacking in this area. We are often in a hurry to make changes and say we will do the documentation later; most of the time, though, that doesn't happen. You should realize that documentation is critical. It eliminates misunderstandings and serves as a trail if something goes wrong down the road. Change documentation should include the following:

▶ Specific details, such as the files being replaced, the configuration being changed, the machines or operating systems affected, and so on

▶ The name of the authority who approved the changes

▶ A list of the departments that are involved in performing the changes and the names of the supervisors in those departments

▶ What the immediate effect of the change will be

▶ What the long-term effect of the change will be

▶ The date and time the change will occur

After the change has occurred, the following should be added to the documentation:

▶ Specific problems and issues that occurred during the process

▶ Any known workarounds if issues have occurred

▶ Recommendations and notes on the event

After the change has been requested, documented, and approved, you should then send out notification to the users so that they know what to expect when the change has been implemented.

Incident Management

Incidents do happen from time to time in most organizations, no matter how strict security policies and procedures are. It is important to realize that proper incident handling is just as vital as the planning stage, and its presence may make the difference between being able to recover quickly and ruining a business and damaging customer relations. Customers need to see that the company has enough expertise to deal with the problem.

Incident response guidelines, change management procedures, security procedures, and many other security-related factors require extensive planning and documentation. Incident response documentation should include the identification of required forensic and data-gathering procedures and proper reporting and recovery procedures for each type of security-related incident.

The components of an incident-response plan should include preparation, roles, rules, and procedures. Incident-response procedures should define how to maintain business continuity while defending against further attacks. Although many organizations have an incident response team (IRT), which is a specific group of technical and security investigators that respond to and investigate security incidents, many do not. If there is no IRT, first responders need to handle the scene and the response. Systems should be secured to prevent as many incidents as possible and monitored to detect security breaches as they occur. The National Institute of Standards and Technology (NIST) has issued a report on incident response guidelines that can help an organization spell out its own internal procedures. These guidelines serve as best practices and can be found at http://csrc.nist.gov/publications/nistpubs/800-61rev2/SP800-61rev2.pdf.

User Rights and Permissions Reviews

After you have established the proper access control scheme, it is important to monitor changes in access rights. Auditing user privileges is generally a two-step process that involves turning auditing on within the operating system and then specifying the resources to be audited. After enabling auditing, you also need to monitor the logs that are generated. Auditing should include both privilege and usage. Auditing of access use and rights changes should be implemented to prevent unauthorized or unintentional access or escalation of privileges, which might allow a guest or restricted user account access to sensitive or protected resources.

Some of the user activities that can be audited include the following:

▶ Reading, modifying, or deleting files

▶ Logging on or off the network

▶ Using services such as remote access or remote desktop services

▶ Using devices such as printers

When configuring an audit policy, it is important to monitor successful and failed access attempts. Failure events enable you to identify unauthorized access attempts; successful events can reveal an accidental or intentional escalation of access rights.

Perform Routine Audits

How much you should audit depends on how much information you want to store. Keep in mind that auditing should be a clear-cut plan built around goals and policies. Without proper planning and policies, you probably will quickly fill your log files and hard drives with useless or unused information.

Note

The more quickly you fill up your log files, the more often you need to check the logs; otherwise, important security events might be deleted unnoticed.

Consider the following items when you are ready to implement an audit policy:

▶ Identify potential resources at risk within your networking environment. These resources typically include sensitive files, financial applications, and personnel files.

▶ After the resources are identified, set up the audit policy through the operating system tools. Each operating system will have its own method for tracking and logging access.

▶ Auditing can easily add an additional 25% load or more on a server. If the policy incorporates auditing large amounts of data, be sure that the hardware has the additional space needed and processing power and memory.

After you have auditing turned on, log files are generated. It is important to schedule regular time to review the logs.

In addition to auditing events on domain controllers and user computers, servers that perform specific roles, such as a Domain Name Service (DNS), Dynamic Host Configuration Protocol (DHCP), SQL, or Exchange server, should have certain events audited. For example, you should enable audit logging for DHCP servers on your network and check the log files for an unusually high number of lease requests from clients. DHCP servers running Windows Server 2008 or later include several logging features and server parameters that provide enhanced auditing capabilities, such as specifying the following:

▶ The directory path in which the DHCP server stores audit log files. By default, the DHCP audit logs are located in the %windir%\System32\ Dhcp directory.

▶ A minimum and maximum size for the total amount of disk space that is available for audit log files created by the DHCP service.

▶ A disk-checking interval that determines how many times the DHCP server writes audit log events to the log file before checking for available disk space on the server.

> **Note**
>
> Turning on all possible audit counters for all objects could significantly affect server performance and overload data storage systems with the constant flood of unnecessary detail.

Enforce Policies and Procedures to Prevent Data Loss or Theft

Many organizations do not have security policies in place, and security policies that are in place are often ineffective. This allows employees to put corporate data at risk. Creating security policies and communicating those policies to employees are important initial steps in protecting organizational assets. Security policies and procedures are only successful when employees understand and follow them. The biggest risk to data loss is the lack of employee awareness of and compliance with existing security policies. Integrating security with business processes and aligning policies with job requirements are good ways to demonstrate that security is central to business success. Policy enforcement is easier, and there is a higher level of compliance, when the organization creates realistic policies. Policy and procedure awareness should begin when employees are first hired.

Critical data must remain secure. One way the organization can help keep data secure is to implement and enforce security policies that prevent unauthorized or inappropriate access and misuse of data. One of the most common polices used to prevent data loss and theft is limiting access to writeable media. The advent of bring your own device (BYOD) presents a challenge for organizations trying to protect critical data. When BYOD is acceptable for the organization, polices such as BYOD, MDM, and MAM must be implemented to protect data exposed by the BYOD, mobile device, and application domain. Another common policy that prevents data loss is one that limits email exposure both internally and externally. The use of personal email accounts of users is often not monitored. Implementing a policy that allows users to communicate through their corporate mail while denying traffic bound for mail servers outside the perimeter will prevent users from using personal email. Microsoft Exchange Server 2013 contains policy templates to help enforce email policies and organizational compliance needs. Other polices that need to be implemented and enforced to prevent data loss and theft include the following: restricting printer access

▶ Disallowing file transfer applications such as instant messaging, P2P file sharing, and FTP file transfer

▶ Restricting the use of unapproved applications and processes from using ports commonly allowed to traverse the perimeter of the network

▶ Controlling wireless access

Enforce Technology Controls

Organizations face growing challenges to safeguarding confidential data and proprietary information. It would appear that if policies and procedures were properly followed data would be protected, but organizations need technology controls in place to supplement policies and procedures. Hardening the network perimeter and implementing proper access controls helps mitigates threats and vulnerabilities from outside threats. Due to the large volumes and mobility of data made available to users, the biggest threat of data loss often comes from inside the organization. Technology and data access have become so intertwined that it is quite easy for users to unintentionally release confidential data. Once users have been granted permission to access information, technological controls need to be put in place to restrict user ability to redistribute or modify data.

Technology controls consist of the type of control and the control points. For example, encryption may be used on devices such as laptop or desktop hard drives. Access controls provide both authentication and authorization, including technology such as web access management and two-factor authentication. Access controls can be implemented at the host level to ensure only authorized users and machines have access to key information. Data controls include encryption, data-loss prevention, and information rights management. Audit controls such as security information and event management (SIEM) systems provide the technological means to show compliance and refine controls.

Data-Loss Prevention

Data loss is a problem faced by all organizations, but it can be especially challenging for global organizations that store a large volume of PII in different legal jurisdictions. Privacy issues differ by country, regions, and states. Organizations implement data-loss prevention tools as a way to prevent data loss. DLP is a way of detecting and preventing confidential data from being exfiltrated physically or logically from an organization by accident or on purpose. DLP systems are basically designed to detect and prevent unauthorized use and transmission of confidential information based on one of the three states of data: in-use, in-motion, or at-rest. DLP systems provide a way to enforce data security policies by providing centralized management for detecting and preventing the unauthorized use and transmission of data the organization deems confidential. A well-designed DLP strategy allows control over sensitive data, reduces the cost of data breaches, and achieves greater insight into organizational data use. International organizations should ensure that they are in compliance with local privacy regulations before implementing DLP tools and processes. DLP is discussed in greater detail in Chapter 9, "Data Security."

Cram Quiz

Answer these questions. The answers follow the last question. If you cannot answer these questions correctly, consider reading this section again until you can.

1. Which of the following would be used to detect and prevent unauthorized transmission of confidential information?

   ○ **A.** Change management

   ○ **B.** Incident management

   ○ **C.** Auditing

   ○ **D.** Data-loss prevention

2. Which of the following could prevent unauthorized or unintentional access or escalation of privileges?

   ○ **A.** Auditing network logons

   ○ **B.** Auditing process tracking

   ○ **C.** Auditing replace a process-level token

   ○ **D.** Auditing bypass traverse checking

3. Technology controls consist of which of the following? (Select two correct answers.)

   ○ **A.** Type of control

   ○ **B.** Control points

   ○ **C.** Policy templates

   ○ **D.** Physical barriers

Cram Quiz Answers

1. **D.** DLP is a way of detecting and preventing confidential data from being exfiltrated physically or logically from an organization by accident or on purpose. DLP systems are basically designed to detect and prevent unauthorized use and transmission of confidential information based on one of the three states of data. Answer A is incorrect because change management provides specific details when system changes are made, such as the files being replaced, the configuration being changed, and the machines or operating systems affected. Answer B is incorrect because incident management includes preparation, roles, rules, and procedures for incident response and how to maintain business continuity while defending against further attacks. Answer C is incorrect because auditing is used to detect unauthorized or unintentional access or escalation of privileges.

2. **A**. Auditing logging on or off the network could prevent unauthorized or unintentional access or escalation of privileges. Answer B is incorrect because auditing process tracking is more closely associated with auditing a developer's computer. Answers C and D are incorrect. These events are never audited, mainly because they are used by processes.

3. **A** and **B**. Technology controls consist of the type of control and the control points. For example, encryption may be used on devices such as laptop or desktop hard drives. Answer C is incorrect because policy templates are used to enforce polices not technology controls. Answer D is incorrect because physical barriers are not technology controls.

Given a Scenario, Implement Basic Forensic Procedures

▶ **Order of volatility**
▶ **Capture system image**
▶ **Network traffic and logs**
▶ **Capture video**
▶ **Record time offset**
▶ **Take hashes**
▶ **Screenshots**
▶ **Witnesses**
▶ **Track man hours and expense**
▶ **Chain of custody**
▶ **Big Data analysis**

CramSaver

If you can correctly answer these questions before going through this section, save time by skimming the Exam Alerts in this section and then completing the Cram Quiz at the end of the section.

1. Why it is necessary to record the time offset when acquiring forensic evidence?

2. Explain the relevance of hashing to acquiring and analyzing forensic evidence.

3. What is the main purpose of chain of custody?

Answers

1. Recording the time offset is critical to an accurate examination when dates and times are at issue and should be done at the beginning of any examination. Just because a computer was seized in a particular time zone does not mean that it is configured for that time zone.

2. You should generate hashes of all data and applications before and after any deep analysis is performed, allowing validation that the forensic analysis itself has not produced unexpected modifications of evidentiary data. When the image of the drive is complete, a hash value of the image is taken and then compared against the hash of the original drive. If they are the same, you didn't change anything.

3. Key to any form of forensic investigation is adherence to standards for the identification, collection, storage, and review of evidence. The chain of custody provides a clear record of the path evidence takes from acquisition to disposal.

Order of Volatility

When a potential security breach must be reviewed, the digital forensics process comes into play. Data of potential evidentiary value can be stored in many different forms within a subject system. Some of these storage locations preserve the data even when a system is powered off, whereas others might hold data for only a very brief interval before it is lost or overwritten. Even the process of evaluation can modify or overwrite these volatile storage areas, and shutting off a running system might completely wipe all data stored in active memory.

In some cases, evidence that is relevant to a case may only temporarily exist. Evidence can be lost when a computer is powered down. By capturing the volatile data before unplugging the computer, you get a snapshot of the system at the time you arrived on the scene. You should collect the following information:

▶ System date and time

▶ Current network connections

▶ Current open ports and applications listening on those ports

▶ Applications currently running

Data capture is highly dependent upon the order of volatility, where capture and examination of more durable storage can eliminate data of potential evidentiary value at more volatile levels.

ExamAlert

The order of volatility follows:

▶ **Registers and caches:** Data stored within the CPU's registers and cache levels might remain only nanoseconds before being overwritten by normal system operations.

▶ **Routing and process tables:** Data stored within networking and other active devices can be modified externally by ongoing operations.

▶ **Kernel statistics:** Data regarding current kernel operations can be in constant transit between cache and main memory.

▶ **Main memory:** Data stored within the system's RAM storage.

▶ **Temporary file systems:** Data stored within elements of system memory allocated as temporary file stores, such as a RAM disk, or within virtual system drives.

▶ **Secondary memory:** Data stored in nonvolatile storage such as a hard drive or other form of media that retains data values after a system shutdown.

> ▶ **Removable media:** Nonvolatile removable media such as backup tape storage media.
>
> ▶ **Write-once storage:** Nonvolatile media not subject to later overwrite or modification, such as CD-ROMs and printouts.

Data capture in running systems is a specialized practice and should not be attempted by untrained responders.

Capture System Image

Drive imaging can be performed in several ways:

▶ Disk to disk image

▶ Disk to image file

▶ Image file to disk

Regardless of whether a direct device-to-device copy of the media or forensic evidence copies are created for examination, the process should be forensically sound, and the examination of media should be conducted in a forensically sound environment. A forensically sound environment is one in which the examiner has complete control. You can use a full system image to further examine data in an operational state, although you must put protections in place to prevent external communication through wired and wireless connectivity to protect against external manipulation or alerting of a suspect. When available, use a write blocking device to access suspect media to capture a system image. You can use software or hardware write blockers. Software write blockers stop any operating system write operations from modifying the media. Hardware write blockers are physical devices that sit between the drive itself and the controller card.

Data storage should be duplicated using verified forensic utilities and then only the duplicate reviewed in subsequent investigations to protect the original against modification or corruption. VM (virtual machine) images are acquired by either using tools specifically designed to capture a VM environment or using vendor built-in tools.

Network Traffic and Logs

Analysts can use data from network traffic to reconstruct and analyze network-based attacks. When deciding what evidence to capture, first identify potential sources where the breach occurred within the networking environment. These resources typically include network traffic and files. Once the resources are identified, gather the logs files that capture network traffic flows, management devices, servers, workstations, and wireless and mobile devices. Network traffic data is usually recorded to a log or stored in a packet capture file and the examiner can collect the logs along with the packet capture. Remote-access logging occurs on the remote-access server or the application server, but in some cases, the client also logs information related to the connection. Each system will have its own method for tracking and logging access, so it is important to capture all related logs files. Collecting network traffic can pose legal issues, such as the capture of information with privacy or security implications. If logs may be needed as court evidence, organizations may want to collect copies of the original log files, the centralized log files, and interpreted log data, in case there are any questions about the accuracy of the copying and interpretation processes.

Capture Video

If at all possible, videotape the entry of all persons into the crime area. By taping the actual entrance of a forensics team into the area, you can help refute claims that evidence was planted at the scene. You might also want to take photographs of the actual evidence and take notes at the scene. For example, in the case of an intrusion, you may want to take a photograph of the monitor. If the computer will be dissembled onsite for imaging, pictures of the computer should be taken from all angles to document the system hardware components and how they are connected. Carefully photograph the inside of the machine and note the serial number, internal drives, and peripheral components. Label the evidence, and then once again photograph the evidence after the labels have been attached. It might be a good idea to use a 35mm camera for your photographs. Digital images are easy to manipulate. Should it be questioned that the images have been altered, the negatives from the film would validate the pictures. Ideally, one person documents while another person handles the evidence. You want to be able to prove that you did not alter any of the evidence.

You can find valuable evidence about physical access through the recordings of CCTV systems, although some organizations must deploy adequate signage to make clear whether camera systems are monitored or merely present for later prosecution of wrongdoing. Otherwise, individuals who have signaled to the cameras for assistance during an emergency might bring suit against the organization due to the expectation of live monitoring of security cameras. Some CCTV systems might employ non-visible-spectrum cameras, such as thermal imaging systems able to spot heat blooms and body heat sources even when otherwise concealed. CCTV systems should be configured to observe access paths as well as locational areas, but not so that displayed data, password entry, and other similar details become remotely observable.

Record Time Offset

Records should be kept of all data and devices collected, including details such as system time offset from a verified time standard, nonstandard hardware or equipment configurations, and codecs available for video manipulation and running services (if the system is in operation). Recording the time offset is critical to an accurate examination when dates and times are at issue and should be done at the beginning of any examination. Just because a computer was seized in a particular time zone does not mean that it is configured for that time zone. Because computers can be moved from one zone to another, incorrectly configured, or deliberately altered, the time and time zone offset may not be accurate. When computers are examined, their date and time settings are recorded and compared with the current time. This may be used to calculate the difference between the two. This difference is then used as an offset and applied to all the time evidence on the computer. For example, when a computer that is imaged in the mountain time zone is analyzed with a tool that is in the eastern time zone, the time zone is adjusted to accurately reflect the time of the imaged drive. To resolve these issues, you need to know the machine's BIOS time and the time zone offset for which it is configured so that you can apply the correct time zone offset to your case. The time zone offset in Windows operating systems is stored in the Registry.

ExamAlert

Time offset adjustments cannot state anything about the accuracy of the events on the computer. The time offset adjustment establishes only the accuracy of the date and time record of the device when it was acquired.

Take Hashes

You should generate hashes of all data and applications before and after any in-depth analysis is performed, allowing validation that the forensic analysis itself has not produced unexpected modifications of evidentiary data. When the image of the drive is complete, a hash value of the image is taken and then compared against the hash of the original drive. If they are the same, you didn't change anything.

The most common method of taking a hash of a drive is to calculate a hash of the entire drive. Most forensic tool sets include a utility to calculate either a cyclic redundancy check (CRC) or Message Digest 5 (MD5) hash value. Other valid methods are available to generate a single value for a file, or collection of files, but the CRC and MD5 hash values are the most common. Both algorithms examine the input and generate a single value. Any changes to the input will result in a different value.

After you have ensured the physical integrity of the media, you can mount the media and access it in read-only mode. It is important that you explicitly separate the suspect media from other media during any access to the data. The only safe way to ensure nothing changes the data on the drive is to use trusted tools to access the media only once. The only reason to directly access suspect media is to copy it for analysis.

Screenshots

You should capture screenshots during the investigation and include them in forensic documentation for later reporting or testimony of the process and resulting findings. These should supplement photographs of the scene prior to evidentiary gathering and video of the collection and analysis process itself. Whenever possible, you should capture and preserve network traffic and logs to aid in the identification of related processes, remote virtual storage systems, and distributed computing functions that might relate to the investigation.

When collecting data, it is important to do the following:

▶ Document an investigation from initial notification through conclusion.

▶ Locate data any devices of potential evidentiary value.

▶ Identify data of interest.

▶ Establish an order of volatility to identify the first level of data capture desired.

▶ Eliminate external mechanisms of modification.

▶ Collect all data of potential evidentiary value.

▶ Create forensic duplicates of data for review.

▶ Store original data and devices in a manner that preserves integrity.

▶ Perform forensic evaluation and document findings or lack thereof.

▶ Report findings as appropriate.

Witnesses

Witnesses are an important part of any crime scene. If you interviewed anyone, you should create a list of whom you interviewed, including their names, email addresses, and what they saw (when, where, and how). The interviewer should ensure that physical distractions, such as noise or the presence of other persons, are minimized. The witness should be encouraged to volunteer information without prompting. In cases such as the release of malware, denial-of-service (DoS) attacks or theft of information, you can sometimes obtain more information than you expect just by asking. You might even end up with a confession if the threat was from an insider.

Track Man-Hours and Expense

The cost of a forensics investigation can run into thousands of dollars. As soon as the work proposal or court order is executed, the tracking of man-hours and administrative work begins. Costs are important part of project planning. Calculating the number of man-hours and other related expenses provides a way to estimate the investigation costs with the budgeted amount. The costs include the acquisition, investigation, and reporting of time and expenses. An organization will assess the costs of the investigation compared with the potential benefits to determine whether it is cost-effective and technically feasible.

Chain of Custody

Key to any form of forensic investigation is adherence to standards for the identification, collection, storage, and review of evidence. Chief among these is the creation of a log of all actions taken, including any inferences and causative details used to identify data of potential evidentiary value. This log should support the chain of custody for any evidentiary data, as well as track man-hours, expense and details of identification, and contact data for any witnesses and statements provided during an investigation. The chain of custody provides a clear record of the path evidence takes from acquisition to disposal.

Similar to other forms of forensics, this process requires a vast knowledge of computer hardware, software, and media to protect the chain of custody over the evidence, avoid accidental invalidation or destruction of evidence, and preserve the evidence for future analysis. Computer forensics review involves the application of investigative and analytical techniques to acquire and protect potential legal evidence. Therefore, a professional within this field needs a detailed understanding of the local, regional, national, and even international laws affecting the process of evidence collection and retention, especially in cases involving attacks that may be waged from widely distributed systems located in many separate regions.

ExamAlert

The practice of forensics analysis is a detailed and exacting one. The information provided in this section enables an entering professional to recognize that precise actions must be taken during an investigation. It is crucial that you do not attempt to perform these tasks without detailed training in the hardware, software, network, and legal issues involved in forensics analysis.

The major concepts behind computer forensics are to

- ▶ Identify the evidence
- ▶ Determine how to preserve the evidence
- ▶ Extract, process, and interpret the evidence
- ▶ Ensure that the evidence is acceptable in a court of law

Each state has its own laws that govern how cases can be prosecuted. For cases to be prosecuted, evidence must be properly collected, processed, and preserved. The corporate world focuses more on prevention and detection, whereas law enforcement focuses on investigation and prosecution.

Forensics analysis involves establishing a clear chain of custody over the evidence, which is the documentation of all transfers of evidence from one person to another, showing the date, time, and reason for transfer and the signatures of both parties involved in the transfer. In other words, it tells how the evidence made it from the crime scene to the courtroom, including documentation of how the evidence was collected, preserved, and analyzed. Every time data of possible evidentiary value is moved, accessed, manipulated, or reviewed, it is critical that the chain of custody be maintained and actions logged. Forensic analysis of information might require further actions with law enforcement, depending on findings and evidentiary data of interest.

If you are asked to testify about data that has been recovered or preserved, it is critical that you, as the investigating security administrator, be able to prove that no other individuals or agents could have tampered with or modified the evidence. This requires careful collection and preservation of all evidence, including the detailed logging of investigative access and the scope of the investigation. Definition of the scope is crucial to ensure that accidental privacy violations or unrelated exposure do not contaminate the evidence trail. After data is collected, you must secure it in such a manner that you, as the investigating official, can state with certainty that the evidence could not have been accessed or modified during your custodial term.

ExamAlert

For evidence to be useful, it must have five properties:

▶ **Admissible:** Evidence must be able to be used in court or within an organization's practices and so must follow all appropriate legal requirements and guidelines for identification, acquisition, examination, and storage.

▶ **Authentic:** Evidence must be proven to relate to the incident, with any changes accounted for in evidence review logs.

▶ **Complete:** In addition to data of evidentiary value, it is critical that evidentiary gathering includes both directly related as well as indirectly related data. An example might include a listing of all accounts logged in to a server when an attack occurred, rather than only logging details of the suspect's login.

▶ **Reliable:** Evidentiary identification, acquisition, review, and storage practices must ensure that the data remains authentic and unmodified to the best extent possible based on the data's order of volatility.

▶ **Believable:** Evidence must be clear and easy to understand, but it must be related to original binary or encrypted data through a process that is equally clear, documented, and not subject to manipulation during transition. Raw hexadecimal data is difficult for juries to review, but a chart illustrating the same information must represent the evidentiary data in a manner able to be replicated by another forensic analyst with the same end result.

Big Data Analysis

Big data describes the rapidly multiplying growth and availability of data. It is a combination of both structured and unstructured data. Structured data is information with a high degree of organization such as office documents, and most database files. Unstructured data is unorganized and not easily searchable, such email, social media, and log files. Big data security initiatives focus on the best way to protect such large stores of data by using multilayer security to deter any malicious activity, emerging threats, and vulnerabilities.

Forensic analysis of big data presents quite a few challenges. Data is spread out among numerous servers and other components. When a crime happens, the location of recoverable data includes the client machine, the equipment of the Internet service provider (ISP), and the data backups of the cloud service provider. This makes acquiring evidence from a crime committed in a diverse environment much more difficult because the environment is not localized like it is in a traditional digital forensic evidence acquisition. In addition to diverse environments, examiners must tackle the fundamental challenge of analyzing vast amounts of data in a reasonable response time while preserving forensic principles for the results to be presented in a court of law. In the examination of large environments, in many cases, the evidence system is in operation and data is fluctuating as it is being collected. The examiner may have difficulty proving that the evidence is original because there is neither a validating hash nor a forensic image of the device.

ExamAlert

As organizations place more and more data on infrastructure that the organization does not own, security and forensic processes and tools require revaluation to properly protect data and gather forensic evidence.

Cram Quiz

Answer these questions. The answers follow the last question. If you cannot answer these questions correctly, consider reading this section again until you can.

1. In which of the following type of analysis might an examiner have difficulty proving that the evidence is original?

   - ○ **A.** Disk to image file
   - ○ **B.** Disk to disk image
   - ○ **C.** Big data
   - ○ **D.** Log files

2. Which of the following information should be collected when collecting volatile data? (Select all correct answers.)

   - ○ **A.** System date and time
   - ○ **B.** Current network connections
   - ○ **C.** Current open ports and applications listening on those ports
   - ○ **D.** Full disk image

3. Which of the following provides a clear record of the path evidence takes from acquisition to disposal?

   - ○ **A.** Video capture
   - ○ **B.** Chain of custody
   - ○ **C.** Hashes
   - ○ **D.** Witness statements

Cram Quiz Answers

1. **C.** Because big data is unstructured and in diverse environments, the examiner may have difficulty proving that the evidence is original because there is neither a validating hash nor a forensic image of the device. Answer A is incorrect because disk to image files are hashed to prove originality. Answer B is incorrect because disk to disk images are hashed to prove originality. Answer D is incorrect because in cases where logs may be needed as court evidence, organizations can collect copies of the original log files, the centralized log files, and interpreted log data.

2. **A, B**, and **C.** The following volatile information should be collected: system date and time, current network connections, current open ports and applications listening on those ports, and applications currently running. Answer D is incorrect because a full disk image is not volatile data.

3. **B.** The chain of custody provides a clear record of the path evidence takes from acquisition to disposal. Answer A is incorrect because videotaping the actual entrance of a forensics team into the area helps refute claims that evidence was planted at the scene. Answer C is incorrect because hashes allow validation that the forensic analysis itself has not produced unexpected modifications of evidentiary data. Answer D is incorrect because witnesses provide statements about what they saw, when, where, and how.

Summarize Common Incident Response Procedures

▶ **Preparation**

▶ **Incident identification**

▶ **Escalation and notification**

▶ **Mitigation steps**

▶ **Lessons learned**

▶ **Reporting**

▶ **Recovery/reconstitution procedures**

▶ **First responder**

▶ **Incident isolation**

▶ **Data breach**

▶ **Damage and loss control**

CramSaver

If you can correctly answer these questions before going through this section, save time by skimming the Exam Alerts in this section and then completing the Cram Quiz at the end of the section.

1. Identify incident response preparation communications items.

2. Describe the information provided in a lessons learned meeting or report.

3. Explain why systems are isolated when an incident occurs.

Answers

1. Communication mechanisms include a variety of information such as contact information for team members within the organization, a system for tracking incident information, encryption software for securing team communications, and a secure storage area for evidence and other sensitive materials.

2. A lessons learned meeting or report provides a chance for incident closure by reviewing what occurred, what action was taken to mitigate and contain the incident, and how well the mitigation worked. A meeting should be held or report filed within a few days of the incident. Lessons learned reports provide valuable information for updating incident response policies and procedures. Post-mortem analysis of incident handling will often reveal a missing step or procedure.

3. Isolating systems or devices involved in an incident provides time for developing a tailored remediation strategy. The infected systems need to be isolated and quarantined. The quarantine phase involves finding each infected machine and disconnecting, removing, or blocking them from the network to prevent them from infecting other unpatched machines on the network.

Preparation

Organizational policies and practices are structural guidance designed to ensure quality and efficiency in the workplace. In an effort to properly preserve evidence, an incident response team (IRT) that knows how to handle incidents must be prepared. Incident response plans are needed so that you can intelligently react to an intrusion. If a plan is not in place and duties are not clearly assigned, the organization could end up in a state of panic. The components of an incident response plan should include preparation, roles, rules, and procedures. Incident response methodologies typically emphasize preparation so that the organization is ready to not only respond to incidents, but also to prevent incidents by ensuring that systems, networks, and applications are sufficiently secure.

Several categories of information are used for incident response preparation. The NIST Computer Security Incident Handling Guide (SP 800-61) provides a wealth of information along with the following recommendations. Communication mechanisms should include

▶ Contact information for internal team members

▶ On-call information for other teams

▶ Incident reporting mechanisms that includes at least one mechanism for anonymous reporting

▶ A system for tracking incident information

▶ Encryption software for securing communications among team members

▶ A war room for central communication and coordination

▶ Secure storage area for evidence and other sensitive materials

Incident analysis hardware and software include the following:

▶ Digital forensic workstations, laptops, and other mobile devices for tasks such as analyzing data, sniffing packets, and writing reports

▶ Blank removable media

▶ A portable printer

▶ Packet sniffers and protocol analyzers

▶ Digital forensic software

▶ Removable media with trusted versions of programs

▶ Evidence-gathering accessories

Incident analysis resources include the following:

▶ Commonly used port lists

▶ Documentation for operating systems, applications, protocols, and intrusion detection and antivirus products

▶ Network diagrams and lists of critical assets

▶ Current baselines of expected network, system, and application activity

▶ Cryptographic hashes of critical files

Incident mitigation software includes access to images of clean operating systems and application installations.

Incident Identification

Many risks to enterprise networks relate to vulnerabilities present in system and service configurations and to network and user logon weaknesses. Signs of an incident fall into one of two categories: precursors and indicators. A precursor is a sign that an incident may occur in the future. An indicator is a sign that an incident may have occurred or may be occurring now. Not every precursor or indicator is guaranteed to be accurate. For example, intrusion detection systems may produce false positives. There can be thousands or millions of indicators generated daily, and each indicator must be evaluated to determine legitimacy. An accurate indicator does not necessarily mean that an incident has occurred, and often determining whether a particular event is actually an incident a matter of judgment. When the response team has determined that an incident has occurred, the next step in incident analysis involves taking a comprehensive look at the incident activity to determine the scope, priority, and threat of the incident. This aids with researching possible response and mitigation strategies.

Escalation and Notification

In incident identification, events from various sources (such as log files, intrusion detection systems, and firewalls) that may produce evidence to help determine whether an event is an incident are gathered. When an incident is analyzed and prioritized, the incident response team needs to notify the appropriate individuals so that all who need to be involved will play their roles.

> **ExamAlert**
>
> Incident response policies should include provisions concerning incident escalation and notification that includes what must be reported to whom and at what times.

The exact reporting requirements vary among organizations, but parties that are typically notified include the CIO, CISO, other internal incident response team members, human resources, public affairs, legal department, and law enforcement when necessary.

Mitigation Steps

Depending on the severity of the incident and the organizational policy, incident response functions can take many forms. The response team might send out recommendations for mitigation, recovery, containment, and prevention to systems and network administrators, who then complete the response steps. The team might perform the mitigation actions themselves.

> **ExamAlert**
>
> *Mitigation* refers to the action of minimizing the impact of an incident. It is important to accurately determine the cause of each incident so that it can be fully contained and the exploited vulnerabilities can be mitigated to prevent similar incidents from occurring in the future.

In keeping with the severity of the incident, the organization can act to mitigate the impact of the incident by containing it and eventually restoring operations to normal. Mitigation is important before an incident damages resources. Because of the quick need to act, mitigation is often based on judgment and quick decision making. Decisions are easier to make if strategies and procedures for incident mitigation are already in place. Organizations should define acceptable risks in dealing with incidents and develop strategies accordingly. The incident type will determine the mitigation. Organizations should create separate mitigation strategies for each major incident type, with criteria clearly documented.

Lessons Learned

The follow-up response can involve sharing information and lessons learned with other response teams and other appropriate organizations and sites. One of the most important parts of incident response is lessons learned.

> ### ExamAlert
>
> A lessons learned meeting should be conducted after a major incident. Alternatively, a lessons learned report can be filed. A lessons learned meeting or report provides a chance for incident closure by reviewing what occurred, what action was taken to mitigate and contain the incident, and how well the mitigation worked.

A meeting should be held or report filed within a few days of the incident. Lessons learned reports provide valuable information for updating incident response policies and procedures. Post-mortem analysis of incident handling will often reveal a missing step or procedure.

Reporting

After the incident is mitigated, the organization issues a report containing details about the incident, such as the cause, cost, and recommendations for preventing future incidents. Incident reporting allows processes to be reviewed and adjusted, enabling an organization to help reduce incidents and losses. Organizations may be subject to industry requirements for reporting certain types of incidents. In this case, there will be requirements and guidelines for external communications and information sharing (for example, what can be shared with whom, when, and over what channels), and the handoff and escalation points in the incident management process. In addition, forensic analysis of information might require further reporting to law enforcement or clients depending on the findings and evidentiary data.

Recovery/Reconstitution Procedures

Depending on the nature of the incident, there may be destruction of physical property, and it might be necessary to rebuild or reconstitute the organization.

Reconstitution options can include continuing to operate from the current alternate site, beginning an orderly phased return to the original site, or beginning to establish a reconstituted organization at another location. In recovery, administrators restore systems to normal operation and confirm that the systems are functioning normally.

ExamAlert

Recovery may involve such actions as restoring systems from clean backups, rebuilding systems from scratch, replacing compromised files with clean versions, installing patches, changing passwords, and tightening network perimeter security.

Higher levels of system logging or network monitoring are often part of the recovery process. Once a resource is successfully attacked, it is often attacked again, or other resources within the organization are attacked in a similar manner.

Eradication and recovery should be done in a phased approach so that remediation steps are prioritized. For large-scale incidents, recovery may take months.

First Responder

How evidence is handled at the scene is often much more important than the laboratory analysis work that is done later. First responders are the first ones to arrive at the incident scene. The success of data recovery and potential prosecution depends on the actions of the individual who initially discovers a computer incident. How the evidence scene is handled can severely affect the ability of the organization to prosecute. Although police officers are trained to have a good understanding of the limits of the Fourth and Fifth Amendments and applicable laws, many system administrators and network security personnel are not. The entire work area is a potential crime scene, not just the computer itself. There might be evidence such as removable media, voicemail messages, or handwritten notes. The work area should be secured and protected to maintain the integrity of the area. Under no circumstances should you touch the computer/device or should anyone be allowed to remove any items from the scene.

Incident Isolation

Isolating systems or devices involved in an incident provides time for developing a tailored remediation strategy. The infected systems need to be isolated and quarantined. The quarantine phase involves finding each infected machine and disconnecting, removing, or blocking them from the network to prevent them from infecting other unpatched machines on the network.

> **ExamAlert**
>
> Although it is generally advised to remove the device from the network, this process may cause additional damage when sophisticated malware is involved.

For example, when a machine running malware that regularly reports back to a designated host fails to report as expected, the malware may overwrite or encrypt all the data on the host's hard drive. Incident response personnel should not assume that further damage to the host has been prevented just because a host has been disconnected from the network. In cases such as this, the organization may redirect the attacker to a sandbox so that they can monitor the attacker's activity to gather additional evidence and more clearly understand the attack. This approach comes with additional risks, including possible legal ramifications.

Data Breach

The 2013 data breach at Target put some 110 million people at risk of credit fraud and identity theft. Companies such as Neiman Marcus, eBay, Home Depot, and Sony have recently made headlines due to large-scale data breaches. One of the most important points about a data breach is that mitigation of further loss of data is necessary, and you should conduct a thorough investigation of the suspected or confirmed loss or theft of account information within 24 hours of the compromise. Data breach notification is very often a requirement in responding to a data breach. Currently, only Alabama, New Mexico, and South Dakota have not enacted laws related to security breach notification. Data breach notification laws provide direction on steps to be taken following a data breach and may define responsibilities and liabilities involved in a breach.

> **ExamAlert**
>
> Federal laws addressing privacy, data protection, and breach notification include
>
> ▶ HIPAA and HITECH
>
> ▶ Gramm-Leach-Bliley Act
>
> ▶ Fair Credit Reporting Act
>
> ▶ Children's Online Privacy Protection Act

A key challenge in responding to a data breach is determining whether and when notification is an appropriate response. This determination will often be made by the legal team. Data breach notification laws are continually changing, and businesses should consider the statutes of all states in which they do business or of whose residents they have personal information.

Damage and Loss Control

Following a data breach, a company typically incurs costs for notifying customers and for processing claims for damages. The following expenses may be incurred when a data breach results in the loss or theft of third-party information:

▶ Forensic examination to determine the severity and scope of the breach

▶ Notification of third parties

▶ Call center hotline support

▶ Credit or identity monitoring

▶ Public relations for damage control

▶ Legal defense

▶ Regulatory proceedings, fines and penalties

In addition, regulatory settlements may require the breached organization to implement a comprehensive written information security program subject to periodic audits.

Cram Quiz

Answer these questions. The answers follow the last question. If you cannot answer these questions correctly, consider reading this section again until you can.

1. Which of the following is a communications mechanism defined in incident response preparation?

   ○ **A.** Blank removable media

   ○ **B.** War room

   ○ **C.** Documentation for OSs

   ○ **D.** Images of clean OS and application installations

2. Which of the following parties are typically notified first when a confirmed incident has occurred? (Select two correct answers.)

   ○ **A.** Press

   ○ **B.** CISO

   ○ **C.** End users

   ○ **D.** Legal

3. Which of the following federal laws address privacy, data protection, and breach notification? (Select all correct answers.)

   ○ **A.** Sarbanes–Oxley Act

   ○ **B.** HIPAA

   ○ **C.** Gramm-Leach-Bliley Act

   ○ **D.** Children's Online Privacy Protection Act

Cram Quiz Answers

1. **B.** Communication mechanisms include a war room (for central communication and coordination) and a secure storage facility for evidence and other sensitive materials. Answer A is incorrect because blank removable media is part of incident analysis hardware and software. Answer C is incorrect because documentation for operating systems is part of incident analysis resources. Answer D is incorrect because incident mitigation software includes access to images of clean OS and application installations.

2. **B and D.** The exact reporting requirements vary among organizations, but parties that are typically notified include the CIO, CISO, other internal incident response team members, human resources, public affairs, legal department, and law enforcement when necessary. Answer A is incorrect because the press is not normally notified when an incident occurs. Answer C is incorrect because the users are not normally notified initially when an incident occurs.

3. **B**, **C**, and **D**. Federal laws addressing privacy, data protection, and breach notification include HIPAA and HITECH, Gramm-Leach-Bliley Act, Fair Credit Reporting Act, and Children's Online Privacy Protection Act. Answer A is incorrect because the Sarbanes-Oxley Act covers responsibilities of a public corporation's board of directors and adds criminal penalties for certain misconduct.

What Next?

If you want more practice on this chapter's exam objectives before you move on, remember that you can access all the Cram Quiz questions on the CD. You can also create a custom exam by objective with the practice exam software. Note any objective that you struggle with and go to the material that covers that objective in this chapter.

CHAPTER 4

Response and Recovery

> **This chapter covers the following official CompTIA Security+ SY0-401 exam objectives:**
>
> ▶ Explain the importance of security-related awareness and training
>
> ▶ Compare and contrast physical security and environmental controls
>
> ▶ Summarize risk management best practices
>
> ▶ Given a scenario, select the appropriate control to meet the goals of security
>
> (For more information on the official CompTIA Security+ SY0-401 exam topics, see the "About the CompTIA Security+ SY0-401 Exam" section in the Introduction.)

Planning and testing of security-awareness programs, disaster recovery plans, and physical security controls are critical prior to an incident to ensure that proper policies are in place to preserve organizational value in the face of disaster recovery practices that must focus first on preservation of human life or on which lines of communication and succession must be well known by those who remain following a large-scale event. This chapter examines the importance of security-awareness training and environmental and physical security controls. It also covers risk management best practices, including the requirements for business continuity/continuity of operations and disaster recovery planning, along with selecting the appropriate control to meet organizational security goals.

Explain the Importance of Security-Related Awareness and Training

▶ Security policy training and procedures

▶ Role-based training

▶ Personally identifiable information

▶ Information classification

▶ Data labeling, handling, and disposal

▶ Compliance with laws, best practices, and standards

▶ User habits

▶ New threats and new security trends/alerts

▶ Use of social networking and P2P

▶ Follow up and gather training metrics to validate compliance and security posture

CramSaver

If you can correctly answer these questions before going through this section, save time by skimming the Exam Alerts in this section and then completing the Cram Quiz at the end of the section.

1. What policy restricts inadvertent data disclosure due to notes left behind?

2. What type of threat is most challenging for a network?

3. Are security posters the best solution for user awareness?

4. An email to ALLSTAFF detailing a new email virus improves what aspect of user security awareness?

5. When a user switches between organizational sections, what type of security training does he or she need to cover encryption and using USB thumb drives?

Answers

1. The clean desk policy assists users in remembering not to write down data nor leave it behind, such as notes of passwords and phrases left under the keyboard.

2. A zero-day threat takes advantage of a previously unaddressed vulnerability so that there is no time to properly protect the network before its resulting threats can come to bear.

3. Passive techniques such as posters and email are much less effective than active delivery of security issues such as introductory training and yearly seminars.

4. **Threat awareness.** Threat awareness includes recognizing attacks and requires constant reminders of newly emergent threat agents to remain current.

5. **Data handling.** Because the policies, procedures, and types of data managed in each organizational section can vary widely, it is important to provide a transferring organizational member with data handling training to ensure her compliance with appropriate protocols and procedures.

The challenge of insider threats (malicious or simply error or accident) continues to expand as more data is made accessible across more types of devices and expressed in more data delivery scenarios.

Before you can properly secure a network, you must understand the security function, purpose of network devices, and technologies used to secure the network. This section introduces the implementation of security configuration parameters as they apply to network devices and other technologies that are used to form the protection found on most networks.

Security Policy Training and Procedures

Human resources (HR) policies and practices should reduce the risk of theft, fraud, or misuse of information facilities by employees, contractors, and third-party users. The primary legal and HR representatives should review all policies, especially privacy issues, legal issues, and HR enforcement language. Legal and HR review of policies is required in many, if not most, organizations.

Security planning must include procedures for the creation and authorization of accounts (provisioning) for newly hired personnel and the planned removal of privileges (deprovisioning) following employment termination. When termination involves power users with high-level access rights or knowledge of service administrator passwords, it is critical to institute password and security updates to exclude known avenues of access while also increasing security monitoring for possible reprisals against the organization.

The hiring process should also include provisions for making new employees aware of acceptable-use and disposal policies and the sanctions that might be enacted if violations occur. An organization should also institute a formal code of ethics to which all employees should subscribe, particularly power users with broad administrative rights.

User education is mandatory to ensure that users are made aware of expectations, options, and requirements related to secure access within an organization's network. Education can include many different forms of communication, including the following:

▶ New employees and contract agents should be provided education in security requirements as a part of the hiring process.

▶ Reminders and security-awareness newsletters, emails, and flyers should be provided to raise general security awareness.

▶ General security policies must be defined, documented, and distributed to employees.

▶ Regular focus group sessions and on-the-job training should be provided for users regarding changes to the user interface, application suites, and general policies.

▶ General online security-related resources should be made available to users through a simple, concise, and easily navigable interface.

ExamAlert

Although all the previously mentioned practices are part of a security-awareness training program, security training during employee orientation combined with yearly seminars is the best method of user security-awareness training because these combined methods raise security awareness. Email and posters are passive and tend to be less effective.

User training should ensure that operational guidelines, restrictions on data sharing, disaster recovery strategies, and operational mandates are clearly conveyed to users and refreshed regularly. Policies may also require refresher training during transfer between organizational components or roles/job duties under the rotation policy. Details such as information classification (high, medium, low, confidential, private, public), sensitivity of data and handling guidelines, legal mandates around data forms such as personally identifiable information (PII) in financial or healthcare settings, best practices, and consumption standards can vary widely between organizational units with the proper protocols for access, storage, and disposal varying accordingly. In response to the continued expansion of electronic technology provided by users themselves in bring-your-own-device (BYOD) settings, security-awareness training is also key to managing user habits and expectations developed due to the prevalence of computing equipment at home and in their mobile devices.

Role-Based Training

For organizations to protect the integrity, confidentiality, and availability of information in today's highly diverse network environments, ensuring that each person involved understands his and her roles and responsibilities and is adequately trained is paramount. NIST Special Publication 800-16 outlines the advantages of role- and performance-based security training and presents models for both role- and performance-based training models. All employees need fundamental training in IT security concepts and procedures. Training can then be broken into three levels: beginning, intermediate, and advanced. Each level is then linked to roles and responsibilities. Because individuals may perform more than one role within the organization, they may need intermediate or advanced level IT security training in their primary job role, but only the beginning level in a secondary role.

Personally Identifiable Information

Privacy-sensitive information is referred to as personally identifiable information (PII). This is any information that identifies or can be used to identify, contact, or locate the person to whom such information pertains.

ExamAlert

Personally identifiable information is information about a person that contains some unique identifier from which the identity of the person can be determined. Examples of PII include name, address, phone number, fax number, email address, financial profiles, Social Security number, and credit card information. PII is not limited to the these examples and includes any other personal information that is linked or linkable to an individual.

For many organizations, privacy policies are mandatory, have detailed requirements, and carry significant legal penalties (for example, entities covered under the Health Insurance Privacy and Portability Act [HIPPA]).

To be considered PII, information must be specifically associated with an individual person. Information provided either anonymously or not associated with its owner before collection is not considered PII. Unique information, such as a personal profile, unique identifier, biometric information, and IP address that is associated with PII, can also be considered PII. The definition of PII is not anchored to any single category of information or technology. It is important for an organization to train employees to recognize that non-PII can become PII whenever additional information is made publicly available (in any medium and from any source) that, when combined with other available information, could be used to identify an individual. Organizations should require that all employees and contractors complete privacy training annually within a set numbers of days after the start of employment.

Information Classification

ISO 17799 can help an organization establish information classification criteria. It is essential to classify information according to its value and level of sensitivity so that the appropriate level of security can be used. A system of classification should be easy to administer, effective, and uniformly applied throughout the organization. Organizational information that is not public should not be disclosed to anyone who is not authorized to access it. The organization should have a strict policy in place for violations that could result in disciplinary proceedings against the offending individual, and all employees should be trained in this policy.

Data is classified first based on impact to the C-I-A triad security objectives: confidentiality, integrity, and availability. Information resources are broken into three categories of risk: low, medium, and high. All information has some level of risk and a minimum level of protection requirements. Some categories of information have higher levels of risk either because of the sensitive nature of the information or because of the value of the information. After the impact has been decided, classification of data is based on its level of sensitivity and the impact to the organization should that data be disclosed, altered, or destroyed without authorization. The classifications are usually broken into the categories of confidential or high, private or medium, and public or low depending on the guidance used by the organization. For example, FIPS Publication 199 Standards for Security Categorization of Federal Information and Information Systems uses the categories high, medium, and low.

High

The unauthorized disclosure of information could be expected to have a severe or catastrophic adverse effect on organizational operations, organizational assets, or individuals. Systems handling restricted data should have the strictest security requirements. This classification level is reserved for information that would, if inadvertently released, have a significant adverse impact to the organization.

Medium

The unauthorized disclosure of information could be expected to have a serious adverse effect on organizational operations, organizational assets, or individuals. Medium sensitivity should be considered the default classification level for nonrestricted data that has not been explicitly made public.

Low

The unauthorized disclosure of information could be expected to have a limited adverse effect on organizational operations, organizational assets, or individuals. The lowest data classification level includes data openly available to the public. This might include low-sensitivity data that, when openly distributed, presents no risk to the organization.

Confidential

Confidential information is internal information that defines the way in which the organization operates. Security should be high. Confidential data is information that, if made available to unauthorized parties, may adversely affect individuals or the organization. This classification also includes data that the organization is required to keep confidential, either by law or under a confidentiality agreement with a third party, such as a vendor. This information should be protected against unauthorized disclosure or modification. Confidential data should be used only when necessary for business purposes and should be protected both when it is in use and when it is being stored or transported.

Private

Private data is information that is unlikely to result in a high-level financial loss or serious damage to the organization but still should be protected. Data should be classified as private when the unauthorized disclosure, alteration, or destruction of that data could result in a moderate level of risk to the organization, its affiliates, or business partners. By default, all data that is not explicitly classified as confidential or public data should be treated as private data. A reasonable level of security controls should be applied to private data.

Public

Public data is information in the public domain. This is a minimal security level. Data should be classified as public when the unauthorized disclosure, alteration, or destruction of that data would results in little or no risk to the organization, its affiliates, or business partners. Examples of public data include press releases, directory information, and any other information that is publicly shared. Little or no controls are required to protect the confidentiality of public data, but some level of control is required to prevent unauthorized modification or destruction of public data.

The important thing to remember here is to document how your data classifications correlate to your security objectives. When classifications are established, they should be adhered to and closely monitored, and employees should be trained so that they understand information classification. Data classifications can also help when submitting discoverable information subject to the Federal Rules of Civil Procedure should the organization be involved in a lawsuit.

Data Labeling, Handling, and Disposal

An organization's information sensitivity policy defines requirements for the classification and security of data and hardware resources based on their relative level of sensitivity. Some resources, such as hard drives, might require very extensive preparations before they can be discarded. Data labeling and cataloging of information stored on each storage device, tape, or removable storage system becomes critical to identifying valuable and sensitive information requiring special handling.

The hiring process should also include provisions for making new employees aware of acceptable use, data handling, and disposal policies and the sanctions that might be enacted if violations occur. An organization should also institute a formal code of ethics to which all employees should subscribe, particularly power users with broad administrative rights.

Compliance with Laws, Best Practices, and Standards

The organization should be sure the security policies and awareness training includes compliance with current state and federal legislation and does not create unnecessary business risk to the company by employee misuse of resources. The most successful organizations implement security-awareness best practices that are documented, accessible, effective, appropriate, and widely accepted. These best practices consist of strategies and approaches in compliance with existing laws and regulations that are developed by knowledgeable bodies and are carried out by adequately trained personnel. This approach is shown to be effective at providing reasonable assurance of desired outcomes, provided that the policies and training are continually reviewed and improved upon as needed. A good security-awareness training program should consist of strategy, planning, program development, program delivery, and administration.

User Habits

I have heard it said that "an enterprise could be nearly perfect, except for all the users." Like a chain, a network is "only as secure as its weakest link," and users present a wide variety of bad habits, a vast range of knowledge and skill, and a varying intent in data access. Proper user education can go a long way to mitigating risk in the enterprise.

Password Behaviors

Users must be instructed in the value of their access credentials and the impact that could result from sharing their passwords and logons, using weak passwords (and the ability to identify a strong password), using easily guessed passwords, and expectations of password expiration schedules to avoid filling up the call center the first Monday morning every 90 days.

Data Handling

User training should address legal or regulatory requirements for accessing, transporting, storing, or disposing of data and data storage devices. This includes encryption systems for mobile and removable storage devices, data access logging requirements under laws such as HIPPA, and review of the retention and destruction policy.

Clean Desk Policies

A clean desk policy is one of the top strategies used when trying to reduce the risk of security breaches in the workplace. Training should include details of the organization's clean desk policy, encouraging users to avoid jotting down hard-to-recall passphrases or details from electronic systems that might contain PII. A clean desk policy can also increase employee's awareness about protecting sensitive information. Users should understand why taping a list of their logons and passwords under their keyboards is a bad idea.

ExamAlert

A clean desk policy can be a vital tool in protecting sensitive and confidential materials in the hands of end users. A clean desk policy requires that users remove sensitive and confidential materials from workspaces and items that are not in use are locked when employees leave their workstations.

Prevent Tailgating

User training should encourage situational awareness at all times. Unbadged individuals wandering in secured areas should be challenged, tailgating at checkpoints (following an authorized individual in closely to avoid having to provide personal authorization credentials) should be prevented, and guidelines for handling other forms of physical and logical security violations must be conveyed and practiced.

Personally Owned Devices

Common mobile computing devices, removable media storage key fobs, file-sharing systems (Dropbox, Box.com, or SkyDrive or OneDrive), peer-to-peer transfer services, and even browser-based social media solutions and games can all introduce a range of vulnerabilities and threat agents to an enterprise without requiring elevated privilege or special equipment. Users must be given training in the proper use of their various personal technologies (or reasons to not use the technologies). Because this area is constantly evolving, convey reminders and updates in the regular security-awareness newsletter.

New Threats and New Security Trends/Alerts

Training reminders are regular memos emailed to users outlining the "best practices" of computer virus protection. These should include how-to tips on email attachments or antivirus software usage, phishing attacks, and zero-day exploits. When a major new virus is seen in the wild or a new zero-day exploit appears, there is an opportunity to tie in news media coverage with specific tips on avoiding these security breaches in your organization.

New Viruses

Emergent viruses, worms, Trojans, rootkits, phishing attacks, and other threats should be identified and conveyed to users as rapidly as possible before dozens of calls come in asking why the "I Love You" email didn't show its attached greeting card properly when opened. This must be tempered, though, as the million-plus new viral versions every year will rapidly overwhelm users into a state of helplessness or disinterest in the face of apparent inevitability.

Phishing Attacks

Personalized spear-phishing attacks are becoming more prevalent, requiring vigilance on the part of the users to avoid the natural response of opening everything that seems to be coming from their family members, boss, or co-workers. Educating users about security is challenging, particularly in the context of phishing, because it is difficult to teach people to make the right online trust decision without increasing their tendency to misjudge nonthreats as threats. An interactive approach is to provide web-based tests that let users assess their own knowledge of phishing. Another option is to send fake phishing emails to test users' vulnerability and then follow up with training.

Zero-Day Exploits

When a new zero-day threat emerges that has not been specifically considered in response planning, the same communication channels can be used to alert users of actions being taken by the IT group to correct, recover, repair, or patch systems and data. In a Windows environment, when there is new zero-day vulnerability on the loose, best practices for mitigation include user access control and educating the users about running files from unknown sources.

> **ExamAlert**
>
> To mitigate zero-day exploits, organizations should employ a layered approach to security that begins with an acceptable use policy and include operating system and application patching. By limiting exposure to threats, blocking malware and viruses, and containing security breaches quickly, zero-day exploits can be better mitigated.

Use of Social Networking and Peer-to-Peer Services

The emergence of new services connecting one person to another (social networking like Facebook and Twitter) or directly connecting one device to another (peer to peer) can bypass traditional network defenses, potentially exposing the enterprise to unexpected avenues by which malware can enter or providing uncontrolled pathways by which data can exfiltrate the enterprise's scope of defensive measures. In addition to the challenges of protecting against accidental data release of intellectual property, social networking can expose business practices and new market exploration by revealing something as simple as the GPS data embedded in a "selfie" picture posted on Facebook. Tracking troop deployments through such means is a common practice for warfighting information services, while a rival company might identify a new fabrication site merely by tracking publicly shared data on its competitor's Vine or Twitter posts.

Users must be trained in critical consideration before providing logon credentials to any service, particularly those that bring personal data interaction into the workplace. Social media services are increasingly used for business purposes, so separation of business and personal accounts become critical in the event of a legal motion for discovery that could otherwise require access to personally controlled data resources. Social media services accessed through encrypted web access also offer a route through which protected information could be inadvertently disclosed without passing in readable form through normal boundary content review systems.

Peer-to-peer (P2P) services also present a danger to intellectual property and system availability protection by allowing direct connections between random endpoints using a wide variety of protocols and service ports, making firewall and packet-shaper management much more difficult for technicians and potentially sharing otherwise secure data stores to unknown parties as in the case of a misconfigured P2P client such as BitTorrent. P2P encrypted data streams can also result in contraband content being placed on a system within an organization without proper review, potentially exposing the organization to legal action based on the type of contraband.

Follow Up and Gather Training Metrics to Validate Compliance and Security Posture

Information security continuous monitoring helps to maintain an ongoing awareness of information security, vulnerabilities, and threats in support of organizational risk management decisions. Real-time monitoring of technical controls can provide an organization with a view of the effectiveness of those controls and the security posture of the organization. It is important to recognize that with any comprehensive information security program, all implemented security controls, including management and operational controls, must be regularly assessed for effectiveness, even if the monitoring of such controls cannot be automated or is not easily automated. Metrics enable you to track and measure the impact of your security-awareness program. The results can be used to validate compliance and evaluate the organizational security posture. SANS has developed a spreadsheet that identifies and documents different options for measuring your security-awareness program. It includes metrics for both measuring impact (change in behavior) and for tracking compliance. You can find the spreadsheet at http://www.securingthehuman.org/resources/metrics.

Cram Quiz

Answer these questions. The answers follow the last question. If you cannot answer
these questions correctly, consider reading this section again until you can.

1. Which of the following individual items are examples of PII? (Choose all correct
   answers.)

   ○ **A.** Social Security number

   ○ **B.** Home address

   ○ **C.** Gender

   ○ **D.** State of residence

2. Which of the following requires that users remove sensitive and confidential materials from workspaces and items that are not in use are locked when
   employees leave their workstation?

   ○ **A.** Data handling policy

   ○ **B.** Clean desk policy

   ○ **C.** Tailgating training

   ○ **D.** Phishing attack training

3. Which of the following is information that is unlikely to result in a high-level financial loss or serious damage to the organization but still should be protected?

   ○ **A.** Public data

   ○ **B.** Confidential data

   ○ **C.** Sensitive data

   ○ **D.** Private data

Cram Quiz Answers

1. **A** and **B**. Examples of PII are name, address, phone number, fax number, email address, financial profiles, Social Security number, and credit card information. PII is not limited to these examples and includes any other personal information that is linked or linkable to an individual. Answers C and D are incorrect because individually they are not considered to be PII, but when combined with other information, may become PII.

2. **B**. A clean desk policy requires that users remove sensitive and confidential materials from workspaces and items that are not in use are locked when an employees leave their workstation. Answer A is incorrect because a data handling policy should address legal or regulatory requirements for accessing, transporting, storing, or disposing of data and data storage devices. Answer C is incorrect because tailgating involves following an authorized individual in closely avoiding having to provide personal authorization credentials. Answer D is incorrect because phishing attacks training teaches users to avoid the natural response of opening everything that seems to be coming from their family members, boss, or co-workers.

3. **D**. Private data is information that is unlikely to result in a high-level financial loss or serious damage to the organization but still should be protected. Answer A is incorrect because the unauthorized disclosure, alteration, or destruction of public data would result in little or no risk to the organization. Answer B is incorrect because confidential information is internal information that defines the way in which the organization operates. Security should be high. Answer C is incorrect because sensitive data is considered confidential data.

Compare and Contrast Physical and Environmental Controls

▶ **Environmental controls**

▶ **Physical security**

▶ **Control types**

CramSaver

If you can correctly answer these questions before going through this section, save time by skimming the Exam Alerts in this section and then completing the Cram Quiz at the end of the section.

1. What is the most important asset that must be protected by physical and environmental security controls?

2. What is TEMPEST?

3. Which type of fire extinguisher should be used for burning magnesium fires?

Answers

1. Human life is always the most important asset when planning for physical and environmental safety controls.

2. TEMPEST is a type of shielding used against electromagnetic interference, generally found in military equipment.

3. Class D extinguishers are used for burning combustible metals such as magnesium and sodium.

Environmental Controls

Not all incidents arise from attacks, illegal activities, or other forms of directed threats to an enterprise. Many threats emerge due to physical and environmental factors that require additional consideration in planning for security controls. The location of everything from the actual building to wireless antennas affects security. When picking a location for a building, an organization should investigate the type of neighborhood, population, crime rate, and emergency response times. This helps in the planning of the physical barriers needed, such as fencing, lighting, and security personnel. An organization must also analyze the potential dangers from natural disasters and plan to reduce their effect when possible.

When protecting computers, wiring closets, and other devices from physical damage due to either natural or manmade disasters, you must select locations carefully. Proper placement of the equipment should cost a company little money upfront but provide significant protection from possible loss of data due to flooding, fire, or theft.

HVAC

You must take into consideration the cooling requirements of computer data centers and server rooms when doing facilities planning. The amount of heat generated by some of this equipment is extreme and highly variable. Depending on the size of the space, age, and type of equipment the room contains, energy consumption typically ranges from 20 to 100 watts per square foot. Newer servers, although smaller and more powerful, might consume more energy. Therefore, some high-end facilities with state-of-the-art technology can require up to 400 watts per square foot. These spaces consume many times more energy than office facilities of equivalent size and must be planned for accordingly. Smaller, more powerful IT equipment is considerably hotter than older systems, making heat management a major challenge.

When monitoring the HVAC system, keep in mind that overcooling causes condensation on equipment and too-dry environments lead to excessive static. The area should be monitored for hot spots and cold spots. This is where one exchange is frigid cold under vent and still hot elsewhere. Water or drain pipes above facilities also raise a concern about upper-floor drains clogging, too. One solution is to use rubberized floors above the data center or server room. Above all else, timely A/C maintenance is required.

Fire Suppression

Fire is a danger common to all business environments and one that must be planned for well in advance of any possible occurrence. The first step in a fire-safety program is fire prevention.

The best way to prevent fires is to train employees to recognize dangerous situations and report these situations immediately. Knowing where a fire extinguisher is and how to use it can stop a small fire from becoming a major catastrophe. Many of the newer motion- and ultrasonic-detection systems also include heat and smoke detection for fire prevention. These systems alert the monitoring station of smoke or a rapid increase in temperature. If a fire does break out somewhere within the facility, a proper fire-suppression system can avert major damage. Keep in mind that laws and ordinances apply to the deployment and monitoring of a fire-suppression system. It is your responsibility to ensure that these codes are properly met. In addition, the organization should have safe evacuation procedures and periodic fire drills to protect its most important investment: human life.

Fire requires three main components to exist: heat, oxygen, and fuel. Eliminate any of these components and the fire goes out. A common way to fight fire is with water. Water attempts to take away oxygen and heat. A wet-pipe fire-suppression system is the one that most people think of when discussing an indoor sprinkler system. The term *wet* is used to describe the state of the pipe during normal operations. The pipe in the wet-pipe system has water under pressure in it at all times. The pipes are interconnected and have sprinkler heads attached at regularly spaced intervals. The sprinkler heads have a stopper held in place with a bonding agent designed to melt at an appropriate temperature. After the stopper melts, it opens the valve and allows water to flow from the sprinkler head to extinguish the fire. Keep in mind that electronic equipment and water don't get along well. Fires that start outside electrical areas are well served by water-based sprinkler systems. Also keep in mind that all these systems should have both manual activation and manual shutoff capabilities. You want to be able to turn off a sprinkler system to prevent potential water damage. Most systems are designed to activate only one head at a time. This works effectively to put out fires in the early stages.

Dry-pipe systems work in exactly the same fashion as wet-pipe systems, except that the pipes are filled with pressurized air rather than water. The stoppers work on the same principle. When the stopper melts, the air pressure is released and a valve in the system opens. One of the reasons for using a dry-pipe system is that when the outside temperature drops below freezing, any water in the pipes can freeze, causing them to burst. Another reason for justifying a dry-pipe system is the delay associated between the system activation and the actual water deployment. Because some laws require a sprinkler system even in areas of the building that house electrical equipment, there is enough of a delay that it is feasible for someone to manually deactivate the system before water starts to flow. In such a case, a company could deploy a dry-pipe system and a chemical system together. The delay in the dry-pipe system can be used to deploy the chemical system first and avoid serious damage to the running equipment from a water-based sprinkler system.

ExamAlert

Know the difference between the different types of fire-suppression systems (see Figure 4.1):

▶ For Class A fires (trash, wood, and paper), water decreases the fire's temperature and extinguishes its flames. Foam is usually used to extinguish Class B fires, which are fueled by flammable liquids, gases, and greases. Liquid foam mixes with air while passing through the hose and the foam.

▶ Class C fires (energized electrical equipment, electrical fires, and burning wires) are put out using extinguishers based on carbon dioxide or Halon. Halon was once used as a reliable, effective, and safe fire-protection tool, but in 1987 an international agreement known as the Montreal Protocol mandated the phase-out of environmentally damaging Halons in developed countries by the year 2000 and in less-developed countries by 2010, due to emissions concerns. Therefore, carbon-dioxide extinguishers have replaced Halon extinguishers in all but a few locations. Carbon-dioxide extinguishers don't leave a harmful residue, and exposure can be tolerated for a time without extreme protective measures, making them a good choice for an electrical fire in a data center or in other electronic devices.

▶ Class D fires are fires that involve combustible metals such as magnesium, titanium, and sodium. The two types of extinguishing agents for Class D fires are sodium chloride and a copper-based dry powder.

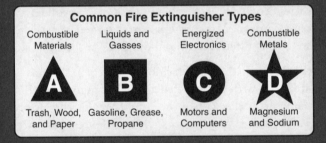

FIGURE 4.1   Labels for common fire extinguisher types

EMI Shielding

One risk that is often overlooked is electronic and electromagnetic emissions. Electrical equipment generally gives off electrical signals. Monitors, printers, fax machines, and even keyboards use electricity. These electronic signals are said to "leak" from computer and electronic equipment. Shielding seeks to reduce this output. The shielding can be local, cover an entire room, or cover a whole building, depending on the perceived threat. We're going to review two types of shielding: TEMPEST and Faraday cages.

TEMPEST is a code word developed by the U.S. government in the 1950s. It is an acronym built from the Transient Electromagnetic Pulse Emanation Standard. It describes standards used to limit or block electromagnetic emanation (radiation) from electronic equipment. TEMPEST has since grown in its definition to include the study of this radiation. Individual pieces of equipment are protected through extra shielding that helps prevent electrical signals from emanating. This extra shielding is a metallic sheath surrounding connection wires for mouse, keyboard, and video monitor connectors. It can also be a completely shielded case for the motherboard, CPU, hard drive, and video display system. This protection prevents the transfer of signals through the air or nearby conductors, such as copper pipes, electrical wires, and phone wires. You are most likely to find TEMPEST-certified equipment in government, military, and corporate environments that process government/military classified information. Because this can be costly to implement, protecting an area within a building makes more sense than protecting individual pieces of equipment.

A more efficient way to protect a large quantity of equipment from electronic eavesdropping is to place the equipment into a well-grounded metal box of conductive material called a Faraday cage, which is named after its inventor, Dr. Michael Faraday. The box can be small enough for a cell phone or can encompass an entire building. The idea behind the cage is to protect its contents from electromagnetic fields. The cage surrounds an object with interconnected and well-grounded metal. The metal used is typically a copper mesh that is attached to the walls and covered with plaster or drywall. The wire mesh acts as a net for stray electric signals, either inside or outside the box. New forms of wall treatment (wall paper) can be used to embed a Faraday mesh atop existing structural materials, retrofitting older buildings with Faraday-style protections to create cell phone-free zones in restaurants and theaters.

Shielding also should be taken into consideration when choosing cable types and the placement of cable. Coaxial cable was the first type of cable used to network computers. Coaxial cables are made of a thick copper core with an outer metallic shield to reduce interference. Coaxial cables have no physical transmission security and are very simple to tap without being noticed or interrupting regular transmissions. The electric signal, conducted by a single core wire, can easily be tapped by piercing the sheath. It would then be possible to eavesdrop on the conversations of all hosts attached to the segment because coaxial cabling implements broadband transmission technology and assumes many hosts are connected to the same wire. Another security concern of coaxial cable is reliability. Because no focal point such as a switch or hub is involved, a single faulty cable can bring the whole network down. Missing terminators or improperly functioning transceivers can cause poor network performance and transmission errors.

ExamAlert

Twisted-pair cable is used in most of today's network topologies. Twisted-pair cabling is either unshielded (UTP) or shielded (STP). UTP is popular because it is inexpensive and easy to install. UTP consists of eight wires twisted into four pairs. The design cancels much of the overflow and interference from one wire to the next, but UTP is subject to interference from outside electromagnetic sources and is prone to radio frequency interference (RFI) and electromagnetic interference (EMI) as well as crosstalk. Longer cable lengths transfer a more significant environmental measure of noise because wires can inadvertently act as an "antenna" for broadcast emanations.

STP differs from UTP in that it has shielding surrounding the cable's wires. Some STP has shielding around the individual wires, which helps prevent crosstalk. STP is more resistant to EMI and is considered a bit more secure because the shielding makes wiretapping more difficult.

Both UTP and STP are possible to tap, although it is physically a little trickier than tapping coaxial cable because of the physical structure of STP and UTP cable. With UTP and STP, a more inherent danger lies in the fact that it is easy to add devices to the network via open ports on unsecured hubs and switches. These devices should be secured from unauthorized access, and cables should be clearly marked so that a visual inspection can let you know whether something is awry. Also, software programs are available that can help detect unauthorized devices and the ports on which they will accept attempts at connection.

The plenum is the space between the ceiling and the floor of a building's next level. It is commonly used to run network cables, which must be of plenum-grade. Plenum cable is a grade that complies with fire codes. The outer casing is more fire-resistant than regular twisted-pair cable.

Fiber-optic cabling was designed for transmissions at higher speeds over longer distances, such as in underwater intercontinental telecommunications applications. Fiber uses light pulses for signal transmission, making it immune to RFI, EMI, and eavesdropping without specialized equipment able to detect transient optical emission at a fiber join or bend. Fiber-optic wire has a plastic or glass center, surrounded by another layer of plastic or glass with a protective outer coating. On the downside, fiber is still quite expensive compared to more traditional cabling, it is more difficult to install, and fixing breaks can be time intensive and costly with hundreds or thousands of individual fibers in a single bundle. As far as security is concerned, fiber cabling eliminates the signal tapping that is possible with coaxial cabling. It is impossible to tap fiber without interrupting the service and using specially constructed equipment. This makes it more difficult to eavesdrop or steal service.

Hot Aisles/Cold Aisles

Data centers and server farms might make use of an alternating arrangement of server racks, with alternating rows facing opposing directions so that fan intakes drawn in cool air vented to racks facing the cold aisle, and then fan output of hot air is vented to the alternating hot aisles for removal from the data center as shown in Figure 4.2. This data center organization allows greater efficiency in thermal management by allowing for supply ducts to serve all cold aisles and exhaust ducts to collect and draw away heated air.

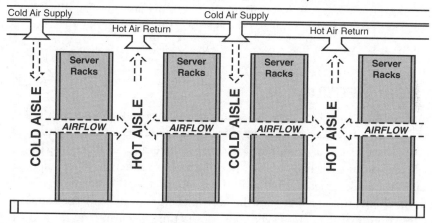

FIGURE 4.2 Simplified hot-aisle/cold-aisle data center layout with overhead HVAC supply and exhaust ducts.

Environmental Monitoring

To allow actions to be taken in response to undesirable environmental conditions, it is necessary to put into place environmental monitoring solutions that can raise alerts or trigger automated responses at need. Alerting systems must be able to sustain operations during the event. So, a water-sensing monitor should be able to function and raise an alert even when the environment is filled with water.

Monitoring systems must also be able to communicate in the event of service disruption so that alerts can be passed to responders even if the email server cluster has shut down due to thermal overload conditions. If the monitoring solution relies on networking for sensor measurement or raising alerts, environmental issues that degrade or prevent network communications might go unnoticed or alerts may not reach responders in a timely manner.

Temperature and Humidity Controls

As mentioned previously, overcooling causes condensation on equipment, and too-dry environments lead to excessive static. In addition to temperature monitoring, humidity should be monitored. Humidity is a measurement of moisture content in the air. A high level of humidity can cause components to rust and degrade electrical resistance or thermal conductivity. A low level of humidity can subject components to electrostatic discharge (ESD), causing damage; at extremely low levels, components might be affected by the air itself. The American Society of Heating, Refrigerating and Air-Conditioning Engineers (ASHRAE) recommends optimal humidity levels in the 40% to 55% range.

Physical Security

When planning security for network scenarios, many organizations overlook physical security. In many smaller organizations, the servers, routers, and patch panels are placed as a matter of convenience because of space restrictions. This can cause security issues. Speaking from experience, this equipment ends up in the oddest places, such as in the coat closet by the receptionist's desk in the lobby, in the room with the copy machine, or in a storage room with a backdoor exit that's unlocked most of the time. Securing physical access and ensuring that access requires proper authentication is necessary to avoid accidental exposure of sensitive data to attackers performing physical profiling of a target organization.

ExamAlert

Be familiar with physical security descriptions indicating potential security flaws. Watch for descriptions that include physical details or organizational processes. Be particularly careful when questions address processes using the same physical area for common business traffic as well as data transport media or where data resources are placed in publically accessible areas.

Physical access to a system creates many avenues for a breach in security for several reasons. Unsecured equipment is also vulnerable to social engineering attacks. It is much easier for an attacker to walk into a reception area, say she is there to do some work on the server, and get access to that server in the closet in the front lobby than to get into a physically secured area with a guest sign-in and sign-out sheet. Physical security controls parallel the data controls. Mandatory physical access controls are commonly found in government facilities and military installations, where users are closely monitored and very restricted. Because they are being monitored by security personnel and devices, users cannot modify entry methods or let others in. Discretionary physical control to a building or room is delegated to parties responsible for that building or room. In role-based access methods for physical control, groups of people who have common access needs are predetermined and access to different locations is allowed with the same key or swipe card. Users in this model generally have some security training and are often allowed to grant access to others by serving as an escort or by issuing a guest badge. The security department coordinates the secure setup of the facility and surrounding areas, identifies the groups allowed to enter various areas, and allows them access based on their group membership.

When physical security is considered, the most obvious element to control is physical access to systems and resources. Your goal is to allow only trusted use of these resources via positive identification that the entity accessing the systems is someone or something that has permission to do so based on the security model you have chosen. The following section briefly describes physical security components used a preventive controls.

Hardware Locks

A variety of hardware locks are available for securing resources. Commonly used mechanical locks include deadbolts, knob locks, and padlocks. Keyless entry door locks can operate as standalone units or be implemented into the network for better control. Access to machines that hold sensitive data might be controlled by physically securing a system within a locked room or cabinet, attaching the system to fixed (nonmovable) furniture using locking cables or restraints, and locking the case itself to prevent the removal of key components. Nonstandard case screws are also available to add another layer of security for publicly accessible terminals. When designing security, hardware lock type; functionality; and adequate ability to protect the resources such as strength, material, and cost should be taken into consideration.

Mantraps

A *mantrap* is a holding area between two entry points that gives security personnel time to view a person before allowing him into the internal building. One door of a mantrap cannot be unlocked and opened until the opposite door has been closed and locked.

Video Surveillance

Closed-circuit television (CCTV) is the most common method of surveillance. The video signal is processed and then transmitted for viewing at a central monitoring point. Traditionally, CCTV has been analog. However, recent technologies are taking advantage of the digital format, including IP video surveillance that uses TCP/IP for remote or wireless recording and monitoring.

Fencing

Another common deterrent is a fence or similar device that surrounds the entire building. A fence keeps out unwanted vehicles and people. One factor to consider in fencing is the height. The higher the fence, the harder it is to get over. Another factor to consider is the material the fence is made of. It is much easier to remove wooden slats or cut a chain-link fence with bolt cutters than it is to drill through concrete or block. One final note: If the fence isn't maintained or the area around it isn't well lit, the fence can easily be compromised.

Proximity Readers

Many organizations protect restricted areas with access control systems that use proximity cards. Proximity cards store details of the user's identity in a manner similar to chip and PIN bank cards. Making actual contact with the card is unnecessary because proximity readers read the information using radio frequency communication. The access information on the card can be read by simply holding the card close to the reader.

Access List

Employees should have access to facilities based on their role or function, including visitor control, and control of access to software programs for testing and revision. Access list restrictions specifically align a person's access to information with his or her role or function in the organization. Functional or role-based access control determines which persons should have access to certain locations within the facility based on their roles or functions.

Proper Lighting

If areas are brightly lit and have cameras, they are less likely to have unauthorized access attempts. Protective lighting improves visibility for checking badges and people at entrances, inspecting vehicles, and detecting intruders both outside and inside buildings and grounds. Protective lighting should be located where it will illuminate dark areas and be directed at probable routes of intrusion.

Guards

Security guards, surveillance cameras, motion detectors, limited-access zones, token-based and biometric access requirements for restricted areas, and many other considerations may be involved in access control planning. In addition, users must be educated about each measure taken to prevent circumvention to improve ease of normal access. Security guards and dogs can be great deterrents to intruders. It is imperative that they are trained properly. They are often used in combination with other measures, such as deterrent signs.

Barricades

To enhance the security of critical or vulnerable facilities, physical access control structures or barricades are used to protect against unauthorized people, vehicles, explosives, and other threats. Barricades provide a high level of protection and can withstand direct impact forces. Often, vehicle barricades are used in restricted areas to stop a vehicle from entering without proper authorization. Examples of vehicle barricades include drop-arm gates, active bollard systems, planters, and crash-barrier gates.

Biometrics

Physical security can also integrate biometric methods into a door-lock mechanism. Biometrics can use a variety of methods. See Table 10.1 in Chapter 10, "Authentication, Authorization, and Access Control," for a review of these technologies. When using biometrics, remember that each method has its own degree of error ratios, and some methods might seem invasive to the users and might not be accepted gracefully. Retinal scans, for example, require that users place their eye in contact with the imaging aperture, causing some users to feel squeamish at the potential for contagious disease or concerned at potential injury.

Protected Distribution (Cabling)

A protected distribution system (PDS) consists of copper or optical cables that are physically protected from unauthorized physical access and separated from regular data transmission to protect against electronic access. The purpose of a PDS is to make physical access difficult by enclosing equipment and make electronic access difficult by using different cables and patch panels. Examples of the use of PDSs include SIPRNET (Secure Internet Protocol Router Network) and NIPRNET (Non-Classified but Sensitive Internet Protocol Router Network). These are private government-run networks used for exchanging sensitive information in a secure manner.

Alarms

Alarm systems detect intrusions and monitor/record intruders. Electronic alarm systems are designed to detect, determine, and deter criminal activity or other threatening situations. An alarm system can detect an event such as an invasion, fire, gas leak, or environmental changes; determine whether the event poses a threat; and then send a notification about the event. Alarm systems may also be combined with CCTV surveillance systems to automatically record the activities of intruders and may interface to access control systems for electrically locked doors.

Motion Detection

Motion detectors can alert security personnel of intruders or suspicious activity on the company's premises. They can be based on light, sound, infrared, or ultrasonic technology. These devices must be properly configured because they are extremely sensitive and can issue false alarms if set too stringently.

> **ExamAlert**
>
> The exam might include questions about the various physical-barrier techniques. Be sure you are familiar with the methods previously listed.

Deterrents don't necessarily have to be designed to stop unauthorized access. As the name implies, they need to help deter the access. That is, the potential attacker might think twice about the attempt, especially as even an attacker considers the concept of risk/reward. Common examples include a sign indicating the property is alarmed or protected by a dog. Lighting, locks, dogs, cleared zones around the perimeter, and even life-sized cutouts of law enforcement officers can make a location appear less inviting to the potential attacker.

Control Types

Controls for providing information security can be deterrent, compensating, technical, or administrative. These categories of controls can be further classified as either preventive or detective. The following section outlines these controls and provides examples of each type of control.

Deterrent

Deterrent controls are intended to discourage individuals from intentionally violating information security policies or procedures. These usually take the form of some type of punishment or consequence that makes it undesirable to perform unauthorized activities. Deterrence involves detecting violations that are attached to some form of punishment that may be what the intruder fears most. An example of deterrent controls are signs such as "No Trespassing," "These premises are under video surveillance," and "Beware of guard dogs."

Preventive

Preventive controls attempt to avoid the occurrence of unwanted events by inhibiting the free use of computing resources. Preventive controls are often hard for users to accept because they restrict free use of resources. Examples of preventive administrative controls include security awareness, separation of duties, security policies and procedures, and disaster recovery plans.

Detective

Detective physical controls warn that physical security measures are being violated. Detective controls attempt to identify unwanted events after they have occurred. Common technical detective controls include audit trails, intrusion-detection methods, and checksums. Common physical detective controls include motion detectors, CCTV monitors, and alarms. Detective administrative controls are used to determine compliance with security policies and procedures. Detective administrative controls include security reviews and audits, mandatory vacations, and rotation of duties.

Compensating

Compensating controls are internal controls that are intended to reduce the risk of an existing or potential control weakness. Compensating controls are often found in organizations that are bound by some type of legislation such as PCI DSS. Compensating controls are not a shortcut to compliance. Compensating controls are used when a business or technological constraint exists and an alternative control is used that is effective in the current security threat landscape. For example, if separation of duties is required and duties cannot be separated due to company size, compensating controls should be in place such as audit trails and transaction logs that are reviewed by someone in a higher position than the employee performing the job function.

Technical

Technical controls are sometimes referred to as logical controls. Preventive technical controls are used to prevent unauthorized personnel or programs from gaining remote access to computing resources. Technical controls include logical access control systems, security systems, encryption, and data classification solutions.

Administrative

Administrative controls consist of management constraints, operational procedures, and supplemental administrative controls established to provide an acceptable level of protection for resources. Administrative controls tend to be things that employees may do, or must always do, or cannot do. Preventive administrative controls are personnel-oriented techniques for controlling people's behavior to ensure the confidentiality, integrity, and availability of computing data and programs.

Consider for a moment the importance of having both detection controls and prevention controls. In a perfect world, we would only need prevention controls. Unfortunately, not all malicious activity can be prevented. As a result, it is important that detection controls are part of one's layered security approach. For example, due to the value of the assets in a bank, the best protected banks use both detective and preventive controls. In addition to the locks, bars, and security signs, the bank probably has various detection controls such as motion detectors and cash register audits.

ExamAlert

Some controls can be both detection controls and preventive controls. A camera (if visible or advertised) or guard, as examples, not only serves as a detection control (if actively monitored) but also serves as a deterrent to a would-be attacker, thus being preventive. Although cameras can serve as a deterrent, without active monitoring by a security guard they are likely only useful for later analysis to identify the actor and means following an incident. Security guards, however, easily serve as both a preventive and detective control. In addition, a security guard can initiate an immediate response to an incident and potentially alert others about the identified threat.

Cram Quiz

Answer these questions. The answers follow the last question. If you cannot answer
these questions correctly, consider reading this section again until you can.

1. Which type of fire extinguisher would be best for putting out burning wires?

   ○ **A.** Foam

   ○ **B.** Carbon dioxide

   ○ **C.** Sodium chloride

   ○ **D.** Copper powder

2. What is the plenum?

   ○ **A.** A mesh enclosure designed to block EMI

   ○ **B.** A mechanism for controlling condensation

   ○ **C.** A type of dry-pipe fire control system

   ○ **D.** A mechanism for thermal management

3. The ASHRAE recommends humidity levels in which range?

   ○ **A.** 25% to 40%

   ○ **B.** 40% to 55%

   ○ **C.** 55% to 70%

   ○ **D.** 70% to 85%

4. Which of these is not a concern for environmental monitoring systems?

   ○ **A.** Able to sustain operations during an environmental disaster

   ○ **B.** Able to communicate even if the email service was involved

   ○ **C.** Able to reach responders in a timely manner

   ○ **D.** Include signage noting live or automated review only

Cram Quiz Answers

1. **B**. The carbon-dioxide extinguisher replaces the Halon extinguisher for putting out electrical (Class C) fires. Answer A is incorrect because foam is used for Class A fires (trash, wood, and paper). Answers C and D are incorrect because both sodium chloride and copper-based dry powder extinguishers are used for Class D (combustible materials) fires.

2. **D**. A plenum is the space below a raised floor or above a drop ceiling that can be used in hot-aisle/cold-aisle server rooms to efficiently manage thermal dissipation. Answer A is incorrect because a grounded mesh enclosure for EMI shielding is called a Faraday cage. Answer B is incorrect because management of condensation is handled as part of the HVAC function as air is cooled. Answer C is incorrect because a dry-pipe system is a fire extinguishing system that uses pressurized air as a triggering mechanism for water.

3. **B**. The Air-Conditioning Engineers (ASHRAE) recommendation for optimal humidity levels between 40% and 55% to minimize electrostatic discharge and condensation. Answer A is incorrect because it specifies a range too low that would be dangerous for static discharge, whereas answers C and D are incorrect because they represent too high a humidity level that would be susceptible to the buildup of condensation on cool components and boards.

4. **D**. Video surveillance might require signage noting whether cameras are monitored live or not, to avoid a legal complaint if someone tries unsuccessfully to signal for aid during an emergency. Answers A, B, and C are valid concerns because environmental monitoring systems must be able to operate even during a disaster and communicate with responders in a timely manner even if the servers hosting the usual communication services (email, SMS, and so on) are involved in the disaster.

Summarize Risk Management Best Practices

▶ **Business continuity concepts**

▶ **Fault tolerance**

▶ **Disaster recovery concepts**

CramSaver

If you can correctly answer these questions before going through this section, save time by skimming the Exam Alerts in this section and then completing the Cram Quiz at the end of the section.

1. Which type of recovery allows a business to sustain operations following an incident?

2. How much time can a service be unavailable to meet a "five nines" uptime requirement?

3. Which form of RAID would be best if single-user performance were the sole consideration?

Answers

1. Business continuity planning (BCP) and continuity of operation planning (COOP) are used to ensure organizational functional restoration in the shortest possible time even if services resume at a reduced level of effectiveness or availability. Disaster recovery plans (DRPs) extend this process to ensure a full recovery of operational capacity following a disaster (natural or manmade). Instructions and details for recovery should occur before an incident. Not only should plans be set forth, but they should be regularly updated and tested, as well, to ensure that communication plans can be implemented and that responders can execute response and recovery plans properly. These should address different scenarios for incident handling responses and notification procedures following identification, short-term recovery of key service, and operational data access functions as part of continuity of operation preparedness, and long-term sustained recovery to full operational status in disaster recovery planning. A business recovery plan, business resumption plan, and contingency plan are also considered part of business continuity planning. In the event of an incident, an organization might also need to restore equipment (in addition to data) or personnel lost or rendered unavailable due to the nature or scale of the disaster.

2. 5.3 minutes per year. Service level agreements (SLAs) have thresholds for acceptable levels of downtime, based on the overall percentage of operational time. Five nines refers to 99.999% of total operational potential. So, for a 24x7 service such as an online auction site available to global consumers, across a year that translates to less than 5.3 minutes of downtime combined.

3. RAID 0 is the best from a performance-only perspective. All other varieties trade additional time calculating and storing parity data to protect redundancy and gain fault tolerance in the event of hardware failure in one or more drives, or to share access loads across multiple drives for high-throughput requirements.

Business Continuity Concepts

In any planning, safety of human life must be paramount. BCP involves identification of risks and threats to operation and implementing strategies to mitigate the effect of each. Beyond backup and restoration of data, disaster recovery planning must include a detailed analysis of underlying business practices and support requirements. This is called business continuity planning. BCP is a more comprehensive approach to provide guidance so that the organization can continue making sales and collecting revenue. As with disaster recovery planning, it covers natural and manmade disasters. BCP should identify required services, such as network access and utility agreements, and arrange for automatic failover of critical services to redundant offsite systems.

Business Impact Analysis

A business impact analysis (BIA) is the process for determining the potential impacts resulting from the interruption of time-sensitive or critical business processes. IT contingency planning for both disaster recovery and operational continuity rely on conducting a BIA as part of the overall DR/BC planning process. Unlike a risk assessment, the BIA is not focused as much on the relative likelihood of potential threats to an organization, but instead focuses on the relative impact on critical business functions due to the loss of operational capability due to the threats. Conducting a business impact analysis involves identification of critical business functions and the services and technologies required for each, along with the cost associated with the loss of each and the maximum acceptable outage period.

For hardware-related outages, the assessment should also include the current age of existing solutions along with standards for the expected mean time between failures based on vendor data or accepted industry standards. Strategies for the DR/BC plan are intended to minimize this cost by arranging recovery actions to restore critical functions in the most effective manner based on cost, legal or statutory mandates, and mean-time-to-restore calculations.

Identification of Critical Systems and Components

BCP must include identification of critical systems and components. In the event that a disaster is widespread or targeted at an Internet service provider (ISP) or key routing hardware point, an organization's continuity plan should include options for alternative network access, including dedicated administrative connections that might be required for recovery. Continuity planning should include considerations for recovery in the event that existing hardware and facilities are rendered inaccessible or unrecoverable. You should include hardware configuration details, network requirements, and utilities agreements for alternative sites (that is, warm and cold sites) in this planning consideration.

Removing Single Points of Failure

A single point of failure is a potential risk posed by a flaw in business continuity planning in which one fault or malfunction causes an entire system or enterprise to stop operating. Single points of failure are avoided by means of redundancy and various fault-tolerance protocols. Examples of removing single points of failure include the use of server clustering technology, redundant switches, and redundant network connections.

Business Continuity Planning and Testing

BCP and COOP are used to ensure organizational functional restoration in the shortest possible time even if services resume at a reduced level of effectiveness or availability. Disaster recovery plans (DRPs) extend this process to ensure a full recovery of operational capacity following a disaster (natural or manmade). Instructions and details for recovery should occur before an incident. Not only should plans be set forth, but they should be regularly updated and tested as well to ensure that communication plans can be implemented and that responders can execute response and recovery plans properly. These should address different scenarios for incident handling responses and notification procedures following identification, short-term recovery of key service and operational data access functions as part of continuity of operation preparedness, and long-term sustained recovery to full operational status in disaster recovery planning. A business recovery plan, business resumption plan, and contingency plan are also considered part of business continuity planning.

In the event of an incident, an organization might also need to restore equipment (in addition to data) or personnel lost or rendered unavailable due to the nature or scale of the disaster.

Risk Assessment

Risk assessments identify potential vulnerabilities and analyze what could happen if an incident occurs. Risk assessments are conducted to plan recovery appropriately, determining the scope and criticality of organizational services and data. In addition, an order (a priority) of recovery must be established, with recovery time and recovery measures of success identified, documented, shared, and tested during training to function properly during the operational window following an incident.

Continuity of Operations

Continuity of operations is an initiative issued by the President of the United States in 2007 to be sure that government departments and agencies are able to continue operation of their essential functions under circumstances involving natural, manmade, and technological threats and national security emergencies. Continuity of operations is generally viewed as the same as business continuity, although it primarily focused on government and public sectors. Policies and procedures are designed to ensure that an organization can recover from a potentially destructive incident and resume operations as quickly as possible following that event.

Disaster Recovery

Disaster recovery involves many aspects, including the following:

▶ **Disaster recovery plan:** A DRP is a written document that defines how the organization will recover from a disaster and how to restore business with minimum delay. The document also explains how to evaluate risks; how data backup and restoration procedures work; and the training required for managers, administrators, and users. A detailed disaster recovery should address various processes, including backup, data security, and recovery.

▶ **Disaster recovery policies:** These policies detail responsibilities and procedures to follow during disaster recovery events, including how to contact key employees, vendors, customers, and the press. They should also include instructions for situations in which it might be necessary to bypass the normal chain of command to minimize damage or the effects of a disaster.

▶ **Service level agreements:** SLAs are contracts with ISPs, utilities, facilities managers, and other types of suppliers that detail minimum levels of support that must be provided (including in the event of failure or disaster).

IT Contingency Planning

IT contingency planning is designed to sustain and recover critical IT services following an emergency. IT contingency planning is a broad plan that includes organizational and business process continuity and recovery planning. Organizations integrate a sequence of plans covering response, recovery, and continuity activities to prepare for disruptions to business processes, loss of IT systems, and damage to the facility. An IT contingency plan requires a long-term planning strategy and program management plan especially when national security matters or military branches are involved. The planning process outlines how the organization will designate resources, define short- and long-term goals and objectives, forecast budgetary requirements, anticipate and address issues and potential obstacles, discuss essential functions, and establish planning milestones.

Succession Planning

BCP must also include contingencies for personnel replacement in the event of loss (death, injury, retirement, termination, and so on) or lack of availability. Succession planning is a process whereby an organization ensures that employees are recruited and developed to fill each key role within the organization. Clear lines of succession and cross-training in critical functions and communications plans for alternative mechanisms of contact to alert individuals as to the need for succession are imperative for meeting recovery time objectives (RTOs) and recovery point objectives (RPOs).

High Availability

One of the best ways to ensure the availability of replacement parts is through SLAs. These are signed contracts between the organization and the vendors with which they commonly deal. SLAs are covered in greater detail in the next chapter. SLAs can be for services such as access to the Internet, backups, restoration, and hardware maintenance. Should a disaster destroy your existing systems, the SLA can also help you guarantee the availability of computer parts or even entire computer systems.

It is important to understand all equipment warranties, especially if the organization decides against SLAs for computer equipment. Often, opening a computer yourself and replacing the parts voids a warranty if the warranty has not expired.

Also confirm that critical suppliers have strict disaster recovery plans. There's no point in having your equipment in the hands of a company that is struggling to get back on its feet after a disaster or merger.

When evaluating SLAs, the expected uptime and maximum allowed downtime on a yearly basis are considered. Uptime is based on 365 days a year, 24 hours a day. Here is an example:

99.999%	5.3 minutes downtime/year
99.99%	53 minutes downtime/year
99.9%	8.7 hours downtime/year
99%	87 hours downtime/year

Redundancy

The main goal of preventing and effectively dealing with any type of disruption is to ensure availability. Of course, you can use RAID, uninterruptible power supply (UPS) equipment, and clustering to accomplish this. But neglecting single points of failure can prove disastrous. A single point of failure is any piece of equipment that can bring your operation down if it stops working. To determine the number of single points of failure in the organization, start with a good map of everything the organization uses to operate. Pay special attention to items such as the Internet connection, routers, switches, and proprietary business equipment. After identifying the single points of failure, perform a risk analysis. In other words, compare the consequences if the device fails to the cost of redundancy. For example, if all your business is web based, it is a good idea to have some redundancy in the event the Internet connection goes down. However, if the majority of your business is telephone based, you might look for redundancy in the phone system as opposed to the ISP. In some cases, the ISP might supply both the Internet and the phone services. The point here is to be aware of where your organization is vulnerable and understand what the risk is so that you can devise an appropriate backup plan.

In disaster recovery planning, you might need to consider redundant connections between branches or sites. Internally, for total redundancy, you might need two network cards in computers connected to different switches. With redundant connections, all devices are connected to each other more than once, to create fault tolerance. A single device or cable failure does not affect the performance because the devices are connected by more than one means. This setup is more expensive because it requires more hardware and cabling. This type of topology can also be found in enterprise-wide networks, with routers being connected to other routers for fault tolerance.

Along with power and equipment loss, telephone and Internet communications might be out of service for a while when a disaster strikes. Organizations must consider this factor when formulating a disaster recovery plan. Relying on a single Internet connection for critical business functions could prove disastrous to your business. With a redundant ISP, a backup ISP could be standing by in the event of an outage at the main ISP. Should this happen, traffic is switched over to the redundant ISP. The organization can continue to do business without any interruptions.

Although using multiple ISPs is mostly considered for disaster recovery purposes, it can also relieve network traffic congestion and provide network isolation for applications. As organizations become global, dealing with natural disasters will become more common. Solutions such as wireless ISPs used in conjunction with Voice over IP (VoIP) to quickly restore phone and data services are being looked at more closely. Organizations might look to ISP redundancy to prevent application performance failure and supplier diversity. For example, businesses that transfer large files can use multiple ISPs to segregate voice and file transfer traffic to a specific ISP. More and more organizations are implementing technologies such as VoIP. When planning deployment, explore using different ISPs for better network traffic performance, for disaster recovery, and to ensure a quality level of service.

Tabletop Exercises

Tabletop exercises involve key personnel participating in an informal, simulated scenario setting. Tabletop exercises are conducted to evaluate an organization's capability to execute one or more portions of a business continuity or disaster recovery plan. Tabletop exercises should be conducted on a regular basis to

▶ Test and evaluate business continuity or disaster recovery policies and procedures to identify plan weaknesses and resource gaps

▶ Train personnel and clearly define roles and responsibilities to improve performance, communication, and coordination

▶ Meet regulatory requirements

A progressive exercise program is made up of gradually more complex exercises, with each one building on the previous, until the exercises are as close to reality as possible. When escalated to a full-scale exercise, it should involve a wide range of organizations to include fire, law enforcement, emergency management, and when necessary, any other entities such as local public health and public safety agencies.

Fault Tolerance

Equipment will fail! As one movie character suggested, "The world is an imperfect place." When a single drive crashes, sometimes the only way to sustain operations is to have another copy of all of the data. This is a form of "desirable redundancy" in enterprise planning in the face of economic cutbacks identifying "undesirable redundancies" for reduction and potential cost savings. Perhaps the biggest asset an organization has is its data. The planning of every server setup should consider how to salvage the data should a component fail. The decision about how to store and protect data is determined by how the organization uses its data. This section examines data-redundancy options.

Hardware

Cross-site replication might be included for high-availability solutions requiring high levels of fault tolerance. Individual servers might also be configured to allow for the continued function of key services even in the case of hardware failure. Common fault-tolerant solutions include RAID solutions, which maintain duplicated data across multiple disks so that the loss of one disk does not cause the loss of data. Many of these solutions might also support the hotswapping of failed drives and redundant power supplies so that replacement hardware can be installed without ever taking the server offline.

RAID

The most common approach to data availability and redundancy is called redundant array of independent disks (RAID). RAID organizes multiple disks into a large, high-performance logical disk. In other words, if you have three hard drives, you can configure them to look like one large drive. Disk arrays are created to stripe data across multiple disks and access them in parallel, which allows the following:

▶ Higher data transfer rates on large data accesses

▶ Higher I/O rates on small data accesses

▶ Uniform load balancing across all the disks

Large disk arrays are highly vulnerable to disk failures. To solve this problem, you can use redundancy in the form of error-correcting codes to tolerate disk failures. With this method, a redundant disk array can retain data for a much longer time than an unprotected single disk. With multiple disks and a RAID scheme, a system can stay up and running when a disk fails and during the time the replacement disk is being installed and data restored. Figure 4.3 shows common types of RAID configurations.

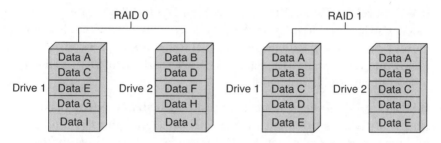

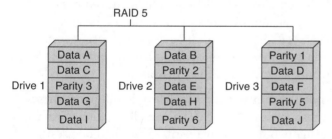

FIGURE 4.3   **Common types of RAID configurations**

The two major goals when implementing disk arrays are data striping for better performance and redundancy for better reliability. There are many types of RAID. Some of the more common ones are as follows:

▶ **RAID Level 0 - Striped disk array without fault tolerance:** RAID 0 implements a striped disk array, the data is broken into blocks, and each block is written to a separate disk drive. This requires a minimum of two disks to implement.

▶ **RAID Level 1 - Mirroring and duplexing:** This solution, called mirroring or duplexing, requires a minimum of two disks and offers 100% redundancy because all data is written to both disks. The difference between mirroring and duplexing is the number of controllers. Mirroring uses one controller, whereas duplexing uses one controller for each disk. In RAID 1, disk usage is 50% and the other 50% is for redundancy.

▶ **RAID Level 2 - Hamming code error correcting code (ECC):** In RAID 2, each bit of a data word is written to a disk. RAID 2 requires the use of extra disks to store an error-correcting code. A typical setup requires 10 data disks and 4 ECC disks. Because all modern disk drives incorporate ECC, this offers little additional protection. No commercial implementations exist today. The controller required is complex, specialized, and expensive, and the performance is not very good.

▶ **RAID Level 3 - Parallel transfer with parity:** In RAID 3, the data block is striped and written on the data disks. This requires a minimum of three drives to implement. In a parallel transfer with parity, data is interleaved bit-wise over the data disks and a single parity disk is added to tolerate any single disk failure.

▶ **RAID Level 4 - Independent data disks with shared parity disk:** Entire blocks are written onto a data disk. RAID 4 requires a minimum of three drives to implement. RAID 4 is similar to RAID 3 except that data is interleaved across disks of arbitrary size rather than in bits.

▶ **RAID Level 5 - Independent data disks with distributed parity blocks:** In RAID 5, each entire block of the data and the parity is striped. RAID 5 requires a minimum of three disks. Because it writes both the data and the parity over all the disks, it has the best small read, large write performance of any redundancy disk array.

▶ **RAID Level 6 - Independent data disks with two independent parity schemes:** This is an extension of RAID 5 and allows for additional fault tolerance by using two-dimensional parity. This method uses Reed-Solomon codes to protect against up to two disk failures using the bare minimum of two redundant disk arrays.

▶ **RAID Level 10 (also called 1+0) - High reliability combined with high performance:** RAID 10 combines RAID 1 and RAID-0 and requires a minimum of four disks to implement. There is also a variant called 0+1. This solution is a striped array that has RAID 1 arrays. Disks are mirrored in pairs for redundancy and improved performance, and then data is striped across multiple disks. Both provide fault tolerance and increased performance.

ExamAlert

Know the different levels of RAID and the number of disks required to implement each one. The most common forms of RAID include the following:

▶ **RAID 0:** Spanned volume, no redundancy, highest write speed.

▶ **RAID 1:** Mirroring, 100% duplication of data across all drives, lowest performance.

▶ **RAID 3:** Parallel transfer with parity bit, minimum three drives, data written to all drives simultaneously while parity is calculated and written to its own non-redundant drive.

▶ **RAID 5:** Parallel transfer with distributed parity, data written to all drives simultaneously, parity written in segments across all drives for redundancy of parity as well as data segments, highest read rates.

▶ **RAID 10 (also called 1+0):** Combines RAID 1 and RAID 0. There is also a variant called 0+1. Both provide fault tolerance and increased performance.

When choosing a method of redundancy, choose a level of RAID that is supported by the operating system. Not all operating systems support all versions of RAID. For example, Microsoft Windows servers support RAID levels 0, 1, and 5. In addition to hardware RAID, software RAID can be used. Software RAID can be used when the expense of additional drives is not included in the budget or if the organization is using older servers. Software RAID can provide more flexibility, but it requires more CPU cycles and power to run. Software RAID operates on a partition-by-partition basis and tends be slightly more complicated to run.

Another point to remember is that even though you set up the server for redundancy, you must still back up your data. RAID does not protect you from multiple disk failures. Regular tape backups enable you to recover from data loss that results from errors unrelated to disk failure (such as human, hardware, and software errors). We discuss the different types and methods of backups later in this chapter.

Clustering

Another way to increase availability is server clustering. A server cluster is the combination of two or more servers so that they appear as one. Clustering increases availability by ensuring that if a server is out of commission because of failure or planned downtime, another server in the cluster takes over the workload. To provide load balancing to avoid functionality loss because of directed attacks meant to prevent valid access, continuity planning might include clustering solutions that allow multiple nodes to perform support while transparently acting as a single host to the user. High-availability clustering might also be used to ensure that automatic failover occurs in the event that hardware failure renders the primary node unable to provide normal service.

Load Balancing

Load balancing is the primary reason server clustering is implemented. Load balancing provides increased availability by distributing workloads across multiple computing resources. Load balancing aims to optimize the use of resources, maximize throughput, minimize response time, and avoid overload of any single resource. This proves especially useful when traffic volume is high. It prevents one server from being overloaded while another sits idle. Load balancing can be implemented with hardware, software, or a combination of both. Typically, load balancing is found in organizations where there is high website traffic and is found in cloud-based environments.

Servers

It might be necessary to set up redundant servers so that the business can still function in the event of hardware or software failure. If a single server hosts vital applications, a simple equipment failure might result in days of downtime as the problem is repaired. In addition, some manufacturers provide redundant power supplies in mission-critical servers.

To ensure availability and reliability, server redundancy is implemented. This means multiple servers are used to perform the same task. For example, if you have a web-based business with more than one server hosting your site, when one of the servers crashes, the requests can be redirected to another server. This provides a highly available website. If you do not host your own website, confirm whether the vendor you are using provides high availability and reliability.

ExamAlert

In today's world, mission-critical businesses demand 100% uptime 24 hours a day 7 days a week. Availability is vital, and many businesses would not be able to function without redundancy. Redundancy can take several forms, such as automatic failover, failback, and virtualization. The most notable advantage of server redundancy, perhaps, is load balancing.

Disaster Recovery Concepts

Too many organizations realize the criticality of disaster recovery planning only after a catastrophic event (such as a hurricane, flood, or terrorist attack). However, disaster recovery is an important part of overall organization security planning for every organization. Natural disasters and terrorist activity can bypass even the most rigorous physical security measures. Common hardware failures and even accidental deletions might require some form of recovery capability. Failure to recover from a disaster might destroy an organization.

Fundamental to any disaster recovery plan is the need to provide for regular backups of key information, including user file and email storage; database stores; event logs; and security principal details such as user logons, passwords, and group membership assignments. Without a regular backup process, loss of data through accidents or directed attack could severely impair business processes.

Disaster recovery planning should include detailed system restoration procedures, particularly in complex clustered and virtualized environments. This planning should explain any needed configuration details that might be required to restore access and network function. These can include items that can either be general or specific.

Also a restoration plan should include contingency planning to recover systems and data even in the event of administration personnel loss or lack of availability. This plan should include procedures on what to do if a disgruntled employee changes an administrative password before leaving. Statistics show that more damage to a network comes from inside than outside. Therefore, any key root-level account passwords and critical procedures should be properly documented so that another equally trained individual can manage the restoration process. This documentation must also include backout strategies to implement in the event that the most recent backup proves unrecoverable or alternative capacity and type of equipment is all that remains available.

The type of recovery site an organization chooses depends on the criticality of recovery and budget allocations. Hot sites are traditionally more expensive, but they can be used for operations and recovery testing before an actual catastrophic event occurs. Cold sites are less costly in the short term. However, equipment purchased after such an event might be more expensive or difficult to obtain.

As part of redundancy and recovery planning, an organization can contract annually with a company that offers redundancy services (for a monthly, or otherwise negotiated, service charge). When contracting services from a provider, the organization should carefully read the contract. Daily fees and other incidental fees might apply. In addition, in a large-scale incident, the facility could very well become overextended.

> **ExamAlert**
>
> Any disaster recovery or business continuity plan including contingencies, backup and recovery, or succession must include regular testing of restoration and recovery processes to ensure that personnel are able to transition and that backup media and procedures are adequate to restore lost functionality.

In the beginning stages of the organizational security plan, the organization must decide how it will operate and how it will recover from any unfortunate incidents that affect its ability to conduct business. Redundancy planning encompasses the effects of both natural and manmade catastrophes. Often, these catastrophes result from unforeseen circumstances.

Backup Plans/Policies

The backup procedures in use might also affect what is recovered following a disaster. Disaster recovery plans should identify the type and regularity of the backup process. The following sections cover the types of backups you can use and different backup schemes.

The different types of backups you can use are full, differential, incremental, and copy. A full backup is a complete backup of all data and is the most time-intensive and resource-intensive form of backup, requiring the largest amount of data storage. In the event of a total loss of data, restoration from a complete backup is faster than other methods. A full backup copies all selected files and resets the archive bit. An archive bit is a file attribute used to track incremental changes to files for the purpose of backup. The operating system sets the archive bit any time changes occur, such as when a file is created, moved, or renamed. This method enables you to restore using just one tape. Theft poses the most risk, however, because all data is on one tape; only encryption can protect the data at that point.

> **ExamAlert**
>
> A differential backup includes all data that has changed since the last full backup, regardless of whether or when the last differential backup was made, because it doesn't reset the archive bit.

This form of backup is incomplete for full recovery without a valid full backup. For example, if the server dies on Thursday, two tapes are needed: the full from Friday and the differential from Wednesday. Differential backups require a variable amount of storage, depending on the regularity of normal backups and the number of changes that occur during the period between full backups. Theft of a differential tape is more risky than an incremental tape because larger chunks of sequential data can be stored on the tape the further away it is from the last full backup.

ExamAlert

An incremental backup includes all data that has changed since the last incremental backup, and it resets the archive bit.

An incremental backup is incomplete for full recovery without a valid full backup and all incremental backups since the last full backup. For example, if the server dies on Thursday, four tapes are needed: the full from Friday and the incremental tapes from Monday, Tuesday, and Wednesday. Incremental backups require the smallest amount of data storage and require the least amount of backup time, but they can take the most time during restoration. If an incremental tape is stolen, it might not be of value to the offender, but it still represents risk to the company.

A copy backup is similar to a full back up in that it copies all selected files. However, it doesn't reset the archive bit. From a security perspective, the loss of a tape with a copy backup is the same as losing a tape with a full backup.

Note

Many organizations have chosen to back up data to a cloud environment using one of the many services available. Cloud services offer continuous backup options so that you can easily recover your files without losing data that is associated with normal backup procedures and not having offsite storage immediately available. Enterprise solutions include options for protecting physical and virtual environments that includes software, appliance, and offsite replication. For example, Barracuda Backup has an extensive range of supported environments and integration with copy file sync and share services so organizations can replicate data from multiple platforms to another Barracuda appliance for private-cloud data protection or secure transfer to the Barracuda cloud.

Backup Execution/Frequency

When choosing a backup strategy, a company should look at the following factors:

▶ **How often it needs to restore files:** As a matter of convenience, if files are restored regularly, a full backup might be chosen because it can be done with one tape.

▶ **How fast the data needs to be restored:** If large amounts of data are backed up, the incremental backup method might work best.

▶ **How long the data needs to be kept before being overwritten:** If used in a development arena where data is constantly changing, a differential backup method might be the best choice.

After the backups are complete, they must be clearly marked or labeled so that they can be properly safeguarded. In addition to these backup strategies, organizations employ tape rotation and retention policies. The various methods of tape rotation include the following:

▶ Grandfather-father-son backup refers to the most common rotation scheme for rotating backup media. The basic method is to define three sets of backups. The first set, son, represents daily backups. A second set, father, is used to perform full backups. The final set of three tapes, grandfather, is used to perform full backups on the last day of each month.

▶ Tower of Hanoi is based on the mathematics of the Tower of Hanoi puzzle. This is a recursive method where every tape is associated with a disk in the puzzle, and the disk movement to a different peg corresponds with a backup to a tape.

▶ Ten-tape rotation is a simpler and more cost-effective method for small businesses. It provides a data history of up to 2 weeks. Friday backups are full backups. Monday through Thursday backups are incremental.

> **Note**
>
> All tape-rotation schemes can protect your data, but each one has different cost considerations. The Tower of Hanoi is more difficult to implement and manage but costs less than the grandfather-father-son scheme.

In some instances, it might be more beneficial to copy or image a hard drive for backup purposes. For example, in a development office, where there might be large amounts of data that changes constantly, instead of spending money on a complex backup system to back up all the developers' data, it might be less expensive and more efficient to buy another hard drive for each developer and have the developer back up data that way. If the drive is imaged, it ensures that if a machine has a hard drive failure, a swift way of getting it back up and running again is available.

Another option available for backups is offsite tape storage with trusted third parties. Vendors offer a wide range of offsite tape-vaulting services. These are highly secure facilities that can include secure transportation services, chain-of-custody control for tapes in transit, and environmentally controlled storage vaults.

Recovery planning documentation and backup media contain many details that an attacker can exploit when seeking access to an organization's network or data. Therefore, planning documentation, backup scheduling, and backup media must include protections against unauthorized access or potential damage. The data should be protected by at least a password, and preferably encryption. When the backups are complete, they must be clearly labeled so that they can be properly safeguarded. Imagine having to perform a restore for an organization that stores its backup tapes unlabeled in a plastic bin in the server room. The rotation is supposed to be on a 2-week basis. When you go to get the needed tape, you discover that the tapes are not marked, nor are they in any particular order. How much time will you spend just trying to find the proper tape? Also, is it a good practice to keep backup tapes in the same room with the servers? What happens if there is a fire?

How backup media is handled is just as important as how it is marked. You certainly don't want to store CDs in a place where they can easily be scratched or store tapes in an area that reaches 110° Fahrenheit during the day. You should ensure that you also have offsite copies of your backups where they are protected from unauthorized access as well as fire, flood, and other forms of environmental hazards that might affect the main facility. Normal backups should include all data that cannot be easily reproduced. Secure recovery services are another method of offsite storage and security that organizations may consider. In military environments, a common practice is to have removable storage media locked in a proper safe or container at the end of the day.

Cold Site

Hot, warm, and cold sites can provide a means for recovery should an event render the original building unusable. These are discussed individually in the following sections.

A cold site is the weakest of the recovery plan options but also the cheapest. These sites are merely a prearranged request to use facilities if needed. Electricity, bathrooms, and space are about the only facilities provided in a cold site contract. Therefore, the organization is responsible for providing and installing all the necessary equipment. If the organization chooses this type of facility, it will require additional time to secure equipment, install operating systems and applications, and contract services such as Internet connectivity. The same distance factors should be considered when planning a cold site as when planning a hot site.

Hot Site

A hot site is a location that is already running and available 7 days a week, 24 hours a day. These sites allow the company to continue normal business operations, usually within a minimal period of time after the loss of a facility. This type of site is similar to the original site in that it is equipped with all necessary hardware, software, network, and Internet connectivity fully installed, configured, and operational. Data is regularly backed up or replicated to the hot site so that it can be made fully operational in a minimal amount of time in the event of a disaster at the original site. The business can be resumed without significant delay. In the event of a catastrophe, all people need to do is drive to the site, log on, and begin working.

Hot sites are the most expensive to operate and are mostly found in businesses that operate in real time, for whom any downtime might mean financial ruin.

The hot site should be located far enough from the original facility to avoid the disaster striking both facilities. A good example of this is a flood. The range of a flood depends on the category and other factors such as wind and the amount of rain that follows. A torrential flood can sink and wash away buildings and damage various other property, such as electrical facilities. If the hot site is within this range, the hot site is affected, too.

Warm Site

A warm site is a scaled-down version of a hot site. The site is generally configured with power, phone, and network jacks. The site might have computers and other resources, but they are not configured and ready to go. In a warm site, the data is replicated elsewhere for easy retrieval. However, you still have to do something to be able to access the data. This "something" might include setting up systems so that you can access the data or taking special equipment over to the warm site for data retrieval. It is assumed that the organization itself will configure the devices, install applications, and activate resources or that it will contract with a third party for these services. Because the warm site is generally office space or warehouse space, the site can serve multiple clients simultaneously. The time and cost for getting a warm site operational is somewhere between a hot and a cold site.

ExamAlert

Be familiar with the various types of site descriptions. Watch for scenarios that require you to choose a hot, warm, or cold site solution. Remember that a hot backup site is a full duplicate of the source data center, so has the fastest recovery time for the highest cost of maintenance. The cold backup site is the opposite: longest recovery window with the lowest cost.

Cram Quiz

Answer these questions. The answers follow the last question. If you cannot answer these questions correctly, consider reading this section again until you can.

1. Which recovery site has only power, telecommunications, and networking active all the time?

   ○ **A.** Hot site

   ○ **B.** Cold site

   ○ **C.** Warm site

   ○ **D.** Shielded site

2. Which type of fault-tolerant RAID configuration provides the lowest disk usage fraction?

   ○ **A.** RAID 0

   ○ **B.** RAID 3

   ○ **C.** RAID 1

   ○ **D.** RAID 5

3. If an organization takes a full backup every Sunday morning and a daily differential backup each morning, what is the fewest number of backups that must be restored following a disaster on Friday?

   ○ **A.** 1

   ○ **B.** 2

   ○ **C.** 5

   ○ **D.** 6

Cram Quiz Answers

1. **C.** The warm site has basics such as power, networking, and telecommunications active all the time. Although alternative computers may be present, they will not be loaded and operations as in a hot site, making Answer A incorrect. Answer B is incorrect because a cold site generally only includes power and physical space when not in use. Answer D is incorrect because any of the recovery site types might or might not be shielded against electromagnetic interference.

2. **C.** RAID 1 (mirroring/duplexing) provides the lowest fraction of total storage for use because every byte of data is written to two devices equally. Answer A is incorrect because RAID 0 does not offer fault protection and spans multiple drives with up to 100% disk usage. RAID 3 and RAID 5 are both incorrect because they both have fault tolerance but have a higher disk use fraction through the use of a parity bit (fixed in RAID 3, distributed in RAID 5) allowing recovery from the loss of a single drive across an array of three or more drives.

3. **B**. With a differential backup scheme, only the last full and last differential backup need to be restored, making answer C incorrect as well. Daily full backups would require only the last full backup, making answer A incorrect in this configuration. Answer D is correct in an incremental rather than a differential backup setting, where the last full and all intervening incremental backups must be restored for recovery.

Given a Scenario, Select the Appropriate Control to Meet the Goals of Security

▶ **Confidentiality**

▶ **Integrity**

▶ **Availability**

▶ **Safety**

CramSaver

If you can correctly answer these questions before going through this section, save time by skimming the Exam Alerts in this section and then completing the Cram Quiz at the end of the section.

1. Which element of the C-I-A triad is addressed by biometric controls?

2. Offsite backup tapes ensure which element of the C-I-A triad?

3. Battery backup power supplies (UPSs) support which element of the C-I-A triad?

Answers

1. Confidentiality. Access control mechanisms such as biometric authentication systems ensure that data confidentiality is maintained.

2. Availability. Backup media is used to restore data lost, corrupted, or otherwise at risk of becoming unavailable.

3. Availability. Loss of power prevents services from remaining available to authorized access requests.

The traditional C-I-A triad of security directives includes maintaining the confidentiality, integrity, and availability of data and services. Threats to these three principles are constantly present and evolving.

Confidentiality

The first principle of information security is that of confidentiality. Confidentiality involves controls to ensure that security is maintained when data is both at rest (stored) and in use (during transport and processing) to protect against unauthorized access or inadvertent disclosure. Confidentiality controls include physical access controls, data encryption, logical access controls, and management controls to put in place policies to protect against shoulder surfing, social engineering, and other forms of observational disclosure. We discuss individual access control mechanisms later in this book; this chapter addresses them only in terms of risk mitigation and selecting the correct control to meet organizational security needs.

Encryption

Encryption is a security control used primarily to provide confidentiality protection for data. Encryption ensures that only the right people (people who know the key) can read the information. Encryption does not guarantee that the data hasn't changed, only that it's been kept private. An example is Secure Sockets Layer / Transport Layer Security (SSL/TLS), a security protocol for communications over the Internet that has been used in conjunction with a large number of Internet protocols to ensure security.

Access Controls

Enforcing file permissions and access control lists to restrict access to sensitive information is a way to ensure information confidentiality. An ACL defines who can access an object. Confidentiality then is achieved by restricting whether a given principal is authorized to execute operations that reveal information.

Steganography

Like many security tools, steganography can be used for a variety of reasons. Legitimate purposes can include watermarking images for copyright protection. Digital watermarks are similar to steganography in that they are overlaid in files, which appear to be part of the original file and are thus not easily detectable by the average person. Steganography can also be used as a way to make a substitute for a one-way hash value. Finally, steganography can be used to maintain the confidentiality of valuable information, to protect the data from possible sabotage, theft, or unauthorized viewing.

ExamAlert

Some questions might include controls that fulfill more than one principle of security, such as access controls that protect both confidentiality and integrity by limiting unauthorized access to examine data (confidentiality) and to modify data (integrity), or malware defenses that protect against keyloggers (confidentiality) as well as drive deletion logic bombs (integrity). In these cases, it is best to look for additional details that can reveal the best answer.

Integrity

The second principle of information security is that of integrity. Integrity involves controls to preserve the reliability and accuracy of data and processes against unauthorized modification. Integrity controls include malware defenses protecting against data corruption or deletion, validation code that protects against incorrect data such as code injection or malformed data input, data hashing validation identifying modifications, and limited user interface options controlling the types of access available to data. As with data confidentiality, cryptography plays a very major role in ensuring data integrity. Cryptographic hash functions, digital signatures, and message authentication codes are used to guarantee integrity.

Hashing

Commonly used methods to protect data integrity include hashing the data you receive and comparing it with the hash of the original message. Hashing algorithms are normally used to create a signature for a message which can be used to verify integrity. Many Internet servers provide message digest 5 (MD5) authentication digests for important files made available for download-ing. Most digital signature systems and secure email system use a digest func-tion to ensure integrity.

Digital Signatures

Digital signatures are used to provide nonrepudiation. Integrity is maintained by protecting a message against any alteration by allowing the receiver to decrypt and verify the signature using the sender's public key and hashing algorithm. The signature uses the message sender's private key and includes the name of the hashing algorithm name used. The creator's public key is then appended to the signature. Digital signatures are commonly used to maintain integrity to prevent forgery or tampering in software distribution and financial transactions.

Certificates

Certificates protect integrity by attesting the identity of an individual to his public key. Certificates form the basis for secure communication and cli-ent and server authentication on the Web. Certificates are used to verify the identity of clients and servers on the Web, encrypt channels to provide secure communication between clients and servers, encrypt messages for secure Internet email communication, and verify the sender's identity for Internet email messages.

Nonrepudiation

Nonrepudiation protects integrity by providing a mechanism whereby one party of a transaction cannot deny having received a transaction nor can the other party deny having sent a transaction. Nonrepudiation is often used for digital contracts, digital signatures, and email messages.

> **ExamAlert**
>
> Integrity is focused on preserving data against unauthorized modification, which might include deletion, but controls for recovery in the case of deletion might fall more accurately into the availability arena. If a question addresses temporarily unavailable data, it is most likely an issue of availability, whereas data outright deleted or overwritten is more likely a case of integrity.

Availability

The final principle of information security is that of availability. Availability involves controls to preserve operations and data in the face of service outages, disaster, or capacity variation. Availability controls include load-balancing systems, redundant services and hardware, backup solutions, and environmental controls intended to overcome outages affecting networking, power, system, and service outages; equipment theft; or data exposure (unless a matter of confidentiality, where regulatory mandates define mandatory control requirements).

Redundancy

The goal of redundancy is to ensure that resources are always available even in the event of a failure. Redundancy increases availability and may be implemented in hardware (RAID), disk drivers or OS (RAID), or at the application/service level (for example, replication, transaction monitors, backup domain controllers). Redundancy is extra hardware or software that can be used as backup if the main hardware or software fails. Redundancy can be achieved via load clustering, failover, RAID, load balancing, and high availability.

Fault Tolerance

Fault tolerance relies on specialized hardware to detect a hardware fault and instantaneously switch to a redundant hardware component. Although this process appears seamless and offers nonstop service, a high premium is paid in both hardware cost and performance because the redundant components do no processing. More important, the fault tolerant model does not address software failures, only hardware failures. Fault tolerance is much harder than high availability in a virtual environment because two copies of a virtual machine must be maintained on separate hosts and be updated as memory and device states change.

Patching

Balancing server patching with maintaining the availability of services can be a difficult task. Systems that must run continuously cannot be shut down for system maintenance. Runtime patching can aid in keeping up running systems by allowing for bug fixes and software upgrades provided that the patches are prepared ahead of time, extensively tested in offline systems, and applied in swift manner.

Safety

Organizations must promote, create, and maintain a safe and secure environment for employees and visitors alike by complying with applicable safety, health, and environmental federal and state rules and regulations. Safety plans should include resources needed to address physical security risks.

Fencing

Fencing provides protection for the perimeter of the organization's property. The type of fencing used determines the facility security and safety of its employees. Fencing is used to reduce physical damage to organizational assets from the impact of weather-related disasters such as floods, chemical-related disasters such as bombs, and human-related incidents including workplace violence. Fencing is an important consideration when designing both operational and physical security.

Lighting

From a safety perspective, too little light can provide an opportunity for a criminal, and too much light can create glare and blind spots, resulting in potential risks. Glare can be minimized through proper placement and positioning of fixtures. Installing lamps with at least a 60 on the color-rendering index in areas where crime is a concern provides better lighter conditions for a safer environment. When designing a lighting strategy considerations should be given to uniformity, glare, CCTV compatibility, and compliance with local ordinances. Proper maintenance and bi-annual audits of all exterior lighting helps ensure the safety and security of people and property.

Locks

Secured-area considerations include ensuring that air ducts, drop ceilings, and raised floors do not provide unauthorized avenues for physical access. You can have the most secure lock on the door with biometric devices for identification, but if the walls don't go up all the way and ceiling tiles can be removed to access rooms with sensitive equipment in them, someone can easily walk off with equipment and sensitive data. Locks must be easy to operate yet deter intruders. Besides the normal key locks, several different types can be considered. A cipher lock has a punch-code entry system. A wireless lock is opened by a receiver mechanism that reads the card when it is held close to the receiver. A swipe card lock requires a card to be inserted into the lock; many hotels use these.

CCTV

Closed-circuit television (CCTV) is a critical component of a comprehensive security program. It is important to appropriately plan and set clear measurable objectives for a CCTV system. Failing to do so from the outset can be costly. There are many different types of CCTV systems available. Technical, administrative, and legal considerations including privacy should be taken into account prior to and during the implementation of a CCTV system.

Escape Plans

Because a physical security plan should start with an examination of the perimeter of the building, it might also be wise to discuss what happens when an evacuation is necessary. You don't want intruders plundering the building while employees are running haphazardly all over the place. The evacuation plans could be a part of the disaster recovery plan and should include what equipment will be shut down and by whom and who will notify the proper authorities or agencies of the incident. Your plan must include a way to alert employees, including disabled workers, to evacuate or take other action, and how to report emergencies, as required.

Drills

Aside from having emergency response plans, every organization should practice emergency drill scenarios to ensure employees are kept as safe as possible during potentially disastrous scenarios. How drills are conducted vary according to the type of drill, ranging from simple operational procedures to more elaborate communication and command post drills.

> **ExamAlert**
>
> Drills are most helpful when they ensure management and staff communicate well with one another and take measures to keep track of and account for everyone in the building.

Escape Routes

Your ability to get out of a building in a timely manner without loss of life depends on advance warning and advance planning. When formulating escape, be sure to include the following items:

▶ A map of the internal building and all exit areas

▶ Which departments will exit through which doors

▶ Who will do a final inspection of each area and make sure that it is secure

▶ Where each department, once evacuated, will go and how far away from the building they will be located

Make sure that all users understand how these plans function and practice orderly evacuation procedures so that an emergency situation does not leave critical systems unguarded or unsecured. Smoke from a cigarette or a purposefully set flame could create an opportunity for an attacker to gain access to highly secure areas if evacuation planning does not include security considerations.

Testing Controls

Policy determines what security controls are needed. Security controls are selected by identifying a risk and choosing the appropriate countermeasure that reduces the impact of an undesirable event. The basic elements of safety controls include written policies and procedures, routine training of employees and supervisors, safety awareness tests and audits, proper communication, pretest safety meetings, and routine surveillance of ongoing activities. An important part of the safety plan is testing security controls.

Security controls are the safeguards that a business uses to reduce risk and protect assets. Evaluating and testing security controls validates whether the controls adequately address organizational policy, industry best practice, and applicable law. Testing can be an invaluable technique to an organization's information security program. Testing security controls for effectiveness and measuring them against standards help meet organizational goals and regulatory responsibilities.

Cram Quiz

Answer these questions. The answers follow the last question. If you cannot answer these questions correctly, consider reading this section again until you can.

1. Which of the principles of security is supported by redundancy?

   ○ **A.** Confidentiality

   ○ **B.** Integrity

   ○ **C.** Availability

   ○ **D.** Sanitization

2. Which of the principles of security is supported by hashing?

   ○ **A.** Confidentiality

   ○ **B.** Integrity

   ○ **C.** Availability

   ○ **D.** Safety

3. Which of the following are used to ensure employees are kept as safe possible during potentially disastrous events?

   ○ **A.** Lighting

   ○ **B.** Fencing

   ○ **C.** Control testing

   ○ **D.** Drill scenarios

Cram Quiz Answers

1. **C.** Availability is concerned with ensuring that access to services and data is protected against disruption including disasters and other events that could require redundancy. Answer A is incorrect because confidentiality involves protecting against unauthorized access. Integrity is concerned with preventing unauthorized modification, making answer B incorrect. Answer D is incorrect because sanitization involves the destruction or overwriting of data to protect confidentiality.

2. **B.** Commonly used methods to protect data integrity include hashing the data you receive and comparing it with the hash of the original message. Answer A is incorrect because confidentiality involves protecting against unauthorized access. Availability is concerned with ensuring that access to services and data is protected against disruption, making answer C incorrect. Answer D is incorrect because safety addresses physical security risks.

3. **D**. Drill scenarios are used to ensure employees are kept as safe possible during potentially disastrous scenarios. Answer A is incorrect a fence keeps out unwanted vehicles and people. Answer B incorrect because proper lighting ensures that the safety and security of both people and property is not compromised. Answer C is incorrect because security control testing is used for program effectiveness and measuring program goals against standards.

What Next?

If you want more practice on this chapter's exam objectives before you move on, remember that you can access all the Cram Quiz questions on the CD. You can also create a custom exam by objective with the practice exam software. Note any objective that you struggle with and go to the material that covers that objective in this chapter.

CHAPTER 5

Attacks

This chapter covers the following official CompTIA Security+ SY0-401 exam objectives:

▶ Explain types of malware

▶ Summarize various types of attacks

▶ Summarize social engineering attacks and associated effectiveness with each attack

▶ Explain types of wireless attacks

▶ Explain types of application attacks

(For more information on the official CompTIA Security+ SY0-401 exam topics, see the "About the CompTIA Security+ SY0-401 Exam" section in the Introduction.)

Because networks today have become so complex and mobile, they have many points of entry. These various points can all be vulnerable, leaving an intruder many points of access. With so many ways of getting into the network, the components must be divided into separate elements so that the security process becomes easier to manage. To make the best decisions when it comes to securing an environment, it is important that you understand the threats and risks associated with the environment. This section explores those threats, risks, and associated attacks to help you understand everyday potential dangers.

In today's network environment, malicious code, or malware, has become a serious problem. The target is not only the information stored on local computers, but also other resources and computers. As a security professional, part of your responsibility is to recognize malicious code and know how to respond appropriately. This section covers the various types of malicious code you might encounter, including viruses, worms, Trojan horses, spyware, rootkits, botnets, and logic bombs.

Explain Types of Malware

▶ **Adware**

▶ **Viruses**

▶ **Worms**

▶ **Spyware**

▶ **Trojan horses**

▶ **Rootkits**

▶ **Backdoors**

▶ **Logic bombs**

▶ **Botnets**

▶ **Ransomware**

▶ **Polymorphic malware**

▶ **Armored virus**

CramSaver

If you can correctly answer these questions before going through this section, save time by skimming the Exam Alerts in this section and then completing the Cram Quiz at the end of the section.

1. How does a virus differ from a worm?

2. What symptoms indicate that a system contains spyware?

3. What is a botnet, and how does a system become part of a botnet?

Answers

1. Although worms and viruses are similar, the biggest difference is that a worm can replicate itself without any user interaction.

2. A system infested with spyware might exhibit various symptoms, such as sluggishness, changes to the web home pages, web pages automatically added to bookmarks, and websites that launch unexpectedly.

3. A botnet consists of a large number of compromised computers that are able to forward transmissions to other computers outside the network. Most computers that are part of a botnet are often compromised via malicious code executed upon the system.

Adware

Advertising-supported software, or *adware*, is another form of spyware. It is an online way for advertisers to make a sale. Companies offer to place banner ads in their products for other companies. In exchange for the ad, a portion of the revenue from banner sales goes to the company that places the ad. However, this novel concept presents some issues for users. These companies also install tracking software on your system, which keeps in contact with the company through your Internet connection. It reports data to the company such as your general surfing habits and which sites you visit. And although the company might state that it will not collect sensitive or identifying data from your system, the fact remains that you have software on your PC that is sending information about you and your surfing habits to a remote location.

U.S. federal law prohibits secretly installing software that forces consumers to receive pop-ups that disrupt their computer use. Adware is legitimate only when users are informed up front that they will receive ads. In addition, if the adware gathers information about users, it must inform them. Even though legitimate adware is not illegal, certain privacy issues arise. For instance, although legitimate adware discloses the nature of data collected and transmitted, users have little or no control over what data is being collected and dispersed. Remember, this technology can send more than just banner statistics.

Viruses

A *virus* is a program or piece of code that runs on your computer without your knowledge. It is designed to attach itself to other code and replicate. It replicates when an infected file is executed or launched. It then attaches to other files, adds its code to the application's code, and continues to spread. Even a simple virus is dangerous because it can use all available resources and bring the system to a halt. Many viruses can replicate themselves across networks and bypass security systems.

Viruses are malicious programs that spread copies of themselves throughout a single machine. They infect other machines only if an infected object is accessed and the code is launched by a user on that machine. There are several types of viruses:

▶ **Boot sector:** This type of virus is placed into the first sector of the hard drive so that when the computer boots, the virus loads into memory.

▶ **Polymorphic:** This type of virus can change form each time it is executed. It was developed to avoid detection by antivirus software.

▶ **Macro:** This type of virus is inserted into a Microsoft Office document and emailed to unsuspecting users.

▶ **Program:** This type of virus infects executable program files and becomes active in memory.

▶ **Stealth:** This type of virus uses techniques to avoid detection, such as temporarily removing itself from an infected file or masking a file's size.

▶ **Multipartite:** This type of virus is a hybrid of boot and program viruses. It first attacks a boot sector and then attacks system files or vice versa.

ExamAlert

Viruses have to be executed by some type of action, such as running a program.

Here are a few of the most notorious viruses:

▶ **Love Bug:** The virus originated in an email titled "I love you." When the attachment was launched, the virus sent copies of the same email to everybody listed in the user's address book. The virus arrived as a Visual Basic Scripting Edition (VBScript) attachment that deleted files, including MP3s, MP2s, and JPGs. It also sent usernames and passwords to the virus author. It infected about 15 million computers and crashed servers around the world.

▶ **Melissa:** Melissa first appeared in March 1999. It is a macro virus, embedded in a Microsoft Word document. When the recipient receives the Word document as an attachment to an email message and opens the document, the virus sends email to the first 50 addresses in the victim's email address book and attaches itself to each message.

▶ **Michelangelo:** Michelangelo is a master boot record virus. It is based on an older virus called Stoned. The Michelangelo virus erases the contents of the infected drive on March 6 (its namesake's birthday) of the current year.

Since 2000, the majority of viruses released are actually worms, which are discussed in the following section.

Worms

Worms are similar in function and behavior to a virus with the exception that worms are self-replicating. A worm is built to take advantage of a security hole in an existing application or operating system and then find other systems running the same software and automatically replicate itself to the new host. This process repeats with no user intervention. After the worm is running on a system, it checks for Internet connectivity. If it finds connectivity, the worm then tries to replicate from one system to the next.

Examples of worms include the following:

▶ **Morris:** This famous worm took advantage of a Sendmail vulnerability and shut down the entire Internet in 1988.

▶ **Nimda:** This worm infects using several methods, including mass mailing, network share propagation, and several Microsoft vulnerabilities. Its name is admin spelled backward.

▶ **Code Red:** A buffer overflow exploit is used to spread this worm.

▶ **Blaster:** This worm made it difficult to patch infected systems as it would restart systems. Blaster exploits a vulnerability in the Remote Procedure Call (RPC) interface.

▶ **Mydoom:** This was a very fast-spreading worm. It spread via email and was used by spammers to send spam.

Worms propagate by using email, instant messaging, file sharing (P2P), and IRC channels. Packet worms spread as network packets and directly infiltrate the RAM of the victim machine, where the code is then executed. Often, worms are used as the mechanism by which to install backdoors on a user's system. These backdoors can provide subsequent access for the attacker or allow the attacker to maintain control of the system as part of a larger network of controlled systems. These systems are collectively known as *botnets*, which are discussed later in this chapter. The individual computers that make up these botnets are known as *zombies*.

Spyware

Undesirable code sometimes arrives with commercial software distributions. *Spyware* is associated with behaviors such as advertising, collecting personal information, or changing your computer configuration without appropriately obtaining prior consent. Basically, spyware is software that communicates information from a user's system to another party without notifying the user.

Like a Trojan horse (which is described in the next section), spyware sends information out across the Internet to some unknown entity. In this case, however, spyware monitors user activity on the system, and in some instances includes the keystrokes typed. This logged information is then sent to the originator. The information, including passwords, account numbers, and other private information, will no longer be private.

Here are some indications that a computer may contain spyware:

▶ The system is slow, especially when browsing the Internet.

▶ It takes a long time for the Windows desktop to come up.

▶ Clicking a link does nothing or goes to an unexpected website.

▶ The browser home page changes, and you might not be able to reset it.

▶ Web pages are automatically added to your favorites list.

ExamAlert

Spyware monitors user activity on the system and can include keystrokes typed. The information is then sent to the originator of the spyware.

Many spyware eliminator programs are available. These programs scan your machine, similarly to how antivirus software scans for viruses; and just as with antivirus software, you should keep spyware eliminator programs updated and regularly run scans.

Trojan Horses

Trojan horses are programs disguised as useful applications. Trojans do not replicate themselves like viruses, but they can be just as destructive. Code hidden inside the application can attack your system directly or allow the system to be compromised by the code's originator. The Trojan is typically hidden, so its ability to spread depends on the popularity of the software and a user's willingness to download and install the software. Trojans can perform actions without the user's knowledge or consent, such as collecting and sending data or causing the computer to malfunction. Trojans are often classified by their payload or function. The most common include backdoor, downloader, infostealer, and keylogger Trojans. Backdoor Trojans open a less-obvious entry (hence backdoor) into the system, for later access. Downloader Trojans download additional software onto infected systems. This software is most often malicious. Infostealer Trojans attempt to steal information from the infected machine. Keylogger Trojans monitor and send keystrokes typed from the infected machine.

Examples of Trojan horses include the following:

- ▶ **Acid Rain:** This is an old DOS Trojan that, when run, deletes system files, renames folders, and creates many empty folders.

- ▶ **Nuker:** This Trojan was designed to function as a denial-of-service (DoS) attack against a workstation connected to the Internet.

- ▶ **Mocmex:** This Trojan is found in digital photo frames and collects online game passwords.

- ▶ **Simpsons:** This Trojan is a self-extracting batch file that attempts to delete files.

- ▶ **Vundo:** This Trojan downloads and displays fraudulent advertisements.

Trojans can download other Trojans, which is part of how botnets are controlled, as discussed later in this chapter.

Rootkits

Rootkits were first documented in the early 1990s. Today, rootkits are more widely used and are increasingly difficult to detect on networks. A *rootkit* is a piece of software that can be installed and hidden on a computer mainly for the purpose of compromising the system and getting escalated privileges, such as administrative rights. A rootkit is usually installed on a computer by first obtaining user-level access. After a rootkit has been installed, it enables the attacker to gain root or privileged access to the computer. Root or privileged access could also allow the compromise of other machines on the network.

A rootkit might consist of programs that view traffic and keystrokes, alter existing files to escape detection, or create a backdoor on the system.

ExamAlert

Rootkits can be included as part of software package, installed by way of an unpatched vulnerability or by the user downloading and installing it.

Attackers are creating more sophisticated programs that update themselves, which makes them that much harder to detect. If a rootkit has been installed, traditional antivirus software cannot always detect the malicious programs. Many rootkits run in the background. Therefore, you can usually easily spot them by looking for memory processes, monitoring outbound communications, and checking for newly installed programs.

Kernel rootkits modify the kernel component of an operating system. These newer rootkits can intercept system calls passed to the kernel and can filter out queries generated by the rootkit software. Rootkits have also been known to use encryption to protect outbound communications and piggyback on commonly used ports to communicate without interrupting other applications that use that port. These "tricks" invalidate the usual detection methods because they make the rootkits invisible to administrators and to detection tools.

Many vendors offer applications that can detect rootkits, such as RootkitRevealer. Removing rootkits can be a bit complex because you have to remove the rootkit itself and the malware that the rootkit is using. Often, rootkits change the Windows operating system itself. Such a change might cause the system to function improperly. When a system is infected, the only definitive way to get rid of a rootkit is to completely format the computer's hard drive and reinstall the operating system. Most rootkits use global hooks for stealth activity. So, if you use security tools that can prevent programs from installing global hooks and stop process injection, you can prevent rootkit functioning. In addition, rootkit functionality requires full administrator rights. Therefore, you can avoid rootkit infection by running Windows from an account with lesser privileges.

Backdoors

Backdoors are application code functions created intentionally or unintentionally that enable unauthorized access to networked resources. Many times during application development, software designers put in shortcut entry points to allow rapid code evaluation and testing. If not removed before application deployment, such entry points can present the means for an attacker to gain unauthorized access later. Other backdoors might be inserted by the application designers purposefully, presenting later threats to the network if applications are never reviewed by another application designer before deployment.

Logic Bombs

A *logic bomb* is a virus or Trojan horse designed to execute malicious actions when a certain event occurs or a period of time goes by. For a virus to be considered a logic bomb, the user of the software must be unaware of the payload. A programmer might create a logic bomb to delete all his code from the server on a future date, most likely after he has left the company. In several cases recently, ex-employees have been prosecuted for their role in this type of destruction. For example, one of the most high-profile cases of a modern-day logic bomb was the case of Roger Duronio. Duronio was a disgruntled computer programmer who planted a logic bomb in the computer systems of UBS, an investment bank. UBS estimated the repair costs at $3.1 million, and that does not include the downtime, lost data, or lost business. The actions of the logic bomb coincided with stock transactions by Duronio, so securities and mail fraud charges were added to the computer crime charges. The logic bomb that he planted on about 1,000 systems deleted critical files and prevented backups from occurring. He was found guilty of leaving a logic bomb on the systems and of securities fraud. He was sentenced to more than 8 years in jail and fined $3.1 million.

ExamAlert

A logic bomb is also referred to as *slag code*. It is malicious in intent and usually planted by a disgruntled employee.

During software development, it is a good idea to evaluate the code to keep logic bombs from being inserted. Even though this is a preventive measure, code evaluation will not guarantee a logic bomb won't be inserted after the programming has been completed.

Botnets

A *bot*, short for robot, is an automated computer program that needs no user interaction. Bots are systems that outside sources can control. A bot provides a spam or virus originator with the venue to propagate. Many computers compromised in this way are unprotected home computers (although many computers in the corporate world are bots, as well). A *botnet* is a large number of computers that forward transmissions to other computers on the Internet. You might also hear a botnet referred to as a *zombie army*.

A system is usually compromised by a virus or other malicious code that gives the attacker access. A bot can be created through a port that has been left open or an unpatched vulnerability. A small program is left on the machine for future activation. The bot master can then unleash the effects of the army by sending a single command to all the compromised machines. A computer can be part of a botnet even though it appears to be operating normally.

This is because bots are hidden and usually go undetected unless you are specifically looking for certain activity. The computers that form a botnet can be programmed to conduct a distributed denial-of-service (DDoS) attack, distribute spam, or to do other malicious acts.

Since the mid-2000s, botnets have flooded the Internet. For example, the Storm botnet started out as an email that began circulating on January 19, 2007. It contained a link to a news story about a deadly storm. Over a year later, Storm had remained the largest, most active botnet on the Internet at the time. It continued to be a large source of spam even years later. Storm was the first to make wide use of peer-to-peer communications. Storm has a self-defense mechanism. When the botnet is probed too much, it reacts automatically and starts a denial-of-service (DoS) attack against the probing entity. While the magnitude of the Storm botnet has subsided over the years, largely due to patching, on any given day today, there are thousands of command and control botnet servers with millions of active connections.

Botnets can be particularly tricky and sophisticated, making use of social engineering. A collection of botnets, known as Zbot, stole millions from banks in four nations. The scammers enticed bank customers to click a link to download an updated digital certificate. This was a ruse, and Zbot installed a program that allowed it to see the next time the user successfully accessed the account. Zbot then automatically completed cash transfers to other accounts while the victims did their online banking.

The main issue with botnets is that they are securely hidden. This enables the botnet masters to perform tasks, gather information, and commit crimes while remaining undetected. Attackers can increase the depth and effect of their crimes by using multiple computers because each computer in a botnet can be programmed to execute the same command.

Ransomware

Just like it sounds, *ransomware* is a form of malware that attempts to hold one ransom, often for monetary gain. Often, the attacker has already compromised a system, and demands payment to prevent a negative consequence. Common examples of these consequences might include deletion of files or taking a website offline. Ransomware is really an evolved and more demanding form of "scareware." Such scare tactics are common with fake antivirus ads that supposedly find malware on one's machine. Thus, making a purchase only serves to remove the annoying notices.

CryptoLocker is an example of ransomware that became prevalent in 2013. It attempts to encrypt a user's data. The malware generates encryption keys and stores the private key on a command-and-control server. Thereafter, the ransomware demands payment in return for allowing access to the files. If payment is not made, the ransomware threatens to delete the private key, which is required to unencrypt the files and thus restore access to the end user.

Polymorphic Malware

Poly is a prefix meaning many. *Morphic* means shape. Thus, *polymorphic* malware is malicious code able to change its shape. As a result, such malware can mutate to evade detection by traditional antivirus software. Historically, detection has been largely signature based. Signature-based detection works great when you know exactly what is being looked for; however, detecting malware that can mutate and change becomes much more difficult. While polymorphic malware is nothing new, such malware has become more sophisticated. Such sophistication often requires layers of security controls to combat, as well as the need for security vendors to adapt. Cryptography is used as a means to hide the code from being detected. Each time a polymorphic virus infects a new file or system, for example, it changes its code. In each instance, a unique key is used to encrypt the malware. As a result, trying to detect the malware becomes difficult without an identifiable pattern or signature to match. Fortunately, security vendors adapt in their techniques as well. Evolving technology by security and antimalware vendors can help combat such attacks. Heuristic scanning is one example. Rather than look for a specific signature, heuristic-based scanning examines the instructions running within a program, which aren't typically associated or found through other techniques.

Armored Virus

Like polymorphic malware, the aim of an *armored virus* is to make it difficult to detect. Further, armored viruses, like the name suggests, seek to make it difficult to analyze the functions (thus creating a metaphorical layer of armor around the virus). Armored viruses use various methods of operation, but most notably not only do they seek to defeat heuristic countermeasures, but they also try to prevent disassembly and debugging. If a virus is successful with these latter aims, security researchers face more difficulty trying to analyze the code and design better countermeasures. Security is ever changing. As the good guys adapt, so will the bad guys, and the cycle repeats.

> **ExamAlert**
>
> Do not confuse the difference between a polymorphic and armored virus. While they both try to defeat countermeasures, remember that armored viruses use mechanisms to keep them from being disassembled and analyzed.

Cram Quiz

Answer these questions. The answers follow the last question. If you cannot answer these questions correctly, consider reading this section again until you can.

1. Which one of the following is designed to execute malicious actions when a certain event occurs or a specific time period elapses?

   ○ **A.** Logic bomb

   ○ **B.** Spyware

   ○ **C.** Botnet

   ○ **D.** DDoS

2. Which one of the following best describes a polymorphic virus?

   ○ **A.** A virus that infects EXE files

   ○ **B.** A virus that attacks the boot sector and then attacks the system files

   ○ **C.** A virus inserted into a Microsoft Office document such as Word or Excel

   ○ **D.** A virus that changes its form each time it is executed

Cram Quiz Answers

1. **A.** Logic bombs are designed to execute malicious actions when a certain event occurs or a specific time period elapses. Spyware, botnets, and DDoS are all threats but do not execute malicious code after a specific event or period.

2. **D.** Polymorphic viruses can change their form each time they are run. The other answers describe different types of viruses—program, multipartite, and macro, respectively.

Summarize Various Types of Attacks

- ▶ **Man-in-the-middle**
- ▶ **DDoS**
- ▶ **DoS**
- ▶ **Replay**
- ▶ **Smurf attack**
- ▶ **Spoofing**
- ▶ **Spam**
- ▶ **Phishing**
- ▶ **Spim**
- ▶ **Vishing**
- ▶ **Spear phishing**
- ▶ **Xmas attack**
- ▶ **Pharming**
- ▶ **Privilege escalation**
- ▶ **Malicious insider threat**
- ▶ **DNS poisoning and ARP poisoning**
- ▶ **Transitive access**
- ▶ **Client-side attacks**
- ▶ **Password attacks**
- ▶ **Typo squatting/URL hijacking**
- ▶ **Watering hole attack**

CramSaver

If you can correctly answer this question before going through this section, save time by skimming the Exam Alerts in this section and then completing the Cram Quiz at the end of the section.

1. Employees internal to an organization might be threats to the organization. Describe the types of insider threats.

Answers

1. The insider threat is typically classified as either a malicious insider or non-malicious insider. The latter is typically unaware of an organization's security policy or is often just trying to accomplish his job. On the other hand, a malicious insider might be motivated by financial gain, be disgruntled, or be looking to gain a competitive advantage.

Man-in-the-Middle

The *man-in-the-middle attack* takes place when an attacker intercepts traffic and then tricks the parties at both ends into believing that they are communicating with each other. This type of attack is possible because of the nature of the three-way TCP handshake process using SYN and ACK packets. Because TCP is a connection-oriented protocol, a three-way handshake takes place when establishing a connection and when closing a session. When establishing a session, the client sends a SYN request, the server sends an acknowledgment and synchronization (SYN-ACK) to the client, and then the client sends an ACK (also referred to as SYN-ACK-ACK), completing the connection. During this process, the attacker initiates the man-in-the-middle attack. The attacker uses a program that appears to be the server to the client and appears to be the client to the server. The attacker can also choose to alter the data or merely eavesdrop and pass it along. This attack is common in Telnet and wireless technologies. It is also generally difficult to implement because of physical routing issues, TCP sequence numbers, and speed. Because the hacker has to be able to sniff both sides of the connection simultaneously, programs such as Juggernaut, T-Sight, and Hunt have been developed to help make the man-in-the-middle attack easier.

If the attack is attempted on an internal network, physical access to the network is required. Be sure that access to wiring closets and switches is restricted; if possible, the area should be locked.

After you have secured the physical environment, protect the services and resources that allow a system to be inserted into a session. DNS can be compromised and used to redirect the initial request for service, providing an opportunity to execute a man-in-the-middle attack. You should restrict DNS access to read-only for everyone except the administrator. The best way to prevent these types of attacks is to use encryption and secure protocols.

> **ExamAlert**
>
> A man-in-the-middle attack takes place when a computer intercepts traffic and either eavesdrops on the traffic or alters it.

Denial of Service

The purpose of a *denial-of-service* (DoS) *attack* is to disrupt the resources or services that a user would expect to have access to. These types of attacks are executed by manipulating protocols and can happen without the need to be validated by the network. An attack typically involves flooding a listening port on your machine with packets. The premise is to make your system so busy processing the new connections that it cannot process legitimate service requests.

Many of the tools used to produce DoS attacks are readily available on the Internet. Administrators use them to test connectivity and troubleshoot problems on the network, whereas malicious users use them to cause connectivity issues.

Here are some examples of DoS attacks:

▶ **Smurf/smurfing:** This attack is based on the Internet Control Message Protocol (ICMP) echo reply function. It is more commonly known as ping, which is the command-line tool used to invoke this function. In this attack, the attacker sends ping packets to the broadcast address of the network, replacing the original source address in the ping packets with the source address of the victim, thus causing a flood of traffic to be sent to the unsuspecting network device.

▶ **Fraggle:** This attack is similar to a Smurf attack. The difference is that it uses UDP rather than ICMP. The attacker sends spoofed UDP packets to broadcast addresses as in the Smurf attack. These UDP packets are directed to port 7 (Echo) or port 19 (Chargen). When connected to port 19, a character generator attack can be run.

▶ **Ping flood:** This attack attempts to block service or reduce activity on a host by sending ping requests directly to the victim. A variation of this type of attack is the ping of death, in which the packet size is too large and the system does not know how to handle the packets.

▶ **SYN flood:** This attack takes advantage of the TCP three-way handshake. The source system sends a flood of SYN requests and never sends the final ACK, thus creating half-open TCP sessions. Because the TCP stack waits before resetting the port, the attack overflows the destination computer's connection buffer, making it impossible to service connection requests from valid users.

▶ **Land:** This attack exploits a behavior in the operating systems of several versions of Windows, UNIX, OS X, and Cisco IOS with respect to their TCP/IP stacks. The attacker spoofs a TCP/IP SYN packet to the victim system with the same source and destination IP address and the same source and destination ports. This confuses the system as it tries to respond to the packet.

▶ **Teardrop:** This form of attack targets a known behavior of UDP in the TCP/IP stack of some operating systems. The Teardrop attack sends fragmented UDP packets to the victim with odd offset values in subsequent packets. When the operating system attempts to rebuild the original packets from the fragments, the fragments overwrite each other, causing confusion. Because some operating systems cannot gracefully handle the error, the system will most likely crash or reboot.

▶ **Bonk:** This attack affects mostly older operating systems by sending corrupt UDP packets to DNS port 53. The attack modifies the fragment offset in the packet. The target machine then attempts to reassemble the packet. Because of the offset modification, the packet is too big to be reassembled and the system crashes.

▶ **Boink:** This is a Bonk attack that targets multiple ports rather than just port 53.

▶ **Xmas Tree:** A Christmas tree is a packet that makes use of each option for the underlying protocol. Because these packets require more processing, they are often used in what's called a Xmas Tree attack to disrupt service.

DoS attacks come in many shapes and sizes. The first step to protecting yourself from an attack is to understand the nature of different types of attacks in the preceding list. Although there are various security solutions designed specifically to help prevent such attacks, you might consider other measures within your organization. Fundamentally, organizations should ensure that they have well-defined processes around such things as auditing, standard operating procedures, and documented configurations. Finally, being well versed on the nature of the different types of attacks will allow for better decision making when it comes to attack recognition and implementing controls such as packet filtering and rights management.

Distributed DoS

Another form of attack is a simple expansion of a DoS attack, referred to as a *distributed DoS* (DDoS) *attack*. Masters are computers that run the client software, and zombies run software. The attacker creates masters, which in turn create a large number of zombies or recruits. The software running on the zombies can launch multiple types of attacks, such as UDP or SYN floods on a particular target. Figure 5.1 shows a typical DDoS.

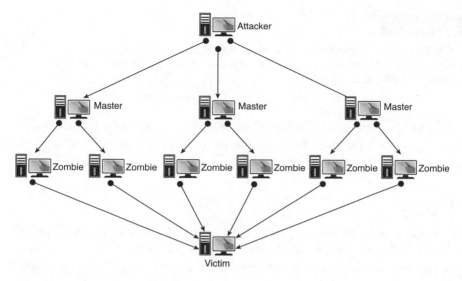

FIGURE 5.1   **A DDoS attack**

In simple terms, the attacker distributes zombie software that allows the attacker partial or full control of the infected computer system.

> **ExamAlert**
>
> When an attacker has enough systems compromised with the installed zombie software, he can initiate an attack against a victim from a wide variety of hosts. The attacks come in the form of the standard DoS attacks, but the effects are multiplied by the total number of zombie machines under the control of the attacker.

Although DDoS attacks generally come from outside the network to deny services, you must also consider the effect of DDoS attacks mounted from inside the network. Internal DDoS attacks allow disgruntled or malicious users to disrupt services without any outside influence.

To help protect your network, you can set up filters on external routers to drop packets involved in these types of attacks. You should also set up another filter that denies traffic originating from the Internet that shows an internal network address. When you do this, the loss of ping and some services and utilities for testing network connectivity is incurred, but this is a small price to pay for network protection. If the operating system allows it, reduce the amount of time before the reset of an unfinished TCP connection. Doing so makes it harder to keep resources unavailable for extended periods of time.

> **Note**
>
> In case of a DDoS attack, your best weapon is to get in touch quickly with your upstream Internet service provider (ISP) and see whether it can divert traffic or block the traffic at a higher level.

Subscribing to newsgroups and checking security websites daily ensures that you keep up with the latest attacks and exploits. Applying the manufacturer's latest operating system patches or fixes can also help prevent attacks.

Replay

In a replay attack, packets are captured by using sniffers. After the pertinent information is extracted, the packets are placed back on the network. This type of attack can be used to replay bank transactions or other similar types of data transfer in the hopes of replicating or changing activities, such as deposits or transfers.

Protecting yourself against replay attacks involves some type of time stamp associated with the packets or time-valued, nonrepeating serial numbers. Secure protocols such as IPsec prevent replays of data traffic in addition to providing authentication and data encryption.

DNS Poisoning

DNS poisoning enables a perpetrator to redirect traffic by changing the IP record for a specific domain, thus permitting the attacker to send legitimate traffic anywhere he chooses. This not only sends a requestor to a different website, but also caches this information for a short period, distributing the attack's effect to the server users. DNS poisoning may also be referred to as *DNS cache poisoning* because it affects the information that is cached.

All Internet page requests start with a DNS query. If the IP address is not known locally, the request is sent to a DNS server. There are two types of DNS servers: authoritative and recursive. DNS servers share information, but recursive servers maintain information in cache. This means a caching or recursive server can answer queries for resource records even if it cannot resolve the request directly. A flaw in the resolution algorithm allows the poisoning of DNS records on a server. All an attacker has to do is delegate a false name to the domain server along with providing a false address for the server. For example, an attacker creates a hostname hack.hacking.biz. After that, the attacker queries your DNS server to resolve the host hacking.biz.

The DNS server resolves the name and stores this information in its cache. Until the zone expiration, any further requests for hacking.biz do not result in lookups but are answered by the server from its cache. It is now possible for the attacker to set your DNS server as the authoritative server for his zone with the domain registrar. If the attacker conducts malicious activity, the attacker can make it appear that your DNS server is being used for these malicious activities.

DNS poisoning can result in many different implications. Domain name servers can be used for DDoS attacks. Malware can be downloaded to an unsuspecting user's computer from the rogue site, and all future requests by that computer will be redirected to the fake IP address. This could be used to build an effective botnet. This method of poisoning could also allow for cross-site scripting exploits, especially because Web 2.0 capabilities allow content to be pulled from multiple websites at the same time.

To minimize the effects of DNS poisoning, check the DNS setup if you are hosting your own DNS. Be sure the DNS server is not open-recursive. An open-recursive DNS server responds to any lookup request without checking where it originates. Disable recursive access for other networks to resolve names that are not in your zone files. You can also use different servers for authoritative and recursive lookups and require that caches discard information except from the com servers and the root servers. From the user perspective, education works best. However, it is becoming more difficult to spot a problem by watching the address bar on the Internet browser. Therefore, operating system vendors are adding more protection. Microsoft Windows User Account Control (UAC) notifies the user that a program is attempting to change the system's DNS settings, thus preventing the DNS cache from being poisoned.

ARP Poisoning

All network cards have a unique 48-bit address that is hardcoded into the network card. For network communications to occur, this hardware address must be associated with an IP address. Address Resolution Protocol (ARP), which operates at Layer 2 (data link layer) of the OSI model, associates MAC addresses to IP addresses. ARP is a lower-layer protocol that is simple and consists of requests and replies without validation. However, this simplicity also leads to a lack of security.

When you use a protocol analyzer to look at traffic, you see an ARP request and an ARP reply, which are the two basic parts of ARP communication. There are also Reverse ARP (RARP) requests and RARP replies. Devices maintain an ARP table that contains a cache of the IP addresses and MAC addresses the device has already correlated. The host device searches its ARP table to see whether there is a MAC address corresponding to the destination host IP address. When there is no matching entry, it broadcasts an ARP request to the entire network. The broadcast is seen by all systems, but only the device that has the corresponding information replies. However, devices can accept ARP replies before even requesting them. This type of entry is known as an *unsolicited entry* because the information was not explicitly requested.

ExamAlert

Because ARP does not require any type of validation, as ARP requests are sent the requesting devices believe that the incoming ARP replies are from the correct devices. This can allow a perpetrator to trick a device into thinking any IP is related to any MAC address.

In addition, they can broadcast a fake or spoofed ARP reply to an entire network and poison all computers. This is known as *ARP poisoning*. Put simply, the attacker deceives a device on your network, poisoning its table associations of other devices.

ARP poisoning can lead to attacks such as DoS, man-in-the-middle, and MAC flooding. DoS and man-in-the-middle attacks were discussed earlier. *MAC flooding* is an attack directed at network switches. This type of attack is successful because of the nature of the way all switches and bridges work. The amount of space allocated to store source addresses of packets is very limited. When the table becomes full, the device can no longer learn new information and becomes flooded. As a result, the switch can be forced into a hub-like state that will broadcast all network traffic to every device in the network. An example of this is a tool called Macof. Macof floods the network with random MAC addresses. Switches can then get stuck in open-repeating mode, leaving the network traffic susceptible to sniffing. Non-intelligent switches do not check the sender's identity, thereby allowing this condition to happen.

A lesser vulnerability of ARP is port stealing. *Port stealing* is a man-in-the-middle attack that exploits the binding between the port and the MAC address. The principle behind port stealing is that an attacker sends numerous packets with the source IP address of the victim and the destination MAC address of the attacker. This attack applies to broadcast networks built from switches.

ARP poisoning is limited to attacks that are local based, so an intruder needs either physical access to your network or control of a device on your local network. To mitigate ARP poisoning on a small network, you can use static or script-based mapping for IP addresses and ARP tables. For large networks, use equipment that offers port security. By doing so, you can permit only one MAC address for each physical port on the switch. In addition, you can deploy monitoring tools or an intrusion detection system (IDS) to alert you when suspect activity occurs.

Spoofing

Spoofing is a method of providing false identity information to gain unauthorized access. This is accomplished by modifying the source address of traffic or source of information.

> **ExamAlert**
>
> Spoofing seeks to bypass IP address filters by setting up a connection from a client and sourcing the packets with an IP address that is allowed through the filter.

In blind spoofing, the attacker sends only data and only makes assumptions of responses. In informed spoofing, the attacker can participate in a session and can monitor the bidirectional communications.

Services such as email, web, and file transfer can also be spoofed. Web spoofing happens when an attacker creates a convincing but false copy of an entire website. The false site looks just like the real one; it has all the same pages and links. However, the attacker controls the false site so that all network traffic between the victim's browser and the site goes through the attacker. In email spoofing, a spammer or a computer virus can forge the email packet information in an email so that it appears the email is coming from a trusted host, from one of your friends, or even from your own email address. If you leave your email address at some Internet site or exchange email with other people, a spoofer might be able to use your email address as the sender address to send spam. File-transfer spoofing involves the FTP service. FTP data is sent in clear text. An attacker can intercept the data. The data could then be viewed and altered before sending it on to the receiver. These forms of attacks are often used to get additional information from network users to complete a more aggressive attack.

You should set up a filter that denies traffic originating from the Internet that shows an internal network address. Using the signing capabilities of certificates on servers and clients allows web and email services to be more secure. The use of IPsec can secure transmissions between critical servers and clients. This will help prevent these types of attacks from taking place.

Spam

Just like junk mail clogs our regular mailboxes, spam clogs our email boxes. *Spam* is a term that refers to the sending of unsolicited commercial email. Email spam targets individual users with direct mail messages. Most spam is commercial advertising, often for products such as "get rich quick" schemes, physical enhancements, and cheap medications. More dangerous spam might include hoaxes and may be combined with forms of social engineering discussed in the next section. Spam costs the sender little to send because the actual costs are paid for by the carriers rather than by the sender. Email spam lists are often created by scanning newsgroup postings, stealing Internet mailing lists, or searching the Web for addresses. Spammers use automated tools to subscribe to as many mailing lists as possible. From those lists, they capture addresses or use the mailing list as a direct target for their attacks. State, federal, and international laws regulate spam.

> **Note**
>
> Requesting to be removed from junk email lists often results in more spam because it verifies that you have a legitimate, working email address.

When dealing with spam, follow this advice:

▶ Never make a purchase from an unsolicited email.

▶ If you do not know the sender of an unsolicited email message, delete it. (Do not be curious and open it.)

▶ Do not respond to spam messages and do not click any links within the message (even to "unsubscribe").

▶ Do not use the preview function of your email software, because if you do, the email message will automatically show as read.

▶ When sending email messages to a number of people, use the blind carbon copy (BCC) field to hide their email addresses.

▶ Be careful about giving out your email address on websites and newsgroups.

▶ Use more than one email address, keeping your personal email address private.

In addition, use software that filters spam. Approximately 75% of the email organizations receive is spam. It is best to filter it before it gets to the users. One method spammers have used to try to circumvent mail filters is sending spam through instant messaging, also known as *spim*. Spim uses bots to simulate being a human on the other side of the instant message. In most cases, spim, like spam, includes links for which the spammer is trying to market.

Phishing and Related Attacks

More and more, social engineering attacks, which are discussed further in the next section, are combined with electronic means. Social engineering conducted via computer systems is given different names based on the target and the method used. One of the more common methods of social engineering via electronic communications is phishing. *Phishing* is an attempt to acquire sensitive information by masquerading as a trustworthy entity via an electronic communication, usually an email. Phishing attacks rely on a mix of technical deceit and social engineering practices. In the majority of cases, the phisher must persuade the victim to intentionally perform a series of actions that will provide access to confidential information. As scam artists become more sophisticated, so do their phishing email messages. The messages often include official-looking logos from real organizations and other identifying information taken directly from legitimate websites. For best protection, you must deploy proper security technologies and techniques at the client side, the server side, and the enterprise level. Ideally, users should not be able to directly access email attachments from within the email application. However, the best defense is user education.

Other related methods with slightly varying differences include the following:

▶ **Spear phishing:** This is a targeted version of phishing. Whereas phishing often involves mass email, spear phishing might go after a specific individual.

▶ **Whaling:** Whaling is identical to spear phishing except for the "size of the fish." Whaling employs spear phishing tactics but is intended to go after high-profile targets such as an executive within a company.

▶ **Vishing:** Also known as voice phishing, the attacker often uses fake caller ID to appear as a trusted organization and attempts to get the individual to enter account details via the phone.

▶ **Smishing:** Also known as SMS phishing, this involves using phishing methods through text messaging.

▶ **Pharming:** This is a term coined based upon farming and phishing. Pharming does not require the user to be tricked into clicking a link. Rather pharming redirects victims to a bogus website, even if the user correctly entered the intended site. To accomplish this, the attacker employs another attack, such as DNS cache poisoning.

> **ExamAlert**
>
> Phishing combines technical deceit with the elements of traditional social engineering. Be sure to know the different variants of phishing attacks.

Privilege Escalation

Programming errors can result in system compromise, allowing someone to gain unauthorized privileges. Software exploitation takes advantage of a program's flawed code, which then crashes the system and leaves it in a state where arbitrary code can be executed, or an intruder can function as an administrator. This is known as *privilege escalation*.

Perhaps the most popular method of privilege escalation is a buffer-overflow attack discussed later in this chapter.

Malicious Insider Threat

Attacks are often thought to be a result of the outside malicious hacker; however, insider threats are a source of many breaches. In many cases, this includes employees who have the right intentions but are unaware of or ignore an organization's security policy. A common example is the well-intentioned employee who uses a personal web-based email account to send home sensitive files to work on later in the evening. These sensitive files have now proliferated unencrypted outside of the organizational network. Another common scenario is the user who brings in USB thumb drives that unknowingly have been infected with malware. Proper training and education is key to help prevent the nonmalicious insider threat.

However, deliberate or malicious insider threats also present a source of attack. These are typically motivated by financial gain, sabotage, and theft to gain a competitive advantage. Or consider events such as that of ex-National Security Agency (NSA) contractor Edward Snowden. Snowden, formerly an insider, later circulated various documents and secrets about the NSA's surveillance program. Protecting against malicious insiders is a daunting and difficult task. Regardless, organizations should have policies in place to help identify risky personnel (for example, those given separation notice), and arguably most important, organizations need to have mechanisms to proactively monitor network and systems activities.

Transitive Access and Client-Side Attacks

Transitive access, in many cases, can be by design. One unintended consequence however, is that certain attacks can take advantage of such configurations. The methods and specifics can vary greatly from system to system, but you should at least be able to understand situations potentially subject to transitive access. Consider that the word *transitive* describes logic in which access or a relationship can be assumed or transferred. For example, if A trusts B and B trusts C, it can be assumed that A also trusts C. While the relationship between A and B and the relationship between B and C are explicit, the relationship between A and C is implied or transitive. Although such access has benefits, it is important to be certain when making connections between systems and organizations that you understand the risk potentially posed by such transitive access.

This relationship is why client-side attacks have seen increased focus from attackers. While the targeted system, such as the server with the confidential data, may be locked down and difficult to attack directly, the transitive relationship between a client machine and the system make the client-side attacks more ideal. Therefore, even the most secured server system is vulnerable to a client system with a single unpatched vulnerability.

Password Attacks

Any resource exposed on a network may be attacked to gain unauthorized access. The most common form of authentication and user access control is the username/password combination, which can be significantly weakened as a security measure if a "weak" password is selected. Automated and social engineering assaults on passwords are easier when a password is short; lacking in complexity; derived from a common word found in the dictionary; or derived from easily guessable personal information such as birthdays, family names, pet names, and similar details.

Successful attacks on passwords often result in immediate unauthorized access to systems and potentially sensitive information. Historically, password attacks are a classic method of obtaining such access. The security of passwords largely relies upon end users. For an end user, the tradeoff of an easy-to-remember password versus a complex one may lean to the simple password, despite putting organizational assets at risk. Even in the instance where technical controls may be put in place to ensure complex passwords, an end user may simply write their passwords down for someone else to find. Fortunately, passwords, which provide the primary means of authentication, have evolved to help thwart attacks (for example, additional controls, such as examining login location or sending a secondary authentication code such as a text message to the user's phone). Of course, a tradeoff always exists between security and usability, which is why such methods are usually based on the perceived risk at that moment.

Before discussing types of password attacks, keep in mind that although passwords can be stored in plain text, they should not be. In fact, most passwords are actually stored as a cryptographic hashed value. In a simplified example, imagine that each letter of the alphabet corresponds to a number (A = 1, B = 2, C = 3, and so on). If our password is ABC, then using our hashing algorithm (that is, adding up the numbers), we arrive at a value of 6. When a password is subsequently entered, it is run through the same algorithm and then compared to the stored value. If we try to enter ABD, the resulting value of 7 will not match the value stored. Of course, actual hashing algorithms and the process is much more complicated than this, but this should help you understand the concepts further.

There are various types of password attacks. In some instances, passwords may be written down and retrieved, improperly shared, or easily guessed. However, various tools are available to automate password hacks. Imagine trying every word in the dictionary to gain access to a system. This is *dictionary attack*. In essence, this is software that automates such a task. Dictionary attacks can often use different and custom dictionaries. Such files could even contain list of passwords that are not typically contained within a traditional dictionary, such as 1234 and abcde. A dictionary attack is most successful on simple passwords, as the attack will go through and try each word within the supplied list.

The word *love*, for example, might easily be compromised through a simple dictionary attack; however, simply changing the letter *o* to a zero may very well counter such an attack. Brute-force attacks, however, are quite capable of defeating such passwords. Brute-force attacks, unlike a simple dictionary attack, rely on cryptoanalysis or algorithms capable of performing exhaustive key searches. Against short passwords, brute-force attacks are very quick and would crack a password quicker than a dictionary attack. However, a brute-force attack can take a lot of time and computing power against larger more complex passwords because it will attempt to exhaust all possible combination of letters, numbers, and symbols.

A dictionary attack might not be successful against a common word with numbers included. Yet, a brute-force attack might take too long for a long word with numbers included. Another attack, known as a *hybrid attack*, not only provides a compromise but is also a useful tool to help identify weak passwords and controls for audit purposes. A hybrid attack uses the dictionary attack method, but builds upon this by doing such things as adding numbers to the end of the words, substituting certain letters for numbers and capitalizing the first letter of each word.

Two well-known methods that are types of brute-force attacks are birthday attacks and the use of rainbow tables. The birthday attack is a cryptographic method against a secure hash. Keep in mind that a dictionary or brute-force attack is successful when each guess is hashed, and then the resulting hash matches a hash being cracked. A birthday attack, instead, finds collisions within hash functions, which results in a more efficient method of brute forcing one-way hashes. So, why is this called a birthday attack? It is based on what is known as the *birthday paradox*. Simply put, if there are 23 people in a room, the probability that two of those people have the same birthday is 50%. Hard to believe? True. That's why it is called a paradox. Without getting into complex math, let's try to simplify the reasoning here (not easy to do!). The birthday paradox is concerned with finding any match, and not necessarily a match for *you*. Consider that you would need 253 people in a room to have a 50% chance that someone else shares *your* birthday. Yet, you only need 23 people to create 253 pairs when cross-matched with one another. That gets us to 50% chance. This same theory applies to finding collisions within hash functions. Just as it would be more difficult to find someone who shares (collides) with your birthday, it is more difficult to find something that would collide with a given hash. However, just as we increase the probability of finding *any* two birthdays that match within the group, it is easier to find two inputs that have the same hash.

A rainbow table is another brute-force method for cracking passwords that have been hashed. Rainbow tables can most easily be thought of as a very large set of precomputed hash values for every possible combination of characters. With the assumption that an attacker has enough resources to store an entire rainbow table in memory, a successful attack on passwords is able to occur with great efficiency.

Various countermeasures exist to help prevent and mitigate such attacks. This includes such things as multiple authentication methods. For example, combining something you know (for example, a password) with something you have (for example, a one-time-use token or code sent to a registered phone, in addition to controls already discussed, such as account lockout after three unsuccessful attempts). Finally, password hashes can use a "salt." Understand that some of the attacks mentioned here work because users who have the same password would also have the same resulting hash. This problem can be overcome by making the hashes more random. Salting uses a prefix consisting of a random string of characters to passwords before they are hashed. Such a countermeasure makes it more difficult or impractical to attack passwords unless the attacker knows the value of the salt that needs to be removed.

> **ExamAlert**
>
> Multifactor authentication mechanisms such as a token that changes every 30 seconds or a text message to a phone are important countermeasures to mitigate password-based attacks. This requires users to have something in their possession in addition to the knowledge of a password or passphrase.

Typo Squatting/URL Hijacking

Typo squatting, also known as *URL hijacking*, is a simple method used frequently for benign purposes but can and is easily used for more malicious attacks. Typo squatting most commonly relies on typographic errors made by users on the Internet. It could be as simple as typing www.gooogle.com accidentally rather than www.google.com. In this particular example, Google actually owns both domain names and redirects the mistyped domain to the correct domain. However, there are many instances where a misspelled URL of a travel website, for instance, might take one to a competing website. Aside from those trying to profit from the mistake, such a mistake could lead to more drastic consequences. While any domain name may be slightly misspelled, some lend themselves to more common and frequent misspellings. Imagine that you unknowingly and mistakenly type in the wrong URL to go to your bank; perhaps you just accidentally transpose a couple letters. But rather than being presented with a generic parked domain for a domain registrar (immediate tip-off that something is wrong), you are presented with what you know and expect to be your bank. While the variations and motives can vary, a simple attack would just be to easily record your login information.

Perhaps after you try to log in, you are simply presented with a message that your bank is undergoing website maintenance and will be back up in 24 hours. Meanwhile, the attacker has access to your credentials and knows which site they can be used on.

Watering Hole Attack

In many ways, a watering hole attack is similar to spear phishing discussed earlier. But instead of using email, the attacker will attack a site frequently visited by the target. The goal is often to compromise the larger environment (for example, the company the target works for).

Just as the lion will wait hidden near the watering hole frequented by the zebras, the attacker is waiting at the sites you frequent. In a typical scenario, the attacker will first profile and understand the victim. This includes what websites are visited and what type of computer and web browser is used. Next, the attacker will look for opportunities to compromise any of these sites based on existing vulnerabilities. Understanding more about the victim (for example, type of browser used and activities) will help compromise the site with the greatest chance of, in turn, exploiting the victim. Finally, such attacks are commonly used in conjunction with a zero-day exploit. By even being able to take advantage of a cross-site scripting vulnerability on the visited site, the attacker can ensure the trusted site helps in delivering an exploit to the victim's machine.

Cram Quiz

Answer these questions. The answers follow the last question. If you cannot answer these questions correctly, consider reading this section again until you can.

1. You're the security administrator for a bank. The users are complaining about the network being slow. It is not a particularly busy time of the day, however. You capture network packets and discover that hundreds of ICMP packets have been sent to the host. What type of attack is likely being executed against your network?

    ○ **A.** Spoofing

    ○ **B.** Man-in-the-middle

    ○ **C.** Password attack

    ○ **D.** Denial-of-service

2. Which one of the following is not an example of a denial-of-service attack?

    ○ **A.** Fraggle

    ○ **B.** Smurf

    ○ **C.** Gargomel

    ○ **D.** Teardrop

3. Users received a spam email from an unknown source and chose the option in the email to unsubscribe and are now getting more spam as a result. Which one of the following is most likely the reason?

    ○ **A.** The unsubscribe option does not actually do anything.

    ○ **B.** The unsubscribe request was never received.

    ○ **C.** Spam filters were automatically turned off when making the selection to unsubscribe.

    ○ **D.** They confirmed that they are a "live" email address.

Cram Quiz Answers

1. **D.** A ping flood is a DoS attack that attempts to block service or reduce activity on a host by sending ping requests directly to the victim using ICMP. Spoofing involves modifying the source address of traffic or source of information. A man-in-the-middle attack is commonly used to gather information in transit between two hosts. A password attack attempts to gain unauthorized access by going after the authentication control for an account. Answers A, B, and C are incorrect.

2. **C**. A Gargomel attack, although cool sounding, does not actually exist. Fraggle, Smurf, and Teardrop are names of specific denial-of-service attacks; therefore, answers A, B, and D are incorrect.

3. **D**. Often, an option to opt out of further email does not unsubscribe users, but rather means "send me more spam" because it has been confirmed that the email address is not dormant. This is less likely to occur with email a user receives that he or she opted into in the first place, however. Answers A, B, and C are incorrect because these are less likely and not the best choices.

Summarize Social Engineering Attacks and the Associated Effectiveness with Each Attack

▶ **Shoulder surfing**

▶ **Dumpster diving**

▶ **Tailgating**

▶ **Impersonation**

▶ **Hoaxes**

▶ **Whaling**

▶ **Vishing**

▶ **Principles (reasons for effectiveness)**

CramSaver

If you can correctly answer these questions before going through this section, save time by skimming the Exam Alerts in this section and then completing the Cram Quiz at the end of the section.

1. Phishing, spear phishing, whaling, vishing, and smishing are commonly used for what purpose, and what are the technical differences between each?

2. Describe several different examples of social engineering attacks.

3. What can an organization do to prevent sensitive information from being divulged via dumpster diving?

Answers

1. Phishing, spear phishing, whaling, vishing, and smishing are all very similar. Each is a technique commonly used as part of a social engineering ploy. Phishing is commonly done through email across a large audience, whereas spear phishing targets an individual. Whaling, in essence, is spear phishing, but instead is directly targeted at a very high-value target. Vishing and smishing are also similar to phishing but use voice and SMS text messaging, respectively.

2. Although there are countless answers, social engineering relies on extracting useful information by tricking the target. Examples include scenarios that involve impersonating someone else, coercing someone else into divulging sensitive information without cause for concern, or convincing someone to install a malicious program to assist you.

3. The proper disposal of data and equipment should be part of an organization's security policy. Such a policy would likely require ongoing end-user
awareness, as well as procedures around the shredding or other proper
disposal of sensitive information.

Social Engineering

Social engineering is nothing new and has been around as long as humans.
Perhaps you recall face-to-face interactions in which one individual fishes for
information in a deceptive way. One area of security planning that is often
considered the most difficult to adequately secure is the legitimate user. *Social
engineering* is a process by which an attacker might extract useful information
from users who are often just tricked into helping the attacker. It is extremely
successful because it relies on human emotions. Common examples of social
engineering attacks include the following:

▶ An attacker calls a valid user and impersonates a guest, temp agent,
or new user asking for assistance in accessing the network or requests
details involving the business processes of the organization.

▶ An attacker contacts a legitimate user, posing as a technical aide
attempting to update some type of information and asks for identifying
user details that can then be used to gain access.

▶ An attacker poses as a network administrator, directing the legitimate
user to reset his password to a specific value so that an imaginary update
can be applied.

▶ An attacker provides the user with a "helpful" program or agent, through
email, a website, or other means of distribution. This program might
require the user to enter login details or personal information useful to
the attacker, or it might install other programs that compromise the system's security.

Another form of social engineering has come to be known as *reverse social
engineering*. Here, an attacker provides information to the legitimate user that
causes the user to believe the attacker is an authorized technical assistant. This
might be accomplished by obtaining an IT support badge or logo-bearing
shirt that validates the attacker's legitimacy, by inserting the attacker's contact
information for technical support in a secretary's Rolodex, or by making
himself known for his technical skills by helping people around the office.

Many users would rather ask assistance of a known nontechnical person who they know to be skilled in computer support rather than contact a legitimate technical staff person who may be perceived as busy with more important matters. An attacker who can plan and cause a minor problem is then able to easily correct this problem, gaining the confidence of the legitimate user while being able to observe operational and network configuration details and login information, and potentially being left alone with an authorized account logged in to the network.

ExamAlert

Social engineering is a common practice used by attackers, and one that is not easily countered via technology. It is important to understand that the best defense against social engineering is a program of ongoing user awareness and education.

Earlier in this chapter, we discussed various attacks such as phishing, whaling, and vishing that can also be classified as social engineering, but rely more on technical methods to accomplish the goals. These attacks, and several of the methods discussed next, are attacks on humans and take advantage of human psychology. People have a tendency to trust others. People tend to want to be helpful to others in need. Because of these tendencies, adequate and ongoing training is required to counteract such things.

Both whaling and vishing by themselves can lead to sensitive data loss. In many cases, as with other methods of social engineering, they are just a means to an end. While in and of itself, information acquired might not have immediate consequences, the cumulative effect combined with other social engineering and technical attacks may lead to dire consequences (either for the individual or the organization he or she is affiliate with).

Shoulder Surfing

Shoulder surfing most literally means looking over someone's shoulder to obtain information. Common situations include entering one's PIN at an automated teller machine (ATM) or typing in a password at a computer system. More broadly, however, shoulder surfing includes any method of direct observation. This could include, for example, a camera located nearby, or even someone using binoculars from a distance. As with many of these types of methods, user awareness and training is key to prevention. However, there are also tools to assist here. Many ATMs now include mirrors to see who might be behind you, as well as better-designed keypads to help conceal one's entry. Even special screen overlays are available for laptop computers, which prevent someone from seeing the screen from an angle. In such situations, the consequences for the perpetrator are low. Simply peering over one's shoulder to learn the combination is less risky than, say, actually breaking the safe open or attempting to open the safe when unauthorized. In fact, the shoulder surfer might not actually be the one to initiate a subsequent attack. Information security attacks have evolved into a ecosystem. The shoulder surfer's job may be complete here, as he or she provides or sells this information to someone else with more nefarious goals.

Dumpster Diving

As humans, we naturally seek the path of least resistance. Instead of shredding documents or walking them to the recycle bin, they are often thrown in the wastebasket. Equipment sometimes is put in the garbage because city laws do not require special disposal. Because intruders know this, they scavenge discarded equipment and documents, in an act called *dumpster diving*, and extract sensitive information from it without ever contacting anyone in the organization.

In any organization, the potential that an intruder can gain access to this type of information is huge. What happens when employees are leaving the organization? They clean out their desks. Depending on how long the employees have been there, what ends up in the garbage can be a goldmine for an intruder.

Other potential sources of information that are commonly thrown in the garbage include the following:

▶ Old company directories

▶ Old QA or testing analysis

▶ Employee manuals

▶ Training manuals

▶ Hard drives

▶ Floppy disks

▶ Optical media

▶ USB flash drives

▶ Printed emails

Proper disposal of data and equipment should be part of the organization's security policy. It is prudent to have a policy in place that requires shredding of all physical documents and secure erasure of all types of storage media before they may be discarded. Secure erasure is often performed via the use of disk-wiping software, which can delete the data according to different standards.

Tailgating

Tailgating is a simple yet effective form of social engineering. It involves piggybacking or following closely behind someone who has authorized physical access within an environment. Tailgating often involves giving off the appearance of being with or part of an authorized group or capitalizing on people's desire to be polite. A common example is having a secured door held open by an authorized person when following from behind. Many high-security facilities employ mantraps (an airlock-like mechanism that allows only one person to pass at a time) to provide entrance control and prevent tailgating.

Impersonation

Impersonation is simply a method whereby one assumes the character or appearance of someone else. They are pretending to be something they are actually not. Impersonation is often used in conjunction with a pretext or invented scenario. For many, images of private detectives come to mind. In fact, there are many great movies, such as *Catch Me if You Can* and *Beverly Hills Cop*, in which the drama or humor unfolds as a result of impersonation and pretexting.

Hoaxes

Hoaxes are interesting because although they present a threat, the threat at face value does not actually exist. Because a hoax seems like it could be legitimate, it is often the resulting actions by people that actualize various threats. For example, the hoax virus email can consume resources as it is forwarded on. In fact, a widely distributed and believed hoax about a computer virus can result in consequences as significant as an actual virus! Such hoaxes, particularly as they manifest themselves in the physical world, can create unnecessary fear and irrational behaviors. Most hoaxes are passed around not just via email but also by social networks and word of mouth. Many times, the same hoax will find ways to make the rounds again even years later, perhaps sometimes slightly altered. Snopes.com is a well-known resource that has been around since the mid-1990s. If you are ever in doubt, or need help in debunking hoaxes, make this site part of your trusted arsenal.

Principles (Reasons for Effectiveness)

Ready for a psychology cram? As stated earlier, social engineering relies much on what is known about human psychology. In particular, the social engineer is looking to influence another to gain something, which is most often not in the target's best interest. In many cases, the social engineering combines influence with manipulation. Given this, let's take a look at the various principles of influence. The following topics are largely based on the work of Robert Cialdini, Regent's Professor Emeritus of Psychology and Marketing at Arizona State University. The key challenge for the various principles of influence is that even while one may recognize the specific principle, it is not easy to see when they are being illegitimately used. The following points summarize key principles of influence and highlight why they are effective:

▶ **Authority:** Job titles, uniforms, symbols, badges, and even specific expertise all represent elements we often equate with authority. With such proclaimed and believed authority, we naturally feel an obligation to comply. This could be the flashing red lights that cause you to pull over. It could be the specific expertise of the IT security administrator or chief information security officer that compels us to divulge our password so that they can troubleshoot. In addition to feeling a sense of obligation, we also tend to trust authoritative symbols (many of which are easily forged).

▶ **Intimidation:** While authority plays to our sense of duty, those with authority or power above us are in a position to abuse that power, which we may feel would have a negative impact. Intimidation does not need to necessarily be so severe that one fears physical harm. A social engineer would more likely use intimidation to play upon a fear of getting in trouble or getting fired, for example.

▶ **Consensus/social proof:** Based on the idea that people tend to trust like-minded people such as friends and family, this is about doing or believing what others around us believe. Think of the cliché "safety in numbers." This is why we are more likely to put a tip in a tip jar when it is not empty, for example, or why we might be hesitant to eat at a restaurant that is empty. A social engineer might mention friends and colleagues—perhaps you might be told that these trusted people mentioned you, or that perhaps they too have already complied with whatever you are being asked for. Requests or situations that might be ambiguous are more likely to be acted on with the belief that others are doing or bought into the same situation.

▶ **Scarcity and urgency:** The idea of scarcity is a tactic commonly used as a marketing ploy (some more effective than others). Surely you have heard the pitch about the special price only available to the first 50 callers. Or perhaps the stories of companies unable to keep up with demand (either real or just an illusion). We will tend to want or value something more if we believe it is less available. We are likely to be more impulsive if we believe it is the last one. The social engineer might use such principle to engage one to more quickly act on a request before giving the request more thought. Scarcity will tend to work when the victim desires something and will, in turn, act with a greater sense of urgency. Likewise, the social engineer can use urgency to gain support. Perhaps there might be dreadful consequences unless action take place immediately.

▶ **Familiarity/liking:** People will tend to comply with requests from those whom they like or have common ground with. Liking often leads to trust. The social engineer might try to use humor or connect more personally through shared interests or through common past events and institutions. This is effective based on our fundamental desire to establish and maintain social relationships with others. The social engineer who can get you to like him often finds that you will be helpful because you, too, want to be liked.

▶ **Trust:** Trust plays a large role in the previous principles. We trust those with assigned authority. We trust those with specific expertise regarding their subject. Trust typically follows liking someone. We trust the consensus. Trust further is established and plays out in the idea of reciprocation. We are taught from an early age the golden rule—to do unto others as you would have them do unto you. As a result, a social norm is established to establish equity in social situations and to return favors and not feel indebted to anyone. The reciprocation that occurs and the equity that is established helps build trust.

ExamAlert

Be sure to understand how a social engineer can use the previously mentioned principles for their gain, and in particular, why these strategies are effective.

Cram Quiz

Answer these questions. The answers follow the last question. If you cannot answer these questions correctly, consider reading this section again until you can.

1. Which of the following is an effective way to get information in crowded places such as airports, conventions, or supermarkets?

   ○ **A.** Vishing

   ○ **B.** Shoulder surfing

   ○ **C.** Reverse social engineering

   ○ **D.** Phishing

2. At your place of employment, you are rushing to the door with your arms full of bags. As you approach, the woman before you scans her badge to gain entrance while holding the door for you, but not without asking to see your badge. What did she just prevent?

   ○ **A.** Phishing

   ○ **B.** Whaling

   ○ **C.** Tailgating

   ○ **D.** Door diving

3. Which one of the following is not a type of phishing attack?

   ○ **A.** Spear phishing

   ○ **B.** Wishing

   ○ **C.** Whaling

   ○ **D.** Smishing

Cram Quiz Answers

1. **B**. Shoulder surfing uses direct-observation techniques. It gets its name from looking over someone's shoulder to get information. Answer A is incorrect because vishing uses a phone to obtain information. Answer C is incorrect because reverse social engineering involves an attacker convincing the user that she is a legitimate IT authority, causing the user to solicit her assistance. Answer D is incorrect because phishing is an attempt to acquire sensitive information by masquerading as a trustworthy entity via an electronic communication, usually an email.

2. **C**. Tailgating involves following closely behind someone with authorized physical access in order to gain access to the environment. Answers A and B are incorrect because these describe methods of acquiring sensitive information by masquerading as a trustworthy source. Answer D is also incorrect.

3. **B**. Wishing is not a type of phishing attack. Answers A, C, and D are incorrect because these all do describe a type of phishing attack. Spear phishing is targeted. Whaling is spear phishing that specifically targets high-profile personnel. Smishing is SMS-based phishing.

Explain Types of Wireless Attacks

▶ **Rogue access points**

▶ **Jamming/Interference**

▶ **Evil twin**

▶ **War driving**

▶ **Bluejacking**

▶ **Bluesnarfing**

▶ **War chalking**

▶ **IV attack**

▶ **Packet sniffing**

▶ **Near-field communication**

▶ **Replay attacks**

▶ **WEP/WPA attacks**

▶ **WPS attacks**

CramSaver

If you can correctly answer these questions before going through this section, save time by skimming the Exam Alerts in this section and then completing the Cram Quiz at the end of the section.

1. What is the difference between bluejacking and bluesnarfing?

2. Which of the following describes a pastime in which wireless networks are marked with a special symbol upon a nearby object?

3. What wireless protocol was subject to an IV attack?

Answers

1. Bluejacking involves sending an unsolicited broadcast message to nearby Bluetooth-enabled devices. In contrast, bluesnarfing is more nefarious in that, if successful, it enables the attacker to gain unauthorized access to the device. Bluejacking is commonly used as a means to enable bluesnarfing.

2. In combination with war driving, war chalking describes the activity of drawing special symbols on nearby objects to describe the state of existing wireless networks.

3. WEP was cracked as a result of an IV attack. Specifically, the IV was too short and had a high probability of repeating itself.

Jamming/Interference

Wireless networks are susceptible to being disrupted by other radio sources. Such disruptions can merely be unintentional interference or a malicious attempt to jam the signal. For example, you may have personally experienced or heard stories about how the operation of one's microwave oven interferes with the wireless access to the Internet. This is the result of specific wireless 802.11 devices operating at or near the same wireless band that the microwave emits. Specific attacks on wireless networks can be performed by setting up a nearby access point, or even through the use of dedicated wireless jamming devices.

> **Note**
>
> According to the Federal Communications Commission (FCC), "Federal law prohibits the operation, marketing, or sale of any type of jamming equipment, including devices that interfere with cellular and Personal Communication Services (PCS), police radar, Global Positioning Systems (GPS) and wireless networking services (Wi-Fi)."

Counteracting a jamming attack can be quite simple, but also complicated. It is simple in that most jamming attacks require close physical proximity. So, for example, in the case of a cell phone, just moving 30 feet away could make a difference. However, moving location is not always a viable option. In such cases, it becomes necessary to be able to locate the source of the jamming or boost the signal being jammed. Many enterprise-grade devices provide power levels that can be configured and the ability to identify and locate rogue devices causing the interference. Such rogue devices are discussed next.

Rogue Access Points

The term *rogue access points* refers to situations in which an unauthorized wireless access point has been set up. In organizations, well-meaning insiders might use rogue access points with the best of intentions. However, rogue access points can also serve as a type of man-in-the-middle attack often referred to as an *evil twin*. Because the request for connection by the client is an omnidirectional open broadcast, it is possible for a hijacker to act as an access point to the client, and as a client to the true network access point, enabling the hijacker to follow all data transactions and have the ability to modify, insert, or delete packets at will. By implementing a rogue access point with stronger signal strength than more-remote permanent installations, the attacker can cause a wireless client to preferentially connect to its own stronger nearby connection using the wireless device's standard roaming handoff mechanism. Fortunately, detecting rogue access points is fairly simple through the use of software. A common method to detect rogue access points is through the use of wireless sniffing applications such as AirMagnet or NetStumbler. The latter was commonly used as the tool of war drivers, which are discussed next. As wireless networks have become ubiquitous and often a requirement, organizations have employed wireless site surveys. These surveys provide a well-defined process for the analysis and planning of wireless networks. Such site surveys are often associated with new deployments, but they are also conducted within existing wireless networks. During such surveys, looking for rogue access points is part of the process because these access points can negatively impact not just security but also quality of service of the legitimate wireless network.

War Driving

A popular pastime involves driving around with a laptop system configured to listen for open 802.1X APs announcing their service set identifier (SSID) broadcasts, which is known as *war driving*. Many websites provide central repositories for identified networks to be collected, graphed, and even generated against city maps for the convenience of others looking for open access links to the Internet. A modification of Depression-era symbols is being used to mark buildings, curbs, and other landmarks to indicate the presence of an available access point (AP) and its connection details. This so-called *war chalking* uses a set of symbols and shorthand details to provide specifics needed to connect using the AP.

Bluejacking/Bluesnarfing

Mobile devices equipped for Bluetooth short-range wireless connectivity, such as laptops, tablets, and cell phones, are subject to receiving text and message broadcast spam sent from a nearby Bluetooth-enabled transmitting device in an attack referred to as *bluejacking*. Although typically benign, attackers can use this form of attack to generate messages that appear to be from the device itself, leading users to follow obvious prompts and establish an open Bluetooth connection to the attacker's device. Once paired with the attacker's device, the user's data becomes available for unauthorized access, modification, or deletion, which is a more aggressive attack referred to as *bluesnarfing*.

> **ExamAlert**
>
> Do not confuse bluejacking and bluesnarfing. Remember that bluesnarfing is more often associated with being a more dangerous attack, which can expose or alter a user's information.

Packet Sniffing

A wireless sniffer includes a hardware or software device capable of capturing the data or packets that traverse across the wireless channel. In situations where traffic being sent across the network is unencrypted, *packet sniffing* enables the attacker to capture the data and decode it from its raw form into readable text.

WEP/WPA Attacks

Chapter 2, "Network Implementation," discussed different types of wireless networks. Recall that both Wired Equivalent Privacy (WEP) and Wi-Fi Protected Access (WPA) provide methods to encrypt wireless traffic between wireless clients and APs. After security flaws were discovered in WEP, WPA was developed to replace the now deprecated WEP. In addition, WPA2 was introduced and provided stricter security standards.

As early as 2001, researchers from Berkeley discovered and published information pertaining to the flaws within WEP. Their research suggested that the "attacks are practical to mount using only inexpensive off-the-shelf equipment." Specifically the research uncovered the following four types of attacks:

▶ Active attacks that allow new traffic to be injected based on known plain text

▶ Active attacks to decrypt the traffic by tricking the AP

▶ Passive attacks using statistical analysis that can decrypt the traffic

▶ Dictionary-building attacks that within 24 hours allow decryption of all traffic

An IV attack is one such attack on WEP using passive statistical analysis. An IV is an input to a cryptographic algorithm, which is essentially a random number. Ideally, an IV should be unique and unpredictable. An IV attack can occur when the IV is too short, predictable, or not unique. The attack on WEP was a result of an IV not long enough, which meant it had a high probability of repeating itself after only a small number of packets. Subsequent wireless encryption algorithms use not only a longer IV, but newer protocols also use a mechanism to dynamically change keys as the system is used. This combination is able to defeat the IV attack used on WEP.

> **ExamAlert**
>
> To prevent an IV attack, an IV must not be repeated with a given key and should appear random. More important, WEP should *never* be used and is deprecated.

Recall that a replay attack occurs when packets are captured, and after the information is extracted the packets are placed back on the network. Address Resolution Protocol (ARP) replay attacks are the foundation of many attacks and provide a successful means for generating new IVs. In this attack, software listens for ARP packets to replay back to the AP. When this occurs, the AP will retransmit the ARP packet along with a new IV. As this occurs over and over, the AP will continue to retransmit the same ARP packet with a new IV. From all these new IVs, the attacker can determine the WEP key.

WPA mostly uses the Temporal Key Integrity Protocol (TKIP). There are known attacks against TKIP. In most cases, these attacks do not necessarily provide access to the network but theoretically could compromise confidentiality by decrypting data in small increments. In addition, even the best security protocols and cryptographic methods are only as good as their implementation. There have been instances of viable attacks against poor implementations that would require a firmware update to patch the vulnerability. Other methods of attacking WPA require brute forcing. WPA supports both AES and RC4 algorithms. The latter is less secure and should be avoided.

WPA2 is similar to WPA, but most important, it does not use TKIP. Instead, it uses the Counter Mode Cipher Block Chaining Message Authentication Code Protocol (CCMP). CCMP provides for greater confidentiality while addressing the shortcomings of TKIP. WPA2 is still subject to both passive and active attacks. Even though a protocol may be cryptographically secure, this does not prevent, as in the case with WPA2, an attacker from using methods such as brute forcing to test passcodes. To accomplish such a goal, however, the attack would be run offline after the attacker has gathered the initial handshake packets between the AP and user during the authentication process.

WPS Attacks

Wi-Fi Protected Setup (WPS), originally known as Wi-Fi Simple Config, is an extension of the wireless standards whose purpose was to make it simple for end users to establish secure wireless home networks. Originally as Wi-Fi devices entered the mainstream, setup was complex, which often resulted in users running with default configurations. Such defaults typically left these wireless networks wide open and easy to exploit. WPS provided two certified modes of operation. The first involves the use of a PIN code, which the user enters when connecting devices. The second method requires the user to simply push a button on the AP and the connecting wireless device. In 2011, however, a major security vulnerability was exposed. In fact, the vulnerability is so severe that the solution is to turn off WPS capabilities. Via brute-force attack, the PIN could be recovered in as little as 11,000 guesses, or within several hours. In some cases, however, disabling WPS might not be enough to prevent such attacks, and a firmware upgrade will be required to completely disable the feature.

ExamAlert

Wi-Fi Protected Setup should not be used to prevent attacks. It should be disabled, at a minimum.

Near-Field Communication

Near-field communication (NFC) is a set of standards for contactless communication between devices. Although NFC is considered contactless, in most practical uses devices will establish communication by being within very close proximity or by touching them. Currently, there are varying use cases for the use of NFC. Most individuals may be familiar with NFC as a feature of their smartphone. NFC is available on most devices running the Android operating system, and recently even Apple's iPhone 6 now includes an NFC chip, albeit at launch time it is only for use with its Apple Pay technology.

NFC chips within mobile devices generate electromagnetic fields. This allows the device to communicate with other devices, or even a tag that contains specific information, which leverages the electromagnetic field as a power supply to send the information back to the device. Consider, for example, an advertisement at a bus stop embedded with a tag, which is then able to communicate with a smart device.

Given NFC's limited range, the types and practicality of attacks becomes limited by distance. Regardless, the following list highlights potential risks of NFC:

▶ **Confidentiality:** Attacks can take advantage of the risk posed by any communications methods. This includes eavesdropping. Any sensitive data must be encrypted to mitigate such concerns.

▶ **Denial of Service:** Similar to our discussion previously on jamming and interference, NFC could be subject to such disruptions, too.

▶ **Main-in-the-middle (MITM):** Theoretically, MITM attacks are possible. But again, given the limitations of proximity, such attacks present their own challenges.

▶ **Malicious Code:** As with any client device, preventing malware and user awareness are key controls.

Specific concerns about NFC that have surfaced are largely due to lenient configurations. In one example, applications of NFC may provide a function to pass information such as contacts and applications, yet no confirmation is required from the receiving end of things. In other applications, such as the pairing of devices, in the absence of any type of confirmation an attacker could easily connect and run further attacks to access the device.

Cram Quiz

Answer these questions. The answers follow the last question. If you cannot answer these questions correctly, consider reading this section again until you can.

1. What is the term given to a rogue access point in which they serve as a man in the middle from which further attacks can be carried out?

   ○ **A.** War driving

   ○ **B.** Evil twin

   ○ **C.** War twinning

   ○ **D.** Twin driving

2. Which of the following best describes packet sniffing?

   ○ **A.** Packet sniffing allows an attacker to capture and decrypt data into readable text.

   ○ **B.** Packet sniffing allows an attacker to smell which network components are transmitting sensitive data.

   ○ **C.** Packet sniffing allows an attacker to capture and decode data from its raw form into readable text.

   ○ **D.** Packet sniffing allows an attacker to encode and transmit packets to disrupt network services.

3. An initialization vector should be which of the following?

   ○ **A.** Unique and unpredictable

   ○ **B.** Unique and predictable

   ○ **C.** Repeatable and random

   ○ **D.** Repeatable and unique

Cram Quiz Answers

1. **B**. An evil twin is a rogue access point used for malicious purposes, in which the attacker is acting as a man in the middle. War driving refers to the act of traveling around looking for unsecured wireless devices, and so answer A is incorrect. Answers C and D are both incorrect.

2. **C**. Packet sniffing is best described as the process of capturing and decoding data from its raw form into readable text. Answer A is incorrect. Encryption protects against revealing information through packet sniffing. Answers B and D are also incorrect.

3. **A**. An IV should be unique and unpredictable. Answers B, C, and D are incorrect.

Explain Types of Application Attacks

▶ **Cross-site scripting**

▶ **SQL injection**

▶ **LDAP injection**

▶ **XML injection**

▶ **Directory traversal/command injection**

▶ **Buffer overflow**

▶ **Integer overflow**

▶ **Zero-day**

▶ **Cookies and attachments**

▶ **LSO (locally shared objects)**

▶ **Flash cookies**

▶ **Malicious add-ons**

▶ **Session hijacking**

▶ **Header manipulation**

▶ **Arbitrary/remote code execution**

CramSaver

If you can correctly answer these questions before going through this section, save time by skimming the Exam Alerts in this section and then completing the Cram Quiz at the end of the section.

1. Identify and explain at least two different types of code injection techniques.

2. Why should HTTP headers not be used to transport important and sensitive data?

3. What is the difference between a tracking cookie and a session cookie?

Answers

1. Common code injection techniques include XSS, SQL injection, LDAP injection, and XML injection. XSS involves including client-side script on a website for malicious purpose to exploit a vulnerability. SQL, LDAP, and XML injection, like XSS, are similar in that they piggyback malicious code through an input field in the application. SQL injection is targeted at databases, LDAP injection at directories, and XML injection at XML documents and code.

> **2.** HTTP headers can easily be manipulated through the use of proxy software. Because headers originate at the client, the end user can modify the data.
>
> **3.** A tracking cookie is a particular type of permanent cookie that sticks around. Spyware, for example, would likely use tracking cookies. Session cookies, in contrast, stay around only for that particular visit to a website.

Browser Threats

The evolution of web network applications, Web 2.0 interactive interfaces, and other browser-based secure and anonymous-access resources available via the HTTP and HTTPS protocols presents an "anytime/anywhere" approach to enterprise network resource availability. As more applications are migrated into the browser, attackers have an increasingly large attack surface area for interception and interaction with user input and for directed attacks against web-based resources. The global nature of the Internet enables attackers to place web-based traps in countries of convenience, where law enforcement efforts are complicated by international legal variance.

ExamAlert

Maintaining operating system, application, and add-on updates helps to reduce the threat posed by many browser-based attack forms. When possible, restricting automatic code execution of JavaScript or ActiveX controls and cookie generation can also strengthen the client's browser security stance.

Browser-based vulnerabilities you should know for the exam include the following:

▶ **Session hijacking:** Because browsers access resources on a remote server using a predefined port (80 for HTTP or 443 for HTTPS), browser traffic is easily identifiable by an attacker who may elect to hijack legitimate user credentials and session data for unauthorized access to secured resources. Although Secure Sockets Layer (SSL) traffic is encrypted between endpoints, an attacker who crafts a web proxy with SSL can allow a user to connect securely to this proxy system and then establish a secured link from the proxy to the user's intended resource, capturing plain-text data transport on the proxy system even though the user receives all appropriate responses for a secured connection.

▶ **Malicious add-ons:** Active content within websites offers an attractive attack space for aggressors, who might craft special "drivers" required for content access that are in fact Trojans or other forms of malware. Other attackers craft malware to take advantage of unpatched add-ons to directly inject code or gain access to a user's system when a vulnerable browser is directed to an infected website.

▶ **Buffer overflows:** Like desktop- and system-based applications, many web browser applications offer an attacker a mechanism for providing input in the form of a crafted uniform resource locator (URL) value. By extending the input values beyond the memory space limitations of the expected input values, an attacker can inject code into adjacent memory space to allow execution of arbitrary code on the web server. Buffer over-flows are discussed further later in this chapter.

Code Injections

Application developers and security professionals need to be aware of the different types of threats from malicious code. Using malicious *code injection*, attackers can perform a variety of attacks on systems. Proper input validation is one primary means of preventing such attacks. These attacks can result in the modification or theft of data. Examples of code injection include the following:

▶ **Cross-Site scripting (XSS):** By placing malicious client-side script on a website, an attacker can cause an unknowing browser user to conduct unauthorized access activities, expose confidential data, and provide logging of successful attacks back to the attacker without the user being aware of her participation. XSS vulnerabilities can be used to hijack the user's session or to cause the user accessing malware-tainted Site A to unknowingly attack Site B on behalf of the attacker who planted code on Site A.

▶ **SQL injection:** Inserts malicious code into strings, which are later passed to a database server. The SQL server then parses and executes this code.

▶ **LDAP injection:** Some websites perform LDAP queries based on data provided by the end user. LDAP injection involves changing the LDAP input so that the web app runs with escalated privileges.

▶ **XML injection:** Uses malicious code to compromise XML applications, typically web services. XML injection attempts to insert malicious content into the structure of an XML message to alter the logic of the targeted application.

Directory Traversal

In most instances, surfing the Web presents the users with web pages filled with images and text. Behind these pages, however, is a system of files and directories. Directory traversal allows one to navigate the directories. In most cases, this directory structure is restricted; however, an attack using *directory traversal* enables the attacker to gain access to otherwise restricted files and directories.

As with code injection, directory traversal vulnerabilities are a result of poor input validation. The potential for these types of attacks requires the developers to focus on building secure websites and applications.

Header Manipulation

HTTP headers are control data used between the web browser and web server. In most cases, websites and applications do not rely on the headers for important data, yet it was a common practice in the past, and it is still used across many less-secure applications and sites. In cases where a developer chooses to inspect and use the incoming headers, it is important to note that the headers originate at the client. As a result, these headers could easily be modified by the user using freely available proxy software.

Zero-Day

A *zero-day* (or zero-hour or day zero) *attack* or threat is a computer threat that tries to exploit computer application vulnerabilities that are unknown to others or the software developer, also called *zero-day vulnerabilities*. Zero-day exploits (actual software that uses a security hole to carry out an attack) are used or shared by attackers before the developer of the target software knows about the vulnerability.

A zero-day attack is more dire and differs from other attacks and vulnerabilities. Most attacks on vulnerable systems involve known vulnerabilities. These include vulnerabilities known by developers, but for which a patch has not been issued. In most cases, however, attacks target known vulnerabilities for which there is a fix or a control but that is not implemented. In the case of zero-day attacks, the software developer has not even had a chance to distribute a fix for his software.

ExamAlert

Remember that zero-day vulnerabilities do not have a patch yet available. Keep this in mind when evaluating techniques to protect your organization. Effective security policies, training, and mitigating controls are more effective, even compared to the most aggressive patch management strategies, when it comes to zero-day exploits.

Buffer Overflows

Buffer overflows cause disruption of service and lost data. This condition occurs when the data presented to an application or service exceeds the storage-space allocation that has been reserved in memory for that application or service. Poor application design might allow the input of 100 characters into a field linked to a variable only capable of holding 50 characters. As a result, the application does not know how to handle the extra data and becomes unstable. The overflow portion of the input data must be discarded or somehow handled by the application; otherwise, it could create undesirable results. Because no check is in place to screen out bad requests, the extra data overwrites some portions of memory used by other applications and causes failures and crashes. A buffer overflow can result in the following:

▶ Overwriting of data or memory storage.

▶ A denial of service due to overloading the input buffer's ability to cope with the additional data.

▶ The originator can execute arbitrary code, often at a privileged level.

Services running on Internet-connected computers present an opportunity for compromise using privilege escalation. Some services require special privileges for their operation. A programming error could allow an attacker to obtain special privileges. In this situation, two possible types of privilege escalation exist: a programming error that enables a user to gain additional privileges after successful authentication, and a user gaining privileges with no authentication.

In the case of buffer overflows, good quality assurance and secure programming practices could thwart this type of attack. Currently, the most effective way to prevent an attacker from exploiting software is to keep the manufacturer's latest patches and service packs applied and to monitor the Web for newly discovered vulnerabilities.

Integer Overflows

An *integer overflow* is closely related to a buffer overflow. It is specific to whole numbers, though, which are known as *integers*. For example, 12 is an integer, but not 12.1. Programs that do not carefully account for integer overflows can result in undesirable behaviors and consequences. Imagine a typical vehicle odometer. Most odometers support only six digits, which go to 999,999 miles or kilometers. Many vehicles are lucky to see 200,000 miles; so, what happens if one drives 1 million miles? The odometer suffers from an integer overflow and will now show that 0 miles have been driven! Put another way, a program designed to hold an integer of 8 bits could support a number up to 255, and would look like the following in binary: 11111111. The number 256 requires an extra bit and would be 100000000. If such a program designed to support only 8 bits accepted the decimal number of 256, it may interpret 256 as 0 (only accepting the last 8 bits) or as 128 (only accepting the first 8 bits).

Cookies

To overcome the limitations of a stateful connection when scaled to global website deployments, the Netscape Corporation created a technology using temporary files stored in the client's browser cache to maintain settings across multiple pages, servers, or sites. These small files are known as *cookies*. They can be used to maintain data such as user settings between visits to the same site on multiple days or to track user browsing habits, such as those used by sites hosting DoubleClick banner advertisements.

Many sites require that browsing clients be configured to accept cookies to store information such as configuration settings or shopping cart data for electronic commerce (e-commerce) sites. Cookies can be used to track information such as the name and IP address of the client system and the operating system and browser client being used. Additional information includes the name of the target and previous URLs, along with any specific settings set within the cookie by the host website.

ExamAlert

Although cookies generally provide benefits to the end users, spyware would be most likely to use a tracking cookie. A *tracking cookie* is a particular type of permanent cookie that sticks around, whereas a *session cookie* stays around only for that particular visit to a website.

If cookies are accessed across many sites, they may be used to track the user's browsing habits and present the user with targeted advertising or content. Many users believe this is a violation of their privacy.

Cookies can also be used to store session settings across multiple actual connections to a web server. This proves helpful when connecting to a distributed server farm, where each page access might be handled by a separate physical server, preventing the use of session variables to maintain details from one page to another.

This is useful in electronic commerce sites, where a shopping cart application might add items from multiple pages to a total invoice before being transferred to a billing application. These cookies are also useful to provide custom user configuration settings on subsequent entries to web portals whose content is presented in a dynamic manner.

The danger to maintaining session information is that sites might access cookies stored in the browser's cache that might contain details on the user's e-commerce shopping habits, along with many user details that could possibly include sensitive information identifying the user or allowing access to secured sites.

> **Note**
>
> Clients should regularly clear their browser cookie caches to avoid exposing long-term browsing habits in this way. Where possible, client browsers can also be configured to block third-party cookies, although many online commerce sites require this functionality for their operation.

Flash cookies, as they are commonly known, are actually *local shared objects* (LSO). The enabling software behind LSOs is Adobe Flash. These objects are simply data files that can be created on a client computer, and like cookies, they help enhance one's experience on the web or provide another useful function. Unlike cookies, which store data in plain text only, LSOs are capable of more complex data stores. These LSOs are commonly used to enhance the authentication experience for banking clients and provide an added level of security. In fact, the risk-based authentication schemes used by these sites is enabled through the use of these LSOs to better understand the client and to create a profile used to evaluate a risk score. At one point, these LSOs were preferred to cookies, as many users were disabling cookies, yet practically every computer had Flash installed. Just like browser configuration settings provide control for cookies, LSOs can also be controlled or even disabled through the Flash security settings. Most concerns about these Flash cookies have largely centered on privacy issues.

Arbitrary/Remote Code Execution

Arbitrary code execution is the process to describe an attacker's ability to execute programs and commands on the attacked machine. Exploits are designed to attack bugs in software that provide such methods for these commands to be run. From a vulnerability standpoint, these types of bugs are significant because they allow the attacker to overtake a particular process. Such capability increases the likelihood that the attacker could then completely take control of the client system. A system vulnerable to such code execution is highly susceptible to malware, which would not require the owner's consent. Rather, the malware can be run arbitrarily (that is, without permission and without restriction). This problem is compounded with *remote code execution*. Specifically, such code could actually be run across networks and even the Internet. Preventing such attacks begins with secure coding practices. Unfortunately, end users are sometimes at the mercy of their software vendors. Therefore, it is important that end users keep their systems patched, and that organization pay particular attention to the types of software vulnerabilities. Often, arbitrary remote code execution vulnerabilities should be prioritized in the remediation process.

Cram Quiz

Answer these questions. The answers follow the last question. If you cannot answer these questions correctly, consider reading this section again until you can.

1. Spyware is most likely to use which one of the following types of cookies?

   - ○ **A.** Session
   - ○ **B.** Transport
   - ○ **C.** Tracking
   - ○ **D.** Poisonous

2. Which of the following types of attacks can result from the length of variables not being properly checked in the code of a program?

   - ○ **A.** Buffer overflow
   - ○ **B.** Replay
   - ○ **C.** Spoofing
   - ○ **D.** Denial of service

3. Which one of the following is a best practice to prevent code injection attacks?

   - ○ **A.** Session cookies
   - ○ **B.** Input validation
   - ○ **C.** Implementing the latest security patches
   - ○ **D.** Using unbound variables

Cram Quiz Answers

1. **C.** Whereas cookies generally provide benefits to the end users, spyware would be most likely to use a tracking cookie. A tracking cookie is a particular type of permanent cookie that stays around, whereas a session cookie stays around only for the particular visit to a website. Therefore, answer A is incorrect. Answers B and D are not types of cookies and are incorrect.

2. **A.** Buffer overflows result from programming flaws that allow for too much data to be sent. When the program does not know what to do with all this data, it crashes, leaving the machine in a state of vulnerability. Answer B is incorrect because a replay attack records and replays previously sent valid messages. Answer C is incorrect because spoofing involves modifying the source address of traffic or the source of information. Answer D is incorrect because the purpose of a DoS attack is to deny the use of resources or services to legitimate users.

3. **B**. Input validation is the one of the most important countermeasures to prevent code injection attacks. Answer A is incorrect because session cookies pertain to maintaining state within a visit to a website. Answer C is incorrect. Although making sure that systems are patched is a good practice, it is not specifically a best practice to prevent code injection attacks. Answer D is incorrect because proper input validation to prevent code injection would rely on bound variables.

What Next?

If you want more practice on this chapter's exam objectives before you move on, remember that you can access all the Cram Quiz questions on the CD. You can also create a custom exam by objective with the practice exam software. Note any objective that you struggle with and go to the material that covers that objective in this chapter.

CHAPTER 6

Deterrents

This chapter covers the following official CompTIA Security+ SY0-401 exam objectives:

▶ Analyze a scenario and select the appropriate type of mitigation and deterrent techniques

▶ Given a scenario, use appropriate tools and techniques to discover security threats and vulnerabilities

▶ Explain the proper use of penetration testing versus vulnerability scanning

(For more information on the official CompTIA Security+ exam topics, see the "About the CompTIA Security+ SY0-401 Exam" section in the Introduction.)

In most situations, it is not possible, nor even prudent, to try to completely eliminate risks. Remember that risk is typically a result of some type of benefit gained. Although you might be able to eliminate the risk of being involved in a vehicle accident, this would mean that you never get inside a vehicle. Of course, an important benefit is derived as a result, and thus a tradeoff: Even deciding instead to walk everywhere brings its own risks. Just as one who drives a vehicle buys insurance and wears a seatbelt, organizations look to reduce or mitigate risks when it comes to information security.

Two commonly used assessment methodologies are vulnerability scanning and penetration testing. Both provide outputs that assist with the detection of and appropriate response to weaknesses.

Analyze a Scenario and Select the Appropriate Type of Mitigation and Deterrent Techniques

▶ **Monitoring system logs**

▶ **Hardening**

▶ **Network security**

▶ **Security posture**

▶ **Reporting**

▶ **Detection controls versus prevention controls**

CramSaver

If you can correctly answer these questions before going through this section, save time by skimming the Exam Alerts in this section and then completing the Cram Quiz at the end of the section.

1. Describe several deterrents used to prevent unauthorized physical access.

2. Aside from the description of an event, what other fields are typical within a system's event log?

3. What are examples of some security deterrents to prevent unauthorized access by hardening a system?

Answers

1. Deterrents do not necessarily have to be designed to stop unauthorized access. As the name implies, they need to help deter the access. That is, the potential attacker might think twice about the attempt, especially because even an attacker considers the concept of risk/reward. Common examples include a sign indicating the property is alarmed or protected by a dog. Lighting, locks, dogs, video surveillance, fencing, cleared zones around the perimeter, and even life-sized cutouts of law enforcement officers can make a location appear less inviting to the potential attacker.

2. Although the exact taxonomy might vary by vendor, the various fields you are likely to find within an event log include the type of event (for example, error, warning), the time the event occurred, the system from which the event occurred, and an event ID.

3. Often, the purpose of a deterrent is to stop an event from happening in the first place. Common examples include disabling unnecessary services, disabling unnecessary accounts, and using adequate password protection.

Monitoring System Logs

Almost every modern system can generate systems logs. These logs contain
all the details pertaining to the operation of the particular system. This
includes operating systems, network devices, and applications. As a result, the
data contained within these files may be more relevant to specific individuals
responsible for specific functions within an organization.

The amount of log data generated can be overwhelming. Fortunately,
automated tools are also available to collect and correlate events across all
these different logs. Regardless, these systems still need proper configuration.
This includes understanding internal policies, in addition to who needs
access to what information. To better understand the data being collected,
it is helpful to establish baselines of what is normal, and depending on the
business, what is considered normal could vary. For example, perhaps one
particular system is accessed only biannually. On a daily basis, it is not normal
for there to be access, but it is normal on a biannual basis. Perhaps it is not
typical that anyone access specific systems after-hours. In this example, alerts
could easily be generated to bring these particular events to the attention of
security personnel. Broadly, system logs help in several ways:

▶ Troubleshooting

▶ Security enforcement and response

▶ Auditing

The methodology to perform system monitoring on each system depends on
the individual operating environment. In Microsoft operating systems, the
Event Viewer records activities in the System event log. Event Viewer enables
you to view certain events that occur on the system. Event Viewer maintains
various log files. These usually include specific logs for system events, security-
related events, application events, in addition to a log to collect forwarded
events sent to the system by another computer.

ExamAlert

The Security log records security events and is available for view only to
administrators. For security events to be monitored, you must enable auditing.

Unlike the Security log, the Application and System logs are available to all
users to view. You can use the Application log to tell how well an application
is running. The System log shows events that occur on the individual

system. You can configure settings such as the size of the file and the filtering of events. Event logging is used for troubleshooting or for notifying administrators of unusual circumstances. It is important to be sure that you have the log file size set properly, that the size is monitored, and that the logs are periodically archived and cleared. Consider carefully where you store log files to make sure that intruders do not have access to them. By doing so, you eliminate the ability for intruders to cover their tracks. Table 6.1 lists the fields and definitions of Windows events.

Table 6.1   Windows Events

Field Name	Field Description
Type	The type of the event, such as error, warning, or information
Time	The date and time of the local computer at which the event occurred
Computer	The computer on which the event occurred
Provider Type	The type of event that generated the event, such as a Windows event log
Provider Name	The name of the event, such as Application or Security
Source	The application that logged the event, such as MSSQL Server
Event ID	The Windows event number
Description	The description of the event

Of these fields, it is important to note the Event ID and the Description Text fields. The event ID is the easiest way to research the event in the Microsoft Knowledge Base, and the description text usually explains what happened in simple language.

There are also built-in and downloadable tools in other operating systems, such as iStat nano for OS X systems. iStat nano is a system monitor widget that enables you to view statistics about the system, such as CPU usage, memory usage, hard drive space, bandwidth usage, temperatures, fan speeds, battery usage, uptime, and the top five processes. In addition, third-party programs are available that provide network health monitoring. These programs can monitor the entire network and include devices such as modems, printers, routers, switches, and hubs.

To monitor the health of all systems, you install agents on the machines and then monitor the agents from a central location. For example, Simple Network Management Protocol (SNMP) is an application layer protocol whose purpose is to collect statistics from TCP/IP devices.

The nuances of system logging and monitoring are varied and detailed, but system logs are broadly classified as follows:

▶ **System event logs:** These logs record the events that occur across the system and most notably are related to the operating system. Keep in mind that these logs are particular to the system, and not to the user interacting with the system. Examples include hardware failures, drivers not loading properly, and issues related to performance.

▶ **Audit logs:** Audit logs help ensure proper process and provide a useful record for auditors. Such logs provide relevant security information, such as successful and unsuccessful login attempts, creation and deletion of users, deletion of log data, user privilege modification, and file access. These logs also provide accountability and, in the case of an incident, a record of what occurred for forensics and recovery purposes.

▶ **Security logs:** Security logs contain the events specific to systems and application security. Security solutions deployed within the network are a major source of such logs. This includes antimalware software, intrusion-detection systems, remote-access software, vulnerability management software, authentication servers, network quarantine systems, routers, and firewalls.

▶ **Access logs:** These logs provide information about requests and connections between systems. This could include connections between a Lightweight Directory Access Protocol (LDAP) client to a directory server, which might include details such as the IP address and records related to the binding operation. Web servers are also another common source of access logs. For example, a web server will log access to each resource, such as a page or image. Included within the log entry will be details such as IP address, browser, operating system, the referring page, and a date and time stamp.

ExamAlert

It is important you understand system logs are varied. Be able to recognize event, audit, security, and access logs. In addition, understand when each would be used given specific scenarios.

Hardening

In security terms, *hardening* a system refers to reducing its security exposure and strengthening its defenses against unauthorized access attempts and other forms of malicious attention. Common methods for hardening a system include the following:

- ▶ Disable unnecessary services

- ▶ Protect management interfaces

- ▶ Protect passwords

- ▶ Disable unnecessary accounts

A "soft" system is one that is installed with default configurations or unnecessary services, or one that is not maintained to include emerging security updates. There is no such thing as a "completely safe" system, so the process of hardening reflects attention to security thresholds.

Systems installed in default configurations often include many unnecessary services that are configured automatically. These provide many potential avenues for unauthorized access to a system or network. Many services have known vulnerabilities that require specific action to make them more secure or ones that might just impair system function by causing additional processing overhead. Default configurations also allow for unauthorized access and exploitation. For example, a denial-of-service (DoS) attack against an unneeded web service is one way a nonessential service could potentially cause problems for an otherwise functional system.

Common default-configuration exploits include both services such as anonymous-access FTP servers and network protocols such as the SNMP.

ExamAlert

When presented with a scenario on the exam, you might be tempted to keep all services enabled to cover all requirements. Be wary of this option; it might cause the installation of unnecessary services or protocols.

Many vendors provide regular updates for installed products, managed through automated deployment tools or by manual update procedures carried out by a system user. Regular maintenance is required to meet emerging security threats, whether applying an updated RPM (Red Hat Package Manager, a file format used to distribute Linux applications and update packages) by hand or through fully automated "call home for updates" options like those found in many commercial operating systems and applications.

Because of the emergence of blended-threat malware, which targets multiple vulnerabilities within a single attack, all major operating systems and application solutions must be considered in system hardening plans. Automated reverse-engineering of newly released patches has significantly reduced the time from an update's initial release until its first exploits are seen in the wild, down from months to hours before unpatched applications can be targeted.

Types of updates you should be familiar with include the following:

▶ **Hotfixes:** Typically, small and specific-purpose updates that alter the behavior of installed applications in a limited manner. These are the most common type of update.

▶ **Service packs:** Major revisions of functionality or service operation in an installed application. Service packs are the least common type of update, often requiring extensive testing to ensure against service failure in integrated network environments before application. Service packs are usually cumulative, including all prior service packs, hotfixes, and patches.

▶ **Patches:** Like hotfixes, patches are usually focused updates that affect installed applications. Patches are generally used to add new functionality, update existing code operation, or to extend existing application capabilities.

Particular attention should be given to management interfaces and applications. Most hardware and software security solutions provide some type of portal or method to interact with and configure the system. In some cases, it might be wise to limit access to only an authorized user who is physically present at the specific system. In lieu of this, additional controls should be put in place, such as making sure that all communication is encrypted, strong authentication is used, and only the necessary personnel have access to the systems.

The latter two examples should be considered not only for management interfaces but also for the hardening of systems in general. Proper password protection is critical. This is often an easy exploit for attackers to mount an attack. Default passwords for systems are easily available. Consider, for example, vendor-supplied default logon/password combinations, such as the Oracle DB default admin: scott/tiger. Many users are aware of the default password phenomenon through the use of home wireless access points in which each specific device shipped with the same username and password. In addition to immediately changing all default passwords, complex passwords or some sort of strong authentication should be used. Complex passwords contain at least eight characters and consist of mix-cased letters, numbers, and symbols.

Finally, just as unnecessary services should be disabled, so should unnecessary accounts. Some systems include default accounts, which provide an attacker with another option for entry. A more common example is users and administrators who are no longer with the organization or no longer require access to a particular system. Often, these accounts are left in place. Such accounts should be disabled immediately.

> **ExamAlert**
>
> System hardening comes down to several key areas. These include disabling unnecessary services and accounts, protecting management interfaces, and changing default passwords.

Network Security

In addition to ensuring individual systems are hardened, care should be given to mitigating risk from a network security standpoint as well. Common methods include the following:

- ▶ Disabling unused interfaces and unused applications service ports
- ▶ Protecting management interfaces
- ▶ MAC limiting and filtering
- ▶ Rogue machine detection
- ▶ 802.1X

Unnecessary services, discussed earlier, use logical ports on a system. A part of ensuring that unnecessary services are disabled is to prevent access via the assigned ports. Just as these unnecessary logical ports or services should be disabled, so should physical ports that are not required. Even in the case of ports that are needed, these should still be closely monitored and should possibly have additional layers of controls in place to prevent improper use.

Each device on the network has a MAC address that identifies the network interface. A common control, albeit one that should not be solely relied on to prevent rogue machine access, is MAC limiting and filtering. This control provides further ability to limit what can access a network or service. Wireless access points, for example, can easily be configured to accept connections from only specific MAC addresses. The reason that additional measures should be in place is that MAC addresses can easily be spoofed. Although it is a worthy control to prevent average users from bringing in their own devices, it is not likely to prevent an attacker who wants to gain access.

Devices that need to connect to a network can also be controlled via the IEEE standard 802.1X. This should not be confused with 802.11. The former provides standards for port-based access control, whereas 802.11 is specific to wireless technology. 802.1X provides a method for authenticating a device to another system via an authentication server. The standard essentially allows various authentication methods such as RADIUS, digital certificates, and one-time password devices to be used.

Security Posture

A *security posture* includes an organization's overall plan for protecting itself against threats. This should also include the activities required for the ongoing monitoring and reaction required of security incidents.

An overall approach is to set baseline standards. To establish effective security baselines, enterprise network security management requires a measure of commonality between systems. Mandatory settings, standard application suites, and initial setup configuration details all factor into the security stance of an enterprise network.

Types of configuration settings you should be familiar with include the following:

- ▶ **Group policies:** Collections of configuration settings applied to a system based on computer or user group membership, which might influence the level, type, and extent of access provided.

- ▶ **Security templates:** Sets of configurations that reflect a particular role or standard established through industry standards or within an organization, assigned to fulfill a particular purpose. Examples include a "minimum-access" configuration template assigned to limited-access kiosk systems, whereas a "high-security" template could be assigned to systems requiring more stringent logon and access control mechanisms.

▶ **Configuration baselines:** Many industries must meet specific criteria, established as a baseline measure of security. An example of this is the healthcare industry, which has a lengthy set of requirements for information technology specified in the Health Insurance Portability and Accountability Act (HIPAA) security standards. Unless the mandated security baseline is met, penalties and fines could be assessed. Security baselines are often established by governmental mandate, regulatory bodies, or industry representatives, such as the Payment Card Industry (PCI) requirements established by the credit card industry for businesses collecting and transacting credit information.

To maintain a strong security posture, organizations should also implement plans for continuous security monitoring and remediation. It is important that security monitoring is not just a one-time or isolated event. It needs to be conducted on an ongoing basis. Furthermore, a plan for ongoing security monitoring actually needs to be monitored. That is, it should not just be a system of systematic logging and monitoring. Instead, mechanisms and procedures need to be in place to ensure that personnel are actively looking at what is taking place and that proper alerts and notifications are set up.

Finally, organizations should have a plan for response and remediation. Although the hope is that the controls in place should prevent a breach or damaging attack, this is not always the case. This is especially evident in recent news, in which organizations are breached despite the many controls they had in place. Many of these instances provide ideal case studies in remediation. This includes, for example, how quickly the issue was identified and controlled, how quickly the damage was repaired, and even how effectively the organization dealt with the public and their customers and clients.

Reporting

Proper and effective reporting is critical to the overall health and security of an organization. The use of reporting should be dictated by a policy based on the overall risk of the infrastructure and data. This will help define what types of reports are required, the frequency of the reports, and how often they are examined. Adequate reporting should also include the following mechanisms:

▶ **Alarms:** The purpose of an alarm is to report a critical event that typically requires some type of immediate response. Consider the common analogy of a bank. Each time the safe is accessed might be part of a report that does not necessitate an alarm; however, a broken window after-hours is cause for alarm, and an immediate response can take place.

▶ **Alerts:** An alert is similar to an alarm, but it is less critical and likely
does not require an immediate response. Several failed logon attempts,
for example, would likely generate an alert. This alert, at a minimum,
should generate a log file, but depending on the situation, it could
also be a notification of some sort to an administrator. Alerts might be
used in conjunction with an alarm. For example, several alerts might
be correlated together to form a condition that would deem an alarm
necessary.

▶ **Trends:** Identifying and understanding trends is vital to detecting and
responding to incidents. Furthermore, trends also help prevent the
unnecessary response to something that initially might seem warranted
but is actually not. Trends become more apparent based on the time-
frame. For example, over a week period, there might be an abnormal
activity on Sunday. Yet, over a month period, it becomes evident that this
activity occurs every Sunday, perhaps due to a weekly processing event.

Detection Controls Versus Prevention Controls

Consider for a moment the importance of having both detection controls
and prevention controls. In a perfect world, we would only need prevention
controls. Unfortunately, not all malicious activity can be prevented. As a
result, it is important that detection controls are part of one's layered security
approach. Using our bank analogy from before, even the best protected banks
in the world use both. In addition to the locks, bars, and security signs, the
bank probably has various other detection controls, such as motion detectors.

As you might have already guessed, some controls can be both detection
controls and preventive controls. A camera (if visible or advertised), for
example, not only serves as a detection control (if actively monitored), but
it also serves as a deterrent to a would-be attacker, thus being preventive.
Although cameras can serve as a deterrent, without active monitoring by a
security guard they are likely only useful for later analysis. Security guards,
however, easily serve as both a preventive and detective control. In addition, a
security guard can initiate an immediate response to an incident.

Information security intrusions might be physical, such as in the case of an
intrusion into a data center. In addition, intrusions can occur through the
more common means of logical access. An intrusion includes any unauthorized
resource access attempt within a secured network. Although it is possible for
human monitoring to identify real-time intrusion events within small, tightly
controlled networks, it is more likely that a human administrator monitors

alerts and notifications generated by intrusion-detection systems (IDS). These software and hardware agents monitor network traffic for patterns that might indicate an attempt at intrusion, called an *attack signature*, or might monitor server-side logs for improper activity or unauthorized access.

Both passive and active forms of IDS exist:

▶ A passive IDS solution is intended to detect an intrusion, log the event, and potentially raise some form of alert.

▶ An active IDS solution acts to terminate or deny an intrusion attempt by changing firewall or IPsec policy settings automatically before logging the event and raising an alert for human operators.

Both active and passive IDSs must first identify an intrusion before altering the network configuration (in an active system), logging the event, and raising an alert.

In contrast, an intrusion-prevention system (IPS) is intended to provide direct protection against identified attacks. Whereas a detection system attempts to identify unauthorized access attempts and generate alerts, a prevention system will provide direct protection against identified attacks. For example, an IPS solution might be configured to automatically drop connections from a range of IP addresses during a DoS attack.

Consider a video camera versus a security guard. Just as a system for intrusion detection will identify that something wrong is occurring, a monitored video camera will also detect an anomaly or attempt to break into a physical location. Once detected, the appropriate response can be considered. In contrast, a security guard, like an IPS, can provide direct protection. Moreover, a security guard serves as a preventive control, deterring would-be attackers.

Analyze a Scenario and Select the
Appropriate Type of Mitigation and
Deterrent Techniques

CramQuiz

Cram Quiz

Answer these questions. The answers follow the last question. If you cannot answer these questions correctly, consider reading this section again until you can.

1. To harden a system, which one of the following is a critical step?

   ○ **A.** Isolate the system in a below-freezing environment

   ○ **B.** Disable all unnecessary ports and services

   ○ **C.** Disable the WWW service

   ○ **D.** Isolate the system physically from other critical systems

2. Which one of the following passwords is the most complex?

   ○ **A.** @nn1e

   ○ **B.** Encryption1

   ○ **C.** 8!m1cT85

   ○ **D.** M!X@199

3. Which one of the following best provides an example of detective controls versus prevention controls?

   ○ **A.** IDS/camera versus IPS/guard

   ○ **B.** IDS/IPS versus Camera/guard

   ○ **C.** IPS/camera versus IDS/guard

   ○ **D.** IPS versus guard

Cram Quiz Answers

1. **B**. One of the most critical steps with regard to system hardening includes disabling unnecessary ports and services. Answer A is incorrect because keeping systems in below-freezing environments is not considered an approach to system hardening, nor is it even good for the systems. Answer C is incorrect because although the web service might be an unnecessary port, it is not considered unnecessary if the system is a web server. Answer D is also incorrect because doing such is not a generally accepted critical step for system hardening.

2. **C**. This password is at least eight characters and contains a combination of mix-cased characters, numbers, and symbols. Answer B is incorrect because it does not contain a special character, despite being over eight characters long. In addition, it includes a word found in a dictionary. Answers A and D are also incorrect. These do not contain eight characters or use mix-cased letters.

3. **A**. Both IDS and a camera are examples of detective controls, whereas IPS and a guard are examples of prevention controls. Answers B, C, and D are incorrect because they do not properly align the detective control against the prevention control.

Given a Scenario, Use Appropriate Tools and Techniques to Discover Security Threats and Vulnerabilities

▶ **Interpret results of security assessment tools**

▶ **Tools**

▶ **Risk calculations**

▶ **Assessment types**

▶ **Assessment technique**

CramSaver

If you can correctly answer these questions before going through this section, save time by skimming the Exam Alerts in this section and then completing the Cram Quiz at the end of the section.

1. A plethora of software provides automatic scanning features to help identify vulnerabilities, which sometimes includes built-in knowledge about the vulnerabilities. Why is it still important to properly interpret the results?

2. Describe a "risky" situation in which you engage, and discuss the process of risk calculation that you might or might not consciously take. Consider threats, vulnerabilities, likelihood, and even how you might mitigate such risks.

Answers

1. Vulnerabilities need to be considered with an overall structure of risk. Assets being protected vary by organization. In addition, threats and the likelihood of the realization of those threats differ by organization. Finally, vulnerabilities must be considered within the overall goals of the organization. As a result, a vulnerability that correlates to a high risk at one place might be low at another.

2. Every day, we engage in various activities that involve some level of risk. These could include such activities from walking to work to engaging in extreme sports. In most of these situations, we engage in them because they provide some type of value or pleasure. In most cases, however, we consider the unique circumstances and take steps to mitigate the risks.

Interpret Results of Security Assessment Tools

Security assessment tools are specialized systems used to test systems for known vulnerabilities, misconfigurations, bugs, or weaknesses. The output of these tools requires careful interpretation. In many cases, several factors need to be considered. The interpretation of the results typically leads to one of three things:

▶ Doing nothing, either because it is a false positive or because no significant risk is presented to the organization

▶ Fixing or eliminating the vulnerability or security gap

▶ Accepting the security gap but implementing mitigating controls

Tools

There are a number of tools that you can use to identify vulnerabilities and that are part of a complete vulnerability management program. These include vulnerability scanners, honeypots, and honeynets. Other tools include protocol analyzers and sniffers, which were introduced in Chapter 2, "Network Implementation."

Protocol Analyzer

Some operating systems have built-in protocol analyzers. The purpose of the discussion in this chapter is to show how you can use them to detect security-related anomalies. Windows Server operating systems come with a protocol analyzer called Microsoft Message Analyzer. In the Unix environment, many administrators use the tools that come with the core operating system, such as ps and vmstat. Oracle Solaris has a popular utility called *iostat* that provides good information about I/O performance. You can also use other third-party programs, such as Wireshark, for network monitoring.

A sniffer and protocol analyzer are generally accepted as one and the same. As software packages continue to add features, the lines between the two blur. Although the two are considered synonymous, a sniffer can be considered as a tool designed to "sniff" the network capturing packets. In the simplest sense, a sniffer relies on the user to conduct further analysis and interpretation. In contrast, the protocol analyzer can take those packets and provide further details and context abound the captured packets.

> **Note**
>
> A protocol analyzer is used to capture network traffic and generate statistics for creating reports. When the packets have been captured, you can view the information.

Vulnerability Scanner

Another common tool is the vulnerability scanner. A *vulnerability scanner* is a software utility that scans a range of IP addresses, testing for the presence of known vulnerabilities in software configuration and accessible services. A traditional vulnerability scanner relies on a database of known vulnerabilities. These automated tools are directed at a targeted system or systems. Unlike a system that tests for open ports, which only test for the availability of services, vulnerability scanners may check for the particular version or patch level of a service to determine its level of vulnerability.

Upon careful examination of the output of vulnerability scans, it is recommended to identify all the false positives and then focus on what's left. Keep in mind that a vulnerability does not necessarily indicate something bad or something that needs to be immediately remediated or even remediated at all. Using an analogy, consider a home as a subject for a vulnerability assessment. A broken dead-bolt lock certainly seems like a vulnerability. Ideally, this might be replaced; however, in some parts of the world, it is common that nobody locks their doors anyway. A smashed window is a vulnerability as well. In some cases, it might make sense to only mitigate this by covering it with plastic to protect against the elements. Even a perfectly functioning window by itself is a vulnerability! The benefit that that window provides typically outweighs the other option of living without windows. Of course, this all depends on what one is trying to protect and protect against.

> **Note**
>
> Within U.S. governmental agencies, vulnerability may be discussed using the Open Vulnerability Assessment Language (OVAL) sponsored by the Department of Homeland Security's National Cyber Security Division (NCSD). OVAL is intended as an international language for representing vulnerability information using a Extensible Markup Language (XML) schema for expression, allowing tools to be developed to test for identified vulnerabilities in the OVAL repository.

As you can see in the previous analogy, there isn't necessarily a quick method for determining risk based on the output of a vulnerability scanner. The relevancy to the business, tradeoffs, and identified threats and likelihoods all need to be considered to accurately interpret the results of a vulnerability scanner.

Honeypots

Honeypots are often used to identify the level of aggressive attention directed at a network and to study and learn from an attacker's common methods of attack. *Honeypots* are systems configured to simulate one or more services within an organization's network and left exposed to network access. When attackers access a honeypot system, their activities are logged and monitored by other processes so that the attacker's actions and methods can be later reviewed in detail, while the honeypot distracts the attacker from valid network resources. Honeypots might be simple targets exposed for identification of vulnerability exposure, or they might interact with the attacker to extend access time and allow tracking and logging of an attacker's activities to build better attack profile data.

A collection of honeypots is known as a *honeynet*. These honeynets are interconnected honeypots to create functional-appearing networks that can be used to study an attacker's behavior within the network. Honeynets make use of specialized software agents to create normal-seeming network traffic. Honeynets and honeypots can be used to distract attackers from valid network content, to study the attacker's methods, and to provide early warning of attack attempts that may later be waged against the more secured portions of the network.

> **ExamAlert**
>
> Honeypots and honeynets can be thought of as a trap. It is another tool to help fight unauthorized system access. Honeynets and honeypots can be used to distract attackers from valid network content, to study the attacker's methods, and to provide early warning of attack attempts that may later be waged against the more secured portions of the network.

Port Scanners

Port scanners are often part of a more comprehensive vulnerability assessment solution. Port scanners may, however, be standalone in that all they do is scan a range of specific ports to determine what ports are open on a system. The results are valuable to system administrators and attackers alike. *Port scanners* typically identify one of two states in which the port can be in: open or closed.

In addition, some port scanners can provide additional information such as the type of operating system running on the targeted system and services running over the ports.

Passive Versus Active Tools

The idea of passive versus active can be applied in many security situations. Perhaps one of the best ways to think about this and remember the difference is that a passive solution will only listen. In contrast, an active solution will talk. Consider, for example, vulnerability scanner solutions. An active scanner sits on the network and when scheduled reaches out across the network to discover systems and performs a series of inquires to try to identify what is running on the system. Based on that discovery, most scanners perform an iterative process of testing the system against known vulnerability signatures. Active scanners, however, are hampered by network and host firewalls. A passive scanner, though, does not actually perform scans. Instead, it sits on the wire and acts as a sniffer, collecting data from the normal flow over the network. As a result, a passive scanner can gather details between systems behind firewalls. Although a passive scanner might not see a system or application that is not "talking," it does provide greater visibility in the sense that it can see systems actively communicating that you might have not otherwise known about. Finally, active tools, even if they are configured to minimize any impact on target systems, are still invasive. A passive scanner, however, does nothing to interrupt the systems or the flow of information.

Banner Grabbing

Banner grabbing describes a technique to identify what operating system is running on a machine and the services that are running. Active vulnerability scanning solutions use this as a mechanism to help identify the OS type and running services, which in turn help narrow down the vulnerability signatures to scan for. An attacker may footprint an organization in much the same way. The more you understand about the specific operating systems, applications, and version information, the more easy it is to identify vulnerable systems and conduct targeted attacks. Telnet is a common tool used to try and perform banner grabs. For example, from a command shell, one might type the following:

```
telnet www.example.com 80
```

After pressing Enter, and after a connection has been established, a bad request just needs to be sent. This could be as simple as typing any letter followed by the Return key. The results, depending on the system, will likely provide information about the host. This information might include the type and version of web server running and the type and version of operating systems running.

For the systems administrator, this provides a handy way to identify assets. Such information also assists with helping vulnerability management tools to be more intelligent. And again, it can also help an attacker know what exploit he needs to use against the system.

Risk Calculation

Chapter 3, "Risk Management," introduced the important concepts related to risk calculation. These concepts are particularly important as related to implementing and interpreting assessment tools. The choice and use of assessment tools and techniques depends on various interrelated concepts:

► Threat versus likelihood

► Risk assessment

► Threat assessment

► Vulnerability assessment

Let's consider a simple analogy. If you live in Iowa (a Midwestern state in the middle of the United States, which is more than 1,000 miles from the nearest ocean), how likely are you to be concerned with implementing a program to deal with a hurricane or tsunami? Although there are countless threats when dealing with physical and information security, it is important to consider the likelihood of them actually occurring.

Such considerations are important to conducting an overall risk assessment. Given what you have learned previously about risk, you should understand that various components combined make up one's risk. Therefore, to properly understand risk, you must also understand threats and vulnerabilities. Organizations, as part of an overall program, should have identified all relevant threats and their likelihood of occurring to the organization. A hurricane, for example, is a real threat to many coastal communities, but even within that context, some are more likely to be hit than others. A financial institution that conducts business online differs in the likelihood of specific threats compared to nonprofit organization that maintains a static web presence.

The results of a vulnerability assessment, within the context of these other variables now, are more actionable. Although the absence of storm shutters exposes a vulnerability, it is not as important to residents in Iowa as it is to a resident in a hurricane-prone home on the coast. Open ports and services (just like doors and windows) present opportunities for attack, yet you must also consider the benefit of what these are providing. A specific vulnerability ultimately correlates to differing levels of risk based on the organization.

Assessment Technique

When assessing for threats and vulnerabilities as part of an overall risk management program, a variety of techniques exist. Mature risk management programs likely use the following techniques:

▶ **Baseline reporting:** There is no one-size-fits-all approach to security, even with a single organization across various systems. However, it is important to consider a minimum or baseline standard of security. Baseline reporting compares existing implementations against these expected baselines. The goal is to identify those systems that do not meet this minimum level of expected requirements.

▶ **Code review:** As applications are developed, it is important to make sure that the resulting code is thoroughly and methodically reviewed by someone other than the developers. Many exploited vulnerabilities within software can be prevented. It is considered a good practice within organizations to ensure that developed applications are examined before being released in production or to the general public. These reviews are usually conducted using automated software programs designed to check code, in addition to manual human checks in which someone not associated with development combs through the code.

▶ **Determine attack surface:** Given how complex writing code can be, the fact that humans make mistakes, and that technology and threats are constantly evolving, it is important to understand how much opportunity there is for an attack. The *attack surface* refers to the amount of running code, services, and user-interaction fields and interfaces. An analogy is the story of a sniper who once used a rifle to hit a coin from 100 meters away. Sounds impressive, unless, of course, the target consists of thousands of coins! To effectively reduce the attack surface to an appropriate level, it is first important to identify just how broad that surface is.

▶ **Architecture review:** An assessment of system architecture considers
the entire system. It enables you to identify faulty components
and interaction between various elements. It also ensures that the
architecture is consistent with the goals of an organization and the
acceptable tolerance of risk. A physical building, for example, needs to
adhere to structurally sound engineering methods as all the pieces are
put together, but must also consider the environment. Moreover, the
design of the building should correlate to the goals of the occupants
and to the risk. About 2,000 years ago, the Roman architect Vitruvius
described a good building as having durability, utility, and beauty.
Certainly within the context of the first two, these principles apply
to information architecture. Beauty is even important, specifically as
it relates to how it is optimized and well documented and how the
complex is simplified. In fact, there are many examples of beauty being
a determining factor in software architecture, considering things beyond
function and quality. Other examples include a system that anticipates
change, and—just like physical architecture—it should delight the users,
which includes the developers and testers. This helps ensure a life cycle
of quality and alignment with evolving goals.

▶ **Design review:** Not to be confused with architecture, design refers
more specifically to the components of the architecture at a more micro
level. A review of design considers various elements such as compatibility, modularity, reusability, and, of course, security. Design assessments
should not be thought of as a one-time event during initial design. It is
important that design be incorporated into a life cycle process in which
design is constantly considered and reviewed. A continuous process of
assessing design helps deal with the challenge of evolving threats, new
information, and changing organizational goals.

Cram Quiz

Answer these questions. The answers follow the last question. If you cannot answer these questions correctly, consider reading this section again until you can.

1. Which one of the following is used to capture network traffic?

    ○ **A.** Honeynet

    ○ **B.** Vulnerability scanner

    ○ **C.** Honeypot

    ○ **D.** Protocol analyzer

2. Reviews of architecture, design, and code, as well as baseline reporting and understanding attack surface, are all considered which one of the following?

    ○ **A.** Control procedure techniques to protect against insider threats

    ○ **B.** Countermeasures designed to eliminate risk

    ○ **C.** Techniques for assessing threats and vulnerabilities

    ○ **D.** Design procedures for creating sustainable and usable applications

3. Which one of the following is not true of port scanners?

    ○ **A.** They are useful for nefarious purposes.

    ○ **B.** They can be standalone or part of a vulnerability assessment solution.

    ○ **C.** They allow interaction with the attacker to enable logging.

    ○ **D.** They can provide operating system information.

Cram Quiz Answers

1. **D.** Protocol analyzers and sniffers are tools used to capture network traffic. Answer B is incorrect because a vulnerability scanner is used to scan and test for known vulnerabilities. Answers A and C are incorrect because these are mechanisms used to trap or deter attackers using an isolated system that appears to be a valuable target.

2. **C.** Each of these is considered an assessment technique, part of an overall risk management program designed to assess threats and vulnerabilities to ensure that systems are designed securely within the goals of an organization. Answers A, B, and D specifically relate to techniques for assessing threats and vulnerabilities.

3. **C.** A system that allows interaction with an attacker to enable logging describes a function of a honeypot. Answers A, B, and D are incorrect in that each of these describes functions of a port scanner.

Explain the Proper Use of Penetration Testing Versus Vulnerability Scanning

▶ **Penetration testing**

▶ **Vulnerability scanning**

▶ **Black box**

▶ **White box**

▶ **Gray box**

CramSaver

If you can correctly answer these questions before going through this section, save time by skimming the Exam Alerts in this section and then completing the Cram Quiz at the end of the section.

1. Which one of the following best describes a penetration test?

   A. A passive evaluation and analysis of operational weaknesses using tools and techniques that a malicious source might use

   B. An evaluation mimicking real-world attacks to identify ways to circumvent security

   C. The monitoring of network communications and examination of header and payload data

   D. A technique used to identify hosts and their associated vulnerabilities

2. What are the differences between a black box, white box, and gray box as they pertain to penetration testing?

Answers

1. **B.** A penetration test or pen test reveals security weaknesses through real-world attacks. The results of which can help prioritize risk and identify areas for improvement. Penetration tests are active evaluations, and so answer A is incorrect. Answer C describes network sniffing, and answer D describes vulnerability scanning. Both of these, however, can be used as part of the penetration process.

2. Each of these refers to testing performed with varying degrees of knowledge about the system or application being tested. Black box testing assumes no knowledge, whereas white box testing provides more transparency about the inner workings. Gray box testing is a combination of both black box and white box testing.

Penetration Testing

In some cases, vulnerability assessments may be complemented by directed efforts to exploit vulnerabilities in an attempt to gain access to networked resources. These are, in essence, "friendly" attacks against a network to test the security measures put into place. Such attacks are referred to as *penetration tests*, or simply *pen tests*, and may cause some disruption to network operations as a result of the actual penetration efforts conducted. Penetration tests can also mask legitimate attacks by generating false data in IDSs, concealing aggression that is otherwise unrelated to the officially sanctioned penetration test. Some tools use passive OS fingerprinting. A passive attack attempts to passively monitor data being sent between two parties and does not insert data into the data stream.

Some systems administrators might perform amateur or ad hoc pen tests against networks in an attempt to prove a particular vulnerability exists or to evaluate the overall security exposure of a network. This is a bad practice because it generates false intrusion data; might weaken the network's security level; and might be a violation of privacy laws, regulatory mandates, or business entity guidelines. Although regularly conducted penetration tests may be a good way to assess the effectiveness of an organization's controls, these tests should always be performed within a defined program of governance, which includes the knowledge of senior management.

The high-level components of a penetration test include the following:

▶ **Verify a threat exists:** A penetration tests seeks to exploit vulnerabilities. As a result, it is necessary to first understand a threat and to what extent that threat exists in the first place. A sheep farmer in an isolated location might be less concerned about locking the front door than about the threat of wolves to the sheep.

▶ **Bypass security controls:** Just as a real attacker would, penetration tests should seek to bypass security controls. Verifying that a battering ram cannot penetrate the stone wall is worthless when the gate 100 meters away around the back is left wide open. Although network firewalls might be protecting the pathways into the network, a rogue wireless access point or modems might present an easier method of entry for an attacker. Another common method of bypassing security controls is to render them ineffective. For example, a DoS attack can be mounted on security controls to overload the control, allowing for potentially easier access.

▶ **Actively test security controls:** Unlike passive techniques, active techniques include direct interaction with a specific target. Passive techniques seek to identify gaps that could lead to missing or misconfigured security controls. Active techniques, however, seek to identify whether controls are implemented properly. Consider a lock on a door. Although passive reviews might show documentation and policies indicating that locks are installed, in an active test someone walks up and tries to open the door.

▶ **Exploit vulnerability:** Executing an attack is the core of a penetration test. Exploiting a vulnerability follows the identification of a potential vulnerability. Unlike vulnerability scanning, penetration tests do not just check for the existence of a potential vulnerability; they attempt to exploit it. A resulting exploit verifies the vulnerability and should lead to mitigation techniques and controls to deal with the security exposure. Most exploited vulnerabilities are likely the result of misconfigurations, kernel flaws, buffer overflow, input validation errors, and incorrect permissions.

Vulnerability Scanning

A penetration test goes beyond vulnerability scanning by actually subjecting a system or network to a real-world attack. Vulnerability scanning, like a port scanner, identifies hosts and open ports, but it takes things a bit further. It looks for specific vulnerabilities and provides information and guidance. As discussed earlier, it is important to note that although vulnerability scanners aid in interpretation, it is very important for the results to be evaluated within the context of one's own business.

ExamAlert

The results of a vulnerability scan should be organized based on the relative security and value associated with each identified threat. As a result, an organization can prioritize what vulnerabilities need to be addressed first.

Vulnerability scanning, unlike penetration testing, does not seek to test or bypass security controls. In addition, after vulnerabilities are discovered by a vulnerability scanner, no attempts are made to exploit the weaknesses. When used with a penetration testing program, an effective vulnerability scanner should serve the following purposes:

▶ **Passively testing security controls:** Passive scanning poses minimal risk to the assessed environment. They are designed to not interfere with normal activity or degrade performance. In contrast, an active scanner is more aggressive, like a penetration test, and is capable of interrupting services.

▶ **Identify vulnerability:** Vulnerability scanners, using their database of vulnerabilities, can quickly identify known vulnerabilities on systems. This includes outdated software versions that contain flaws or even missing patches.

▶ **Identify lack of security controls:** Identifying vulnerabilities provides for the opportunity to remediate the weakness. In some cases, it highlights the needs for further implementation of security controls to mitigate the risk.

▶ **Identify common misconfiguration:** Vulnerability scanners can identify many common misconfigurations. Some scanners are even capable of remediation. Checking for misconfigurations is most beneficial when compared against an organization's security policies and standards.

▶ **Intrusive versus nonintrusive:** Many network scanners are designed to be nonintrusive to the target systems. Regardless, a series of tests against the system can still affect network and system performance. In fact, it is actually not the vulnerability tests that disrupt systems; rather, it is the initial port scans that typically causes a system to fail (particularly where the implementation of a particular service does not follow proper standards). Intrusive scans will combine verification of actual vulnerabilities by actually trying to exploit the vulnerability. Such tests can be highly intrusive, and due care should be taken before initiating such tests.

▶ **Credentialed versus noncredentialed:** Credentials provide authorized access to the system. Scanners may be configured to run in either mode. Noncredentialed scans are less invasive and provide an outsider's point-of-view. With credentialed scans, however, the system can ascertain greater information, which results in a more complete vulnerability status and greater certainty.

▶ **False positive:** Both credentialed and noncredentialed scans can mistakenly identify vulnerability when there is none, but credentialed scans tend to reduce such false positives. False positives can be time-consuming to confirm and a burden on IT resources.

> **ExamAlert**
>
> Although penetration tests are always considered active, vulnerability scans may use active and passive attempts to identify weaknesses.

Testing

Penetration testing can be conducted using various techniques. Each of these techniques is commonly known as one of the following:

▶ Black box

▶ White box

▶ Gray box

Each of these refers to varying degrees of knowledge about the systems or applications being tested. A black box test is conducted with the assessor having no information or knowledge about the inner workings of the system or knowledge of the source code. The assessor simply tests the application for functionality. An easy way to think about this is that you cannot see through or inside the black box. White box testing, also called *clear box* or *glass box*, provides more transparency. The assessor has knowledge about the inner workings of the system or knowledge of the source code. Because white box techniques are often more efficient and cost-effective, they are the more commonly used technique. Gray box testing uses a combination of both white and black box techniques. This can be more easily thought of as being translucent.

> **ExamAlert**
>
> Remember your boxes! A black box you cannot see inside (no knowledge). A white box is see-through (provides complete knowledge of inner workings). A gray box is a combination of the two (limited knowledge).

Cram Quiz

Answer these questions. The answers follow the last question. If you cannot answer
these questions correctly, consider reading this section again until you can.

1. After conducting a vulnerability assessment, which of the following is the best
   action to perform?

   ○ **A.** Disable all vulnerable systems until mitigating controls can be
      implemented

   ○ **B.** Contact the network team to shut down all identified open ports

   ○ **C.** Immediately conduct a penetration test against identified
      vulnerabilities

   ○ **D.** Organize and document the results based on severity

2. You are conducting a penetration test on a software application for a client.
   The client provides you with details around some of the source code and
   development process. What type of test will you likely be conducting?

   ○ **A.** Black box

   ○ **B.** Vulnerability

   ○ **C.** White box

   ○ **D.** Answers A and C

3. Which of the following is a reason to conduct a penetration test?

   ○ **A.** To passively test security controls

   ○ **B.** To identify the vulnerabilities

   ○ **C.** To test the adequacy of security measures put in place

   ○ **D.** To steal data for malicious purposes

Cram Quiz Answers

1. **D.** After an assessment, the results should be organized based on the severity
   of the risk to the organization. Answer A is incorrect. Although in rare situations
   this might be appropriate on a case-by-case basis, this would otherwise be
   considered extreme. Answer B is incorrect. Many ports are required to be
   opened for a network to function. Answer C is incorrect. Although a penetration
   test might and often does follow a vulnerability scan, it is not necessary to do
   this immediately and certainly not against all identified vulnerabilities.

2. **C.** White box testing is more transparent. Because you are provided with source
   code, you have more knowledge about the system before beginning your
   penetration testing. Answer A is incorrect because black box testing assumes no
   prior knowledge, and answer B is incorrect because this refers to a weakness;
   therefore, answer D is also incorrect.

3. **C**. A penetration tests helps quantify the adequacy of security measures put in place and to create understanding of the effect that a threat might have against the environment. Answers A and B are incorrect because these describe the purpose of a vulnerability scan. Answer D is incorrect. A penetration test is a "friendly" attack to help safeguard an organization from a real attack. A penetration test, even one that is successful in deeply penetrating an organization, should never maliciously harm critical assets and intellectual property.

What Next?

If you want more practice on this chapter's exam objectives before you move on, remember that you can access all the Cram Quiz questions on the CD. You can also create a custom exam by objective with the practice exam software. Note any objective that you struggle with and go to the material that covers that objective in this chapter.

CHAPTER 7

Application Security

This chapter covers the following official CompTIA Security+ SY0-401 exam objectives:

▶ Explain the importance of application security controls and techniques

(For more information on the official CompTIA Security+, SY0-401 exam topics, see the "About the CompTIA Security+ SY0-401 Exam" section in the Introduction.)

When establishing operational security baselines, it is important to harden all technologies against as many possible avenues of attack as possible. The three basic areas of hardening are the following:

▶ **Application:** Security of applications and services such as Domain Name Service (DNS), Dynamic Host Configuration Protocol (DHCP), web servers, and user client-side applications and integration suites.

▶ **Host:** Security of the operating system through hardware and software implementations such as firewalls and antimalware programs, along with logical security involving access control over resources and virtualization.

▶ **Data:** Security of data and mitigating risks on laptops, PCs, removable media, mobile devices, and static environments.

These areas are discussed in the next few chapters. The focus of this chapter is application security, which has become a major focus of security as we rely on more web-based application-as-a-service business models and as exploits such as cross-site scripting and SQL injections become an everyday occurrence. Web-based applications and application servers contain a wealth of valuable data. Internally, application servers store a variety of data, from web pages to critical data and sensitive information. Regulatory compliance issues make it necessary to have sound procedures in place for the security of application data.

Explain the Importance of Application Security Controls and Techniques

▶ **Fuzzing**

▶ **Secure coding concepts (error and exception handling, input validation)**

▶ **Cross-site scripting prevention**

▶ **Cross-site request forgery (XSRF) prevention**

▶ **Application configuration baseline (proper settings)**

▶ **Application hardening**

▶ **Application patch management**

▶ **NoSQL databases versus SQL databases**

▶ **Server-side versus client-side validation**

CramSaver

If you can correctly answer these questions before going through this section, save time by skimming the Exam Alerts in this section and then completing the Cram Quiz at the end of the section.

1. Explain what fuzzing is and how it is used in application security.

2. Explain what steps can be taken to mitigate cross-site scripting (XSS) attacks.

3. Explain what steps can be taken to mitigate cross-site request forgery (XSRF) attacks.

4. Explain what steps can be taken to harden a web-based application.

5. Explain what steps can be taken for proper application patch management.

Answers

1. Fuzzing is a process by which semi-random data is injected into a program or protocol stack for detecting bugs. The idea behind fuzzing is based on the assumption that there are bugs within every program. A systematic discovery approach should find them sooner or later. The data generation part consists of generators. Generators usually use combinations of static fuzzing vectors or totally random data. The vulnerability identification relies on debugging tools.

2. Never insert untrusted data except in allowed locations. Use HTML escape before inserting untrusted data into HTML element content, use attribute escape before inserting untrusted data into HTML common attributes, implement JavaScript escape before inserting untrusted data into HTML JavaScript data values, use CSS escape before inserting untrusted data into HTML style property, apply URL escape before inserting untrusted data into HTML URL parameter, use an HTML policy engine to validate or clean user-driven HTML in an outbound way, and prevent DOM-based XSS. To help mitigate the effect of an XSS flaw on your website, it is also good practice to set the HTTPOnly flag on the session cookie and on any custom cookies that are not accessed by your own JavaScript.

3. To mitigate this type of attack, the most common solution is to add a token for every POST or GET request that is initiated from the browser to the server. When a user visits a site, the site generates a cryptographically strong, pseudorandom value and sets it as a cookie on the user's machine. The site requires every form submission to include this pseudorandom value as a form value and also as a cookie value. When a POST request is sent to the site, the request is considered valid only if the form value and the cookie value are the same. Another solution is to use the unique identifiers that are provided as part of the session management. One extra check can be added to the validation subroutines and the requests modified to include the necessary information.

4. Access control may be accomplished at the operating system or application level by including a requirement for regular update of Secure Sockets Layer (SSL) certifications for secured communications. Regular log review is critical for web servers to ensure that submitted URL values are not used to exploit unpatched buffer overruns or to initiate other forms of common exploits.

5. Proactive patch management is necessary to keep your technology environment secure and reliable. As part of maintaining a secure environment, organizations should have a process for identifying security vulnerabilities and responding quickly. This involves having a comprehensive plan for applying software updates, configuration changes, and countermeasures to remove vulnerabilities from the environment and lessen the risk of computers being attacked. It might include using automated tools that make administrators aware of critical updates and allow them to manage and control installation.

Fuzzing

Just as script kiddies require little talent to run exploits, an attacker with moderate skills can reverse engineer executable programs to find major vulnerabilities without ever examining source code. Some of the tools available use a technique called *fuzzing*, which enables an attacker to inject random-looking data into a program to see whether it can cause the program to crash.

> **ExamAlert**
>
> Fuzzing is a black box software testing process by which semi-random data is injected into a program or protocol stack for detecting bugs. The idea behind fuzzing is based on the assumption that there are bugs within every program.

A systematic discovery approach should find application bugs sooner or later. The data-generation part consists of generators. Generators usually use combinations of static fuzzing vectors or totally random data. The vulnerability identification relies on debugging tools. Most fuzzers are either protocol/file-format dependent or data-type dependent. New-generation fuzzers use genetic algorithms to link injected data and observed impact. OWASP's Fuzz Vector's resource (https://www.owasp.org/index.php/Fuzzing) is great for fuzzing methodology and real-life fuzzing vectors examples.

There are several different types of fuzzing:

▶ **Application fuzzing:** Attack vectors are within its I/O, such as the user interface, the command-line options, URLs, forms, user-generated content, and Remote Procedure Call (RPC) requests.

▶ **Protocol fuzzing:** Forged packets are sent to the tested application, which can act as a proxy and modify requests on-the-fly and then replay them.

▶ **File-format fuzzing:** Multiple malformed samples are generated and then opened sequentially. When the program crashes, debug information is kept for further investigation.

An advantage of fuzzing is that the test design is generally very simple without any presumptions about system behavior. This approach makes it possible to find bugs that would have often been missed by human testing. In some closed application instances, fuzzing might be the only means of reviewing the security quality of the program. The simplicity can be a disadvantage because more advanced bugs will not be found. In addition, if a fuzzer is very protocol aware, it tends to miss odd errors. A random approach is still a good idea for best results. Fuzzing can add another dimension to normal software-testing techniques.

Secure Coding Concepts

Attacks against software vulnerabilities are becoming more sophisticated. Many times, a vulnerability might be discovered that is not addressed by the vendor for quite some time. The vendor decides how and when to patch a vulnerability. As a result, users have become increasingly concerned about the integrity, security, and reliability of commercial software. *Software assurance* is a term used to describe vendor efforts to reduce vulnerabilities, improve resistance to attack, and protect the integrity of their products. Software assurance is especially important in organizations where users require a high level of confidence that commercial software is as secure as possible. Secure software is something that may be achieved when software is created using best practices for secure software development.

The security of software code has come to the forefront in recent years, and coalitions have been formed to improve the security of code. In addition, certifications are offered in this software security. The Software Assurance Forum for Excellence in Code (SAFECode) works to identify and promote best practices for developing and delivering more secure and reliable software, hardware, and services. It was founded by EMC Corporation, Juniper Networks, Inc., Microsoft Corporation, SAP AG, and Symantec Corporation. Organizations such as (ISC)² offer a certification specifically geared toward secure code design, such as the Certified Secure Software Lifecycle Professional (CSSLP). The various stages of secure software include design, coding, source code handling, and testing.

It is important that security be implemented from the very beginning. In the early design phase, potential threats to the application must be identified and addressed. You must also consider ways to reduce the associated risks. You can accomplish these objectives through a variety of ways, such as threat modeling and mitigation planning, including analysis of potential vulnerabilities and attack vectors from an attacker's point of view. After the design is complete, the secure programming practices must be implemented. Secure coding skills require the inspection of an application's source code to identify vulnerabilities created by coding errors.

ExamAlert

You should implement secure programming practices that reduce the frequency and severity of errors. You should also perform source code review using a combination of manual analysis and automated analysis tools.

Using automated tools along with manual review can help reduce the vulnerabilities that might be missed using only one method.

After the coding is done and has been reviewed, you must carefully handle the source code. Procedures for secure handling of code include strict change management, tracking, and confidentiality protection of the code. To prevent malicious insiders from introducing vulnerabilities, only authorized persons should be permitted to view or modify the code contents. Additional consideration for the protection of code includes protecting the systems and code repositories from unauthorized access. In cases where the development is outsourced, you should conduct internal design and code reviews to prevent malicious code from being introduced. The final step in secure code development is testing. In the testing phase, pay particular attention to validating that the security requirements were met and the design and coding specifications were followed. Testing processes can include the use of testing techniques such as fuzzing and using a variety of inputs to identify possible buffer overflows or other vulnerabilities. Some software vendors submit their products for external testing, in addition to doing internal testing, because an unbiased, independent test might uncover vulnerabilities that would not be detectable using internal processes. The secure code testing phase discussed previously can include the important black box, white box, or gray box testing methods discussed in previous chapters.

Error and Exception Handling

Many of the software exploits seen in the past few years resulted directly from poor or incorrect input validation or mishandled exceptions. Common programming flaws include trusting input when designing an application and not performing proper exception checking in the code. These practices allow attacks such as buffer overflows, format string vulnerabilities, and utilization of shell-escape codes. To reduce these programming flaws, authentication, authorization, logging and auditing, code dependencies, and error messages and code comment practices should be reviewed.

Authentication strength is vital to the security of the application. You should relinquish common practices such as hardcoding credentials into an application or storing them in clear text in favor of the practice of encrypting authentication credentials. This is especially important for a web application that uses cookies to store session and authentication information. In web applications or multilayered systems where the identity is often propagated to other contexts, authorization control should form a strong link to the identity through the life cycle of the authenticated session. Logging and auditing should be designed to include configurable logging and auditing capabilities. This will allow the flexibility of collecting detailed information when necessary. Using libraries from established vendors will minimize the risk of unknown vulnerabilities especially when using object-oriented programming that relies on the use of third-party libraries.

Take care when programming error messages. Although error messages are important to determine the problem, they should not divulge specific system or application information. Because attackers usually gather information before they try to break into an application, outputting detailed error messages can provide an attacker with the necessary information to escalate an attack. Information output in error messages should be on a need-to-know basis. Exception handling should log the error and provide the user with a standard message. You should not use comments in public viewable code that could reveal valuable information about the application or system, especially in web applications where the code and associated comments reside on the browser.

Input Validation

Input validation tests whether an application properly handles input from a source outside the application destined for internal processing.

> **ExamAlert**
>
> The most common result of improper input validation is buffer overflow exploitation. Additional types of input validation errors result in format string and denial-of-service (DoS) exploits.

Application field input should always include a default value and character limitations to avoid these types of exploits. Although software developers can overlook input validation, testing the code by sending varying amounts of both properly and improperly formatted data into the application helps determine whether this application is potentially vulnerable to exploits. There are various methods used to test input validation, such as automated testing, session management validation, race condition analysis, cryptographic analysis, and code coverage analysis.

An automated program can randomly perform input validation against the target based on the program's ability to handle input without any established criteria for external interfaces of the application. This means that any component of the application can be tested with randomly generated data without set order or reason. Testing an application for session management vulnerabilities consists of attempting to modify any session state variables to invoke undesirable results from the application. Access can be gained to other communication channels through modified variables, leading to privilege escalation, loss of data confidentiality, and unauthorized access to resources. When a window of time exists between a security operation and the general function it applies to, a window of opportunity is created that might allow security measures to be circumvented. This is known as a *race condition*. Testing for race conditions attempts to access the file between the time the application creates the file and when the application actually applies the security. Sensitive data, such as passwords and credit card information, are often protected by cryptographic methods. Knowing what algorithm an application uses might lead to exploitation of its weaknesses. In addition, if strong encryption is used, but the vendor implementation is incorrect, the data might not be properly protected and can result in errors such as improper creation or storage of the cryptographic keys and key management. Code coverage analysis is used to verify that proper security measures are taken on all possible paths of code execution. Paths might exist that enable security to be bypassed, leaving the system in a vulnerable state. This type of analysis can be resource intensive and should be done in stages during the development of an application.

Cross-Site Scripting Prevention

Web security includes client-side vulnerabilities presented by ActiveX or JavaScript code running within the client's browser; server-side vulnerabilities such as Perl, Active Server Pages (ASP), and Common Gateway Interface (CGI) scripting exploits and buffer overflows used to run undesirable code on the server; and other forms of web-related security vulnerabilities such as those involving the transfer of cookies or unsigned applets. By placing malicious executable code on a website, an attacker can cause an unknowing browser user to conduct unauthorized access activities, expose confidential data, and provide logging of successful attacks back to the attacker without the user being aware of his participation. *Cross-site scripting* (XSS) vulnerabilities can be used to hijack the user's session or to cause the user accessing malware-tainted Site A to unknowingly attack Site B on behalf of the attacker who planted code on Site A. Much of this scenario stems from accepting untrusted data. From a security perspective, although untrusted data most often comes from an HTTP request, some data that comes from other sources such as databases and web services can be considered untrusted as well. The proper way to treat untrusted data is as though it contains an attack. This concept is extremely important because applications are becoming more interconnected and trusted, opening up the real possibility of an attack being executed downstream.

Traditionally, input validation has been the preferred approach for handling untrusted data. However, input validation is not a great solution for injection attacks because it is typically done before the destination is known and potentially harmful characters must be accepted by applications. Input validation is important and should always be performed, but it is not a complete solution. OWASP has formulated the following rules to prevent XSS in your applications:

▶ Never insert untrusted data except in allowed locations.

▶ Use HTML escape before inserting untrusted data into HTML element content.

▶ Use attribute escape before inserting untrusted data into HTML common attributes.

▶ Implement JavaScript escape before inserting untrusted data into HTML JavaScript Data Values.

▶ Use CSS escape before inserting untrusted data into HTML style properties.

▶ Apply URL escape before inserting untrusted data into HTML URL parameters.

▶ Use an HTML policy engine to validate or clean user-driven HTML in an outbound way.

▶ Prevent DOM-based XSS.

To help mitigate the effect of an XSS flaw on your website, it is also good practice to set the HTTPOnly flag on the session cookie as well as any custom cookies that are not accessed by your own JavaScript.

ExamAlert

When presented with a question that relates to mitigating the danger of buffer overflows or XSS attacks, look for answers that relate to input validation. By restricting the data that can be input, application designers can reduce the threat posed by maliciously crafted URL references and redirected web content.

Cross-Site Request Forgery Prevention

An end user can be tricked into loading information from or submitting information to a web application in a number of ways.

ExamAlert

Cross-site request forgery (XSRF) is an attack in which the end user executes unwanted actions on a web application while she is currently authenticated.

An XSRF attack tricks the victim into loading a page that contains a malicious request, usually through sending a link via email or chat. The attacker uses the identity and privileges of the user to execute an undesired function. This can be as simple as changing the victim's email address or as malicious as making purchases on the victim's behalf. A successful attack can compromise end-user data, and if the targeted end user is the administrator account, this can compromise the entire web application. Although XSRF attacks generally target functions that cause a state change on the server, they can also be used to access sensitive data, as in the case of targeting the administrator account.

Most browsers automatically include any credentials associated with the site, such as the user's session cookie and basic authentication credentials, with such requests, so when a user is presently authenticated to the site, the site has no way to distinguish the malicious request from a legitimate user request. Another way this attack can happen is when the XSRF attack is stored on the vulnerable site itself by using an IMG or IFRAME tag in a field that accepts HTML. When an XSRF attack is stored on the site, the victim is more likely to view the page containing the attack because the victim is already authenticated to the site.

Using a secret cookie to mitigate this type of attack does not work well because the secret cookies are submitted with each request. The authentication tokens are submitted whether or not the end user was tricked into submitting the request. Session identifiers are used to associate the request with a specific session object, not to verify that the end user intended to submit the request. Only accepting POST requests does not work well either because, although applications can be developed to only accept POST requests, several methods are available whereby an attacker can trick a victim into submitting a forged POST request. For example, a simple form hosted in the attacker's website with hidden values can be triggered automatically by the victim who thinks the form will do something else.

The key element to understanding XSRF is that attackers are betting that users have a validated login cookie for the website already stored in their browser. All they need to do is get that browser to make a request to the website on their behalf. This can be done by either convincing the users to click an HTML page the attacker has constructed or by inserting arbitrary HTML in a target website that the users visit. To mitigate this type of attack, the most common solution is to add a token for every POST or GET request that is initiated from the browser to the server. When a user visits a site, the site generates a cryptographically strong, pseudorandom value and sets it as a cookie on the user's machine. The site requires every form submission to include this pseudorandom value as a form value and also as a cookie value. When a POST request is sent to the site, the request is considered valid only if the form value and the cookie value are the same. Although it sounds easy, the web application that is developed needs to contain another layer of security that handles the random tokens generation and their validation. Another solution is using the unique identifiers that are provided as part of the session management. One extra check can be added to the validation subroutines and the requests modified to include the necessary information.

Application Configuration Baseline (Proper Settings)

Baselines must be updated on a regular basis and certainly when the network has changed or new technology has been deployed. *Application baselining* is similar to operating system baselining in that it provides a reference point for normal and abnormal activity. As with operating system hardening, default configurations and passwords must be changed in applications such as database- and web-based applications. Applications must also be maintained in a current state by regularly reviewing applied updates and applying those that are required for the network configuration solutions in use. An initial baseline should be done for both network and application processes so that you can tell whether you have a hardware or software issue. Sometimes applications have memory leaks, or a new version might cause performance issues. Not only must applications be maintained, but access rights should be reviewed regularly and permissions granted on a group structure similar to Active Directory.

> **ExamAlert**
>
> Referencing baselines for established patterns of use help to spot variations that can identify unauthorized access attempts.

Security monitoring during baselining is important because an ongoing attack during the baselining process could be registered as the normal level of activity. As with operating system hardening, default configurations and passwords must be changed in network hardware such as routers and managed network devices. Routing hardware must also be maintained in a current state by regularly reviewing applied firmware updates and applying those that are required for the network configuration and hardware solutions in use. The sections that follow examine mechanisms for identifying vulnerabilities and hardening vulnerable applications revealed during this process. Failure to update applications on a regular basis or to update auditing can result in an unsecure solution that provides an attacker access to additional resources throughout an organization's network. In addition, without having a baseline on applications, you may spend a long time trying to figure out what the problem is.

Application Hardening

Each application and service that may be installed within a network must also be considered when planning security for an organization. Applications must be maintained in an updated state through the regular review of hotfixes, patches, and service packs. Many applications, such as antivirus software, require regular updates to provide protection against newly emerging threats.

> **ExamAlert**
>
> Default application administration accounts, standard passwords, and common services installed by default should also be reviewed and changed or disabled as required.

Web Services

Access restrictions to Internet and intranet web services might be required to ensure proper authentication for nonpublic sites, whereas anonymous access might be required for other pages. Access control can be accomplished at the operating system or application level, with many sites including a requirement for regular update of Secure Sockets Layer (SSL) certifications for secured communications.

Regular log review is critical for web servers to ensure that submitted URL values are not used to exploit unpatched buffer overruns or to initiate other forms of common exploits. Many web servers may also be integrated with security add-ins provided to restrict those URLs that may be meaningfully submitted, filtering out any that do not meet the defined criteria. Microsoft's URLScan for the Internet Information Services (IIS) web service is one such filtering add-in.

Email Services

Email servers require network access to transfer Simple Mail Transfer Protocol (SMTP) traffic. Email is often used to transport executable agents, including Trojan horses and other forms of viral software. Email servers might require transport through firewall solutions to allow remote Post Office Protocol 3 (POP3) or Internet Message Access Protocol (IMAP) access or might require integration with VPN solutions to provide secure connections for remote users. User authentication is also of key importance, especially when email and calendaring solutions allow delegated review and manipulation. Inadequate hardware may be attacked through mail bombs and other types of attack meant to overwhelm the server's ability to transact mail messages. Email service hardening also includes preventing SMTP relay from being used by spammers and limiting attachment and total storage per user to prevent denial-of-service attacks using large file attachments.

FTP Services

File Transfer Protocol (FTP) servers are used to provide file upload and download to users, whether through anonymous or authenticated connection. Because of limitations in the protocol, unless an encapsulation scheme is used between the client and host systems, the login and password details are passed in clear text and might be subject to interception by packet sniffing. Unauthorized parties can also use FTP servers that allow anonymous access to share files of questionable or undesirable content while also consuming network bandwidth and server processing resources.

DNS Services

Domain Name Service (DNS) servers responsible for name resolution may be subject to many forms of attack, including attempts at DoS attacks intended to prevent proper name resolution for key corporate holdings. Planning to harden DNS server solutions should include redundant hardware and software solutions and regular backups to protect against loss of name registrations. Technologies that allow dynamic updates must also include access control and authentication to ensure that registrations are valid. Unauthorized zone transfers should also be restricted to prevent DNS poisoning attacks.

NNTP Services

Network News Transfer Protocol (NNTP) servers providing user access to newsgroup posts raise many of the same security considerations risks as email servers. Access control for newsgroups may be somewhat more complex, with moderated groups allowing public anonymous submission (and authenticated access required for post approval). Heavily loaded servers may be attacked to perform a DoS, and detailed user account information in public newsgroup posting stores like those of the AOL and MSN communities may be exploited in many ways.

File and Print Services

User file-storage solutions often come under attack when unauthorized access attempts provide avenues for manipulation. Files can be corrupted, modified, deleted, or manipulated in many other ways. Access control through proper restriction of file and share permissions, access auditing, and user authentication schemes to ensure proper access are necessary. Network file shares are not secure until you remove default access permissions.

Distributed file system and encrypted file system solutions might require bandwidth planning and proper user authentication to allow even basic access. Security planning for these solutions may also include placing user access authenticating servers close to the file servers to decrease delays created by authentication traffic.

Print servers also pose several risks, including possible security breaches in the event that unauthorized parties access cached print jobs. DoS attacks might be used to disrupt normal methods of business, and network-connected printers require authentication of access to prevent attackers from generating printed memos, invoices, or any other manner of printed materials.

DHCP Services

Dynamic Host Configuration Protocol (DHCP) servers share many of the same security problems associated with other network services, such as DNS servers. DHCP servers might be overwhelmed by lease requests if bandwidth and processing resources are insufficient. This can be worsened by the use of DHCP proxy systems relaying lease requests from widely deployed subnets. Scope address pools might also be overcome if lease duration is insufficient, and short lease duration might increase request traffic. If the operating system in use does not support DHCP server authentication, attackers might also configure their own DHCP servers within a subnet, taking control of the network settings of clients and obtaining leases from these rogue servers. Planning for DHCP security must include regular review of networks for unauthorized DHCP servers.

Data Repositories

Data repositories of any type might require specialized security considerations based on the bandwidth and processing resources required to prevent DoS attacks, removal of default password and administration accounts such as the SQL default sa account, and security of replication traffic to prevent exposure of access credentials to packet sniffing. Placement of authentication, name resolution, and data stores within secured and partially secured zones such as an organization's demilitarized zone (DMZ) may require the use of secured VPN connections or the establishment of highly secured bastion hosts.

ExamAlert

You can use role-based access control (RBAC) to improve security, and eliminating unneeded connection libraries and character sets might help to alleviate common exploits.

Take care to include data repositories beyond the obvious file, email, and database stores. Hardening efforts must also address security of the storage and backup of storage-area networks (SAN), network access server (NAS) configurations, and directory services such as Microsoft Active Directory and Novell eDirectory.

Application Patch Management

Organizations sometimes overlook patch installation and management. Because recent worms have the capability of traveling quickly and causing much damage, being proactive in security patch management is necessary to keep your environment secure, reliable, and functional. As part of maintaining a secure environment, organizations should have a process for identifying security vulnerabilities and responding quickly. This involves having a comprehensive plan for applying software updates, configuration changes, and countermeasures to remove vulnerabilities from the environment and lessen the risk of computers being attacked. It might include using automated tools that make administrators aware of critical updates and allow them to manage and control installation.

The term *patch management* describes the method for keeping computers up-to-date with new software releases that are developed after an original software product is installed.

Improperly programmed software can be exploited.

> **ExamAlert**
>
> *Software exploitation* is a method of searching for specific problems, weaknesses, or security holes in software code. It takes advantage of a program's flawed code.

The most effective way to prevent an attacker from exploiting software bugs is to keep the latest manufacturer's patches and service packs applied and to monitor the Web for new vulnerabilities.

NoSQL Databases Versus SQL Databases

With the use of cloud computing environments rapidly expanding, organizations such as financial services, healthcare, utilities, and telecommunications are moving toward the management of big data through the use of NoSQL database technologies. NoSQL encompasses a wide variety of different database technologies. When compared to relational databases, NoSQL systems are more scalable and provide superior performance.
The main database types or models found in NoSQL are key-value stores, document databases, wide-column stores, and graph databases. Protecting NoSQL data from both internal and external breaches is a concern because the NoSQL design does not place security as a high priority, lacking confidentiality and integrity. This means that the application accessing the data is relied on to provide confidentiality and integrity. Relational database security, in contrast, includes features that protect confidentiality, integrity, and availability such as role-based security, encryption, and access control through user-level permissions on stored procedures. Best practices for protecting NoSQL databases include changing the default ports, binding the interface to only one IP, and encrypting data in the application before writing it to the database. Databases such as MongoDB have added support for Kerberos authentication, more granular access controls, and SSL encryption. Should the organization select a NoSQL database technology that is lacking security, it is recommended that organizations implement their own authorization, authentication, and auditing methodologies.

Server-Side Versus Client-Side Validation

Client-side validation occurs when the data entered into a form is validated through a web-page script via the user's browser before the form is posted back to the originating server. Client-side validation is often used for convenience because it allows immediate feedback to the user if incorrect data is input. Client-side validation is an unsecure form of validation in web applications because it places trust in the browser. This form of validation allows validation to be executed by the client and can be easily bypassed or altered and allows the user to view the page code through built-in browser capabilities. When an application accepts input from the client, the input should be validated on the server for type, length, and range.

Server-side validation occurs on the server where the application resides. Server-side validation helps protect against malicious attempts by a user to bypass validation or submit unsafe input information to the server. Server-side checks are more difficult to bypass and are a more secure form of input validation. Several techniques can be used on the server side to improve validation, including identifying the acceptable data input type that is being passed from the client, defining the input format and type, building a validator routine for each input type, and situating the validator routines at the trust boundary of the application. A recommended approach is initially performing client-side validation, then after the input form has posted to the server, performing the validation a second time using server-side validation.

Cram Quiz

Answer these questions. The answers follow the last question. If you cannot answer
these questions correctly, consider reading this section again until you can.

1. Which of the following is a process by which semi-random data is injected into a
   program or protocol stack for detecting bugs?

   ◯ **A.** Cross-site scripting

   ◯ **B.** Fuzzing

   ◯ **C.** Input validation

   ◯ **D.** Cross-site request forgery

2. Joe tricks Jane into submitting a request via link in an HTML email. Jane is
   authenticated with the application when she clicks the link. As a result, money is
   transferred to Joe's account. Which of the following attacks has occurred?

   ◯ **A.** Buffer overflow

   ◯ **B.** Cross-site scripting

   ◯ **C.** Cross-site request forgery

   ◯ **D.** Input validation error

3. Which of the following are steps to mitigate XSRF attacks?

   ◯ **A.** Hardcode the authentication credentials into the application

   ◯ **B.** Always include a default value and character limitations

   ◯ **C.** Set the HTTPOnly flag on the session cookie

   ◯ **D.** Add a token for every POST or GET request that is initiated from the
   browser to the server

4. Which of the following are steps to mitigate XSS attacks? (Choose two
   correct answers.)

   ◯ **A.** Set the HTTPOnly flag on the session cookie

   ◯ **B.** Always include a default value and character limitations

   ◯ **C.** Never insert untrusted data except in allowed locations

   ◯ **D.** Hardcode the authentication credentials into the application

5. Which of the following are steps that can be taken to harden DNS services? (Choose two correct answers.)

   ○ **A.** Anonymous access to share files of questionable or undesirable content should be limited.

   ○ **B.** Regular review of networks for unauthorized or rogue servers.

   ○ **C.** Technologies that allow dynamic updates must also include access control and authentication.

   ○ **D.** Unauthorized zone transfers should also be restricted.

6. Which of the following are steps that can be taken to harden NoSQL databases? (Choose two correct answers.)

   ○ **A.** Binding the interface to multiple IP addresses

   ○ **B.** Encrypting data in the application prior to database writes

   ○ **C.** Changing the default database ports

   ○ **D.** Setting the default encryption to SSL

Cram Quiz Answers

1. **B**. Fuzzing is a process by which semi-random data is injected into a program or protocol stack for detecting bugs. The idea behind fuzzing is based on the assumption that there are bugs within every program. Answer A is incorrect because XSS vulnerabilities can be used to hijack the user's session or to cause the user accessing malware-tainted Site A to unknowingly attack Site B on behalf of the attacker who planted code on Site A. Answer C is incorrect because input validation tests whether an application properly handles input from a source outside the application destined for internal processing. Answer D, XSRF, is an attack in which the end user executes unwanted actions on a web application while he is currently authenticated.

2. **C**. XSRF is an attack in which the end user executes unwanted actions on a web application while she is currently authenticated. Answer A is incorrect because a buffer overflow is the direct result of poor or incorrect input validation or mishandled exceptions. Answer B is incorrect because XSS vulnerabilities can be used to hijack the user's session or to cause the user accessing malware-tainted Site A to unknowingly attack Site B on behalf of the attacker who planted code on Site A. Answer D is incorrect because input validation errors are a result of improper field checking in the code.

3. **D**. To mitigate XSRF attacks, the most common solution is to add a token for every POST or GET request that is initiated from the browser to the server. Answer A is incorrect because common practices such as hardcoding credentials into an application are addressed in secure coding practices. Answer B is incorrect because it describes input validation coding practices. Answer C is incorrect because setting the HTTPOnly flag on the session cookie is used to mitigate XSS attacks.

4. **A** and **C**. The first rule of mitigating XSS errors is to never insert untrusted data except in allowed locations. It is also good practice to set the HTTPOnly flag on the session cookie. Answer B is incorrect because it describes input validation coding practices. Answer D is incorrect because common practices such as hardcoding credentials into an application are addressed in secure coding practices.

5. **C** and **D**. Planning to harden DNS server solutions should include redundant hardware and software solutions and regular backups to protect against loss of name registrations. Technologies that allow dynamic updates must also include access control and authentication to ensure that registrations are valid. Unauthorized zone transfers should also be restricted to prevent DNS poisoning attacks. Answer A is incorrect because it is a hardening practice for FTP services. Answer B is incorrect because it is a hardening practice for DHCP services.

6. **B** and **C**. Best practices for protecting NoSQL databases include changing the default ports, binding the interface to only one IP, and encrypting data in the application prior to writing it to the database. Answer A is incorrect because it is recommended to bind the interface to only one IP address, not to multiple IP addresses. Answer D is incorrect because encryption is not built in to NoSQL databases. Confidentiality and integrity have to be provided entirely by the application accessing the data.

What Next?

If you want more practice on this chapter's exam objectives before you move on, remember that you can access all the Cram Quiz questions on the CD. You can also create a custom exam by objective with the practice exam software. Note any objective that you struggle with and go to the material that covers that objective in this chapter.

CHAPTER 8

Host Security

This chapter covers the following official CompTIA Security+ SY0-401 exam objectives:

▶ Summarize mobile security concepts and technologies

▶ Given a scenario, select the appropriate solution to establish host security

(For more information on the official CompTIA Security+ SY0-401 exam topics, see the "About the CompTIA Security+ SY0-401 Exam" section in the Introduction.)

As technology advances, we add more device types to the network. Most organizations have some type of handheld mobile devices that connect to the network, such as a smartphones or tablets. With these devices becoming more popular, organizations will not only incorporate them into the network but also will have to determine security policies for these devices, especially when the device belongs to the employee. When dealing with host security issues, two general areas need to be covered. The first one involves using protocols and software to protect data. This covers software that can help protect the internal network components, such as personal firewalls and antivirus software. The second one addresses the physical components such as hardware, network components, and physical security designs that can be used to secure the devices.

Summarize Mobile Security Concepts and Technologies

▶ Device security

▶ Application security

▶ BYOD concerns

CramSaver

If you can correctly answer these questions before going through this section, save time by skimming the Exam Alerts in this section and then completing the Cram Quiz at the end of the section.

1. Explain what measures can be taken to secure handheld mobile devices.

2. Explain what measures can be taken to secure applications on handheld mobile devices.

3. Explain what areas should be taken into consideration when implementing a BYOD program.

Answers

1. A screen lock or passcode is used to prevent access to the device. Because passwords are one of the best methods of acquiring access, password length is an important consideration for mobile devices. Just like the data on hard drives, the data on mobile devices can be encrypted. Remote wipe allows the handheld's data to be remotely deleted in the event the device is lost or stolen. Mobile voice encryption allows executives and employees alike to discuss sensitive information without having to travel to secure company locations. In the event a mobile device is lost, GPS tracking can be used to find the location of the device.

2. Recommendations for application security include restricting which applications may be installed through white listing, digitally signing applications to ensure that only applications from trusted entities are installed on the device, and distributing the organization's applications from a dedicated mobile application store.

3. Formulating a BYOD program requires a security model that provides differentiated levels of access by device, user, application, and location. Implementation of a BYOD program and related policies fall into several realms that include general technical considerations, financial responsibility, technical support, and corporate liability.

Device Security

There are specific steps for mitigating mobile device attacks. Both enterprise administrators and users need to be aware of the growing risks associated with the convenience of having the Internet and the corporate network data in the palm of your hand. The most effective way to secure restricted data is not to store it on mobile devices. In many organizations, this does not happen. The commingling of personal and organizational data is inevitable unless some safeguards are in place, such as keeping sensitive data only on secure servers and accessing it remotely using secure communication techniques outlined in the security policy. Another option is to have the user and organizational data separated on the device. This limits business risk associated with enterprise data on mobile devices by compartmentalizing the data. It leaves employees' private information untouched and enforces policies and compliance at the application level. The risk areas associated with mobile devices are physical risk, including theft or loss, unauthorized access risk, operating system or application risk, network risk, and mobile device data storage risk.

To mitigate these risks, many of the same protections that apply to computers apply to mobile devices. Safeguards include screen locks, encryption, remote wipes, GPS tracking, and proper access.

Full Device Encryption

Just like the data on hard drives, the data on mobiles can be encrypted but can present some challenges. First, it is difficult to enter complex passwords on small keyboards, and multifactor authentication is unfeasible. The limited processing power of mobiles also means that the extra computation required for encryption may cause them to suffer performance issues, and the always-on nature of these devices means that encryption can easily break functionality. Another consideration is that because of the variety of devices, a company may have to implement various encryption methods. For example, BlackBerry Enterprise Server can be used to manage built-in data encryption, whereas Windows Android and Windows mobile devices can use a third-party encryption solution.

Mobile voice encryption can allow executives and employees alike to discuss sensitive information without having to travel to secure company locations. A number of options are available for voice encryption. Secusmart makes microSD flash cards that fit into certain Nokia devices. The software is installed on the phone when the card is first inserted into a device. Another hardware option is what is called *embedded encryption*. KoolSpan's TrustChip is one such solution. TrustChip consists of three main components:

▶ Embedded encryption software on the chip

▶ Linux-based management server

▶ TrustChip software development kit (SDK)

Third-party software applications can provide secure VoIP communication for iPhone, Android, and BlackBerry devices by using 256-bit AES military-grade encryption to encrypt calls between users. For added security, 1024-bit RSA encryption can be used during the symmetric key exchange. This type of application can provide VoIP connectivity for secure calls over several networks including 3G, 4G, and Wi-Fi.

One thing to keep in mind when using voice encryption software is that it must be installed on each mobile phone to create a secure connection. You cannot create a secure encrypted connection between a device that has software installed and one that does not. This includes hardware solutions as well. For example, TrustChip encrypts voice only when the phone calls another TrustChip phone. The user sees an icon on his display that informs him that the call is encrypted.

As with many other solutions, using voice encryption is not an end-all solution. It has been discovered that many commercially available mobile voice encryption products can be intercepted and compromised using a little ingenuity and creativity. Some applications can be compromised in as little as a few minutes.

Enterprise-level encryption solutions are also available that encompass a number of different devices. For example, Sophos Mobile Control provides device protection on iOS, Android, and Windows mobile devices. It can secure mobile devices by centrally configuring security settings and enabling lockdown of unwanted features; and it offers remote over-the-air lock or wipe if a device is lost or stolen in addition to having a self-service portal that allows end users to register new devices and lock or wipe lost or stolen phones.

Remote Wiping

The data stored on a mobile device is worth a lot more than the device itself. Mobile device carry a variety of personal and business information, so it's imperative to prevent them from getting into the wrong hands. Many of today's smartphones support a mobile kill switch or remote wipe capability.

Several vendors offer services to Apple users that allow a remote wipe on a lost or stolen iPhone. There are also options to erase all data on the iPhone after a certain number of failed passcode attempts. iPhone models 3GS and newer include hardware encryption, and all data is encrypted on-the-fly. This means that for newer iPhone models you do not need to actually wipe the phone's entire contents; remote wiping the encryption key works. Via remote administration, any BlackBerry Enterprise Server (BES) handset can be erased, reset to factory default settings, or set to retain the IT policy it previously had. This is done via the Erase Data and Disable Handheld command over the wireless network. By default, the device deletes all data after ten bad password attempts. Microsoft's My Phone Windows Phone service enables users to locate lost handhelds via GPS and erase their data remotely. To enable remote wipe on enterprise Android phones, the phone must have the Google Apps Device Policy app installed. This is similar in functionality to the remote control features for a BES. In fact, soon Androids and iPhones will be able to be managed through a BES-like solution.

Remote wipes aren't fail-safe. If someone finds the phone before the remote wipe occurs and either takes the device off the network or force-reboots and restores the device, sensitive data can still be recovered. In the case of BlackBerry devices, if the device is turned off or outside the coverage area, the remote wipe command is queued on the BES until the device can be contacted. If a user is removed from the BES before the command has reached the smartphone, data will not be erased from the device.

In addition to enterprise or built-in remote wiping tools, third-party products can be used to remove sensitive information. Some products are good solutions for a particular device type, whereas others cover all three major mobile device types. Most solutions can securely wipe media cards, be configured to wipe data remotely from a device that has been lost or stolen, automatically wipe the device clean when there is an attempt to insert another SIM card, or disable the phone function.

Lockout

Most mobile phones have the ability to lock the phone, requiring the user to input a passcode or password to access the phone and applications. Figure 8.1 shows the passcode unlock screen of a mobile device.

FIGURE 8.1 **Passcode unlock screen**

Passcodes are a first line of defense and should be required on all devices that access corporate resources. The number of times a user can attempt to input a password or code will depend on the OS or corporate policy. For example, by default the vendor may allow seven bad attempts before the device is locked. If the user fails to enter the correct passcode or password on the screen after seven attempts, the phone will prompt the user to wait for 30 seconds before he can try again. For a reset, the user is required to provide the original email account name and password used to set up the phone. Corporate policies may be more restrictive and tend to lean more toward five bad attempts before the phone becomes locked.

Screen Locks

A screen lock or passcode is used to prevent access to the device. Screen locks can be set on just about any mobile device, such as smartphones or tablets. This feature is used as a most basic form of security. It is done using a pattern lock or a passcode to secure the device. It's similar to a password-protected screensaver on a computer. The lock code usually consists of a four-digit code or PIN. Screen lock only locks users out of the user interface. It does not encrypt data.

Screen locks should be configured to lock the device screen automatically after a brief period of about 10 or 15 minutes of inactivity. Androids can use a pattern on the screen instead of a passcode. Figure 8.2 shows the pattern unlock screen of a mobile device.

FIGURE 8.2 **Pattern unlock screen**

One caveat: You need your Gmail/Google account credentials to reset the security lock should you forget it, so be sure to set up a valid Gmail/Google account beforehand. There are also a number of applications available in the Android application marketplace that can add additional security measures.

GPS

If a mobile device is lost, you can use Global Positioning System (GPS) tracking to find the location. More commonly, employers use this feature to locate employees via their devices.

> **ExamAlert**
>
> GPS tracking features can be used on company-issued devices as a deterrent to prevent the unauthorized, personal use of vehicles and the taking of unauthorized, unscheduled breaks. If a mobile device is lost, you can also use GPS tracking to find the location of the device.

In the case of serious crimes, such as the hijacking of an armored vehicle, GPS-enabled devices can help locate and recover the stolen vehicle and possibly save the lives of the guards.

There are a number of ways to track the location of a mobile phone. Applications such as FlexiSPY use General Packet Radio Service (GPRS) and allow the GPS coordinates to be downloaded in a variety of formats. This makes it easy to import the coordinates into mapping software or create archives. Some software programs use a BES and BlackBerry's push technology to enable IT administrators to track devices through a web-based mapping platform, accessible from any computer or cell phone with an Internet connection. Phone Tracker for iPhones can reveal any geographic locations visited. Applications such as My Tracks or InstaMapper can also be used with Android or iOS.

In addition to applications, there are also services that provide GPS tracking for devices. For example, AccuTracking online GPS cell phone tracking service allows viewing of real-time device locations for about $6 per month. Software is installed on the phone, a PC is used to add the device to the vendor's web interface, the phone communicates with the server, and then the device is tracked with viewing done through the vendor website.

Application Control

Both iOS and Android isolate applications and sensitive operating system features using a method called sandboxing. *Sandboxing* is a security method used to keep running applications separate. Although this design reduces the threat surface, there is still the potential for malware or spyware to be installed. The mobile threat landscape is increased by applications that are more ambiguous in nature such as those that require excessive privileges or that access sensitive data.

> **ExamAlert**
>
> In a corporate environment, applications can be managed through provisioning and controlling access to available mobile applications. This is called *mobile application management* (MAM).

One of the biggest security risks is applications that share data across environments such as Dropbox, Box, Google Drive, OneDrive, and iCloud. Organizations should carefully consider what apps to allow on their production networks.

Storage Segmentation

Storage segmentation separates personal and business content on the device.

> **ExamAlert**
>
> Storage segmentation allows protection of business content from security risks introduced by personal usage.

Security and data protection policies are applied to a segmented business container on a personal or company-owned device.

Applications such as those provided by Good Technology offer a security container that separates company and personal information. The enterprise container is an encrypted envelope that securely houses enterprise data and applications on the device, encrypting all data with strong Advanced Encryption Standard (AES) 192-bit encryption. This solution also encrypts any data that's in transit between the device and servers behind the organization's firewall.

Asset Tracking and Inventory Control

Asset tracking provides effective management of assets in the field so that the device location is known at all times. Applications that allow the use of an asset's ID or barcode provide reliable inventory control and an up-to-date status on assets. Asset tracking is important to quickly identify a device when it is lost or stolen. Inventory control helps the organization keep a firm handle on how many devices are on hand, how many are issued, and to monitor that devices are returned upon employment termination.

Mobile Device Management

Mobile device management (MDM) differs from mobile application management.

MDM provides functionality and control over enterprise devices by allowing the enrollment of enterprise devices for management functions such as provisioning devices, tracking inventory, changing configurations, updating, managing applications, and enforcing policies. For example, VPN and passcode settings can be pushed out to users, saving support a lot of time and effort.

Device Access Control

Employees and guests routinely connect personal devices to corporate networks. To avoid unauthorized devices on the network, an organization can enforce access control through solutions such as mobile endpoint security. Other alternatives for device access control include Next Generation Firewall (NGFW) and intrusion-prevention systems (IPS) because they have the capability to enforce policies blocking certain mobile devices and high-risk applications at the network level.

When an employee is terminated, access can be removed remotely.

Removable Storage

Most mobile devices have an external media card used for storage. In addition to encryption of the data in the device, the data on the media card needs to be encrypted as well. Full device encryption is an added feature that enables users to secure sensitive information on a mobile device's removable flash memory storage card. The data is accessible only when the card is installed in a particular mobile device. If the card is ever lost or stolen, the information remains secure because it is encrypted.

Disabling Unused Features

Unused features on the mobile devices should be disabled. Depending on the organizational needs, it might be advisable to disable other features on the devices as well. For example, if an employee works with highly confidential or trade secret information, the organization may require the camera on corporate devices to be disabled.

> **ExamAlert**
>
> If Bluetooth is necessary for an organization's mobile devices, it should be set to nondiscoverable.

Application Security

In addition to device security, you need to consider mobile application security. The primary attack points on mobiles devices are data storage, key stores, the application file system, application databases, caches, and configuration files. Recommendations for application security include restricting which applications may be installed through white listing, digitally signing applications to ensure that only applications from trusted entities are installed on the device, and distributing the organization's applications from a dedicated mobile application store. This section discusses these recommendations and provides some defense-in-depth strategies to prevent related security breaches.

Key Management

When data is encrypted, key management and key recovery procedures must be in place. Encryption key management systems can be either console-based software or hardware appliances.

> **ExamAlert**
>
> Key management is intended to provide a single point of management for keys and to enable users to manage the life cycle of keys and to store them securely, while also making key distribution easier.

Some mobile operating systems have application key management features built in. In iOS, the keychain provides storage for encryption keys and certificates. After an application requests access to a keychain, it can store and retrieve sensitive data. Android also has a similar keychain capability. On a mobile device, it is quite easy to extract a key and decrypt data when the key is stored either with the encrypted data or as a file private to the application, especially if the device is rooted. This weakness could allow unauthorized applications access to sensitive information. To better protect the keys, one solution is not to store keys but to derive them from user-entered passwords.

Credential Management

Access controls rely on the use of credentials to validate the identities of users, applications, and devices. Credentials for applications such as usernames and passwords are stored in databases on the device, and many times the credentials are not encrypted. MDM solutions allow organizations to employ solutions for managing application credentials that reduce the risk of compromised credentials, protect data more effectively, reduce operational costs, and improve efficiency.

Authentication

Security best practice requires strong authentication credentials so that a device can be trusted on the enterprise's network and with access to enterprise applications. Passwords are one of the primary methods of acquiring access. For applications that require authentication, password length and complexity is an important consideration. Using strong passwords lowers the overall risk of a security breach, but strong passwords do not replace the need for other effective security controls.

> **ExamAlert**
>
> Using static passwords for authentication has a few security flaws because passwords can be guessed, forgotten, or written down.

Mobile phones that are capable of running Java applets are common, so a mobile phone can be used as an authentication token. Many vendors offer one-time passwords (OTP) as an authentication solution for Java-capable mobile devices. An application may require an OTP for performing highly sensitive operations such as fund transfers. OTPs can be either Short Messaging Service (SMS) generated or device generated. Device-generated OTPs are better than SMS OTPs because they eliminate the sniffing and delivery time issues associated with SMS OTP.

Geotagging

Geotagging location services are based on positions and coordinates provided by a GPS.

> **ExamAlert**
>
> The security risks associated with geotagging are unwanted advertising, spying, stalking, and theft. Some social networking sites and services show the location of the logged-on user.

Geotagging enables location data to be attached to images, videos, SMS messages, and website postings, providing permanent and searchable data. Geotagging can be limited by turning off features in social network accounts, disabling location services, and using location features selectively.

Encryption

There are several reasons why you might want to encrypt data from a mobile application. Application data is encrypted to make sure that files exported to shared storage, such as the device's SD card, are not easily accessible to other applications. Some applications store sensitive data on mobile devices and require encryption. Application encryption is used to encrypt sensitive information stored by the app or limit content accessibility to users who have the appropriate access key. Some encryption options for encrypting applications are to use MDM to allow the data to be encrypted by the device itself, allowing the application to provide its own encryption scheme, or to use a MDM application wrapping technology that wraps system calls and automatically performs encryption and decryption on the application data.

Application White Listing

Managing mobile applications is a top security concern for organizations. Applications can be managed by white listing or black listing. The general concept behind application white listing is that instead of attempting to block malicious files and activity as black listing does, application white listing permits only known good apps.

> **ExamAlert**
>
> When security is a concern, white listing applications is a better option because it allows organizations to maintain strict control over the apps employees are approved to use.

White listing apps can be controlled through various degrees of MDM polces. One of the most effective techniques for managing a whitelist is to automatically trust certain publishers of software. White listing increases administrative overhead but offers better control, and in a highly secure environment, maintaining a whitelist may entail exerting strict device control, preventing pairing over USB, deploying only in-house enterprise apps, and removing user capability for installing or deleting apps.

Transitive Trust/Authentication

The concept of transitive trust for mobile devices is very similar to identity federation but can cross boundaries of authentication domains at the application layer. Identity federation defines a set of technologies used to provide authentication (sign-in) services for applications. Transitive trusts enable decentralized authentication through trusted agents.

> **ExamAlert**
>
> Application transitive trusts and authentication can be used to improve availability of service access but can present security issues. When applications interact with each other, restricting one application may create an environment for data to still leave the mobile device through the other application. An application with only local permissions may send sensitive data through third-party applications to external destinations.

BYOD Concerns

Bring your own device (BYOD) focuses on reducing corporate costs and increasing productivity by allowing employees, partners, and guests to connect to the corporate network for access to resources. More employees are using personal devices for critical job functions, requiring organizations to examine methods for better control over mobile devices and implement solutions such as MDM and MAM.

> **ExamAlert**
>
> Formulating a BYOD program requires a security model that provides differentiated levels of access by device, user, application, and location.

Implementation of a BYOD program and related policies requires consideration in several realms, including general technical considerations, financial responsibility, technical support, and corporate liability. This section covers those areas and the security concerns that need to be addressed in BYOD policies.

Data Ownership

Data ownership on an employee-owned device used on a corporate network becomes a combination of corporate data and personal data. Many organizations approach this issue by using either containerization or MDM solutions. When formulating a BYOD policy, the organization should clearly state who owns the data stored on the device, specifically addressing what data belongs to the organization. The policy should include language stipulating the organization will remote wipe data if the employee violates the BYOD policy, terminates employment, or purchases a new device. Some organizations also reiterate user responsibility for backing up of any personal data stored on the device.

Support Ownership

Many organizations save IT support costs because implementing BYOD programs have less device support obligations. Support time is minimal and mostly limited to helping employees initially getting the devices up and running on the network. Most BYOD policies establish what types of devices are permitted to access the network and state that employees are responsible for voice and data plan billing and maintenance of their devices.

Patch and Antivirus Management

When corporate data resides on a personal device, there is risk due to viruses, malware, and OS-related vulnerabilities.

> **ExamAlert**
>
> In a BYOD environment, the organization sets minimum security requirements or mandates security as a condition for allowing personal devices access to network resources.

Policy should be clear on the requirements for installing updates, patches, and antivirus software. Policy options might include the approval of updates and patches or specific antivirus and mandatory reporting of any suspected instances of malware infection. In addition, the inclusion of policy compliance, notification that IT may push updates as required, and responsibility for antivirus software costs may be part of the policy.

Forensics

A key issue in BYOD is the handling of device data when an investigation is required. Any captured data is likely to include personal information of the employee along with corporate data. Although tools can be used to record WLAN data from capture points for forensics, many times the device itself may require imaging. Organizations can try to limit the scope of an investigation or data capture when a personal device is involved. But there are prevailing litigation consequences for failing to preserve data.

ExamAlert

In a BYOD environment, legal requirements take precedence. In the event of an investigation, the employee may be temporarily unable to use the personal device during the investigation period.

Organizations need to address this scenario when creating a BYOD policy, being sure that proper BYOD incident response procedures are formulated and communicated to the users.

Privacy

Data privacy is a concern (not only for the individual but also for the organization) when employees bring their own devices to the corporate network. This holds especially true in organizations that are bound by legal requirements regarding the storage of private personal information, such as in the medical and financial industries. Privacy concerns should be addressed in a BYOD policy. The BYOD policy may need to contain language prohibiting or limiting remote access for certain categories of sensitive data.

The employees should be notified of the monitoring and personal data access capability of the organization. The BYOD policy should clearly disclose how the organization will access an employee's personal data, and in instances where the organization offers device data backup, it should state whether personal data will be stored on backup media or otherwise. In many cases, the organizational BYOD policy will clearly indicate that the organization does not guarantee employee privacy once an employee chooses to be a part of the BYOD workforce.

Onboarding/Offboarding

Onboarding is a term describing the process of registering an asset and provisioning the asset so it can be used to access the corporate network.

Offboarding is the opposite process. In BYOD cases, many organizations use a self-service method through a preconfigured profile to minimize IT intervention. As part of best practice onboarding procedures, some solutions offer integration with Active Directory. This allows a simplified way to identify domain user groups that are permitted to onboard their devices. When an employee is terminated, retires, or quits, it might be difficult to segregate and retrieve organizational data and applications. The BYOD policy should address how data and corporate-owned applications will be retrieved during the offboarding process. In some instances, the organization may opt for a total device wipe.

Adherence to Corporate Policies

When implementing a BYOD policy, employees need to be made aware of, understand, and accept the BYOD policy as it relates to an organization's policies. Many organizations stipulate that they have the right to wipe a device at any time and will not assume responsibility for any loss of data if the device is wiped. Some organizations require employees to install software that provides additional security. Corporate policies may ban rooted or jailbroken devices and the use of file-sharing sites such as Dropbox, Google Drive, OneDrive, or iCloud. Users who are part of the BYOD program are expected to adhere to all corporate policies.

User Acceptance

Employee consent or user acceptance of the BYOD policy helps protect the organization in the event security measures need to be implemented that affect the device. These measures can include seizure of the device or deleting all device data.

ExamAlert

The employees should sign a written consent agreeing to all terms and conditions of the BYOD policy so the organization can easily refute any claim of policy unawareness.

The signed agreements should be kept on file in case the organization needs to take future action that pertains to the device.

Architecture/Infrastructure Considerations

Implementing a BYOD program requires planning and understanding of the access methods and device management options for the devices. In addition to the 802.11 infrastructure, bandwidth, network saturation, and scalability should be considered. There might be a need for manual provisioning of devices, but the design architecture usually includes some type of MDM solution so that security, management of mobile endpoints, self-service for enterprise applications, and onboarding can more easily be managed. Most MDM solutions offer management capabilities through virtualization architecture, identity-based access and provisioning, device identification, authentication, authorization, and policy enforcement. When choosing a centralized MDM strategy, the organization can use a solution offered by mobile device vendor or use a product from a third party. Both approaches are similar, using a typical client/server architecture.

Legal Concerns

Legal concerns for implementing a BYOD program and related policies include whether the policies will be enforceable, whether data privacy laws will restrict security controls and required user consent, whether laws and regulations might limit the capability to audit and monitor activity on personally owned devices, and consent to access the device for business purposes. Furthermore, some legal ramifications relate to the ability to determine the liability of the organization for application usage, licensing, removing sensitive data and organizational applications, and wiping data from a personal device. All legal concerns should be addressed prior to program implementation.

Acceptable-Use Policy

In a BYOD environment, an organization may choose to use a personal device use policy in addition the organizational acceptable-use policy. A personal device use policy defines responsibilities, guidelines, and terms of use for employee-owned devices accessing the organizational network. Often, a personal device use policy is created to address expense limitations and because access to the Internet, applications, and peer-to-peer file sharing is subject to different policies when the use is for personal purposes rather than corporate purposes.

Onboard Camera/Video

Many organizations produce and store proprietary information. Allowing employee-owned devices on the network that can instantly take pictures and record video and audio pose security risks. BYOD policies should cover the use of camera, video, and audio recordings as they relate to the organizational work environment.

> **ExamAlert**
>
> A comprehensive BYOD policy should clearly state restrictions on the usage of cameras, video, audio, or other applications and services.

Although employees may be trustworthy, if the device is lost or stolen, proprietary information could compromised. In high-security areas, the mobile device may have to be surrendered if it is equipped with any of these features.

Cram Quiz

Answer these questions. The answers follow the last question. If you cannot answer these questions correctly, consider reading this section again until you can.

1. Which of the follow methods would be the most effective method to automate management of mobile devices, such as tracking inventory, changing configurations, updating, and enforcing policies?

   ○ **A.** Mobile application management

   ○ **B.** Onboarding

   ○ **C.** Mobile device management

   ○ **D.** Device access controls

2. Which of the following is included in a BYOD policy?

   ○ **A.** Key management

   ○ **B.** Data ownership

   ○ **C.** Credential management

   ○ **D.** Transitive trusts

3. An organization is looking to add a layer of security and maintain strict control over the apps employees are approved to use. Which of the following fulfills this requirement?

   ○ **A.** Black listing

   ○ **B.** Encryption

   ○ **C.** Lockout

   ○ **D.** White listing

4. An organization is looking for a mobile solution that will allow executives and employees alike to discuss sensitive information without having to travel to secure company locations. Which of the following fulfills this requirement?

   ○ **A.** GPS tracking

   ○ **B.** Remote wipe

   ○ **C.** Voice encryption

   ○ **D.** Passcode policy

5. Which of the following is needed to implement an effective BYOD program? (Choose two correct answers.)

   ○ **A.** Key management

   ○ **B.** Legal considerations

    ○   **C.** Infrastructure considerations

    ○   **D.** Storage limitations

Cram Quiz Answers

1. **C**. MDM allows the enrollment of enterprise devices for management functions such as provisioning devices, tracking inventory, changing configurations, updating, managing applications, and enforcing policies. Answer A is incorrect because mobile application management focuses on application management. Answer B is incorrect because onboarding is a term describing the process of registering an asset and provisioning the asset so that it can be used to access the corporate network. Answer D is incorrect because device access controls are used to control network access, not to manage devices.

2. **B**. When formulating a BYOD policy, the organization should clearly state who owns the data stored on the device, specifically addressing what data belongs to the organization. Answer A is incorrect because key management is intended to provide a single point of management for keys and to enable users to manage the life cycle of keys and to store them securely, while also making key distribution easier. Answer C is incorrect because the use of credentials is to validate the identities of users, applications, and devices. Answer D is incorrect because transitive trusts enable decentralized authentication through trusted agents.

3. **D**. Application white listing permits only known good apps. When security is a concern, white listing applications is a better option because it allows organizations to maintain strict control over the apps employees are approved to use. Answer A is incorrect because although black listing is an option, it is not as effective as white listing. Answer B is incorrect because encryption has nothing to do with restricting application usage. Answer C is incorrect because lockout has to do with number of times a user can enter a passcode.

4. **C**. Mobile voice encryption can allow executives and employees alike to discuss sensitive information without having to travel to secure company locations. Answer A is incorrect because if a mobile device is lost, GPS tracking can be used to find the location. Answer B is incorrect because remote wipe allows the handheld's data to be remotely deleted if the device is lost or stolen. Answer D is incorrect because a screen lock or passcode is used to prevent access to the phone.

5. **B** and **C**. To establish an effective BYOD program, all legal concerns should be addressed prior to program implementation. Implementing a BYOD program requires planning and understanding of the access methods and device management options for the devices. Answer A is incorrect because key management is intended to provide a single point of management for keys and to enable users to manage the life cycle of keys and to store them securely, while also making key distribution easier. Answer D is incorrect because storage limitations are not a primary consideration in BYOD.

Given a Scenario, Select the Appropriate Solution to Establish Host Security

▶ **Operating system security and settings**

▶ **OS hardening**

▶ **Anti-malware**

▶ **Patch management**

▶ **White listing versus black listing applications**

▶ **Trusted OS**

▶ **Host-based firewalls**

▶ **Host-based intrusion detection**

▶ **Hardware security**

▶ **Host software baselining**

▶ **Virtualization**

CramSaver

If you can correctly answer these questions before going through this section, save time by skimming the Exam Alerts in this section and then completing the Cram Quiz at the end of the section.

1. Explain how virtualization is used for host security.

2. Explain what devices can be used for physical security of host machines.

3. Explain what is included in hardening a host operating system.

4. Explain what is needed to establish effective security baselines for host systems.

5. Explain what procedures should be used to properly protect a host from malware.

Answers

1. The flexibility of being able to run a Windows guest operating on top of a Linux-based host operating system allows security as well as access to both environments without having to dual boot the machine. Virtualization improves enterprise desktop management and control with faster deployment of desktops and fewer support calls due to application conflicts. Virtualization reduces an entire functioning computer down to just a couple of files, which is obviously much easier to manage than the thousands and thousands of files in the Windows directory alone. With virtualization, it is not only practical, but also logical to simply discard an old or infected virtual machine (VM) in favor of a fresh copy.

2. Security cables with combination locks can provide physical security and are easy to use. PC Safe Barlock Tower and server cages, which have all-steel construction and a lever locking system, are designed to bolt to the floor and prevent theft. A locked cabinet is another alternative for mobile devices that are not used or do not have to be physically accessed on a regular, daily basis. Vendors provide solutions such as security cabinet lockers that secure CPU towers. The housing is made of durable, heavy-duty steel for strength that lasts.

3. Hardening of the operating system includes planning against both accidental and directed attacks, such as the use of fault-tolerant hardware and software solutions. In addition, it is important to implement an effective system for file-level security, including encrypted file support and secured file system selection that allows the proper level of access control. For example, the Microsoft New Technology File System (NTFS) allows file-level access control and encryption, whereas older File Allocation Table (FAT)-based file systems allow only share-level access control and no encryption. It is also imperative to include regular update reviews for all deployed operating systems to address newly identified exploits and apply security patches, hotfixes, and service packs.

4. To establish effective security baselines, enterprise network security management requires a measure of commonality between systems. Mandatory settings, standard application suites, and initial setup configuration details all factor into the security stance of an enterprise network.

5. All host devices must have some type of malware protection. A necessary software program for protecting the user environment is antivirus software. Antivirus software is used to scan for malicious code in email and down-loaded files. Anti-spam and anti-spyware software can add another layer of defense to the infrastructure. Pop-up blocking software programs are available through browsers. Desktops and mobile devices need to have layered security just like servers do. However, many organizations stop this protection at antivirus software, which in today's environment might not be enough to ward off malware, phishing, and rootkits. One of the most common ways to protect desktops and mobile devices is to use a personal firewall.

Operating System Security and Settings

In security terms, *hardening* a system refers to reducing its security exposure and strengthening its defenses against unauthorized access attempts and other forms of malicious attention. A "soft" system is one that is installed with default configurations or unnecessary services or one that is not maintained to include emerging security updates. There is no such thing as a "completely safe" system, so the process of hardening reflects attention to security thresholds.

Systems installed in default configurations often include many unnecessary services that are configured automatically. These provide many potential avenues for unauthorized access to a system or network. Many services have known vulnerabilities that require specific action to make them more secure or ones that might just impair system function by causing additional processing overhead. Default configurations also allow for unauthorized access and exploitation.

> **Note**
>
> A denial-of-service (DoS) attack against an unneeded web service is one example of how a nonessential service could potentially cause problems for an otherwise functional system.

Common default-configuration exploits include both services such as anonymous-access FTP servers and network protocols such as the Simple Network Management Protocol (SNMP). Others may exploit vendor-supplied default logon/password combinations, such as the Oracle DB default admin: scott/tiger.

> **ExamAlert**
>
> When presented with a scenario on the exam, you might be tempted to keep all services enabled to cover all requirements. Be wary of this option; it might cause the installation of unnecessary services or protocols.

To establish effective security baselines, enterprise network security management requires a measure of commonality between systems. Mandatory settings, standard application suites, and initial setup configuration details all factor into the security stance of an enterprise network.

Types of configuration settings you should be familiar with include the following:

▶ **Group policies:** Collections of configuration settings applied to a system based on computer or user group membership, which may influence the level, type, and extent of access provided.

▶ **Security templates:** Sets of configurations that reflect a particular role or standard established through industry standards or within an organization, assigned to fulfill a particular purpose. Examples include a "minimum-access" configuration template assigned to limited-access kiosk systems, whereas a "high-security" template could be assigned to systems requiring more stringent login and access control mechanisms.

▶ **Configuration baselines:** Many industries must meet specific criteria established as a baseline measure of security. An example of this is the healthcare industry, which has a lengthy set of requirements for information technology specified in the Health Insurance Portability and Accountability Act (HIPAA) security standards. Unless the mandated security baseline is met, penalties and fines could be assessed. Security baselines are often established by governmental mandate, regulatory bodies, or industry representatives, such as the Payment Card Industry Data Security Standard (PCI DSS) requirements established by the credit card industry for businesses collecting and transacting credit information.

OS Hardening

Hardening of the operating system includes planning against both accidental data deletion and directed attacks, such as the use of fault-tolerant hardware and software solutions. In addition, it is important to implement an effective system for file-level security, including encrypted file support and secured file system selection that allows the proper level of access control. For example, the Microsoft New Technology File System (NTFS) allows file-level access control and encryption, whereas most File Allocation Table (FAT)-based file systems allow only share-level access control and no encryption.

It is also imperative to include regular update reviews for all deployed operating systems to address newly identified exploits and apply security patches, hotfixes, and service packs. Many automated attacks make use of common vulnerabilities, often ones for which patches and hotfixes are already available but not yet applied. Failure to update applications on a regular basis or perform regular auditing can result in an unsecure solution that provides an attacker access to additional resources throughout an organization's network.

IP Security (IPsec) and public key infrastructure (PKI) implementations must also be properly configured and updated to maintain key and ticket stores. Some systems may be hardened to include specific levels of access, gaining the C2 security rating required by many government deployment scenarios. The Trusted Computer System Evaluation Criteria (TCSEC) rating of C2 indicates a discretionary access control environment with additional requirements such as individual login accounts and access logging.

Operating system hardening includes configuring log files and auditing, changing default administrator account names and default passwords, and the institution of account lockout and password policies to guarantee strong passwords that can resist brute-force attacks. File-level security and access control mechanisms serve to isolate access attempts within the operating system environment. Make sure to understand the *principle of least privilege*, which states that every user or service of a system should only operate with the minimal set of privileges required to fulfill their job duty or function.

Anti-malware

All host devices must have some type of malware protection. According to the 2014 Sophos Security Threat report, malware and related IT security threats have grown and matured in the past few years. Malicious code authors are much more adept at camouflaging their work. Malicious actors use the dark parts of the Internet and are creating new threats that are smarter, shadier, and stealthier.

Antivirus

A necessary software program for protecting the user environment is antivirus software. *Antivirus software* scans for malicious code in email and downloaded files. Antivirus software actually works backward. Virus writers release a virus, it is reported, and then antivirus vendors reverse-engineer the code to find a solution. After the virus has been analyzed, the antivirus software can look for specific characteristics of the virus. Remember that for a virus to be successful, it must replicate its code.

The most common method used in an antivirus program is scanning. Scanning searches files in memory, the boot sector, and on the hard drive and removable media for identifiable virus code. Scanning identifies virus code based on a unique string of characters known as a signature. When the virus software detects the signature, it isolates the file. Then, depending on the software settings, the antivirus software quarantines it or permanently deletes it. Interception software detects virus-like behavior and then pops up a warning to the user. However, because the software looks only at file changes, it might also detect legitimate files.

In the past, antivirus engines used a heuristic engine for detecting virus structures or integrity checking as a method of file comparison. A false positive occurs when the software classifies an action as a possible intrusion when it is actually a nonthreatening action.

> **ExamAlert**
>
> *Heuristic scanning* looks for instructions or commands that are not typically found in application programs. The issue with these methods is that they are susceptible to false positives and cannot identify new viruses until the database is updated.

Antivirus software vendors update their virus signatures on a regular basis. Most antivirus software connects to the vendor website to check the software database for updates and then automatically downloads and installs them as they become available. Besides setting your antivirus software for automatic updates, you should set the machine to automatically scan at least once a week.

If a machine does become infected, the first step is to remove it from the network so that it cannot damage other machines. The best defense against virus infection is user education. Most antivirus software used today is fairly effective, but only if it is kept updated and the user practices safe computing habits, such as not opening unfamiliar documents or programs. Despite all of this, antivirus software cannot protect against brand new viruses, and often users do not take the necessary precautions. Users sometimes disable antivirus software because it might interfere with programs that are currently installed on the machine. Be sure to guard against this type of incident.

Anti-spam

Although the security industry has made strides in preventing spam, a large amount of the email organizations receive daily contains spam. Spam is defined several ways, the most common being unwanted commercial email. Although spam may merely seem to be an annoyance, it uses bandwidth, takes up storage space, and reduces productivity. Spam spread on social networking sites has become a big problem, and social media postings fit within the definition of "commercial electronic mail message" under the federal CAN-SPAM Act of 2003 (Controlling the Assault of Non-Solicited Pornography and Marketing Act of 2003). The CAN-SPAM act makes it unlawful for persons to initiate the transmission of commercial electronic mail messages that contain materially false or misleading header information.

Anti-spam software can add another layer of defense to the infrastructure. You can install anti-spam software in various ways. The most common methods are at the email server or the email client. When the software and updates are installed on a central server and pushed out to the client machines, this is called a *centralized solution*. When the updates are left up to the individual users, you have a *decentralized environment*. The main component of anti-spam software is *heuristic filtering*. Heuristic filtering has a predefined rule set that compares incoming email information against the rule set. The software reads the contents of each message and compares the words in that message against the words in typical spam messages. Each rule assigns a numeric score to the probability of the message being spam. This score is then used to determine whether the message meets the acceptable level set. If many of the same words from the rule set are in the message being examined, it is marked as spam. Specific spam filtering levels can be set on the user's email account. If the setting is high, more spam will be filtered, but it might also filter legitimate email as spam, thus causing false positives.

> ### ExamAlert
>
> It is important to understand that the software cannot assign meaning to the words examined. It simply tracks and compares the words used.

Additional settings can be used in the rule set. In general, an email address added to the approved list is never considered spam. As mentioned previously, this is also known as a *whitelist*. Using whitelists allows more flexibility in the type of email you receive. For example, putting the addresses of your relatives or friends in your whitelist allows you to receive any type of content from them. An email address added to the blocked list is always considered spam. This is also known as a *blacklist*. Other factors might affect the ability to receive email on a whitelist. For example, if attachments are not allowed and the email has an attachment, the message might be filtered even if the address is on the approved list.

Anti-spyware

Many spyware eliminator programs are available. These programs scan your machine, similarly to how antivirus software scans for viruses. Just as with antivirus software, you should keep spyware eliminator programs updated and regularly run scans. Configuration options on anti-spyware software allow the program to check for updates on a regularly scheduled basis. The anti-spyware software should be set to load upon startup and set to automatically update spyware definitions.

Pop-Up Blockers

A common method for Internet advertising is using a window that pops up in the middle of your screen to display a message when you click a link or button on a website. Although some pop-ups are helpful, many are an annoyance, and others can contain inappropriate content or entice the user to download malware.

There are several variations of pop-up windows. A pop-under ad opens a new browser window under the active window. These types of ads often are not seen until the current window is closed. Hover ads are Dynamic Hypertext Markup Language (DHTML) pop-ups. They are essentially "floating pop-ups" in a web page.

Most online toolbars come with pop-up blockers; various downloadable pop-up blocking software programs are available; and the browsers included with some operating systems, such as Windows, can block pop-ups. Pop-up blockers, just like many of the other defensive software discussed so far, have settings that you can adjust. You might want to try setting the software to medium so that it will block most automatic pop-ups but still allow functionality. Keep in mind that you can adjust the settings on pop-up blockers to meet the organizational policy or to best protect the user environment.

Several caveats apply to using pop-up blockers. There are helpful pop-ups. Some web-based programmed application installers use a pop-up to install software.

ExamAlert

If all pop-ups are blocked, the user might not be able to install applications or programs.

Field help for fill-in forms is often in the form of a pop-up. Some pop-up blockers might delete the information already entered by reloading the page, causing users unnecessary grief. You can also circumvent pop-up blockers in various ways. Most pop-up blockers block only the JavaScript; therefore, technologies such as Flash bypass the pop-up blocker. On many Internet browsers, holding down the Ctrl key while clicking a link will allow it to bypass the pop-up filter.

Patch Management

Improperly programmed software can be exploited. Software exploitation is a method of searching for specific problems, weaknesses, or security holes in software code. It takes advantage of a program's flawed code. The most effective way to prevent an attacker from exploiting software bugs is to keep the latest manufacturer's patches and service packs applied and to monitor the Web for new vulnerabilities.

Because of the emergence of blended-threat malware, which targets multiple vulnerabilities within a single attack, all major operating systems and application solutions must be considered in system-hardening plans. Automated reverse-engineering of newly released patches has significantly reduced the time from an update's initial release until its first exploits are seen in the wild, down from months to hours before unpatched applications can be targeted.

Types of updates you should be familiar with include the following:

▶ **Hotfixes:** Typically small and specific-purpose updates that alter the behavior of installed applications in a limited manner. These are the most common type of update.

▶ **Service packs:** Major revisions of functionality or service operation in an installed application. Service packs are the least common type of update, often requiring extensive testing to ensure against service failure in integrated network environments before application. Service packs are usually cumulative, including all prior service packs, hotfixes, and patches.

▶ **Patches:** Like hotfixes, patches are usually focused updates that affect installed applications. Patches are generally used to add new functionality, update existing code operation, or extend existing application capabilities.

ExamAlert

To make the patching process easier, Microsoft releases its patches or hotfixes on a monthly schedule. Any system running Microsoft products in your enterprise should be evaluated for the patch requirements.

Because updates are now released on a schedule, it might be easier to put a sensible plan into place. Should an attacker learn of a vulnerability and release an exploit for it before the update date, the hotfix will be posted ahead of schedule if the situation warrants.

The patch management infrastructure of an organization includes all the tools and technologies that are used to assess, test, deploy, and install software updates. This infrastructure is an essential tool for keeping the entire environment secure and reliable, and therefore it is important that it is managed and maintained properly. When it comes to managing your infrastructure, chances are good that you might have many different types of clients in your network and that they might be at many different levels in regard to the service packs and hot fixes that are applied to them. The most efficient way to update client machines is to use automated processes and products. Many vendors provide regular updates for installed products, managed through automated deployment tools or by manual update procedures carried out by a system user. Regular maintenance is required to meet emerging security threats, whether applying an updated RPM (Red Hat Package Manager, a file format used to distribute Linux applications and update packages) by hand or through fully automated "call home for updates" options such as those found in many commercial operating systems and applications.

Systems Management Server (SMS) assists you in security patch management by its ability to scan computers remotely throughout your network and report the results to a central repository. The results can then be assessed and compared to determine which computers need additional patches.

Microsoft maintains the Automatic Updates website, which contains all the latest security updates. You can configure your Windows host computers to automatically download and install the latest updates on a schedule that you specify. Alternatively, you can choose to download and install the updates yourself. You can configure these settings using Automatic Updates or Windows Update in Windows-based computers. Figure 8.3 shows the Windows update configuration screen.

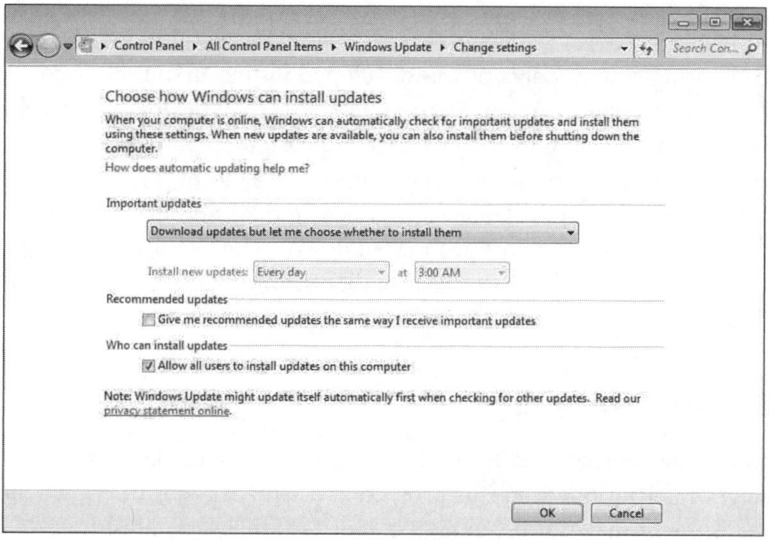

FIGURE 8.3   Windows Update configuration screen

White Listing Versus Black Listing Applications

Organizations control application installations by either black listing or white listing them. Black listing applications consists of listing all applications the organization deems undesirable or banned and then preventing those applications from being installed. The concept of black listing applications is similar to the way antivirus software works. Black listing is generally done to reduce security-related issues, but organizations may blacklist time-wasting or bandwidth-intensive applications. File-sharing apps are the most common blacklisted apps in the enterprise. The top blacklisted apps include Dropbox, SugarSync, Box, Facebook, and Google Drive.

> **ExamAlert**
>
> White listing applications tends to make an environment more closed by only allowing approved applications to be installed.

A whitelist approach uses a list of approved applications. If the application is not on the approved list of software, the application installation is denied or restricted. Application white listing is the preferred method of restricting applications because the approved applications can be allowed to run using numerous methods of trust. This decreases the risk of infection and improves system stability.

Trusted OS

The trusted operating system concept was developed in the early 1980s and is based on technical standards of the Department of Defense (DoD) Trusted Computer System Evaluation Criteria (TCSEC). Trusted operating systems are security-enhanced operating system versions and have access segmented through compartmentalization, role, least privilege, and kernel-level enforcement. Individual components are locked down to protect memory and files, restrict object access, and enforce user authentication. Some applications will not work on a trusted OS because of the strict security settings.

Host-Based Firewalls

Desktops and mobile devices need to have layered security just like servers. However, many organizations stop this protection at antivirus software, which in today's environment may not be enough to ward off malware, phishing, and rootkits. One of the most common ways to protect desktops and mobile devices is to use a personal firewall. Firewalls can consist of hardware, software, or a combination of both. This discussion focuses on software firewalls that you can implement in the user environment.

The potential for hackers to access data through a user's machine has grown substantially as hacking tools have become more sophisticated and difficult to detect. This holds especially true for the telecommuter's machine. Always-connected computers, typical with cable modems, give attackers plenty of time to discover and exploit system vulnerabilities. Many software firewalls are available, and most operating systems now come with them readily available. You can choose to use the OS vendor firewall or to install a separate one.

Like most other solutions, firewalls have strengths and weaknesses. By design, firewalls close off systems to scanning and entry by blocking ports or nontrusted services and applications. However, they require proper configuration. Typically, the first time a program tries to access the Internet, a software firewall asks whether it should permit the communication. Some users might find this annoying and disable the firewall or not understand what the software is asking and allow all communications. Another caveat is that some firewalls monitor only for incoming connections and not outgoing. Remember that even a good firewall cannot protect you if you do not exercise a proper level of caution and think before you download. No system is foolproof, but software firewalls installed on user systems can help make the computing environment safer. Figure 8.4 shows a picture of the Windows Firewall rules.

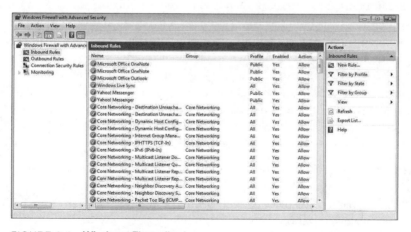

FIGURE 8.4   **Windows Firewall rules**

> **ExamAlert**
>
> Make sure that you can identify the difference between a host-based and a network-based firewall.

Host-Based Intrusion Detection

Host intrusion-detection systems (HIDS) are installed locally on every network computer that has external access. HIDSs monitor communications on a host-by-host basis and try to filter malicious data by means of a locally installed agent. HIDSs can do log analysis, event correlation, integrity checking, policy enforcement, rootkit detection, and alerting. These types of IDSs are good at detecting unauthorized file modifications and user activity. *Host intrusion-prevention systems* (HIPS) are a necessity in any enterprise environment. HIPSs protect hosts against known and unknown malicious attacks from the network layer up through the application layer. HIPS technologies can be categorized by what they scan for, how they recognize an attack, and at what layer they attempt to detect the attack. HIPSs encompass many technologies to protect servers, desktops, and laptops. They are often used as an all-in-one solution that includes everything from traditional signature-based antivirus to behavior analysis.

Hardware Security

Physical access to a system creates many avenues for a breach in security. Many tools can be used to extract password and account information that can then be used to access secured network resources. Given the ability to reboot a system and load software from a USB drive, attackers might be able to access data or implant Trojan horses and other applications intended to weaken or compromise network security. Unsecured equipment is also vulnerable to social-engineering attacks. It is much easier for an attacker to walk into a reception area, say she is there to do some work on the server, and get access to that server in the closet in the front lobby than to get into a physically secured area with a guest sign-in and sign-out sheet.

A more serious threat is theft or loss. Laptops and handheld devices are easy targets for thieves. According to datalossdb.org, stolen laptops account for 11% of all data breaches. To prevent theft or loss, you must safeguard the equipment in your organization.

Cable Locks

To protect organizational resources and minimize liability costs, it is important for each employee to take responsibility for securing office equipment. Laptops should never be left in an area that is open where anyone can have easy access to them. Laptops, Apple iMacs, and any easily transportable office computers should be physically secured. Security cables with combination locks can provide such security and are easy to use. The cable is used to attach the computer to an immovable object. Computers have one and sometimes two security cable slots. The security cable slots allow you to attach a commercially available antitheft device to the computer. Computer locks commonly use steel cables to secure the PC to a desk. They are most commonly found in computer labs and Internet cafes. Laptop locks are meant to protect both privacy and the computer. A number of different types of laptop locks are available: cable locks, case locks, and twist locks. The most common type of antitheft devices for portable computers usually includes a length of metal-stranded cable with an attached locking device and associated key. The cable is looped around an immovable object, and the locking device is inserted into a security cable slot. Antitheft devices differ in design, so be sure that it is compatible with the security cable slot on the computer. Never leave a laptop unsecured. If the area is not safe, do not leave a laptop even if it is secured by a cable-locking device. Thieves have driven off with whole ATM machines, so they can find a way to bypass the lock.

Safe

Tower-style computers can also be targets of thieves, not only for a higher resale value than laptops but also for the data they might hold. For example, financial businesses have been hit hard by theft of desktop computers because they hold a lot of personal data. Secure computer towers and server cages that are designed to bolt to the floor can improve physical security and prevent theft. For machines that are bolted to the floor, drive access can be either completely restricted or left available for ease of use.

There are also laptop safe security cases used to protect an organization's computers and data out in the field. For example, Flexysafe Digital makes a safe that is designed for people who take their laptop computers home from work. Also available are high-security laptop safes, which store laptops in a manner similar to bank vault storage. There is individual storage for laptops in locking compartments, which can then be additionally secured behind the high-security main safe door when required. The open compartment version offers open shelves (usually one laptop per shelf) for storage that can be secured by the safe's main door. Other computer safe options include types made to securely store laptops and carry cases plus other valuable equipment in reception areas, mobile car safes made to prevent smash-and-grab attacks, and a home computer safe with an electronic lock similar to the safes provided in hotel rooms.

Locking Cabinets

A locked cabinet is another alternative for laptop equipment that is not used or does not have to be physically accessed on a regular daily basis. Vendors provide solutions such as a security cabinet locker that secures CPU towers. The housing is made of durable, heavy-duty steel for strength that lasts. The sides and door are ventilated to reduce risk of overheating. Another option is a wood laminate security computer cabinet that provides a computer workstation that can be locked away into a cabinet for space as well as security. Computer cabinets include a keyboard drawer and adjustable top shelf. A slide-out bottom shelf accommodates a CPU and printer. It has built-in cable management grommets. Depending on what needs to be secured, there are computer cabinets designed to hold everything from LCD/LED flat screens to entire systems. This type of security is often used for training rooms, to secure the computers without the inconvenience of removing them after each training session.

Host Software Baselining

The measure of normal activity is known as a *baseline*. This gives you a point of reference when something on the computer goes awry. Without a baseline, it is harder to see what is wrong because you do not know what is normal. Baselines must be updated on a regular basis and certainly when the computer has changed or new technology has been deployed. Baselining should be done for both host and application processes so that you can tell whether you have a hardware or software issue. Host software baselining can be done for a variety of reasons, including malware monitoring and creating system images. Generally, the environment needs of an organization fall into a legacy, enterprise, or high-security client. A legacy client has the lowest lockdown level. It is important that there is a good baseline for these computers because of their vulnerability and lack of ability to configure tightened security settings. The enterprise client environment is designed to provide solid security for the organization and allows the use of more restrictive security templates for added security. Using security templates also allows the organization to introduce additional roles on top of the baseline template for easier implementation of these new roles. In a high-security environment, the settings are very restrictive, and many applications might not function under this type of configuration. Therefore, it is very important to have a baseline.

Virtualization

Virtualization has many benefits, from the data center to the desktop. For example, when working in a development environment, running the new system as a guest avoids the need to reboot the physical computer whenever a bug occurs. A "sandboxed" guest system can also help in computer-security research, which enables the study of the effects of some viruses or worms without the possibility of compromising the host system.

The use of desktop virtualization allows an organization to run multiple operating systems, such as Windows and Linux, on a single computer. With technology permeating every facet of modern life, the flexibility of being able to run a Windows guest operating on top of a Linux-based host operating system allows an added layer of security as well as access to both environments without having to dual boot the machine.

ExamAlert

Virtualization improves enterprise desktop management and control with faster deployment of desktops and fewer support calls because of application conflicts.

Virtualization reduces an entire functioning computer down to just a couple of files, which is obviously much easier to manage than the thousands and thousands of files found in the Windows directory alone. With virtualization, it is not only practical but also logical to simply discard an old or infected virtual machine (VM) in favor of a fresh copy. Virtualized environments are typically subject to the same types of threats as traditional environments. However, virtualization itself may provide an additional attack vector.

Snapshots

A *snapshot* preserves the entire state and data of the virtual machine at the time it is taken. A snapshot includes the VM settings and the state of the machine's virtual drives. The contents of the VM's memory can also be included in the snapshot, but it is not recommended and rarely needed.

> **ExamAlert**
>
> Snapshots may capture sensitive data present on the system at the time the snapshot was taken and can present a situation where personal information is inadvertently put at risk.

Snapshots are useful for eliminating the need to create multiple VMs if there is a need repeatedly return a machine to the same state. In an environment where VM templates are used, disk-based snapshots are a quick way to make a new VM from the template for provisioning.

Patch Compatibility

Some VM products may not certify an operating system for use as a guest OS based on availability of product updates or patch releases. For any guest OS used in a VM environment, OS patches and updates are required. Most VM vendors offer a way to automate host patch management and eliminate common patching problems before they occur. This feature is important when an OS patch or update causes an incompatibility issue with a currently installed application or configuration. Snapshots can be taken and stored so that administrators can easily roll back the VM when a patch causes a compatibility issue.

Host Availability/Elasticity

When dealing with virtualized environments, host availability is a concern. This is where elasticity comes in. The National Institute of Standards and Technology (NIST) defines *elasticity* as the capability for rapid, automatic, and elastic provisioning of resources to quickly scale out and be rapidly released to quickly scale in.

> **ExamAlert**
>
> Elasticity is most often found in cloud environments, where resources can be purchased for a short period of time based on demand and then deleted when no longer needed.

Organizations that have cyclical business periods where the majority of business is done in a few months may choose this option because it saves costs and administrative overhead. Security challenges in an elastic model include enforcing proper configuration, enforcing change management, and adequate administrative separation between virtual customer environments.

Security Control Testing

Virtualization introduces an additional layer of complexity that may require additional security controls and policy management. Appropriate security controls should be implemented in a virtualized environment that provides the same level of security in a physical environment. Additional security controls to be tested in a virtualized environment include hardened VMs, hardened hypervisors, and virtualized network security features.

Sandboxing

Sandboxes and VMs are two different technologies. The basic idea of *sandboxing* is to provide a safe execution environment for untrusted programs. Running a program in a sandbox contains it so that it can be tested, thus reducing some security issues because it cannot harm the host. Virtualized environments are sometimes used as sandboxes. In most browsers, all HTML rendering and JavaScript executions are isolated in their own class of processes.

> ### ExamAlert
>
> Web applications are launched in a sandbox, meaning they run in their own browser windows without the ability to read or write files from sensitive areas.

This is considered sandboxing. Another common use for sandboxing is malware analysis.

Cram Quiz

Answer these questions. The answers follow the last question. If you cannot answer these questions correctly, consider reading this section again until you can.

1. Which of the following methods would be the most effective method to physically secure computers that are used in a lab environment that is not frequently used?

   ○ **A.** Security cables

   ○ **B.** Server cages

   ○ **C.** Locked cabinet

   ○ **D.** Hardware dongles

2. Which of the following is included in hardening a host operating system?

   ○ **A.** A policy for antivirus updates

   ○ **B.** An effective system for file-level security

   ○ **C.** An efficient method to connect to remote sites

   ○ **D.** A policy for remote wipe

3. An organization is looking to add a layer of security and improve enterprise desktop management. Which of the following fulfills this requirement?

   ○ **A.** Roaming profiles

   ○ **B.** Network storage policies

   ○ **C.** VPN remote access

   ○ **D.** Desktop virtualization

4. Which of the following is needed to establish effective security baselines for host systems? (Choose two correct answers.)

   ○ **A.** Cable locks

   ○ **B.** Mandatory settings

   ○ **C.** Standard application suites

   ○ **D.** Decentralized administration

5. Which of the following procedures should be used to properly protect a host from malware? (Choose two correct answers.)

   ○ **A.** Web tracking software

   ○ **B.** Antivirus software

   ○ **C.** Content filtering software

   ○ **D.** Pop-up blocking software

Cram Quiz Answers

1. **C.** A locked cabinet is an alternative for equipment that is not used or does not have to be physically accessed on a regular daily basis. Vendors provide solutions such as a security cabinet locker that secures CPU towers. The housing is made of durable, heavy-duty steel for strength. Answer A is incorrect because security cables with combination locks can provide such security and are easy to use but are used mostly to secure laptops and leave the equipment exposed. Answer B is incorrect because secure computer towers and server cages are designed to bolt to the floor and are meant to be used in an environment that is static. Answer D is incorrect because a hardware dongle, also known as a software copy protection dongle, is used for license enforcement.

2. **B.** Hardening of the operating system includes planning against both accidental data deletions and directed attacks, such as the use of fault-tolerant hardware and software solutions. In addition, it is important to implement an effective system for file-level security, including encrypted file support and secured file system selection that allows the proper level of access control. Answer A is incorrect because it is a host protection measure, not an OS hardening measure. Answer C is incorrect because this is a secure communication measure. Answer D is incorrect because this is a feature associated with data security, not with host hardening.

3. **D.** Virtualization adds a layer of security and improves enterprise desktop management and control with faster deployment of desktops and fewer support calls due to application conflicts. Answer A is incorrect because roaming profiles do not add a layer of security. Answer B is incorrect because network storage policies have nothing to do with desktop management. Answer C is incorrect because VPN remote access will not improve enterprise desktop management.

4. **B** and **C.** To establish effective security baselines, enterprise network security management requires a measure of commonality between the systems. Mandatory settings, standard application suites, and initial setup configuration details all factor into the security stance of an enterprise network. Answer A is incorrect because cable locks have nothing to do with effective security baselines. Answer D is incorrect because decentralized management does not have anything to do with security baselines.

5. **B** and **D.** All host devices must have some type of malware protection. A necessary software program for protecting the user environment is antivirus software. Antivirus software is used to scan for malicious code in email and downloaded files. Anti-spam and anti-spyware software can add another layer of defense to the infrastructure. Pop-up blocking software programs are available through browsers. Answer A is incorrect because web tracking software merely tracks the sites a person visited. Answer C is incorrect because content filtering is done at the server level to keep host machines from accessing certain content.

What Next?

If you want more practice on this chapter's exam objectives before you move on, remember that you can access all the Cram Quiz questions on the CD. You can also create a custom exam by objective with the practice exam software. Note any objective that you struggle with and go to the material that covers that objective in this chapter.

CHAPTER 9

Data Security

This chapter covers the following official CompTIA Security+ SY0-401 exam objectives:

► Implement the appropriate controls to ensure data security

► Compare and contrast alternative methods to mitigate security risks in static environments

(For more information on the official CompTIA Security+ SY0-401 exam topics, see the "About the CompTIA Security+ SY0-401 Exam" section in the Introduction.)

Organizations often approach security as a defense strategy targeting the perimeter of the network. This approach might ignore sensitive data stored on the network, mobile devices, and other devices. The security of organizational data is imperative to prevent attackers from obtaining access to confidential information and to protect sensitive data from employees with high-level access from exploiting this data.

The following section discusses the states of data, how they differ, and how to use and protect data in each particular state. But it is also just as important to have some type of data security life cycle implemented. For example, a data security life cycle might include stages such as create, store, use, archive, and destroy.

Implement the Appropriate Controls to Ensure Data Security

▶ **Cloud storage**

▶ **SAN**

▶ **Handling big data**

▶ **Data encryption**

▶ **Hardware-based encryption devices**

▶ **Data in-transit, data at-rest, data in-use**

▶ **Permissions/ACLs**

▶ **Data policies**

CramSaver

If you can correctly answer these questions before going through this section, save time by skimming the Exam Alerts in this section and then completing the Cram Quiz at the end of the section.

1. Explain the states of data and how they affect data-loss prevention policies.

2. Explain when full disk encryption should be used.

3. Explain what TPM is and how it can be used to secure data.

4. Explain the advantages of using hardware-based USB encryption.

5. Explain how encryption is implemented in a SaaS cloud environment.

Answers

1. Data can generally be considered to be in one of three states: in-use, in-transit, or at-rest. Data-loss prevention (DLP) policies and systems are basically designed to detect and prevent unauthorized use and transmission of confidential information based on one of these three states. Protection of data in-use is considered to be an endpoint solution, and the application is run on end-user workstations or servers in the organization. Protection of data in-transit is considered to be a network solution, and either a hardware or software solution is installed near the network perimeter to monitor for and flag policy violations. Protection of data at-rest is considered to be a storage solution and is generally a software solution that monitors how confidential data is stored.

2. Full disk encryption (FDE), also called whole disk encryption, has gained popularity in recent years to help mitigate the risks associated with lost or stolen mobile devices and accompanying disclosure laws. FDE is most useful when you are dealing with a machine that is being taken on the road, such as the computers used by traveling executives, sales managers, or insurance agents. Because encryption adds overhead, it is less productive for a computer in a fixed location where there is strong physical access control, unless the data is extremely sensitive and must be protected at all costs.

3. Trusted Platform Module (TPM) refers to a secure cryptoprocessor used to authenticate hardware devices such as a PC or laptop. The idea behind TPM is to allow any encryption-enabled application to take advantage of the chip. Therefore, it has many possible applications, such as network access control (NAC), secure remote access, secure transmission of data, whole disk encryption, software license enforcement, digital rights management (DRM), and credential protection. Part of what makes TPM effective is that the TPM module is given a unique ID and master key that even the owner of the system does not control or have knowledge of.

4. No matter how great the encryption algorithm is, if the key is found, the data can be decrypted. When software encryption is used, the key is stored either in the flash memory of the USB drive or on the computer that originated the file encryption. A more secure method is to use a USB drive that stores the encryption key on a separate controller on the device and physically protects the internal contents with a tamper-resistant shell such as the IronKey or LOK-IT. This type of device encrypts all user data stored on the drive using up to 256-bit AES encryption implemented in Cipher Block Chaining (CBC) mode.

5. If using a SaaS environment, the service provider usually encrypts the data. It is essential to enquire where and how the data is encrypted. In some instances, the only encryption provided is basic folder encryption, whereas in other instances data is encrypted using a unique key for every customer. In a SaaS environment, application-level encryption is preferred because the data is encrypted by the application before being stored in the database or file system. The advantage is that it protects the data from the user all the way to storage. To properly secure data stored through a SaaS platform, the organization needs to understand how the provider manages data and the terms of the service contracts.

Cloud Storage

Cloud computing includes various flavors and uses of technology such as desktops-as-a-service and streaming operating systems. The use of these types of environments has a huge potential for a dramatically simplified IT infrastructure with more cost-effective IT management and utilization. But along with that comes the potential for enormous data loss if the data is not properly encrypted. Having highly available cloud data is risky because multiple copies of your data can be in various locations. When you delete files, successful deletion of trace data becomes next to impossible.

Traditional encryption solutions for the purpose of data security protection cannot be adopted for the cloud due to the loss of control of data. Because various kinds of data are stored in the cloud and because of the need for long-term continuous assurance of data security, verifying the correctness of data stored in the cloud becomes even more challenging. Although encryption is far from a total solution for all cloud data security issues, when used properly and in combination with other controls, it provides effective security. In cloud implementations, encryption might help alleviate the security issues related to multitenancy, public clouds, and remote or outsourced hosting. Encrypting data stored in the cloud also helps prevent data from being modified and can reduce the risk of a compromise when sold cloud storage devices still contain organizational information.

The methods used for encryption vary based on the service provider type. Remember from Chapter 1, "Secure Network Design," that cloud computing can be classified as platform-as-a-service (PaaS), software-as-a-service (SaaS), or infrastructure-as-a-service (IaaS). In addition, cloud vendors might have hardware-based solutions in place. In a cloud environment, virtual cryptography-as-a-service deployments are a reality, and some cloud service providers implement a solution with robust security mechanisms, such as centralized key management, granular encryption, and strong access controls. It is best practice to ensure that encryption keys are kept secure and separate from the data.

Because PaaS mainly provides the organization with a development platform, encryption implementation depends on the available application programming interfaces (API) and development environment. Generally speaking, in cloud implementations, data should be encrypted at the application layer rather than within a database, because of the complexity involved. Media encryption is managed at the storage layer.

If using a SaaS environment, the service provider usually encrypts the data. It is essential to enquire where and how the data is encrypted. In some instances, the only encryption provided is basic folder encryption; in other instances, data is encrypted using a unique key for every customer.

> **ExamAlert**
>
> In a SaaS environment, application-level encryption is preferred because the data is encrypted by the application before being stored in the database or file system. The advantage is that it protects the data from the user all the way to storage.

To properly secure data stored through a SaaS platform, the organization needs to understand how the provider manages data and the terms of the service contracts. When using IaaS, virtual private storage is an option. *Virtual private storage* is a method used to protect remote data when there is not complete control of the storage environment. The organization encrypts the data before sending it off to the cloud provider, allowing control over keys and access control lists (ACL). The organization maintains control while still retaining the benefits of cloud-based storage. Many cloud backup solutions use this design. Encrypted virtual machines (VM) are another option. Encryption of a complete VM on IaaS could be considered media encryption.

Several cloud providers have been moving toward the concept of enabling on-premise hardware security modules (HSM) for securing their cloud-hosted applications. This type of environment enables providers to move their applications to the cloud and still keep a root of trust within the HSM. The HSM and cloud machines can both live on the same virtual private network, through the use of a virtual private cloud (VPC) environment. This type of solution is mainly found in private data centers that manage and offload cryptography with dedicated hardware appliances. Using an HSM solution that is properly implemented in a cloud data center can provide the organization a reasonably high level of data protection.

SAN

The main purpose of a storage-area network (SAN) is to allow for high availability of data. Having highly available data at-rest presents security risks. The configuration of a SAN commonly allows connectivity for various types of devices using a SAN fabric. Fabrics were discussed in Chapter 2, "Network Implementation," in the section on Fibre Channel (FC). Weak authentication methods used to send and receive data between the separate components cause SANs to have inherent security problems. When a SAN is not properly protected, it can be compromised through application servers, management systems, the host bus adapter (HBA), or network communications. Because many SANs use IP-based communication, they are susceptible to the same types of attacks as any other IP-based communication.

Organizations can take several steps to better secure SANs. SAN security begins with enhancing the security around the SAN by using filters and ACLs on internal firewalls or routers and hardening all interfacing servers. When addressing the security of the SAN itself, concentrating on physical device security, administrative controls, Fibre Channel access, and vulnerabilities in TCP/IP and Simple Network Management Protocol (SNMP) provides the organization with a better chance of fending off attacks. In addition, other technologies such as data encryption and file access rights are industry best practices and can help protect the environment.

Segregating the FC SAN from the local-area network (LAN) by creating a separate physical network offers a first line of defense. The SAN should be protected against any physical access. As long as physical security is maintained, the only physical security risk is when any type of media is removed from the data center. Device access can be restricted to single zones or shared zones. Zoning can be accomplished through hardware (hard zoning) or software (soft zoning). *Hard zoning*, also called *port zoning*, manages access of the zone members on a port-by-port basis. The FC switch maintains a list of valid port addresses and restricts communication to ports within the zone. *Software zoning* uses stored World Wide Numbers (WWN) from the switch's name server database. The switch checks the WWNs of the source and destination. If the source and destination belong to the same zones, the data is forwarded. Software zoning is more flexible but less secure. A rogue device can connect to the network because WWN can be spoofed. Once the zoning is set up, the SAN can be further locked down by setting up logical unit number (LUN) masking. LUN masking binds the WWN of the HBA on the host server to a specific SCSI identifier, or LUN. LUN masking is a way for the SAN to prevent certain devices from seeing a specific LUN that it is hosting. LUN masking is generally used to hide partitions, so that an application server can see only a designated partition. A final way to secure a SAN is by securing the relationships between SAN subsystems such as host to fabric, management to fabric, and fabric to fabric.

Handling Big Data

Big data is data with a greater volume than can easily be processed using current technology. Big data consists of unstructured data that can be from both internal and external sources. The security issues presented by big data include the following:

▶ Access controls due to arbitrary aggregation

▶ Integrity due to the volume and variety of data

▶ Lack of scalability for data security and compliance

▶ Exposure of sensitive data in data aggregation

Many organizations use platforms like Hadoop for big data and deploy Hadoop alongside their existing database systems. Big data environments such as Hadoop require the same security protections as traditional database systems. Big data environment controls include classification of sensitive data, data access and change controls, data activity monitoring and auditing, data protection, and vulnerability management. Organizations should have a data classification schema in place, but when dealing with big data, it becomes important to know where sensitive data is and how it is related to other data so that once it is moved to a platform such as Hadoop, proper security policies can be put into place. Polices should include user and application access policies, along with real-time monitoring and auditing, to protect from data loss. As in many other areas of data at-rest, data should be protected using either masking or encryption. General recommendations for securing big data are moving security controls as close to the data as possible, using existing technologies for control and protection, monitoring user and application behavior, defining and enforcing concise data-archiving and data-disposal policies, and controlling access to big data resources.

Data Encryption

In many situations, encryption can make a huge difference in how secure your environment is. This is true from the workstation level, to the server level, to how data is transferred to and from your business partners. Data encryption has become more and more important in light of the number of data breaches and leakages that have occurred in the past few years, which include everything from the Target, Home Depot, and JPMorgan Chase credit card breaches to the release of classified material by Edward Snowden. Although encryption might be the most practical method of protecting data stored or transmitted electronically, when the data is sensitive, encryption is a necessity. Should a security breach happen that involves sensitive data, failure to have that data encrypted can result in criminal or civil liabilities as well as irreparable harm to the reputation of the organization. The next couple of chapters cover many different types of data encryption. Data encryption schemes generally fall into two categories: symmetric and asymmetric. Encryption requires thought and preparation prior to implementation. Consideration should be given to answer the following questions:

▶ How will data encryption affect the performance on the network and the servers and workstations attached to that network?

▶ In what ways will the end users interact with encryption? What type of encryption will they experience on an end-user level? What methods of encryption will be needed and in what capacity?

▶ What additional costs will data encryption bring to the organization and the department that manages it? What additional hardware/software will be needed?

▶ Do the business partners or other organizations we communicate with use encryption? If so, what do they use, and how do we integrate with them?

▶ How will the encryption algorithm, software, and other methods we implement today scale with what we want to do tomorrow and with the long-term IT and business goals of our organization?

The answers to these questions help determine how to properly select the encryption methods that best protect the organization's sensitive data.

Full Disk

Full disk encryption (FDE), also called *whole disk encryption*, has gained popularity in recent years to help mitigate the risks associated with lost or stolen mobile devices and accompanying disclosure laws.

ExamAlert

Whole disk encryption can either be hardware or software based, and, unlike file- or folder-level encryption, whole disk encryption is meant to encrypt the entire contents of the drive (even temporary files and memory).

FDE involves encrypting the operating system partition on a computer and then booting and running with the system drive encrypted at all times. If the device is stolen or lost, the operating system and all the data on the drive becomes unreadable without the decryption key.

Unlike selective file encryption, which might require the end user to take responsibility for encrypting files, encrypting the contents of the entire drive takes the onus off individual users. It is not unusual for end users to sacrifice security for convenience, especially when they do not fully understand the associated risks. Nevertheless, along with the benefits of whole disk encryption come certain tradeoffs. For example, key management becomes increasingly important; loss of the decryption keys could render the data unrecoverable.

In addition, although whole disk encryption might make it easier for an organization to deal with a stolen or otherwise lost device, the fact that the entire drive is encrypted could present management challenges, including not being able to effectively control who has unauthorized access to sensitive data.

> **ExamAlert**
>
> The important thing to understand is that after the device is booted and running, it is just as vulnerable as a drive that had no encryption on it.

To effectively use whole disk encryption products, you should also use a preboot authentication mechanism. That is, the user attempting to log in must provide authentication before the actual operating system boots. Thus, the encryption key is decrypted only after another key is input into this preboot environment. Most vendors typically offer different options, such as the following:

▶ Username and password (usually the least secure)

▶ Smart card or smart card–enabled USB token along with a PIN (which provides two-factor functionality and can often be the same token or smart card currently used for access elsewhere)

▶ A Trusted Platform Module (TPM) to store the decryption key (discussed more later in this chapter)

FDE is most useful when you are dealing with a device that is being taken on the road by people such as traveling executives, sales managers, or insurance agents. Because encryption adds overhead, it is less productive for a computer in a fixed location where there is strong physical access control, unless the data is extremely sensitive and must be protected at all costs.

Database

Databases are the largest repository of sensitive information in many organizations. Organizational databases contain data ranging from personally identifiable customer information to intellectual property. Lost or stolen customer data can ultimately result in such severe, permanent damage that the organization goes out of business.

ExamAlert

Although database security is a top priority for organizations, traditional database security methods such as firewalls are no longer sufficient to protect organizational data, especially against insider threat. Database encryption can be used to mitigate security breach risk and to comply with regulations.

For example, in the financial sector, organizations must comply with the Payment Card Industry Data Security Standard (PCI DSS). PCI DSS creates policies that define what data needs to be encrypted and how it is to be encrypted and defines requirements for key management. One of the biggest challenges associated with database encryption is key management. This holds especially true for organizations that have to meet policies requiring Federal Information Processing Standard (FIPS) validated key storage. Database encryption is most often accompanied by a centralized method of defining key policy and enforcing key management, creating a center of trust. If this trust is breached, the ramifications can be far reaching, as seen with the RSA breach and subsequent Lockheed Martin attack.

Although a defense-in-depth strategy can help, encryption of data should occur both at rest and in transit. For example, you can use application-level encryption to encrypt information before it is stored in the database. This can prevent sensitive database information from being disclosed by either unauthorized access or theft. Database-level encryption by means of encrypting the entire contents written to the database can have unintended consequences such as limiting access control and auditing capabilities, so it is important to evaluate any solution before implementation.

ExamAlert

Database encryption must also be accompanied by key management to provide a high level of security. Other solutions to protect encrypted databases include permission restrictions on database and root administrators and restrictions on encryption key administration.

Hardware security modules (HSM), which are discussed in detail later in the chapter, can provide enforcement of separation of duties for key management by separating database and security administration.

Individual Files

File- or folder-level encryption differs from FDE. In FDE, the entire partition or drive is encrypted. In file- or folder-level encryption, individual files or directories are encrypted by the file system itself. Perhaps one of the most common examples of this type of encryption is the Encrypting File System (EFS) available in newer Microsoft operating systems.

> **ExamAlert**
>
> EFS encryption occurs at the file system level as opposed to the application level. This makes the encryption and decryption process transparent to the user and to the application.

If a folder is marked as encrypted, every file created in or moved to the folder will be encrypted. Applications do not have to understand EFS or manage EFS-encrypted files any differently than unencrypted files. EFS-encrypted files do not remain encrypted during transport if saved to or opened from a folder on a remote server. In other words, the file is decrypted, traverses the network in plain text, and then, if saved to a folder on a locally encrypted drive, is encrypted locally.

In file-level encryption, the file system metadata is not usually encrypted, so anyone who has access to the physical drive can see what data is stored on the disk, even though they cannot access the contents. If EFS is used, metadata such as filenames and ownership are all stored encrypted on the disk, while metadata about the storage pool is still stored in the clear. This allows certain information to still be viewable, but not directory information or stored file content.

File-level encryption allows flexible key management, individual management of encrypted files, and shorter memory holding periods for cryptographic keys. Additional uses for file-level encryption include laptops that only periodically hold sensitive data, email attachments, and sensitive information stored on a server in a file that is shared among several employees.

Removable Media

USB flash drives, iPods, and other portable storage devices are pervasive in the workplace and a real threat. They can introduce viruses or malicious code to the network and be used to store sensitive corporate information. Sensitive information is often stored on thumb and external hard drives, which then are lost or stolen. In many instances, the banning of these types of devices is not an acceptable solution. For example, in November 2008, thumb drives were banned after thousands of military computers and networks became infected by malicious software. The ban was a major inconvenience for those who relied on thumb drives. Aircraft and vehicle technicians were storing manuals on thumb drives. Medical records of wounded troops were sometimes stored on thumb drives and accompanied patients from field hospitals in foreign countries to their final U.S.-based hospitals. Pilots used thumb drives to transfer mission plans from operations rooms to aircraft computers. These scenarios highlight the importance of finding a way to secure data that is taken outside of a managed environment as opposed to banning the devices entirely. With the capability to carry organizational data on portable storages, encryption is essential. Some disk encryption products protect only the local drive and do not protect USB devices, whereas other encryption products automatically encrypt data copied or written to removable media.

When choosing an enterprise encryption method, it is important to evaluate how it will integrate with any other encryption solutions already in place. For example, most removable media encryption products can be configured to restrict access to devices by means of an authorized list. Some encryption products support a profile approach to creating user permissions such as those in an Active Directory Windows operating system environment. When this type of solution is used, the network authorizes the device, checks the content on the device, and then digitally marks the device before granting access. When evaluating a removable-media encryption product, in addition to authorized device access, access to personal devices, authorized file copy, encryption keys, and ease of use should be evaluated.

USB drives can also be set up to run as portable environments. This option provides a portable virtual environment that allows applications and operating systems to be carried on a USB drive. This eliminates the need to use public kiosks while away from the office. The USB device runs a virtual environment, thereby leaving the original system intact, but there is more of a risk for the data on the USB drive if it is not encrypted. If the USB drive were lost or stolen and it were unencrypted, there would be access to more than just files. The accessible information would include browser history, File Transfer Protocol (FTP) access, passwords, and email.

All USB flash drives can have their contents encrypted using third-party encryption software. These programs should be evaluated before implementation because many programs, such as TrueCrypt, require the user to have administrative rights on the computer it is run on. In the case where a traveling employee can only take a USB thumb drive, use an encryption method designed for on-the-fly disk encryption. Several free, open source, on-the-fly disk encryption programs can be run directly from the USB drive without any host machine installation. This enables a user to securely access corporate resources through hotel kiosks without the risk of data being left behind.

Mobile Devices

Handheld devices have become very popular in recent years. Many organizations are now faced with either allowing users to use their personal mobile devices on the network or managing and issuing these devices. This is also known as *bring your own device* (BYOD). From an administrative standpoint, it is simpler to allow the users to use their own devices, but then the organization is faced with figuring out a way to not only separate personal data from corporate data but also how to protect the corporate data. Remember from the preceding chapter that applications such as Good are mobile device management (MDM) corporate administration solutions that offer a security container that separates company and personal information, and enterprise encryption solutions are also available that encompass a number of different devices, including iOS, Android, and Windows Phone mobile devices.

ExamAlert

Expanding on these concepts, encryption technology is becoming an important element of any security solution as critical information is increasingly found on mobile devices and in the cloud.

Because most smartphones include the capability to have wireless and cellular communications, you can take different approaches. Some solutions include only voice encryption, and some provide only data encryption. Organizations often implement an endpoint solution depending on policy and devices that are used on the network. For example, Symantec's Mobile Security Suite offers a combination of mobile security and data protection by including virus protection with encryption of sensitive data and logging file accesses. Some platforms include their own encryption solution. If an organization is using a BlackBerry Enterprise Server (BES), devices can be protected via policies. A BES uses a symmetric key encryption algorithm that is designed to protect data in transit between a BlackBerry device and the BES. Standard BlackBerry encryption is designed to encrypt messages that a BlackBerry device sends or that the BES forwards to the BlackBerry device. Data protection is a feature available for iOS devices that offer hardware encryption on iPhone, iPod touch (third generation or later), and iPad models.

The factors organizations should consider when evaluating smartphone encryption products include cost, platform support, how the product meets the organizational policy needs, ease of centralized management, and how the encryption is implemented.

Hardware-Based Encryption Devices

Due to factors such as the need for a highly secure environment, the unreliability of software, and increased frequency of complex attacks, some organizations turn to the use of hardware-based encryption devices. Hardware-based encryption basically allows IT administrators to move certificate authentication (CA) software components to hardware. Authentication is performed based on the user providing a credential to the hardware on the machine. This provides a hardware-based authentication solution for wireless networks and virtual private networks (VPN) and eliminates the possibility of users sharing keys.

TPM

The Trusted Computing Group is responsible for the Trusted Platform Module (TPM) specification.

> **ExamAlert**
>
> TPM refers to a secure cryptoprocessor used to authenticate hardware devices such as PCs, laptops, or tablets.

At the most basic level, *TPM* provides for the secure storage of keys, passwords, and digital certificates. It is hardware based and is typically attached to the circuit board of the system. In addition, TPM can be used to ensure that a system is authenticated and to ensure that the system has not been altered or breached.

TPM is composed of various components. You should be familiar with some key TPM concepts, including the following:

▶ **Endorsement key (EK):** A 2048-bit asymmetric key pair created at the time of manufacturing and that cannot be changed

▶ **Storage root key (SRK):** A 2048-bit asymmetric key pair generated within a TPM and used to provide encrypted storage

▶ **Sealed storage:** Protects information by binding it to the system, which means the information can be read only by the same system in a particular described state

▶ **Attestation:** Vouching for the accuracy of the system

Computers using a TPM can create and encrypt cryptographic keys through a process called *wrapping*. Each TPM has a root wrapping key, called the *storage root key* (SRK), which is stored within the TPM itself. In addition, TPM-enabled computers can create and tie a key to certain platform measurements. This type of key can be unwrapped only when the platform measurements have the same values that they had when the key was created. This process is called *sealing* the key to the TPM. Decrypting it is called *unsealing*. Attestation or any other TPM functions do not transmit personal information of the user.

The idea behind TPM is to allow any encryption-enabled application to take advantage of the chip. Therefore, it has many possible applications, such as network access control (NAC), secure remote access, secure transmission of data, whole disk encryption, software license enforcement, digital rights management (DRM), and credential protection. Interestingly, part of what makes TPM effective is the TPM module is given a unique ID and master key that even the owner of the system neither controls nor has knowledge of. Critics of TPM argue, however, that this security architecture puts too much control into the hands of those who design the related systems and software. So, concerns arise about several issues, including DRM, loss of end-user control, loss of anonymity, and interoperability. If standards and shared specifications do not exist, components of the trusted environment cannot interoperate, and trusted computing applications cannot be implemented to work on all platforms. It is also important to understand that TPM can store pre-run-time configuration parameters but does not control the software that is running on a device. If something happens to the TPM or the motherboard, you need a separate recovery key to access your data simply when connecting the hard drive to another computer.

ExamAlert

A TPM can offer greater security protection for processes such as digital signing, mission-critical applications, and businesses where high security is required. Trusted modules can also be used in mobile phones and network equipment.

The nature of hardware-based cryptography ensures that the information stored in hardware is better protected from external software attacks. A TPM

Management console is incorporated into newer Windows systems. This function can be used to administer the TPM security hardware through a TPM Management console and an API called TPM Base Services (TBS). Figure 9.1 shows the TPM console for a Lenova laptop with BitLocker enabled.

HSM

A *hardware security module* (HSM) can be described as black box combination hardware and software/firmware that is attached or contained inside a computer used to provide cryptographic functions for tamper protection and increased performance.

> ### ExamAlert
>
> Basically, an HSM is a type of cryptoprocessor that manages digital keys, accelerates cryptographic processes, and provides strong access authentication for critical-application encryption keys. HSMs come mainly in the form of slotted cards or external devices that can be attached directly to a network but can also be embedded.

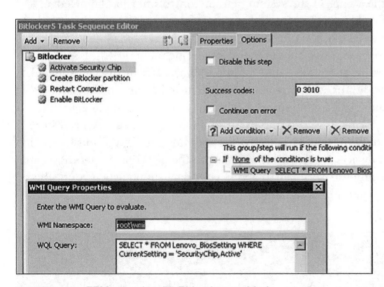

FIGURE 9.1 **TPM console with BitLocker enabled**

The basic cryptographic operations are the same for the different types of HSMs, but the administration structure and authorization models can vary.

Typically, an HSM is installed inside a server box or within an Ethernet cluster. The HSM is then wrapped by the software that provides access to the cryptographic functionality within the HSM. Traditionally, HSMs have been used in the banking sector to secure numerous large, bulk transactions. HSM security requirements were derived from existing ISO, ANSI, federal standards, and accepted best practice recognized by the financial industry. HSMs are also found in public key infrastructure (PKI) deployments to secure CA keys, Secure Sockets Layer (SSL) acceleration, and the storing pf Domain Name Service Security Extensions (DNSSEC) keys along with encrypting zone records.

PKCS (Public-Key Cryptography Standards) #11 provides for access to public and private asymmetric keys, symmetric keys, X.509 certificates, and application data. PKCS #11 is the de facto standard for platform applications, although some newer HSMs include more advanced authentication and authorization models. PKCS #11 was initially designed for accessing smart cards and defines two roles: security officer and user. Each PIN is unique. The security officer PIN is used to manage the user role, and the user PIN is used to authorize token-usage operations.

As mentioned in the previous section, hardware can better protect encryption keys for several reasons: The application does not directly handle the key; the key does not leave the device; and because the host operating system is not storing the key, it cannot be compromised on the host system.

Keep in mind that there are two types of HSMs: ones that are PC based, such as PCI-e cards, and ones that are network based. The main advantages of the network-attached HSM types are similar to the advantages of using network-area storage (NAS). They are essentially platform independent and can be used simultaneously from several clients. Because HSMs are often part of a mission-critical infrastructure such as a PKI or online banking application, HSMs can typically be clustered for high availability, and some HSMs feature dual power supplies. Host HSM systems are also hardware cryptographic accelerators by nature due to the fact that the keys do not leave devices in an unencrypted form. The HSM must perform the common cryptographic operations, so it will accelerate the intense math functions, offering better performance than a normal software-based crypto system.

HSM systems can securely back up their keys either in a wrapped form or externally. Keys protected by HSM are truly hardware protected only if they were generated inside the hardware itself. If a standard software-protected key is imported into an HSM, a non-hardware-protected copy of the key could still exist on old backups.

USB Encryption

As mentioned earlier, sensitive information is often stored on a thumb and external hard drives, which then are lost or stolen. Storing sensitive data on USB drives is always a risk, but many organizations simply cannot ban them. Losing sensitive data can have severe consequences. For example, flash drives carrying sensitive and classified information turned up for sale in a bazaar outside Bagram, Iraq, and a single malware-infected USB stick led to huge compromise of U.S. Central Command's classified and unclassified systems in Iraq. A survey by Ponemon Institute revealed that 51% of respondents said that they use USB sticks to store sensitive data, 57% believe others within their organization routinely do it, and 87% said that their company has policies against it.

Instead of a software-based solution, organizations can choose to approve or purchase and issue flash drives that have hardware encryption.

> **ExamAlert**
>
> All encryption algorithms used for encrypted flash drives have a single key that is used to both encrypt and decrypt the data.

It is imperative to protect this key because no matter how great the encryption algorithm is, if the key is found, the data can be decrypted. When software encryption is used, the key is stored either in the flash memory of the USB drive or on the computer that originated the file encryption. A more secure method is to use a USB drive that stores the encryption key on a separate controller on the device and physically protects the internal contents with a tamper-resistant shell such as the IronKey or LOK-IT. This type of device encrypts all user data stored on the drive using up to 256-bit AES encryption implemented in Cipher Block Chaining (CBC) mode. This can help the organization comply with cryptography requirements such as the U.S. Federal Information Processing Standard (FIPS) 140-2 Level 3 requirements. In a drive such as the IronKey, a cryptochip generates the encryption keys used to protect the data when the drive is first activated. The advantage to this solution is that the encryption keys are never stored or loaded onto the PC. The onboard cryptochip manages the keys and performs the encryption routines. USB drive encryption is discussed in further detail later in the chapter.

Another option for USB encryption is biometrics. Some USB devices feature a sensor strip that allows users to access protected data by simply scanning their fingerprint. One factor to consider while evaluating this solution is that the fingerprint-scanning portion relies on the host operating system to validate the fingerprint via a software driver. This restricts the use to machines where the driver can be installed and is mainly for Microsoft Windows computers. However, some USB drives with fingerprint scanners use controllers that allow access to protected data without any authentication. These drives incorporate a fingerprint scanner that serves as the passcode to the drive, such as the Stealth MXP Bio Gen II. It offers an advanced fingerprint-recognition technology with one-, two-, or three-factor authentication; PKI token services; and OATH one-time password (OTP) onboard key generation.

Hard Drive

Hard drive encryption is divided into three main categories: software-based; hardware-based on the storage device itself; and hardware-based elsewhere, such as the CPU or host bus adaptor. With device theft and loss being primary reasons of data loss, it is important that hardware comes loaded with encryption functionality to safeguard confidential data. By now it should be apparent that when hardware-based encryption is implemented correctly, it is superior to software-based encryption. Hardware vendors are now integrating basic encryption functionality on their drives. But hardware-based encryption products can also vary in the level of protection they provide against attacks such as offline parallel attacks or other cryptanalysis attacks. Hardware drive encryption is similar to other hardware-based solutions in that the encryption key is maintained independently from the computer, preventing the memory from being an attack vector.

The Trusted Computing Group (TCG) security subsystem storage standard Opal provides industry-accepted standardization for *self-encrypting drives* (SED). SEDs automatically encrypt all data in the drive, preventing attackers from accessing the data through the operating system. SED vendors include Seagate Technology, Hitachi, Ltd., Western Digital, Samsung, and Toshiba.

> **ExamAlert**
>
> With hardware drive encryption, authentication happens on power-up of the drive through either a software preboot authentication environment or with a BIOS password. Enhanced firmware and special-purpose cryptographic hardware are built in to the hard drive.

The firmware and hardware implement common cryptographic functions. Disk encryption that is embedded in the hard drive provides performance that is very close to that of unencrypted disk drives and to the user; there is no noticeable difference from using an unencrypted disk. Boot drive solutions require a preboot authentication component that is available from a number of vendors. The authentication credentials are usually a major potential weakness, and some solutions leave the master boot record (MBR) unencrypted. Seagate uses a solution where the authentication software provides the authentication login and then uses a secure and hardened version of Linux to perform the preboot authentication. Some hardware-based FDE systems encrypt the entire boot disk, including the MBR. For example, FlagStone hard drives encrypt and decrypt data immediately, but come in the form of a direct replacement for the computer's standard hard drive.

Advantages of hardware hard drive encryption include faster setup time, enhanced scalability, improved portability, and better system performance. Disadvantages include lack of management software and weak authentication components. Coupled with the TPM's PKI capability, an SED can achieve very strong authentication. You can use hardware drive encryption to protect data at-rest because all the data, even the operating system, is encrypted with a secure mode of AES.

Data In-Transit, Data At-Rest, Data In-Use

One of the biggest challenges for chief information security officers (CISO) and for IT security departments is how to keep data from leaving the organization. This can happen as a result of authorized users causing inadvertent data breaches and as a result of the wrong people having access to sensitive information. When confidential organizational data is exposed, it can severely damage the organization financially and destroy its public image. This section discusses the states of data, how they differ, and how to use and protect data in each particular state. But it is also just as important to have some type of data security life cycle implemented. For example, a data security life cycle might include stages such as create, store, use, archive, and destroy.

Many businesses must now adhere to strict regulatory compliance where data security is concerned. As a result, organizations are increasingly turning to data-loss prevention (DLP) strategies to protect and control the disclosure of sensitive information.

Data can generally be considered to be in one of three states: in-use, in-transit, or at-rest. *Data in-transit* is all data being transferred between two nodes of a network, whether internal or external. *Data in-use* is data being processed, primarily active data being used by an application and held in RAM, swap, or processor cache. *Data at-rest* is stored data, mainly data stored in persistent storage. From a vulnerability standpoint, data at-rest is an organization's most vulnerable data. Figure 9.2 shows the three states of data.

Data in-transit
Data being transferred between two nodes of a network, internal or external

---

Data in-use
Data that constantly changes because it is being processed, primarily active data

---

Data at-rest
Stored data, mainly data stored in persistent storage

FIGURE 9.2   **Three states of data**

ExamAlert

You should know the difference between data in-transit, data at-rest, and data in-use and at which stage data is most vulnerable.

DLP systems are basically designed to detect and prevent unauthorized use and transmission of confidential information based on one of these three states. Protection of data in-use is considered to be an endpoint solution, and the application is run on end-user workstations or servers in the organization. Endpoint systems also can monitor and control access to physical devices such as mobile devices and tablets. Protection of data in-transit is considered to be a network solution, and either a hardware or software solution is installed near the network perimeter to monitor for and flag policy violations. Protection of data at rest is considered to be a storage solution and is generally a software solution that monitors how confidential data is stored.

For an organization to properly implement a DLP solution, the organization has to understand what kind of sensitive data it has and then perform a risk assessment to determine what happens if data is exposed or gets in the wrong hands. After the sensitive data has been identified and the risk determined, the organization can begin DLP product integration. DLP products include ways to identify confidential or sensitive information. It is important to accurately identify sensitive data to lower instances of false positives and negatives.

When evaluating DLP solutions, key content filtering capabilities to look for are high performance, scalability, and the ability to accurately scan nearly anything. High performance is necessary to keep the end user from having lag time and delays. The solution must readily scale as the volume of traffic increases and bandwidth needs increase. The tool should also be able to accurately scan nearly anything.

Using an endpoint solution, here are some examples of when a user can be alerted to security policy violations to keep sensitive information from leaving the user's desktop:

▶ Inadvertently emailing a confidential internal document to external recipients

▶ Forwarding an email with sensitive information to unauthorized recipients inside or outside of the organization

▶ Sending attachments such as spreadsheets with personally identifiable information (PII) to an external personal email account

▶ Accidentally selecting "reply all" and emailing a sensitive document to unauthorized recipients

In addition to DLP, organizations must also address data leakage. Data leakage can occur when a data distributor gives sensitive data to a third party. Sensitive organizational data is sometimes discovered in unauthorized places that can range from wide exposure such as the Internet or in more obscure areas such as on a user's laptop. To avoid data leakage, accurate detection and the capability to define granular policies are required of content scanning tools. To properly prevent sensitive information from falling into the wrong hands, organizations need to focus on the filtering and blocking of all electronic communications including instant messaging (IM), web-based email, and HTTP traffic.

ExamAlert

You should avoid a high reliance on automated content scanners to correctly interpret the information and apply the right protection because of the possibility that the DLP product will either block nonsensitive data or mistakenly release sensitive data.

Permissions/ACL

Appropriate security controls for data permissions pertain to allowing only the required access. It enables the system to ensure that users have access only to the resources for which access has been granted. Permissions allow the setting of who has access to resources and what actions they can perform on those resources. Permissions are a simplified form of ACLs. Permissions can be either user based or resource based. User-based permissions are assigned based on what functions the specific user, group, or role can perform. Resource-based permissions are assigned to a resource and specify who can access the resource and what performable actions are allowed. Data security under permissions applies to permission lists and the users, roles, or resources assigned in the permissions lists. File-level permissions are often used in combination with ACLs.

Access control is the method or mechanism of authorization to enforce what requests to a system resource should be granted. In its broadest sense, an ACL is the underlying data associated with a network resource that defines the access permissions. The most common privileges are read, write to, delete, and execute a file. ACLs most often apply to routers and other devices. The two basic types of access controls that provide protection to the system files are discretionary access control and mandatory access control. Devices such as routers, in particular Cisco routers, have several types of ACLs, which are defined for a distinct purpose or protocol. The two most widely used types of ACLs are standard and extended. Only one type can be applied to an interface at time, and for proper security each access list must have its own number range and applications. Standard access lists match packets by examining the source IP address field in the packet's IP header. Extended access lists can match source and destination addresses and different TCP and UDP ports, allowing greater flexibility and control over network access. Advanced ACLs include reflexive ACLs and dynamic ACLs. Reflexive access lists are based on dynamic packet-filtering technology. Reflexive access lists allow a network administrator to dynamically enable a network filtering router to manage session traffic. The dynamically generated ACL is removed after the session ends. Reflexive ACLs are used on border routers or firewall routers. Dynamic ACLs allow user access to a specific source/destination host by means of a user authentication process. Dynamic ACLs are used for allowing specific remote users access to a host within the internal network through a connection from a remote host via the Internet for a finite period of time. Dynamic ACLs are also used in a similar fashion to allow a subset of hosts on a local network to access a host on a remote network protected by a firewall. The best approach for using permissions and ACLs is to use the easiest-to-maintain and the least ambiguous method. Access control is discussed in further detail in Chapter 11, "Account Management."

Data Policies

Data policies are based on organizational needs and regulatory compliance. Data policies are also used to govern overall IT administrative tasks. Organizational data assets might fall under legal discovery mandates, so a careful accounting is vital to ensure that data can be located if requested and is protected against destruction or recycling in case it must be provided at a later time. Proper data handling also ensures that data storage media can be properly processed for reuse or disposal, where special requirements for sensitive data might require outright destruction of the storage device and logging of its destruction in the inventory catalog.

Wiping and Disposing

ISO 17799, particularly sections 7 and 8, has established standards for dealing with the proper disposal of obsolete hardware. Standards dictate that equipment owned/used by the organization should be disposed of only in accordance with approved procedures, including independent verification that the relevant security risks have been mitigated. This policy addresses issues that should be considered when disposing of old computer hardware, either for recycle, disposal, donation, or resale.

The most prominent example of a security risk involved is that the hard drive inside the computer has not been completely or properly wiped. There are some concerns about data erasure sufficiency in new solid-state drives (SSD) that may require organizations to totally destroy drives rather than simply erasing them for normal disposal channels.

When implementing a policy on the secure disposal of outdated equipment, a wide range of scenarios need to be considered, such as the following:

▶ Breaches of health and safety requirements

▶ Inadequate disposal planning results in severe business loss

▶ Remnants of legacy data from old systems may still be accessible

▶ Disposal of old equipment that is necessary to read archived data

▶ Theft of equipment in use during cleanup of unwanted equipment

Besides properly disposing of old hardware, removable media disposal is just as important. There is a proper way to handle removable media when either the data should be overwritten or is no longer useful or pertinent to the organization. As a general rule, all electronic storage media should be sanitized when it is no longer necessary for business use and prior to sale, donation, or transfer of ownership. The following methods are acceptable to use for some forms of media sanitation:

▶ **Declassification:** A formal process of assessing the risk involved in discarding particular information.

▶ **Sanitization:** The process of removing the contents from the media as fully as possible, making it extremely difficult to restore.

▶ **Degaussing:** This method uses an electrical device to reduce the magnetic flux density of the storage media to zero.

▶ **Overwriting:** This method is applicable to magnetic storage devices and writes over all data on the media, destroying what was originally recorded.

▶ **Destruction:** The process of physically destroying the media and the information stored on it. For USB flash drives and other solid-state non-ferric removable storage, this may prove the only solution acceptable under certain controls and legal mandates.

> **ExamAlert**
>
> An organization's information sensitivity policy will define requirements for the classification and security of data and hardware resources based on their relative level of sensitivity. Some resources, such as hard drives, might require very extensive preparations before they may be discarded.

Storage and Retention

Retention and storage documentation should outline the standards for storing each classification level of data. Take, for example, the military levels of data classification used in their mandatory access control (MAC) strategy. Here, documentation would include directions and requirements for handling and storing the following types of data:

▶ Unclassified

▶ Sensitive

▶ Confidential

▶ Secret

▶ Top secret

ExamAlert

You should know the various data classifications and their meanings.

Policies for data should include how to classify, handle, store, and destroy it. The important point to remember here is to document your security objectives. Then, change and adjust that policy when and as needed (with emphasis on when and as needed). There may be a reason to make new classifications as business goals change, but make sure that this gets into your documentation. This is an ongoing, ever-changing process.

Log files, physical records, security evaluations, and other operational documentation should be managed within an organization's retention and disposal policies. These should include specifications for access authorization, term of retention, and requirements for disposal. Depending on the relative level of data sensitivity, retention and disposal requirements may become extensive and detailed.

Note

Laws may also affect the retention and storage of data, log files, and audit logs. For example, in the United States, changes to the Federal Rules of Civil Procedure (FRCP) have implications for data-retention policies. This governs the conduct and procedure of all civil actions in federal district courts. Organizations may face issues relating to the discovery, preservation, and production of "electronically stored information." For example, if an organization is sued by a former employee for wrongful termination, the department may be compelled during the discovery phase of the suit to produce all documents related to that individual's work performance. This used to mean the personnel records and copies of any written correspondence (memos, letters, and so on) concerning the performance of that employee. Over the past several years, there has been some level of debate over what a "document" is, given that most records now reside in electronic format. The FRCP changes establish that electronic data is now clearly subject to discovery. It goes further to say that all data is subject to discovery regardless of storage format or location: Email, instant messaging, mobile devices, voice mail, and so on all fall under this.

The organization should have a legal hold policy in place, understand statutory and regulatory document retention requirements, understand the varying statues of limitations, and maintain a records-retention and records-destruction schedule.

Cram Quiz

Answer these questions. The answers follow the last question. If you cannot answer
these questions correctly, consider reading this section again until you can.

1. Your organization is exploring data-loss prevention solutions. The proposed
   solution is an endpoint solution. This solution is targeting which of the following
   data states?

   ○ **A.** In-motion

   ○ **B.** In-use

   ○ **C.** At-rest

   ○ **D.** At-flux

2. Which of the following uses a secure cryptoprocessor to authenticate hardware
   devices such as PC or laptop?

   ○ **A.** Trusted Platform Module

   ○ **B.** Full disk encryption

   ○ **C.** File-level encryption

   ○ **D.** Public key infrastructure

3. Which of the following is one of the biggest challenges associated with database
   encryption?

   ○ **A.** Weak authentication components

   ○ **B.** Platform support

   ○ **C.** Multitenancy

   ○ **D.** Key management

4. Which of the following standards is used in HSMs?

   ○ A. PKCS #7

   ○ B. PKCS #11

   ○ **C.** AES

   ○ **D.** EFS

5. Which of the following is the preferred type of encryption used in SaaS
   platforms?

   ○ **A.** Application level

   ○ **B.** HSM level

   ○ **C.** Media level

   ○ **D.** Database level

Cram Quiz Answers

1. **B**. Protection of data in-use is considered to be an endpoint solution, and the application is run on end-user workstations or servers in the organization. Answer A is incorrect because protection of data in-motion is considered to be a network solution, and either a hardware or software solution is installed near the network perimeter to monitor for and flag policy violations. Answer C is incorrect because protection of data at-rest is considered to be a storage solution and is generally a software solution that monitors how confidential data is stored. Answer D is incorrect because there is no such data state.

2. **A**. A TPM refers to a secure cryptoprocessor used to authenticate hardware devices such as PC or laptop. The idea behind a TPM is to allow any encryption-enabled application to take advantage of the chip. Answer B is incorrect because full-disk encryption involves encrypting the operating system partition on a computer and then booting and running with the system drive encrypted at all times. Answer C is incorrect because in file- or folder-level encryption, individual files or directories are encrypted by the file system itself. Answer D is incorrect because PKI is a set of hardware, software, people, policies, and procedures needed to create, manage, distribute, use, store, and revoke digital certificates.

3. **D**. One of the biggest challenges associated with database encryption is key management. Answer A is incorrect because lack of management software and weak authentication components are associated with hardware hard drive encryption. Answer B is incorrect because cost and platform support are concerns with smartphone encryption products. Answer C is incorrect because multitenancy is a security issue related to cloud computing implementations.

4. **B**. The PKCS #11 standard provides for access to public and private asymmetric keys, symmetric keys, X.509 certificates, and application data. PKCS #11 is the de facto standard for platform applications, although some newer HSMs include more advanced authentication and authorization models. Answer A is incorrect because PKCS #7, Cryptographic Message Syntax Standard, describes the syntax for data streams, such as digital signatures, that may have cryptography applied to them. Answer C is incorrect because AES is most commonly found on USB drive encryption. Answer D is incorrect because EFS is the Encrypting File System available in newer Microsoft operating systems.

5. **A**. In a SaaS environment, application-level encryption is preferred because the data is encrypted by the application before being stored in the database or file system. The advantage is that it protects the data from the user all the way to storage. Answer B is incorrect because an HSM solution is mainly found in private data centers that manage and offload cryptography with dedicated hardware appliances. Answer C is incorrect because encryption of a complete virtual machine on IaaS could be considered media encryption. Answer D is incorrect because, due to the complexity involved, data should be encrypted at the application layer in cloud implementations rather than being encrypted within a database.

Compare and Contrast Alternative Methods to Mitigate Security Risks in Static Environments

▶ **Environments**

▶ **Methods**

CramSaver

If you can correctly answer these questions before going through this section, save time by skimming the Exam Alerts in this section and then completing the Cram Quiz at the end of the section.

1. Explain the best way to mitigate security risks for SCADA systems.

2. Explain how to mitigate security risks associated with embedded systems.

3. Explain how network segmentation is used to secure data.

Answers

1. Ideally, two separate security and IT groups would manage the network infrastructure and the SCADA network. One of the first line of defenses against attacks on SCADA systems is to implement physical segregation of internal and external networks to reduce the attack surface by segregating the SCADA network from the corporate LAN. The SCADA LAN can be further segregated from the field device network containing the remote terminal units (RTU) and programmable logic controllers (PLC) by establishing an electronic security perimeter.

2. The best protections for maintaining embedded device security include requiring software and hardware vendors to provide evidence that the software is free of security weaknesses, perform remote attestation to verify that firmware has not been modified, and maintain secure configuration management processes when servicing field devices or updating firmware. In addition, provide proper security oversight and monitoring of contractors and vendors that perform work on installed systems.

3. Network segmentation is one of the most effective controls an organization can implement to mitigate the effect of a network intrusion. Properly implemented, segmentation is a preventive measure to protect sensitive information. Applying segmentation in layers, from the data link layer through the application layer, can go a long way toward protecting vital infrastructure services. Segmentation also includes restricting intersystem communication to specific ports or protocols.

Environments

There are some areas where an organization may be able to exert better control over the management of security risks because the environment is considered static or less fluid than cloud or virtualized environments. Environments such as SCADA systems, some embedded systems, and mainframe sytems may be considered static because the technology behind them has been around for a long time. Due to business needs and vendor access, many of these sytems that previously were on their own secure network have now become targets because they are connected to the Internet. This section discusses these environments.

SCADA

Supervisory control and data acquisition (SCADA) *systems* include those considered to be critical infrastructure systems such as manufacturing, logistics and transportation network, energy and utilities, telecommunication services, agriculture, and food production networks. Ideally, two separate security and IT groups would manage the network infrastructure and the SCADA network. Because SCADA security requirements are different, IT architects and managers without previous experience on SCADA systems need to be trained specifically in SCADA security and be familiar with guidance documents. Otherwise, the stronger security controls required for SCADA systems may be inadvertently missed, putting both the organization and the community at increased risk.

One of the first line of defenses against attacks on SCADA systems is to implement physical segregation of internal and external networks to reduce the attack surface by segregating the SCADA network from the corporate LAN. The SCADA LAN can be further segregated from the field device network containing the remote terminal units (RTU) and programmable logic controllers (PLC) by establishing an electronic security perimeter.

Guidance for proper security and established best practices for SCADA systems can be found in ISA99: Industrial Automation and Control Systems Security, North American Electric Reliability Corporation (NERC): Critical Infrastructure Protection (CIP), and NIST Special Publication 800-82: Guide to Industrial Control Systems (ICS) Security.

ExamAlert

A key control against attacks on SCADA systems is to implement physical segregation of internal and external networks to reduce the attack surface by segregating the SCADA network from the corporate LAN.

Embedded (Printer, Smart TV, HVAC Control)

Embedded systems that are used to capture, store, and access data of a sensitive nature pose several unique and interesting security challenges. Embedded systems are found in printers, smart TVs, HVAC (heating, ventilation, and air conditioning) control systems, among other devices. Security protocols and encryption address security considerations from a functional perspective, but most embedded systems are constrained by the environments they operate in and resources in which they are used. Attacks against embedded systems rely on exploiting security vulnerabilities in the software and hardware components of the implementation and are susceptible to timing and side-channel attacks. Nonvolatile memory chips are found in many hardware devices, including TV tuners, fax machines, cameras, radios, antilock brakes, keyless entry systems, printers and copiers, modems, HVAC controls, satellite receivers, barcode readers, point-of-sale terminals, medical devices, smart cards, lock boxes, and garage door openers. The best protections for maintaining embedded device security include requiring software and hardware vendors to provide evidence that the software is free of security weaknesses, performing remote attestation to verify that firmware has not been modified, and maintaining secure configuration management processes when servicing field devices or updating firmware. In addition, you need to provide proper security oversight and monitoring of contractors and vendors that perform work on installed systems.

Android and iOS

Both iOS and Android isolate applications and sensitive operating system features using a method called *sandboxing*. Both natively support enterprise-level security controls, including device-level access control, remote wipe, and encryption to protect data at-rest and data in-transit. From a risk management standpoint, iOS provides better security, but it is still vulnerable to browser exploits. Although Android's security approach is more flexible when it comes to risk mitigation, it is easier for malware to exploit the Android operating system than to exploit iOS. Vulnerabilities such as mobile cross-site scripting and request forgery allow an unauthorized party to obtain a mobile user's Facebook/Dropbox authentication credentials and record text input. Risk mitigation for iOS and Android begins with minimizing installed applications. Additional mitigation techniques include applying software updates, leveraging device security features, and granting the least privilege necessary for users to perform tasks.

ExamAlert

Mobile devices are subject to vulnerabilities such as mobile cross-site scripting and request forgery for obtaining a mobile user's authentication credentials. Risk mitigation for iOS and Android begins with minimizing installed applications.

Mainframe

The mainframe has long been a secure, isolated, large-scale data processing environment. Security has always been a fundamental strength of the mainframe, offering an architecture that provides protection against the risks and exposures that other platforms experience. However, present-day mainframes host websites, allow PC client applications to access and update data, and constantly exchange bulk data files with other operating environments. Mainframe security management provides the basis for effective security by ensuring that only the appropriate level of access rights to resources is granted and that the rights are properly enforced. An effective technique to mitigate risks associated with crossing organizational boundaries is to implement identity and role-based administration, along with provisioning of user IDs.

Game Consoles

Game consoles have become powerful processing devices. A modified Xbox One has the potential to be used as a personal computer, file server, or web server. Current-generation gaming consoles were built with security in mind. Most gaming consoles only run signed code, encrypt memory, and use firmware updates to patch vulnerabilities. In addition, the PlayStation 4 uses a layered operating system and secure processors for privilege separation. Software exploits are mainly memory overflows or bugs, but most exploits are hardware based and cannot be fixed via firmware updates, leaving a system vulnerable until a new console is released. The trend in gaming is that vendors are shifting to an entirely online platform, allowing console security to be managed by the gaming network vendor.

ExamAlert

In gaming consoles, software exploits are mainly memory overflows or bugs, but most exploits are hardware based and cannot be fixed via firmware updates, leaving a system vulnerable until a new console is released.

In-Vehicle Computing Systems

Automobile in-vehicle computing systems have been inaccessible to attackers.
But with the implementation of wireless networks such as Global System
for Mobile Communications (GSM) and Bluetooth being integrated into
automobiles, the attack landscape is changing. Current in-vehicle systems can
produce and store data necessary for vehicle operation and maintenance, safety
protection, and emergency contact transmission. Most in-vehicle systems have
a wireless interface connecting to the Internet, and an onboard diagnostics
interface for physical access. All communication between controllers is done
in plain text. Because in-vehicle communications do not follow basic security
practices, some of the risks include unauthorized tracking, wireless jamming,
and spoofing. Risk-mitigation suggestions include secure system software
design practices, basic encryption, authentication of incoming data, and
implementation of a firewall on the wireless gateway.

Methods

The previous section discussed environments such as SCADA systems,
embedded systems, mainframe systems, and other environments that the
CompTIA Security+ objectives consider to be static. In many instances, the
standard security fix-all is data encryption. Encryption might not be the best
solution or may not be feasible when dealing with some of these environments.
This section discusses alternative methods to mitigate security risks when
faced with situations where methods such as encryption do not provide the
best possible solution.

Network Segmentation

The network should be segmented to separate information and infrastructure
based on organizational security requirements. *Network segmentation* is one
of the most effective controls an organization can implement to mitigate
the effect of a network intrusion. Properly implemented, segmentation is
a preventive measure to protect sensitive information. In sensitive systems
such as SCADA networks, applying segmentation in layers, from the data
link layer through the application layer, can go a long way toward protecting
vital infrastructure services. Segmentation entails more than just segmenting
networks via firewalls. Segmentation also includes restricting intersystem
communication to specific ports or protocols.

> **ExamAlert**
>
> Some key considerations for implementing good network segmentation are knowing how users and systems interact and communicate with each other, implementing least privilege and need-to-know principles, using whitelisting rather than blacklisting, and segmenting through all layers of the OSI model.

Security Layers

With layered security, the idea is to create rational security layers within the environment for improved security. Security layers can be logical or physical or a combination of both, allowing proper alignment between resources and security requirements. For example, applications can be monitored for anomalous activity by being placed behind heuristic engines. Implementing layered security begins with understanding the organization's current risk, mapping the architecture, and then implementing security layers. Layered security could be a good alternative solution for mainframes. Enforcing security policies, using perimeter devices with ACLs, detecting malicious activity, mitigating vulnerabilities, and patching systems can all be considered layers of security.

Application Firewalls

An ever-increasing threat landscape requires the deployment of multiple detection and protection tools, such as intrusion prevention systems (IPS) and web application firewalls (WAF). A firewall is the first line of defense against attacks. It protects the private network from the public network. Network firewalls operate at Layers 3 and 4 of the OSI model. They do not adequately protect the network at the application layer. An application firewall examines all traffic to check for OSI application layer protocols that are allowed. Although purchased code has the advantage of being readily available, when security vulnerabilities are found the organization can do little except wait for a patch. Application firewalls are a means to mitigate the cost of an application compromise.

> **ExamAlert**
>
> An application firewall examines all traffic to check for OSI application layer protocols that are allowed, thus providing a means to mitigate the cost of an application compromise.

Manual Updates

Often a vendor will require remote access to a system or data for maintenance or diagnostic purposes. Protecting the system during remote reprogramming updates and upgrades requires a secure communications channel. When the possibility exists that the communications channel is unsecure and that the system data is sensitive, manual updates may be required. Manual updates, although inconvenient, may also be necessary when the system contains sensitive data and is segmented. Gaming console vendors sometimes issue manual software updates for controllers and USB ports.

Firmware Version Control

When patches or updates for firmware are missing, serious vulnerabilities and risks can result, allowing embedded devices that have unused features and functions to be exploited. Many organizations have no idea when firmware version changes were last done. Organizations should have a version control system in place similar to what is used in software development versioning. Firmware version control is important in systems like gaming consoles because many vulnerabilities cannot be fixed via firmware updates, leaving a system vulnerable until a new console is released. Firmware version control can often be implemented based on vendor service profile policies and templates.

Wrappers

Wrappers are used in several types of implementations such as smart grids, integration of legacy systems, and reducing the risk of web-based attacks. As a defense against data security threats, code wrappers can be used as a countermeasure to reduce the risk of web-based attacks by restricting requests to port 80 and enforcing rules for well-formed HTTP requests. TCP wrappers can be used in conjunction with a firewall to provide another layer of protection in the implementation of a security policy. In smart grids, systems can be extended to a new set of devices through the use of a wrapper that allows the adding of new hardware in a plug-and-play fashion. In SCADA systems, security wrappers are used around legacy data protocol transmissions.

Control Redundancy and Diversity

Redundancy and diversity are commonly applied principles for fault tolerance against accidental faults. *Redundancy* is replication of a component in identical copies to compensate for random hardware failures. Redundancy is usually dispersed geographically and through backup equipment and databases, or hot sparing of system components. *Diversity* refers to having multiple versions of software packages in which redundant software versions are different. Multiple versions are used as opposed to multiple copies of the same version to protect against software failures. With diverse versions, one hopes that any faults each particular version contains will be sufficiently covered by maintaining multiple versions. Redundancy and diversity should be designed into critical facilities and applications.

For risk mitigation, some redundancy and diversity controls that can be implemented against threats are replication to different data centers, replication to different geographic areas, redundant components, replication of software systems, distinct security zones, different administrative control, and different organizational control.

Cram Quiz

Answer these questions. The answers follow the last question. If you cannot answer these questions correctly, consider reading this section again until you can.

1. A vulnerability assessment revealed that legacy internal heart monitors of a hospital's intensive care unit (ICU) are visibly exposed to the Internet. Which of the following should be implemented?

   ○ **A.** Network segmentation

   ○ **B.** Code wrappers

   ○ **C.** Control diversity

   ○ **D.** Manual updates

2. An application that is used on a regular basis has vulnerability in the current version that will not be fixed until the next software update, 6 months from now. Which of the following implementations would mitigate this vulnerability?

   ○ **A.** Firmware version control

   ○ **B.** Control diversity

   ○ **C.** Manual updates

   ○ **D.** Control redundancy

3. Which of the following is most likely to use firmware version control as an alternate security method?

   ○ **A.** SCADA systems

   ○ **B.** Mainframes

   ○ **C.** Android

   ○ **D.** Gaming consoles

Cram Quiz Answers

1. **A.** Sensitive internal devices should not be exposed to the Internet. There is a segmentation problem with the way the ICU devices are protected. Network segmentation is one of the most effective controls an organization can implement to mitigate the effect of a network intrusion. In sensitive systems such as SCADA networks, applying segmentation in layers, from the data link layer through the application layer, can go a long way toward protecting vital infrastructure services. Answer B is incorrect because wrappers are used in several types of implementations such as smart grids, integration of legacy systems, and reducing the risk of web-based attacks. Answer C is incorrect because control diversity refers to having multiple versions of software packages in which redundant software versions are different. Answer D is incorrect because manual

updates, although inconvenient, may also be necessary when the system contains sensitive data and is segmented.

2. **B**. Control diversity refers to having multiple versions of software packages in which redundant software versions are different. With diverse versions, one hopes that any faults each particular version contains will be sufficiently covered by maintaining multiple versions. Rolling back to an earlier version that does not contain the vulnerability of the current version may be the best option. Answer A is incorrect because firmware version control is important in systems like gaming consoles because many vulnerabilities cannot be fixed via firmware updates, leaving a system vulnerable until a new console is released. Answer C is incorrect because manual updates, although inconvenient, may also be necessary when the system contains sensitive data and is segmented. Answer D is incorrect because control redundancy is replication of a component in identical copies to compensate for random hardware failures.

3. **D**. Most gaming consoles only run signed code, encrypt memory, and use firmware updates to patch vulnerabilities. Answer A is incorrect because SCADA systems would most likely use network segmentation. Answer B is incorrect because mainframes would most likely use security layers. Answer C is incorrect because Android would most likely use security layers.

What Next?

If you want more practice on this chapter's exam objectives before you move on, remember that you can access all the Cram Quiz questions on the CD. You can also create a custom exam by objective with the practice exam software. Note any objective that you struggle with and go to the material that covers that objective in this chapter.

CHAPTER 10

Authentication, Authorization, and Access Control

This chapter covers the following official CompTIA Security+ SY0-401 exam objectives:

▶ Compare and contrast the function and purpose of authentication services

▶ Given a scenario, select the appropriate authentication, authorization, or access control

(For more information on the official CompTIA Security+ SY0-401 exam topics, see the "About the CompTIA Security+ SY0-401 Exam" section in the Introduction.)

The traditional C-I-A triad of security directives includes maintaining the confidentiality, integrity, and availability of data and services. To protect against unauthorized access or modification and to ensure availability for legitimate access requests, you must put in place a mechanism that allows the identification of an authorized request. This overall process is called *access control*, although it is actually three subprocesses that must occur in sequence:

1. **Authentication:** Presenting and verifying credentials or keys as authentic

2. **Authorization:** Checking credentials or keys against a list of authorized security principles

3. **Access Control:** Limiting access to resources based on a defined set of allowed actions and areas of access

This chapter focuses on the fundamental concepts and best practices related to authentication services and selecting the appropriate authentication, authorization, or access control method for given situations. Chapter 11, "Account Management," focuses on security controls for account management and control measure best practices regarding account management.

ExamAlert

The exam might use the term *access control* to refer to the entire process or only to the type of controls being implemented in the third subprocess. Questions asking for answers of a particular type of control (for example, time based, role based, or discretionary) are talking about the subprocess, whereas questions covering more than one function (for example, multifactor and Kerberos) are referring to the overall process itself.

Compare and Contrast the Function and Purpose of Authentication Services

▶ **RADIUS**

▶ **TACACS+**

▶ **Kerberos**

▶ **LDAP**

▶ **XTACACS**

▶ **SAML**

▶ **Secure LDAP**

CramSaver

If you can correctly answer these questions before going through this section, save time by skimming the Exam Alerts in this section and then completing the Cram Quiz at the end of the section.

1. Which authentication protocol provides protection against man-in-the-middle data interception attacks?

2. Which of the following protocols provides accounting of access requests and is an open standard: TACACS, TACACS+, or Extended TACACS?

3. Which type of authentication is named for the three-headed dog that guarded the gates to Hades?

Answers

1. The Kerberos protocol supports mutual authentication between two systems, protecting against man-in-the-middle forms of data interception or manipulation by ensuring that both network endpoints are authenticated to one another.

2. The TACACS+ protocol is a replacement for the legacy variations of the TACACS protocol and is not backward compatible. Like RADIUS, the TACACS+ protocol adds accounting of access requests to the authentication and authorization functions of legacy TACACS solutions. TACACS+ is an open standard just as its predecessor, TACACS, whereas XTACACS is a proprietary version created by Cisco.

3. The Kerberos authentication protocol was named for the three-headed dog, Cerberus, who guarded the gates of Hades in myth. It is so-named due to the three-phase process of mutual authentication it uses.

The process of authentication involves the offer and acceptance of credentials to establish the identity of the originator behind a service or data request. More specifically, the authentication process involves the exchange of credentials, sometimes referred to as *identification*, and subsequent comparison to a database containing all authorized credentials related to the requested service. Both the exchange of information and verification of it against a credential store together define authentication. If the provided credentials match those in the validation data set, further actions involve service access (authorization) and functional limitations during the session (access control). There may also be a listing of credentials entirely blocked from access outright, but this is discussed later with regard to authorization and access control measures.

RADIUS

The Remote Authentication Dial-In User Service (RADIUS) remote-access control system provides authentication and access control within an enterprise network using UDP transport to a central network access server, which in turn provides credentials for access to resources within the extended enterprise. Developed originally for use in dial-up connectivity over telephonic modems, you might still find RADIUS servers in larger enterprises where logons must span resources located in multiple logon realms.

A protected network segment might implement a virtual private network (VPN) or remote-access server (RAS) gateway connection to allow an authenticated external service request to reach a protected server by communicating with a RADIUS server. The requesting account must provide its credentials to the RADIUS server, which then authorizes the access request.

ExamAlert

The RADIUS service provides authentication and authorization functions in addition to network access accounting functions but does not provide further access control.

The RADIUS service can forward authentication and authorization requests between authentication domains (called *realms*) and so can facilitate cross-enterprise authentication, often as part of a single sign-on (SSO) solution.

TACACS+

The Terminal Access Controller Access Control System (TACACS) remote-access control system provides authentication and authorization primarily in Unix networks, where a client service could accept a logon and password from an access requester, forward those credentials to the TACACS server, and receive a response approving the credentials. The original TACACS protocol used either TCP or UDP connectivity over port 49. Two other variations of this protocol have since been introduced: TACACS+ and XTACACS.

Terminal Access Controller Access-Control System Plus (TACACS+) is a protocol developed by Cisco and released as an open standard beginning in 1993. Although derived from TACACS, TACACS+ is a separate protocol that handles authentication, authorization, and accounting (AAA) services. TACACS+ is similar to RADIUS but uses TCP instead of RADIUS's UDP transport. TACACS+ and other flexible AAA protocols have largely replaced their predecessors.

Kerberos

The most basic aspects of authentication within a completely isolated network include only the need to determine the identity of an account (without the third access control subprocess). If a network is physically or logically accessible to external parties that might seek to sniff (capture and examine) data being transacted between systems, the problem arises as to how to keep the authentication keys themselves safe.

Here is an example: A basic File Transfer Protocol (FTP) access session involves the client sending a logon identifier and a password to the FTP server, which accepts or rejects this access. The logon account and password, by default in the FTP protocol, are sent in plain-text form and so are readable by any agent with access to the data as it is transmitted from the client to the server. An unauthorized party, pretending to be the authorized user, might use this information later to gain access to the server.

To avoid sending the open plain-text logon information across an unsecured network, one solution is the symmetric-key authentication protocol known as *Kerberos* (created by the Athena project at MIT and named for the three-headed dog Cerberus that guarded Hades). A symmetric key means that both the client and server must agree to use a single key in both the encryption and decryption processes.

ExamAlert

Kerberos is primarily a UDP protocol, although it falls back to TCP for large Kerberos tickets. Kerberos clients send UDP and TCP packets on port 88 and receive replies from the Kerberos servers. Port 88 is the standard port for Kerberos V5. You might also see references to ports 749 and 750 used by earlier versions of Kerberos.

In Kerberos authentication, a client sends its authentication details not to the target server, but rather to a key distribution center (KDC), as follows:

1. The client first contacts a certification authority (CA).

2. The CA creates a time-stamped session key with a limited duration (by default, 8 hours) using the client's key and a randomly generated key that includes the identification of the target service.

3. This information is sent back to the client in the form of a ticket-granting ticket (TGT).

4. The client then submits the TGT to a ticket-granting server (TGS).

5. This server then generates a time-stamped key encrypted with the service's key and returns both to the client.

6. The client then uses its key to decrypt its ticket, contacts the server, and offers the encrypted ticket to the service.

7. The service uses its key to decrypt the ticket and verify that the time stamps match and the ticket remains valid.

8. The service contacts the KDC and receives a time-stamped session keyed ticket that it returns to the client.

9. The client then decrypts the keyed ticket using its key. When both agree that the other is the proper account and that the keys are within their valid lifetime, communication is initiated.

ExamAlert

The short lifespan of a ticket ensures that if someone attempts to intercept the encrypted data to try to break its keys, the key will have changed before he or she can reasonably be able to break the key using cryptographic algorithms. The handshaking between the client and the KDC and between the service and the KDC provides verification that the current session is valid, without requiring the transmission of logons or passwords between client and service directly.

Kerberos V5 includes support for a process known as mutual authentication, in which both client and server verify that the computer with which they are communicating is the proper system. This process helps to prevent man-in-the-middle attacks, in which an unauthorized party intercepts communications between two systems and pretends to be each to the other, passing some data intact, modifying other data, or inserting entirely new sets of values to accomplish desired tasks.

In mutual authentication, one system creates a challenge code based on a random number and then sends this code to the other system. The receiving system generates a response code using the original challenge code and creates a challenge code of its own, sending both back to the originating system. The originating system verifies the response code as a value and returns its own response code to the second system, generated from the challenge code returned with the first response code. After the second system has verified its returned response code, it notifies the originating system, and both systems consider themselves mutually authenticated.

The strength of Kerberos authentication comes from its time-synchronized connections and the use of registered client and service keys within the KDC. These also create some drawbacks, such as the need to use a standard synchronized time base for all systems involved. Difficulties arise if the KDC is unavailable or the cached client and service credentials were accessed directly from the granting servers. An important advantage of time-stamped credentials is that they help prevent spoofing and replay attacks.

> **ExamAlert**
>
> Not all authentication services provide the same functions, so aligning the proper service with the right environment requires knowledge of the basics of each service. Remember that Microsoft Active Directory networks rely on Kerberos for credentials exchange, so all systems must share a common time service to maintain synchronization.

LDAP

The Lightweight Directory Access Protocol (LDAP) provides access to directory services, including those used by the Microsoft Active Directory. LDAP was created as a "lightweight" alternative to earlier implementations of the X.500 Directory Access Protocol and communicates on port 389. Its widespread use influences many other directory systems, including the Directory Service Markup Language (DSML), Service Location Protocol (SLP), and Microsoft Active Directory and Secure LDAP variations.

Variations of LDAP share many common vulnerabilities, including the following:

▶ Buffer overflow vulnerabilities may be used to enact arbitrary commands on the LDAP server.

▶ Format string vulnerabilities might result in unauthorized access to enact commands on the LDAP server or impair its normal operation.

▶ Improperly formatted requests may be used to create an effective denial-of-service (DoS) attack against the LDAP server, preventing it from responding to normal requests.

LDAP uses an object-oriented access model defined by the Directory Enabled Networking (DEN) standard, which is based on the Common Information Model (CIM) standard.

XTACACS

A proprietary version of the original TACACS protocol was developed by Cisco and is called the Extended Terminal Access Controller Access Control System (XTACACS) protocol. XTACACS is a newer variation that is not backward-compatible with the legacy TACACS standard. This protocol extended the original TACACS by adding support for accounting and auditing but has since been displaced by the TACACS+ and RADIUS protocols. TACACS and XTACACS both allow a remote access server to communicate with an authentication server in order to determine whether the user has access to the network.

SAML

Security Assertion Markup Language (SAML) is an Extensible Markup Language (XML) framework for creating and exchanging security information between online partners. Most cloud and software-as-a-service (SaaS) service providers, including Salesforce.com, WebEx and Google Apps, favor SAML because it provides authentication assertion, attribute assertion, and authorization assertion. Authentication assertion validates the user's identity. Attribute assertion contains information about the user, and authorization assertion identifies what the user is authorized to do. The main difference between SAML and other identity mechanisms is that SAML relies on assertions about identities. The weakness in the SAML identity chain is the integrity of users. To mitigate risk, SAML systems need to use timed sessions, HTTPS, and SSL/TLS.

Secure LDAP

LDAP is used to read from and write to Active Directory. By default, LDAP traffic is transmitted unsecured. You can make LDAP traffic confidential and secure by using Secure Sockets Layer (SSL) / Transport Layer Security (TLS) technology. You can enable LDAP over SSL (LDAPS) by installing a properly formatted certificate from either a Microsoft certification authority (CA) or a non-Microsoft CA. Reasons for enabling LDAP over SSL/TLS include protection the authentication session when an application authenticates with Active Directory Domain Services (AD DS) through simple BIND; use of proxy binding or password change over LDAP, which requires LDAPS; and encrypted communications are required by applications that integrate with LDAP servers (such as Active Directory or Active Directory domain controllers). You can find implementation guidelines at http://support.microsoft.com/kb/321051.

Cram Quiz

Answer these questions. The answers follow the last question. If you cannot answer these questions correctly, consider reading this section again until you can.

1. Which of the following would be implemented for secure communications if the organization is using an application that authenticates with Active Directory Domain Services (AD DS) through simple BIND?

   ○ **A.** TACACS+

   ○ **B.** SAML

   ○ **C.** Secure LDAP

   ○ **D.** XTACACS

2. An organization that relies heavily on cloud and SaaS service providers, such as Salesforce.com, WebEx, and Google, would have security concerns about which of the following?

   ○ **A.** TACACS+

   ○ **B.** SAML

   ○ **C.** Secure LDAP

   ○ **D.** XTACACS

3. Which of the following is a nonproprietary protocol that provides authentication and authorization in addition to accounting of access requests against a centralized service for authorization of access requests?

   ○ **A.** TACACS+

   ○ **B.** SAML

   ○ **C.** Secure LDAP

   ○ **D.** XTACACS

Cram Quiz Answers

1. **C.** Reasons for enabling LDAP over SSL/TLS, also known as LDAPS, include protection of the authentication session when an application authenticates with AD DS through simple BIND. Answer A is incorrect because the TACACS+ protocol provides authentication and authorization in addition to accounting of access requests against a centralized service for authorization of access requests. Answer B is incorrect because SAML is an XML framework for creating and exchanging security information between online partners. Answer D is incorrect because XTACACS is a proprietary version of the original TACACS protocol that was developed by Cisco.

2. **B**. SAML is an XML framework for creating and exchanging security information between online partners. The weakness in the SAML identity chain is the integrity of users. To mitigate risk, SAML systems need to use timed sessions, HTTPS, and SSL/TLS. Answer A is incorrect because the TACACS+ protocol provides authentication and authorization in addition to accounting of access requests against a centralized service for authorization of access requests. Answer C is incorrect because secure LDAP is a way to make LDAP traffic confidential and secure by using SSL/TLS technology. Answer D is incorrect because XTACACS is a proprietary version of the original TACACS protocol that was developed by Cisco.

3. **A**. TACACS+, released as an open standard, is a protocol that provides authentication and authorization as well as accounting of access requests against a centralized service for authorization of access requests. TACACS+ is similar to RADIUS but uses TCP instead of RADIUS's UDP transport. Answer B is incorrect because SAML is an XML framework for creating and exchanging security information between online partners. Answer C is incorrect because secure LDAP is a way to make LDAP traffic confidential and secure by using SSL/TLS technology. Answer D is incorrect because XTACACS is a proprietary version of the original TACACS protocol that was developed by Cisco.

Given a Scenario, Select the Appropriate Authentication, Authorization, or Access Control

▶ **Identification versus authentication versus authorization**

▶ **Authorization**

▶ **Authentication**

▶ **Authentication factors**

▶ **Identification**

▶ **Federation**

▶ **Transitive trust/authentication**

CramSaver

If you can correctly answer these questions before going through this section, save time by skimming the Exam Alerts in this section and then completing the Cram Quiz at the end of the section in this section and then completing the Cram Quiz at the end of the section.

1. What are the five basic categories of authentication?

2. Would a high-security biometric sensor measuring palm geometry, fingerprints, blood vessel patterns, and blood oxygenation be a multifactored authentication solution?

3. What distinguishes single-factor from multifactor authentication?

4. What are the two meanings of RBAC controls?

5. At what category is discretionary access control specified?

6. Which type of access control involves comparing labels such as SENSITIVE or PUBLIC?

Answers

1. The five basic categories of authentication involve verification of "something you know," "something you have," "something you are," "something you do," and "somewhere you are."

2. No, all of the measures are of a biological nature and so represent a complex but single-factor (biometric) "something you are" authentication mechanism. If a personal identification number (PIN) or smart card "something you have" type of validator was also required, the solution would be considered multifactor.

3. Multifactor identification involves two or more types of authentication (something you have versus something you know, for example). Two or more of the same type of authentication remains a single-factor solution (as in the case of username and password, which are both something you know).

4. RBAC refers to rule-based access control or role-based access control. The exam will expect you to use role-based access control anytime RBAC is paired with DAC (discretionary access control) and MAC (mandatory access control) measures.

5. According to the TCSEC criteria, DAC is defined in Category C, with sub-categories specifying additional criteria (for example, data segmentation, authenticated logons, and logged access audit controls are in subcategory C2 [Controlled Access Protection]).

6. Comparing the requestor's assigned labels with those of the requested resource is the process used in MAC, which is Category B.

Identification Versus Authentication Versus Authorization

It is necessary to discern the difference between identification, authentication, and authentication because you will be tested on all three concepts. Identification occurs when a user or device presents information such as a username, a process ID, a smart card, or other unique identifier claiming an identity. Authentication is the process of validating an identity. This occurs when the user provides appropriate credentials such as the correct password with a username. Authentication provides proof of a claimed identity. Once identification through the presentation and acceptance of credentials is accomplished, the credentials must be measured against a listing of all known credentials by the authentication service to determine authorization of the request before access rights during the session can be established.

Authorization

Authorization is any mechanism by which a system grants or revokes the right to access some resource or perform some action. Often, a user must log on to a system by using some form of authentication before there is authorization. Authentication and access control measures should ensure appropriate access to information and resources while preventing inappropriate access to such resources.

Least Privilege

Least privilege is an access control practice wherein a logon is provided only the bare minimum access to resources required to perform its tasks. Remember the phrase *less is more* when considering security principles: Grant no more access than is necessary to perform assigned tasks. Whenever confronted by a solution involving the determination of proper levels of access, remember the phrase *less is more*.

Separation of Duties

Separating duties is an access control practice involving both the separation of logons and the separation of roles. Separation of logons is having a day-to-day regular user account separate from an admin account that are both assigned to the same network admin. Separation of roles such as security assignment and compliance audit procedures prevents the same individual from being able to verify or record the success or failure of their own work. Separation of account functionality protects the network by ensuring that an inadvertent malware execution during normal unprivileged daily operations cannot attack the network with full administrative privileges possible under the alternative admin-only logon. Separation of role duties ensures that validation is maintained apart from execution to protect the network against fraudulent actions or incomplete execution of security mandates. This is commonly practiced in application development, where the process of coding and testing is handled separately from the actual rollout of final code to the production environment.

ACLs

The mechanism for assigning authorization (allow/deny) privileges for a particular account or group of accounts involves assigning those rights to an access control list (ACL). In its broadest sense, an ACL is the underlying data associated with a network resource that defines its related access permissions. The most common privileges are Read, Write, Read & Execute, Modify, Full Control, and List Folder Contents. ACLs can apply to routers and other devices in addition to individual data resources and services. For purposes of this discussion, the definition is limited to operating system objects. Every operating system object created has a security attribute that matches it to an ACL. The ACL has an entry for each system user that defines the account's access privileges to that object.

ACLs are used in addition to physical security controls to limit access to data. This design helps ensure the integrity of information, preserve the confidentiality of data, and maintain the availability of information. In addition, it helps the organization conform to laws, regulations, and standards.

Access control generally refers to the process of making resources available to accounts that should have access, while limiting that access to only what is required. The forms of access control you need to know include the following:

▶ Mandatory access control (MAC)

▶ Discretionary access control (DAC)

▶ Rule-based access control (RBAC)

▶ Role-based access control (RBAC)

Mandatory Access

The most basic form of access control involves the assignment of labels to resources and accounts (examples include SENSITIVE, SECRET, and PUBLIC). If the labels on the account and resource do not match, the resource remains unavailable in a nondiscretionary manner. This type of access control is called *mandatory access control* (MAC, also referred to as *multilevel access control*) and is often used within governmental systems where resources and access may be granted based on categorical assignment such as classified, secret, or top secret. Mandatory access control applies to all resources within the network and does not allow users to extend access rights by proxy.

ExamAlert

Note that in the Security+ exam the acronym MAC can refer both to mandatory access control and to the Media Access Control sublayer of the data link layer (Layer 2) in the OSI model. When the question involves access control, MAC applies to mandatory controls over access rather than Layer 2 networking.

Discretionary Access

A slightly more complex system of access control involves the restriction of access for each resource in a discretionary manner. Discretionary access control (DAC) scenarios allow individual resources to be made available or secured from access individually. Access rights are configured at the discretion of accounts with authority over each resource, including the ability to extend administrative rights through the same mechanism. In DAC, a security principal (account) has complete control over the objects that it creates or otherwise owns unless restricted through group or role membership. The owner assigns security levels based on objects and subjects and can make his own data available to others at will.

These types of access control and access control best practices are covered in the following sections. These methods and best practices are based on security criteria set by various efforts. Trusted Computer System Evaluation Criteria (TCSEC) and Information Technology Security Evaluation Criteria (ITSEC) are major security criteria efforts. The Common Criteria is based on both TCSEC and ITSEC.

ExamAlert

The TCSEC specification used by many government networks explicitly specifies only the MAC and DAC forms of access control. Because of the color of the original printed manual's cover (DoD 5200.28-STD), the TCSEC is sometimes referred to as the *Orange Book*. The TCSEC is the first book in the Department of Defense (DoD)-published Rainbow series of security criteria, released in 1983. The TCSEC specification identifies levels of security based on the minimum level of access control used in a network environment. The four divisions of access control are the following:

▶ A = Verified

▶ B = Mandatory

▶ C = Discretionary

▶ D = Minimal

Category A is the highest level, essentially encompassing all elements of Category B, in addition to formal design and verification techniques.

You should be aware that individual categories are subdivided based on the complexity of implementation. For example, Category C (Discretionary Access Control) contrasts between basic separation of user data and controlling access to resources (C1 [Discretionary Security Protection]) from environments using data segmentation, authenticated logons, and logged access audit controls (C2 [Controlled Access Protection]).

Rule-Based Access Control

The designation RBAC is sometimes used to refer to *rule-based access control* in addition to *role-based access control*.

Rule-based access control dynamically assigns roles to users based on criteria defined by the data custodian or system administrator. Rule-based access control includes controls such as those based on time of day, day of the week, specific terminal access, GPS coordinates of the requester, and other factors that may overlay a legitimate account's access request. Implementation of rule-based access control may require that rules programmed using code as opposed to traditional access control by checking a box.

Role-Based Access Control

In a role-based access control (RBAC) scenario, access rights are first assigned to roles and accounts are then associated with these roles without direct assignment of resource access rights. This solution provides the greatest level of scalability within large enterprise scenarios, where the explicit granting of rights to each individual account could rapidly overwhelm administrative staff and the potential for accidental granting of unauthorized permissions increases.

RBAC combines some direct access aspects of mandatory access control and varying discretionary access rights based on role membership. Delegation of administration over rights granted through RBAC is itself managed by specialized administration roles, rather than through ownership or direct control over the individual resources as in strictly DAC solutions.

ExamAlert

Remember that the exam may include alternative uses for the RBAC acronym that refers to rule-based access controls. In a rule-based access control solution, access rights can vary by account, by time of day, only from a trusted OS, or through other forms of conditional testing. Exam items dealing with conditional testing for access (for example, time-of-day controls) are examining rule-based access control. Items involving assignment of rights to groups for inheritance by group member accounts are focused on role-based access control.

Time-of-Day Restrictions

Besides password restrictions, you can restrict logon hours in many operating systems. By default, all domain users can log in at any time. Many times, it is necessary to restrict logon hours for maintenance purposes. For example, at 11:00 p.m. each evening, the backup is run; therefore, you might want to be sure that everyone is off of the system. Or if databases get re-indexed on a nightly basis, you might have to confirm that no one is changing information or locking records during the re-indexing process.

This is also a good way to be sure that a hacker is not logging in with stolen passwords during off-peak hours. You can restrict logon hours by days of the week, hours of the day, or both. You can also assign time-of-day restrictions to ensure that employees use computers only during specified hours. This setting proves useful for organizations where users require supervision, where security certification requires it, or where employees are mainly temporary or shift workers.

ExamAlert

Each OS is different, so the effect of the restrictions differs if the user is currently logged on when the restriction time begins. In a Microsoft environment, whether users are forced to log off when their logon hours expire is determined by the Automatically Log Off Users setting. In other environments, the user might be allowed to stay logged on, but once logged off, the user cannot log back on. The logon schedule is enforced by the Kerberos Group Policy setting Enforce User Logon Restrictions, which is enabled by default in Windows Active Directory environments.

The account expires attribute specifies when an account expires. You can use this setting under the same conditions as mentioned previously for the time-of-day restrictions. Temporary or contract workers should have user accounts that are valid only for a certain amount of time. This way, when the account expires, it can no longer be used to log on to any service. Statistics show that a large number of temporary accounts are never disabled. Limiting the time an account is active for such employees should be part of the policies and procedures. In addition, user accounts should be audited on a regular basis for de-provisioning or re-provisioning based on role change.

Authentication

Before authorization can occur for anything other than anonymous access to public resources, the identity of the account attempting to access a resource must be determined. This process is known as *authentication*. The most common form of authentication is the use of a logon account and password in combination to access resources and services. Access is not possible without both parts required for account authentication.

Authentication and access control policies are typically technical controls over access rights assignment and group membership, as discussed in Chapter 11.

ExamAlert

The exam might contrast *identification* (the presenting of credentials or keys) with *authentication* (the verification of presented credentials or keys as being valid and present in the authorization system's database).

The relative strength of an authentication system involves the difficulty involved in falsifying or circumventing its process. Anonymous or open access represents the weakest possible form of authentication, whereas the requirement for both a logon identifier and password combination might be considered the simplest form of actual account verification. The highest levels of authentication might involve not only account logon, but also criteria measuring whether the logon is occurring from specific network addresses or whether a security token such as an access smart card is present.

In theory, the strongest security would be offered by identifying biometric (body-measuring) keys unique to a particular user's physical characteristics, such as fingerprints and retinal or iris patterns, combined with other authentication methods involving access passwords or token-based security requiring the possession of a physical smart card key.

Tokens

One of the best methods of "something you have" authentication involves the use of a token, which might either be a physical device or a one-time password issued to the user seeking access. Or in the case of credit cards, an embedded chip in the card itself that must be paired with a "something you know" PIN code to avoid the type of issue vendors like Target suffered in 2013. Tokens include solutions such as a chip-integrated smart card or a digital token such as RSA Security's SecurID token that provides a numeric key that changes every few minutes and is synchronized with the authentication server. Without the proper key or physical token, access is denied. Because the token is unique and granted only to the user, it is harder to pretend to be (spoof) the properly authorized user. Digital tokens are typically used only one time or are valid for a very short period of time to prevent capture and later reuse. Most token-based access control systems pair the token with a PIN or other form of authentication to protect against unauthorized access using only a lost or stolen token.

Telecommuters might also use an electronic device known as a key fob that provides one part of a three-way match to log on over an unsecure network connection to a secure network. This kind of key fob might have a keypad on which the user must enter a PIN to retrieve an access code, or it could be a display-only device such as a VPN token that algorithmically generates security codes as part of a challenge/response authentication system.

Common Access Card

The common access card (CAC) is a credit card-sized "smart" card. This is the standard identification for active duty uniformed service personnel, selected reserve, DoD civilian employees, and eligible contractor personnel. It is also the principal card used to enable physical access to buildings and controlled spaces, and it provides access to DoD computer networks and systems. Homeland Security Presidential Directive 12 (HSPD 12) establishes the policies for a common identification standard for federal employees and contractors. DoD Instruction (DoDI) 1000.13 states that the CAC shall serve as the federal personal identity verification (PIV) card for DoD implementation of HSPD 12. When a CAC is inserted into a smart card reader and the associated PIN entered, the information on the card's chip is compared with data on a government server and access is either granted or denied.

Smart Card

Smart cards are a form of "something you have" authentication that uses a standard wallet card with an embedded chip that can automatically provide an authenticating cryptographic key to its reader, or it might contain data useful for other forms of authentication, such as biometric measures, which can be too large for high-volume remote authentication solutions.

ExamAlert

The exam might include questions regarding two new forms of smart card required for U.S. federal service identity verification under the HSPD 12:

▶ **Common access card (CAC):** A smart card used in military, reserve officer, and military-contractor identity authentication systems

▶ **Personal identity verification (PIV) card:** A smart card used for federal employees and contractors

---

Multifactor Authentication

Obviously, the needs for authentication are going to be relative to the value assigned to a particular resource's security. Additional authentication layers required for access increase both the administrative overhead necessary for management and the difficulty users have trying to access needed resources. Consider, for example, the differences in authentication requirements for access to a high-security solution such as the Department of Energy's power grid control network as opposed to those needed to access an unprivileged local account in a public kiosk.

In the first scenario, to establish authentication for rightful access, the use of a combination of multiple biometric, token-based, and password-form authentication credentials might be mandatory. You can also use these access methods with even more complex forms of authentication, such as the use of dedicated lines of communication, time-of-day restrictions, synchronized shifting-key hardware encryption devices, and redundant-path comparison. You use these to ensure that each account attempting to make an access request is properly identified. In the second scenario, authentication might be as simple as an automatic anonymous guest logon shared by all visitors.

Each mechanism for authentication provides different levels of identification, security over data during the authentication exchange, and suitability to different authentication methods such as wireless or dial-up network access requests. Multiple authentication factors can be combined to improve the overall strength of the access control mechanism.

A common example of a multi-factor authentication system is used at automated teller machines (ATMs), which require both a "something you have" physical key (your ATM card) in combination with a "something you know" PIN. Similar issues with payment card systems arose following public attacks on vendors such as Target, resulting in expansion of the effort to enable two-factor authentication using electronic chips in the cards (something you have) and a PIN (something you know). By combining two or more types of authentication, you improve access security above a single-factor authentication such as your "something you have" car key, which could be used alone without any additional credentials beyond possession of the physical key or its duplicate.

The difficulty involved in gaining unauthorized access increases as more types of authentication are used, although the difficulty for users wanting to authenticate themselves is also increased similarly. Administrative overhead and cost of support also increase with the complexity of the authentication scheme, so a solution should be reasonable based on the sensitivity of data being secured.

ExamAlert

The exam might ask you to distinguish between single-factor and multifactor authentication solutions. A multifactor authentication scenario involves two or more of the *types* of authentication (something you know, have, are, or do or somewhere you are), not simply multiple credentials or keys of the same type. The common logon/password combination is a single-factor ("something you know") authentication using two separate keys of the same authentication type.

TOTP

One-time passwords (OTP) are passwords that can be only used one time. An OTP is considered safer than a regular password because the password keeps changing, providing protection against replay attacks. The two main standards for generating OTPs are TOTP and HOTP. Both standards are governed by the Initiative for Open Authentication (OATH). The time-based one-time password (TOTP) algorithm relies on a shared secret and a moving factor or counter, which is the current time. The moving factor constantly changes based on the time passed since an epoch.

HOTP

The HMAC-based one-time password (HOTP) algorithm relies on a shared secret and a moving factor or counter. When a new OTP is generated, the moving factor is incremented, generating a different password each time. The main difference between HOTP and TOTP is that HOTP passwords can be valid for an unknown amount of time. In contrast, TOTP passwords keep on changing and are only valid for a short period of time. Because of this difference, TOTP is considered more secure.

CHAP

The Challenge-Handshake Authentication Protocol (CHAP) can be used to provide on-demand authentication within an ongoing data transmission. CHAP uses a one-way hashing function that first involves a service requesting a CHAP response from the client. The client creates a hashed value that is derived using the message digest (MD5) hashing algorithm and sends this value to the service, which also calculates the expected value itself. The server, referred to as the authenticator, compares these two values. If they match, the transmission continues. This process is repeated at random intervals during a session of data transaction. CHAP functions over Point-to-Point Protocol (PPP) connections. There are also two forms of CHAP that are Microsoft specific (MS-CHAP and MS-CHAPv2) that you should be able to recognize.

PAP

Password Authentication Protocol (PAP) is a simple authentication protocol in which the username and password are sent to the remote-access server in plain-text form. Using PAP is strongly discouraged because user passwords are easily readable from the PPP packets exchanged during the authentication process. PAP is typically used only when connecting to older Unix-based remote-access servers that do not support more secure authentication protocols.

Single Sign-On

Distributed enterprise networks often include many different resources, each of which might require a different mechanism or protocol for authentication and access control. To reduce user support and authentication complexity, a single sign-on (SSO) capable of granting access across multiple services might be desirable. SSO solutions can use a central meta-directory service or can sequester services behind a series of proxy applications as in the service-oriented architecture (SOA) approach.

In the SOA network environment, the client-facing proxy application provides a standard mechanism for interacting with each service (called a *wrapper*), handling specialized logon, authentication, and access control functions "behind the scenes" and out of sight of the consuming user or service.

Access Control

Enterprise access control systems or identity management systems provide an integrated set of tools to manage access control. Access control manages what resources a user can access physically, electronically, and virtually. Access control mechanisms provide an audit trail of user interactions with the enterprise resources. An access control policy should be established, documented, and periodically reviewed based on business needs and external requirements. Planning for access control might affect the methods used in the authentication process. For example, if there is a need only for anonymous access to a public read-only HTML document, the simple access control mandates eliminate the need for a complex authentication process.

Implicit Deny

Implicit deny is an access control practice wherein resource availability is restricted to only those logons explicitly granted access, remaining unavailable even when not explicitly denied access. This practice is used commonly in Cisco networks, where most ACLs have a default setting of *implicit deny*. This ensures that when access is not explicitly granted, it is automatically denied by default.

Trusted OS

An operating system is called *trusted* if it meets the intended security requirements. A certain level of trust can be assigned to an operating system depending on the degree to which it meets a specific set of requirements. A trusted operating system is designed from the beginning with security in mind. The evaluation of the level of trust depends on the enforcement of security policy, and the sufficiency of the operating system's measures and mechanisms. Trusted operating system authentication is a feature that allows the existing OS authentication to log on to system architecture. The user is not prompted for a user logon to connect the second architecture. For example, IBM Rationale Directory Server has options that allow supported tools to use the existing operating system authentication to log on to IBM Rational Directory Server.

Authentication Factors

A method for authenticating users must be designed and implemented properly for the organization to achieve established business goals and security control objectives. There are several common factors used for authentication: something you know, something you have, something you are, something you do, and somewhere you are. Authentication factors provide a means for implementation of multifactor authentication. Multifactor authentication provides additional security because account access is no longer possible with only a password.

ExamAlert

Forms of authentication credentials can be generally broken into five basic categories, depending on what is required to identify the access requester:

▶ Something you **know** (passwords, account logon identifiers)

▶ Something you **have** (smart cards, synchronized shifting keys)

▶ Something you **are** (fingerprints, retinal patterns, hand geometry)

▶ Something you **do** (gait and handwriting kinematics)

▶ Some**where** you **are** (you are in a trusted or less-trusted location)

Location-specific logons from a particular GPS zone, time-of-day restrictions, or restricted console terminal requirements can also factor in limiting access to requests.

Identification

The proper identification of a person, device, or group is important to protect and maintain the confidentiality, integrity, and availability of the organization's assets and infrastructure. Based on business policies, identification access controls can be created for authenticating users and devices.

> **ExamAlert**
>
> The exam will expect you to group identification together with authentication as a single step.

Biometrics

The most unique qualities of an individual can be obtained by measuring and identifying his or her unique physical characteristics in "something you are" forms of bio measurement (biometric) authentication such a fingerprints, retinal patterns, iris patterns, blood vessel patterns, bone structure, and other forms of physiological qualities unique to each person. Other "something you do" values may be measured, such as voice-pattern recognition, movement kinematics, or high-resolution cardiac patterns, but because these might change based on illness, injury, or exertion, they suffer high rates of false rejection (valid attempts at authentication that are returned as failures).

New systems are becoming available to allow authentication of users by their body measurements (biometrics), which are compared to values stored within an authorization system's database to provide authentication only if the biometric values match those previously measured. Another alternative is to store biometric data on smart card tokens, which can then be paired by the localized authentication service with the requisite physical measurement without requiring a centralized database for comparison. Under this scenario, users must be authenticated within a widely distributed scheme where transactions against a central server storing large and complex biometric values might be difficult.

Biometric devices are susceptible to false acceptance and false rejection rates. The false acceptance rate (FAR) is a measure of the likelihood that the access system will wrongly accept an access attempt (in other words, allow access to an unauthorized user).

The false rejection rate (FRR) is the percentage of identification instances in which false rejection occurs. In false rejection, the system fails to recognize an authorized person and rejects that person as unauthorized.

Table 10.1 describes some of the most common biometric methods.

TABLE 10.1 **A Comparison of Common Biometric Measures**

Method	Process	Issues
Fingerprint	Scans and identifies the swirls and loops of a fingerprint.	Injury, scars, or loss of a finger might create false rejection results. Unless paired with other measures, pattern alone can be easily counterfeited.
Hand/palm geometry	Measures the length and width of a hand's profile, including hand and bone measures.	Loss of fingers or significant injury might create false rejection results.
Voiceprint	Measures the tonal and pacing patterns of a spoken phrase or passage.	Allergies, illnesses, and exhaustion can distort vocal patterns and create false rejection results.
Facial recognition	Identifies and measures facial characteristics, including eye spacing, bone patterns, chin shape, and forehead size and shape.	Subject to false rejection results if the scanner is not aligned precisely with the scanned face.
Iris	Scans and identifies the unique patterns in the colored part of the eye that surrounds the pupil.	Lighting conditions, alcohol, and medications can affect the pupil's dilation and present false rejections.
Retina	Scans and identifies the unique blood vessel and tissue patterns at the back of the eye.	Illness or inaccurate placement of the eye against the scanner's cuff can result in false rejection results.
Blood vessels	Identifies and measures unique patterns of blood vessels in the hand or face.	Environmental conditions, clothing, and some illnesses can render false rejection results due to measurement inaccuracies.
Signature	Records and measures the speed, shape, and kinematics of a signature provided to an electronic pad.	Variations in personal signature due to attitude, environment, injury, alcohol, or medication might render false rejection results.
Gait	Records and measures the unique patterns of weight shift and leg kinematics during walking.	Variations in gait due to attitude, environment, injury, alcohol, or medication might render false rejection results.

> **ExamAlert**
>
> The exam might include questions about the various biometric methods, so be sure you are familiar with each of the descriptions in Table 10.1 and the limitations of each. Remember that combinations of biometric solutions, such as readers for both hand geometry and blood vessel patterns, remain a single-factor "something you are" authentication solution unless also paired with something else, such as a "something you have" key card.

Personal Identification Verification Card

A personal identity verification (PIV) card is a smart card used for identification of federal employees and contractors. NIST developed the standard "Personal Identity Verification (PIV) of Federal Employees and Contractors," published as Federal Information Processing Standards (FIPS) Publication 201. A PIV card contains the necessary data for the cardholder to be granted access to federal facilities and information systems that includes separation of roles and strong biometric binding. A smart card becomes a CAC if it is used by the U.S. Department of Defense; CAC is for DoD users. A PIV card is for civilian users working for the federal government.

Username

The most common form of authentication combines two "something you know" forms of authentication: a username and a password or passphrase. This form is easily implemented across many types of haptic interface, including standard keyboards and assistive technology interfaces. If both values match the credentials associated within the authorization system's database, the credentials can be authenticated and authorized for a connection. Password strength is a measure of the difficulty involved in guessing or breaking the password through cryptographic techniques, rainbow tables, or library-based, automated, brute-force testing of alternative values.

Federation

A political federation involves a myriad of equal participants, collaborating through agreements and agreed-upon rules or mediators who can represent their own political agenda. In the United Nations, for example, each governmental body assigns its own ambassador, who can speak for their country's interests. A federated authentication solution transfers this idea into technology by assigning an administrative account capable of enumerating local security principals and resources, with the federation system accessible from each domain, so that accounts in one area can be granted access rights to any other resource whether it be local or remote within the communicating domains.

Transitive Trust/Authentication

Several mechanisms exist for provisioning accounts for authorization and applying access controls across an enterprise or multiple enterprises facilitate connecting resources with user principals across multiple resource pools. Two domains can be configured to share a trust of one another by configuring the administrative connection between two resource pools. A one-way trust (Domain A trusts Domain B) allows resources in Domain A to be accessed by security principals (users, services, and so on) in Domain B. A two-way trust allows each domain to trust members of either domain. (Domain A and Domain B resources can be accessed by authorized requests from user accounts in either Domain A or Domain B.)

Within compatible domains, a limited form of interoperation can be assigned directly between two resource pools through administrative actions within each specifically designating the other as a trusted resource pool and allowing enumeration of accounts and available resources, so that access control over any resource can be granted or denied to any account in either domain. This connection is termed a *trust*, which is like an agreement between allied countries directly. If the trust is configured so that any domain trusting Domain A will in turn trust all other domains Domain A trusts in turn, this connection is called a *transitive trust*. This is like a friend of your father being trusted by your siblings and then becoming transitive if you and your siblings agree to trust everyone your father trusts.

Cram Quiz

Answer these questions. The answers follow the last question. If you cannot answer these questions correctly, consider reading this section again until you can.

1. If you have a smart card that contains details of your iris coloring and retinal patterns, which two types of authentication would be involved in a successful access request?

   ○ **A.** Something you have and something you do

   ○ **B.** Something you do and something you are

   ○ **C.** Something you are and something you know

   ○ **D.** Something you have and something you are

2. Which type of "something you have" factor is employed by U.S. federal governmental employees and contractors under HSPD 12?

   ○ **A.** Smart card

   ○ **B.** CAC

   ○ **C.** PIV

   ○ **D.** SecurID

3. What is the proper order of operations during the access control process?

   ○ **A.** Identification, authorization, access control

   ○ **B.** Authentication, authorization, access control

   ○ **C.** Authorization, authentication, accounting

   ○ **D.** Identification, authentication, access control

4. Which biometric measure involves scanning tissue patterns at the back of the eye?

   ○ **A.** Retina

   ○ **B.** Iris

   ○ **C.** Facial recognition

   ○ **D.** Signature

Cram Quiz Answers

1. **D**. The smart card is an example of "something you have," and the biometric measures are an example of "something you are." Answer A is incorrect because there are no biometrics relating to "something you do," only simple measurements of bodily configuration. Answer B is incorrect for the same reason; there is no "something you do" metric present. Answer C is incorrect because no PIN or password is employed as a "something you know" factor.

2. **C**. The PIV card is used by U.S. federal employees and contractors under HSPD 12. Answer A is incorrect because A, B, and C are all smart card variations, but only C is specifically used for federal employees and contractors under HSPD 12. Answer B is incorrect because the CAC is used by U.S. military, military reserve, and military contractors. Answer D is incorrect because the RSA SecurID is an example of a time-shifting key token.

3. **B**. The correct order of operations is the authentication of provided credentials or keys, followed by authorization of the presented credentials, and finally the application of access controls. Answer A is incorrect because identification involves only the presentation of credentials and not the requirement for verifying those credentials as valid. Answer C is incorrect because accounting of access is a function of the authentication and authorization service rather than a required operation for the process of authorization alone. Answer D is incorrect because identification is included along with authentication and authorization is missing.

4. **A**. Retinal biometric identification involves the scanning and identification of blood vessels and tissues in the back of the eye. Answer B is incorrect because iris biometric systems analyze only the external colored part of the eye around the pupil. Answer C is incorrect because facial recognition systems measure the overall proportions of facial features and bones. Answer D is incorrect because signature biometric analysis involves the gross motions and patterns of a written signature rather than those of the scanned back of the eye.

What Next?

If you want more practice on this chapter's exam objectives before you move on, remember that you can access all the Cram Quiz questions on the CD. You can also create a custom exam by objective with the practice exam software. Note any objective that you struggle with and go to the material that covers that objective in this chapter.

CHAPTER 11

Account Management

This chapter covers the following official CompTIA Security+ SY0-401 exam objectives:

▶ Install and configure security controls when performing account management, based on best practices.

(For more information on the official CompTIA Security+ SY0-401 exam topics, see the "About the CompTIA Security+ SY0-401 Exam" section in the Introduction.)

To protect against unauthorized access or modification and to ensure availability for legitimate access requests, you must put a mechanism into place that allows the identification of an authorized request from an unauthorized one. This overall process is called *access control*.

The previous chapter covered the fundamental concepts and best practices related to authentication services and selecting the appropriate authentication, authorization, or access control. This chapter focuses on account management controls and account management best practices.

Install and Configure Security Controls When Performing Account Management, Based on Best Practices

▶ Mitigate issues associated with users with multiple account/roles and/or shared accounts

▶ Account policy enforcement

▶ Group-based privileges

▶ User-assigned privileges

▶ User access reviews

▶ Continuous monitoring

CramSaver

If you can correctly answer these questions before going through this section, save time by skimming the Exam Alerts in this section and then completing the Cram Quiz at the end of the section.

1. What is the best model for access rights assignment in a large, distributed enterprise?

2. Which type of groups are assigned for non–security-related functions?

3. What policy prevents accidental access or denial rights continuing after role reassignment?

4. Which type of account policy is set for accounts created for temporary employees or contractors?

5. What is best practice for handling the user account of a user that has been terminated?

Answers

1. The *role/group-based* model is best for large, complex enterprises because each group can have associated access rights that are inherited by individuals and other groups assigned to that group.

2. Distribution groups are used for non–security-related groups such as email distribution lists.

3. User access reviews allow the identification of misapplied changes or other access control adjustments through direct assignment or inherited nesting of role access rights. Through regular reviews, accidents or malicious attempts to gain unauthorized access rights can be identified and rectified.

4. In the normal course of business, you might sometimes create domain user accounts for a short duration. This type of account is typically used for contractors or temporary employees. With this kind of user, accounts should be created that automatically expire after a specified date.

5. Disable user accounts as soon as a user leaves the company. The advantage of disabling user accounts is all of its settings, files, and folders remain intact and you can access information tied to the user account anytime by reenabling the account.

Mitigate Issues Associated with Users with Multiple Account/Roles and/or Shared Accounts

The access level that users are given directly affects the level of network protection you have. Even though it might sound strange that the network should be protected from its own users, the internal user has the greatest access to data and the opportunity to either deliberately sabotage it or accidentally delete it. Upon logon, showing a logon banner statement to the effect that network access is granted under certain conditions and that activities might be monitored helps the organization be sure that legal ramifications are covered and that users can be expected to follow security policy protocols.

One of the first steps that must be taken to provide a secure account access environment is to eliminate the use of shared accounts, whose use cannot be attributed to a particular user's credentials and so precludes determination of specific access rights and audit of access use. By providing each set of access credentials to a single principal, either a user or a machine service, every use of data access can be measured to determine a baseline of expected and acceptable use and then monitored for variations that may indicate potential misuse of enterprise resources or data access.

Users with administrative functions should not rely on their with-privileges accounts for everyday use (email and so on) because an unexpected piece of malware encountered through the course of normal business functions will run under the access control restrictions of the accessing account. By issuing these users a common account for normal access and a separate administrative credential set used when needed, this limits the span of control for their operational account. Linux users have been doing this for some time, using **sudo** *(superuser do)* to perform administrative functions from their session account.

Account Policy Enforcement

As the number of systems and users grows in an organization, account policy enforcement becomes critical. Therefore, you should set account policies that define strong security for your systems. Account policies are a subset of the policies configurable in Group Policy.

Credential Management

Credentials must also be assigned for a given time period, with an automatic failover to access denial if not renewed to ensure that provisioned accounts are used or cease to operate. This is often necessary in workforces consisting of short-term or temporary workers, whose accounts could otherwise be left intact and unmonitored after the workers rotate to new positions. Such an account presents a target for brute-force types of attacks on logon passwords, which can then be spread over a long period of time to avoid detection by intrusion-prevention measures. All credentials, whether simple logon passwords or complex encryption keys, should carry a built-in lifetime that ensures their termination even if otherwise lost or forgotten. Auditing procedures should reveal long-term inactive accounts and machine accounts that should be routinely expired and reestablished to protect against long-term attacks and limit exploitation if compromised during the normal period of use.

Group Policy

Active Directory domains use Group Policy objects (GPO) to store a wide variety of configuration information, including password policy settings. Domains have their own password policy in addition to the local password policy. Domain password policies can control password settings. The Account Policies settings in Group Policy are applied at the domain level. The domain Account Policies settings become the default local Account Policies settings of any Windows-based computer that is a member of the domain. The only exception to this rule is when another Account Policies setting is defined for an organizational unit (OU). The Account Policies settings for the OU affect the local policy on any computers that are contained in the OU.

> **ExamAlert**
>
> In organizations that use Windows or a similar directory service architecture for enterprise management, Group Policy assignment of access controls can mandate the application of security configuration technical controls based on organizational unit or domain membership to handle all accounts within an organization or to establish default configuration settings.

Password policy settings for the domain are defined in the root container for the domain. The default domain policy is linked to the root container. It contains a few critical domain-wide settings including the default password policy settings.

Password Complexity

Because passwords are one of the best methods of gaining successful access to services and resources, password length, duration, history, and complexity requirements are all important to the security of the network. When setting up user accounts, take into account proper planning and policies. Passwords are one of the first pieces of information entered by a user. Passwords that contain only alphanumeric characters are easy to compromise by using publicly available tools. To prevent this, passwords should contain additional characters and meet complexity requirements.

The Password Must Meet Complexity Requirements policy setting in Windows operating systems determines whether passwords meet certain criteria for a strong password. Enabling this policy setting requires passwords to meet the following requirements:

▶ The password may not contain the user's account or full name value

▶ The password contains three of the following: uppercase letters, lower-case letters, numbers, nonalphanumeric characters (special characters), and any Unicode character that is categorized as an alphabetic character but is not uppercase or lowercase.

Complexity requirements are enforced when passwords are changed or created. This policy setting, combined with a minimum password length of 8, ensures that there are at least 218,340,105,584,896 different possibilities for a single password. This makes a brute-force attack difficult, but still not impossible.

Expiration

In the normal course of business, you might sometimes create domain user accounts for a short duration. This type of account is typically used for contractors or temporary employees. With this kind of user, accounts should be created that automatically expire after a specified date. When an account expires, the user is no longer allowed to log on to the domain and the operating system displays an error message informing the user that the account has been expired.

Account provisioning policies for creation, update, and removal must be integrated into an organization's HR process and regularly audited to ensure continued compliance. Legacy access groups should be similarly expired when no longer appropriate to the organization's operational structure, helping to eliminate potential avenues of unauthorized access through normal line-of-business operations. During separation procedures, passwords and other security credentials should be automatically expired to prevent unauthorized access after no longer appropriate. During termination proceedings, this is typically coordinated between managers and the IT department to protect organizational resources from retributive or exploitive actions attempted by the terminated employee.

Recovery

When a user forgets a password, generally there are two options: password recovery or a password reset. Password resets are also performed when a new account is created, to set an initial password. There are many ways in which password recovery and resets can happen that range from an in-person visit with an IT staff member to a fully automated self-service utility. If the identity of the user requesting a password recovery or reset is not properly verified, an attacker could easily pose as a user and gain access to that user's password. All recovery and reset mechanisms should first verify the user's identity using appropriate methods. Common methods include predetermined challenge response questions set during account creation, emailing recovery information, or texting a code to the user's cell phone.

Never store passwords or access credentials in an unsecure location or use a reversible form of encryption. Sometimes a company might want a list of machine accounts or fundamental server recovery administrative passwords. This list might end up in the wrong hands if not properly secured along with the disaster recovery documentation. If a user forgets his password, administrators should not be able to recover the old password, but instead should issue new credentials after the proper identity has been verified.

Disablement

Rename or disable the administrator account and guest account in each domain to prevent attacks on your domains. Disable user accounts as soon as a user leaves the company. The advantage of disabling user accounts is that all of its settings, files, and folders remain intact and that you can access information tied to the user account anytime by reenabling the account. It is good policy to not reuse or rename the account of a terminated user. When a user leaves the organization, the account can be disabled and moved if necessary. Depending on company policy, the user account may need to be kept for a certain period of time. For example, some organizations keep disabled accounts for 90 days. Once 90 days is over, the account is deleted.

Lockout

The account lockout policy settings help you to prevent attackers from guessing users' passwords and decreases the likelihood of successful attacks on your network. An account lockout policy disables a user account when an incorrect password is entered a specified number of times over a specified period. Account lockout policy settings control the threshold for this response and the actions to be taken after the threshold is reached.

The account lockout duration policy setting determines the number of minutes that a locked-out account remains locked out before automatically becoming unlocked. The available range is from 1 through 99,999 minutes. A lockout duration value of 0 specifies that the account will be locked out until an administrator explicitly unlocks it. The lockout threshold can be set to any value from 0 to 999. If the lockout threshold is set to 0, accounts will not be locked out due to invalid logon attempts. The Reset Account Lockout Counter After policy setting determines the number of minutes that must elapse from the time a user fails to log on before the failed logon attempt counter is reset to 0. If the account lockout threshold is set to a number greater than 0, this reset time must be less than or equal to the value of account lockout duration. A disadvantage to configuring these settings too restrictive is that users may make excessive help desk calls. General best practices dictate that you should lock user accounts out after 3 to 5 failed logon attempts. This policy stops programs from deciphering the passwords on locked accounts by repeated brute-force attempts.

Password History

The Maximum Password Age policy setting determines the number of days that a password can be used before the system requires the user to change it. You can set passwords to expire after a number of days between 1 and 999, or you can specify that passwords never expire by setting the number of days to 0. In Microsoft operating systems, there is both a maximum password age and a minimum password age. If the maximum password age is set, the minimum password age must be less than the maximum password age. When the maximum password age is set to 0, the minimum password age can be any value between 0 and 998 days. Good policy is to set the maximum password age to a value between 30 and 90 days, depending on your environment. Try to expire the passwords between major business cycles to prevent work loss.

Configure minimum password age so that you do not allow passwords to be changed immediately. This way, an attacker has a limited amount of time in which to compromise a user's password and have access to your network resources.

Password Reuse

Password reuse is an important concern in any organization. When allowed, users tend to reuse the same password over a long period of time. The longer the same password is used for a particular account, the greater the chance that an attacker will be able to determine the password through brute-force attacks. Allowing users to reuse an old password greatly reduces the effectiveness of a good password policy.

Most operating systems have settings that do not allow users to reuse a password for a certain length of time or number of password changes. The enforce password history policy setting in Windows operating systems determines the number of unique new passwords that must be associated with a user account before an old password can be reused. Specifying a low number for enforce password history allows users to continually use the same small number of passwords repeatedly. Configure the server to not allow users to use the same password over and over again. Setting the enforce password history to 24 helps mitigate vulnerabilities that are caused by password reuse.

Password Length

Making the password length at least eight characters and requiring the use of combinations of uppercase and lowercase letters, numbers, and special characters is good practice. In Windows operating systems, the Minimum Password Length policy setting determines the least number of characters that can make up a password for a user account. You can set a value of between 1 and 14 characters, or you can establish that no password is required by setting the number of characters to 0.

In most environments, an eight-character password is recommended because it is long enough to provide adequate security and still short enough for users to easily remember. Adding complexity requirements will help reduce the possibility of a dictionary attack. Although longer passwords are more effective against attacks, requiring long passwords can cause account lockouts due to mistyping and can actually decrease the security of an organization because users might be more likely to write down their passwords to avoid forgetting them. User education on the proper way to make long passwords that they can easily remember is the best solution.

ExamAlert

The key aspects of password controls include required complexity, password length, and account lockout/expiration terms.

Consider the following suggested minimum standards when developing password policies for the exam:

ExamAlert

Password policies help secure the network and define the responsibilities of users who have been given access to company resources. You should have all users read and sign security policies as part of their employment process. Domain password policies affect all users in the domain. The effectiveness of these policies depends on how and where they are applied. The three areas that can be configured are password, account lockout, and Kerberos policies.

You can use the account lockout policy to secure the system against attacks by disabling the account after a certain number of attempts, for a certain period of time. Use the Kerberos policy settings for authentication services. In most environments, the default settings should suffice. If you do need to change them, remember that they are applied at the domain level and more finely controlled by access denial for the particular Group Policy applied for specific groups.

Require users to change passwords every 90 to 180 days, depending on how secure the environment needs to be. Remember that the more often users are required to change passwords, the greater the chance that they will write them down, potentially exposing them to unauthorized use.

Generic Account Prohibition

Certain groups are installed by default. As an administrator, you should know what these groups are and know which accounts are installed by default. In dealing with individual accounts, the administrative account should be used only for the purpose of administering the server. Granting users this type of access is a disaster waiting to happen. An individual using the administrative account can put a company's entire business in jeopardy if the user accesses a malware-infected website or reads the wrong email. In addition, generic accounts that are used by multiple users must be prohibited.

By knowing which accounts are installed by default, you can determine which are really needed and which can be disabled, thereby making the system more secure. You should also know which accounts, if any, are installed with blank or well-established passwords. Common machine accounts used in web-based access systems are common targets for unauthorized access attempts, particularly when left in default or well-known configuration states such as the Oracle database Scott/Tiger access credential combination.

The security settings in many of the newer operating systems do not allow blank passwords. However, there might still be accounts in older operating systems that have a blank password or a well-known default like the *admin/admin* logon in older routers. User rights are applied to security groups to determine what members of that group can do within the scope of a domain or forest. The assignment of user rights is through security options that apply to user accounts.

ExamAlert

The User Account Control (UAC) technology used by the Windows 7/8 and later operating systems ensures that software applications cannot perform privileged access without additional authorization from the user. Within the Microsoft environment, lesser accounts may perform privileged processes using the "run as" option to specify the explicit use of a privileged account from within the unprivileged account logon. This is similar to the sudo shell operation under Unix operating systems.

Default credentials and unmonitored accounts such as the "guest" or "admin" account commonly established in older equipment and software create a softening effort on security because they provide one component of access credentials to potential attackers or their tools. Replacing a default administrative account named admin with one using a nonsense term or autogenerated value such as R0und$b0ut!2LLYHan50ut67 adds another obstacle to account comprise. Instead of having the account name admin already provided and only requiring the passcode to be broken, attempts to secure access authentication require compromise both of the account and its associated authentication keys.

Key-generating keys in public-key encryption infrastructures (PKI) should similarly be guarded to prevent access to resources protected by the subordinate keys through compromise of the base keys used by the certificate authority. No logical access should ever allow access to these base key sets, which should ideally be kept offline and in environmentally stabilized protected storage to prevent both directed and purposeful access and damage due to environmental threats (fire, flood, earthquake, and so forth).

Group-Based Privileges

When working with groups, remember a few key items: No matter what OS you are working with, if you are giving a user full access in one group and denying access in another group, the result is deny access. However, group permissions are cumulative, so if a user belongs to two groups and one has more liberal access, the user will have the most liberal access, except where the deny access permission is involved. If a user has difficulty accessing information after he or she has been added to a new group, the first item you might want to check for is conflicting permissions.

> **ExamAlert**
>
> When assigning user permissions, if the groups the user is assigned to have liberal access and another group has no access, the result is no access.

When dealing with user access, a fine line often exists between sufficient access to get the job done and too much access. In this section, you examine how to manage user access by using groups and group policies. Keep the "least privilege" best practice in mind when comparing access control options.

A user account holds information about the specific user. It can contain basic information such as name, password, and the level of permission the user has in her associated access control lists (ACL). It can also contain more specific information, such as the department the user works in, a home phone number, and the days and hours the user is allowed to log on to specific workstations. Groups are created to make the sharing of resources more manageable. A group contains users who share a common need for access to a particular resource; it can be nested in other groups in turn to better aggregate access permissions for multiple roles. Even though the connotations might differ with each operating system, all of these terms still refer to the access that a user or group account is granted or specifically denied.

> **ExamAlert**
>
> When working with logical controls, there are two models for assignment of permissions and rights: user based and role or group based.

Access control over large numbers of user accounts can be more easily accomplished by managing the access permissions on each group, which are then inherited by the group's members. In this type of access, permissions are assigned to groups, and user accounts become members of the groups based on their organizational roles. Each user account has access based on the combined permissions inherited from its various group memberships. These groups often reflect divisions or departments of the company, such as human resources, sales, development, and management. In enterprise networks, groups may also be nested. Group nesting can simplify permission assignment if you know how to use hierarchical nesting, or it can complicate troubleshooting when you do not know what was set up for each level or why and so do not know where a deny or allow permission is assigned.

User-Assigned Privileges

Within a user-based model, permissions are uniquely assigned to each user account. One example of this is a peer-to-peer network or a workgroup where access is granted based on individual needs. This access type is also found in government and military situations and in private companies where patented processes and trademark products require protection. User-based privilege management is usually used for specific parts of the network or specific resources. This type of policy is time-consuming and difficult for administrators to handle, plus it does not work well in large environments. You will find that making groups and assigning users to these groups will make the administration process much easier.

In addition to permissions, user rights can be assigned. Although user rights can apply to individual user accounts, they are best administered by using group accounts. The user rights assignment is twofold: It can grant specific *privileges*, and it can grant *logon rights* to users and groups in your computing environment:

▶ **Logon:** Logon rights control who and how users log on to the computer, such as the right to log on to a system locally.

▶ **Privilege:** Privileges allow users to perform system tasks, such as the right to back up files and folders.

▶ **Implicit deny:** This ensures that when access is not explicitly granted, it is automatically denied by default.

ExamAlert

In Windows environments, Active Directory Domain Services provides flexibility by allowing two types of groups: security groups and distribution groups:

▶ Security groups are used to assign rights and permissions to groups for resource access.

▶ Distribution groups are assigned to a user list for applications or non–security-related functions, such as an email distribution list that functions like a LISTSERV in the Unix environment.

User Access Reviews

User access reviews allow the identification of misapplied changes or other access control adjustments through direct assignment or inherited nesting of role access rights. Through regular reviews, accidents or malicious attempts to gain unauthorized access rights can be identified and rectified. Periodic access reviews for access management can help ensure the necessary personnel have access to essential systems and unauthorized employees don't. Best practices dictate that access to high-risk applications should be reviewed quarterly and every application should have a review conducted at least on an annual basis. A baseline must be established to account for normal line-of-business operations and be updated regularly to reflect changes in organization processes and software applications. Examples include identifying the business owners of every application and classifying the data within applications. This allows unusual activity to be identified, while regular reviews of all accounts (including "permanent" machine and service accounts) will ensure that unneeded credentials can be disabled and removed from service. Access reviews should also be conducted for group membership and role/group alignment for organization assignment. This allows accidental access rights assignment through role and group membership to be corrected. Users should also be notified of their access rights and the need to alert the IT staff if their access appears to be more than allowed by their role.

Education and regular operational control reviews should be part of the organization's continuous improvement program to ensure that security protections are complied with and that users understand the requirements demanded by their acceptance and use of data access credentials. Understanding requirements is inherent in any attempt to control data access to conform to those requirements. Technical controls must be continuously monitored to protect against violation of policy through purposeful or accidental access. An important best practice is to make sure separation of duties among developers, data custodians, and IT administration is well defined and documented.

Continuous Monitoring

The purpose of continuous monitoring is to ensure that the processes for user account provisioning, life cycle management, and termination are followed and enforced. Continuous monitoring begins with knowing what user account activity should be present. By continuously monitoring user access, detection of unauthorized access and user account creation that may be used by attackers as a system backdoor is possible, averting a wide-scale incident.

Industry regulations may require continuous monitoring. For example, PCI DSS compliance requires that an organization have well-defined processes in place to review and reassess security practices, even in highly dynamic business environments.

Monitoring practices should consist of a process to record and monitor significant changes to user accounts and groups to ensure that access is not granted outside of a formal approval process. Activities that should be monitored and reviewed include the business need for each active account, reconciliation of existing active accounts with account access requests, and account and privilege updates with close attention paid to administrative privilege updates as these may signify compromised accounts.

Cram Quiz

Answer these questions. The answers follow the last question. If you cannot answer these questions correctly, consider reading this section again until you can.

1. Which type of password policy will protect against reuse of the same password over and over again?

   ○ **A.** Account lockout

   ○ **B.** Password complexity

   ○ **C.** Expiration

   ○ **D.** Password history

2. A user calls the help desk saying that she changed her password yesterday, did not get any email on her mobile phone last night, and cannot log on this morning. Which password policy is most likely at fault for her difficulties?

   ○ **A.** Account lockout

   ○ **B.** Password complexity

   ○ **C.** Expiration

   ○ **D.** Password history

3. Which of the following reduces the effectiveness of a good password policy?

   ○ **A.** Account lockout

   ○ **B.** Password recovery

   ○ **C.** Account disablement

   ○ **D.** Password reuse

4. Which of the following is considered best practice when formulating minimum standards for developing password policies?

   ○ **A.** Password length set to 6 characters

   ○ **B.** Require password change at 90 days

   ○ **C.** Maximum password age set to 0

   ○ **D.** Account lockout threshold set to 0

5. Which of the following is one of the first steps that must be taken to provide a secure account access environment?

   ○ **A.** Set user-assigned privileges

   ○ **B.** Implement user access reviews

   ○ **C.** Eliminate the use of shared accounts

   ○ **D.** Initiate continuous account monitoring

Cram Quiz Answers

1. **D**. The password history policy prevents reuse of the same passwords over and over again. Account lockout deactivates an account after a number of failed access attempts, making answer A incorrect. Answer B is incorrect because password complexity is a policy that determines how many types of characters must be used to create a strong password (lower- and uppercase letters, numbers, and symbols being the four general types of characters possible on a standard keyboard). Account expiration policies ensure that unused or no-longer-used accounts are properly disabled, making answer C incorrect.

2. **A**. If the user failed to also change her password on her phone, its repeated attempts to access email during the night would have triggered the account lockout protections and temporarily disabled her account. Password complexity and history would not lock out her account after successfully changing it, making answers B and D incorrect. Answer C is incorrect because, although account expiration is possible, it is unlikely without specifying this was near the end of her employment.

3. **D**. The longer the same password is used for a particular account, the greater the chance that an attacker will be able to determine the password through brute-force attacks. Allowing users to reuse an old password greatly reduces the effectiveness of a good password policy. Answer A is incorrect because making the password length at least eight characters and requiring the use of the account lockout policy settings help you to prevent attackers from guessing users' passwords, and they decrease the likelihood of successful attacks on your network. Answer B is incorrect because it is used when a user forgets a password. Generally there are two options for this: password recovery or a password reset. Answer C is incorrect because disabling user accounts is used when there might be a need for keeping the settings, files, and folders intact to access information tied to the user account anytime by reenabling the account.

4. **B**. Require users to change passwords every 90 to 180 days, depending on how secure the environment needs to be. Remember that the more often users are required to change passwords, the greater the chance that they will write them down, potentially exposing them to unauthorized use. Answer A is incorrect because making the password length at least eight characters and requiring the use of combinations of uppercase and lowercase letters, numbers, and special characters is good practice. Answer C is incorrect because good policy is to set the maximum password age to a value between 30 and 90 days. Answer D is incorrect because if the lockout threshold is set to 0, accounts will not be locked out due to invalid logon attempts.

5. **C**. One of the first steps that must be taken to provide a secure account access environment is to eliminate the use of shared accounts, whose use cannot be attributed to a particular user's credentials and so preclude determination of specific access rights and audit of access use. Answers A, B, and D are incorrect because they should be considered after original configuration and the shared accounts eliminated. Answer A is incorrect because in a user-based model, permissions are uniquely assigned to each user account and happens after any shared accounts are eliminated. This access type is also found in government and military situations and in private companies where patented processes

and trademark products require protection. Answer B is incorrect because user access reviews allow the identification of misapplied changes or other access control adjustments through direct assignment or inherited nesting of role access rights and are done after accounts are created. Answer D is incorrect because the purpose of continuous monitoring is to ensure that the processes for user account provisioning, life cycle management, and termination are followed and enforced. This process happens after the accounts have been secured.

What Next?

If you want more practice on this chapter's exam objectives before you move on, remember that you can access all the Cram Quiz questions on the CD. You can also create a custom exam by objective with the practice exam software. Note any objective that you struggle with and go to the material that covers that objective in this chapter.

CHAPTER 12

Cryptography Tools and Techniques

This chapter covers the following official CompTIA Security+ SY0-401 exam objectives:

▶ Given a scenario, utilize general cryptography concepts

▶ Given a scenario, use appropriate cryptographic methods

(For more information on the official CompTIA Security+ exam topics, see the "About the CompTIA Security+ Certification Exam" section in the Introduction.)

A *cryptosystem* or *cipher system* provides a method for protecting information by disguising (encrypting) it into a format that can be read only by authorized systems or individuals. The use and creation of such systems is called *cryptography*, which is often considered to be both an art and a science.

Cryptography dates back to the ancient Assyrians and Egyptians. In the beginning, the systems of cryptography were manually performed, but during the twentieth century, machine and mechanical cryptography was born. The cryptography that is the focus of this chapter and the exam is modern cryptography, which began with the advent of the computer.

Recently, modern cryptography has become increasingly important and ubiquitous. There has been increasing concern about the security of data, which continues to rapidly grow across information systems and traverses and resides in many different locations. This, combined with more sophisticated attacks and a growing economy around computer-related fraud and data theft, makes the need to protect the data itself even more important than in the past.

One practical way to secure this data is to use cryptography in the form of encryption algorithms applied to data that is passed around networks and to data at rest.

> **Note**
>
> As related to cryptography, an *algorithm* is the mathematical procedure or sequence of steps taken to perform the encryption and decryption. Practically speaking, however, you can think of an algorithm as a cooking recipe, which provides the ingredients needed and step-by-step instructions.

This chapter discusses the concepts of cryptography and many popular encryption methods and their applications. In addition to being able to explain these fundamental cryptography concepts, you will begin to understand how cryptography can be used as a tool to protect and authenticate all types of information and to protect the computers and networks in information security systems.

Given a Scenario, Utilize General Cryptography Concepts

- ▶ **Symmetric versus asymmetric**
- ▶ **Session keys**
- ▶ **In-band versus out-of-band key exchange**
- ▶ **Fundamental differences and encryption methods**
- ▶ **Transport encryption**
- ▶ **Nonrepudiation**
- ▶ **Hashing**
- ▶ **Key escrow**
- ▶ **Steganography**
- ▶ **Digital signatures**
- ▶ **Use of proven technologies**
- ▶ **Elliptic curve and quantum cryptography**
- ▶ **Ephemeral key**
- ▶ **Perfect forward secrecy**

CramSaver

If you can correctly answer these questions before going through this section, save time by skimming the Exam Alerts in this section and then completing the Cram Quiz at the end of the section.

1. What are the differences between symmetric and asymmetric cryptography?

2. What is the fundamental difference between a block cipher and a stream cipher?

Answers

1. Symmetric cryptography uses a shared key, and asymmetric uses different mathematically related keys. Symmetric key cryptography is more efficient, yet asymmetric cryptography helps overcome the challenges associated with key management and key distribution.

2. Block ciphers operate on a fixed-length group of bits, which are called blocks. The resulting cipher text corresponds to the input length. Stream ciphers are more efficient and plain-text bits are encrypted one at a time.

Symmetric Versus Asymmetric

Symmetric key cryptography is a system that uses a common shared key between the sender and receiver. The primary advantages to such a system are that it is easier to implement than an asymmetric system and is typically faster. However, the two parties must first somehow exchange the key securely. Assume, for example, that you have a friend located thousands of miles away from you, and to exchange secured messages you send messages back and forth in a secured lockbox; you both have a copy of the key to the lockbox. Although this works, how did you securely deliver the key to your friend? Somehow the key must have be communicated or delivered to your friend, which introduces additional challenges around logistics and ensuring that the key was not compromised in the process. Asymmetric cryptography helps overcome these challenges.

Now imagine a system in which more than two parties are involved. In this scenario, every party participating in communications must have the exact same key to compare the information. If the key is compromised at any point, it is impossible to guarantee that a secure connection has commenced.

> **Note**
>
> Symmetric key algorithms are often referred to as *secret key algorithms*, *private key algorithms*, and *shared secret algorithms*.

Even given the possible risks involved with symmetric key encryption, the method is used often today mainly because of its simplicity and easy deployment. In addition, it is generally considered a strong encryption method as long as the source and destination that house the key information are kept secure.

> **ExamAlert**
>
> A symmetric key is a single cryptographic key used with a secret key (symmetric) algorithm. The symmetric key algorithm uses the same private key for both operations of encryption and decryption.

The asymmetric encryption algorithm has two keys: a public key and a private key. The public key is made available to whoever is going to encrypt the data sent to the holder of the private key. The private key is maintained on the host system or application. Often, the public encryption key is made available in a number of fashions, such as email or centralized servers that host a pseudo address book of published public encryption keys. One of the challenges, however, is ensuring authenticity of the public key. To address this, a public key infrastructure (PKI) is often used. A PKI uses trusted third parties that certify or provide proof of key ownership. PKI is discussed in greater detail in Chapter 13, "Public Key Infrastructure." Figure 12.1 illustrates the asymmetric encryption process.

FIGURE 12.1 **An example of asymmetric encryption**

Asymmetric algorithms are often referred to as *public key algorithms* because of their use of the public key as the focal point for the algorithm.

As an example of asymmetric encryption, think about the secure exchange of an email. When someone wants to send a secure email to someone else, he or she obtains the target user's public encryption key and encrypts the message using this key. Because the message can be unencrypted only with the private key, only the target user can read the information held within. Ideally, for this system to work well, everyone should have access to everyone else's public keys.

Imagine a postal mailbox that enables the letter carrier to insert your mail via an open slot, but only you have the key to get the mail out. This is analogous to an asymmetric system in which the open slot is the public key. If you are concerned about the security of your mail, this is much easier than ensuring every letter carrier has a copy of your mailbox key! The letter carrier is also thankful he or she isn't required to carry hundreds of different keys to complete mail-delivery duties.

Public key encryption has proven useful on networks such as the Internet. This is primarily because the public key is all that needs to be distributed. Because nothing harmful can be done with the public key, it is useful over unsecured networks where data can pass through many hands and is vulnerable to interception and abuse. Symmetric encryption works fine over the Internet, too, but the limitations on providing the key securely to everyone that requires it can be difficult. In addition, asymmetric key systems are also used to verify digital signatures, which provide assurance that communications have not been altered and that the communication arrived from an authorized source.

Symmetric encryption uses two primary types of methods for encrypting plain-text data, as follows:

▶ **Stream cipher:** The plain-text bits are encrypted a single bit at a time. These bits are also combined with a stream of pseudorandom characters. Stream ciphers are known for their speed and simplicity.

▶ **Block cipher:** Plain text is encrypted in blocks, which is a fixed-length group of bits. The block of plain text is encrypted into a corresponding block of cipher text. So, a 64-bit block of plain text would output as a 64-bit block of cipher text.

Elliptic Curve and Quantum Cryptography

Two emerging cryptosystems are elliptic curve cryptography (ECC) and quantum cryptography. ECC is a public-key cryptosystem based on complex mathematical structures. ECC uses smaller key sizes than traditional public-key cryptosystems. As a result, it is faster and consumes fewer resources, making it more ideal for mobile and wireless devices.

Unlike elliptic curves and other cryptosystems, quantum cryptography does not rely on mathematics. Quantum cryptography instead relies on physics. Although slower, the primary advantage provided by quantum cryptography is increased security. Quantum mechanics protects against data being disturbed because one cannot measure the quantum state of the photons. The mere observation of a quantum system changes the system.

In-Band Versus Out-of-Band Key Exchange

An important concept in any discussion of encryption is understanding the importance of key exchange. The challenge historically is that to share a secret you must share a secret. Let's take a simple analogy. Imagine the clubhouse as a kid, which requires the secret password to gain secret access. Perhaps that password (or key) is "open sesame." The problem is that, at some point, that secret password had to be shared with you. However, when that password was shared, it was likely not secure and subject to eavesdropping. Of course, it could have been whispered to you at one point (still subject to eavesdropping). Even in this scenario, the challenge is you had to meet face to face. Regardless, at some point, you likely received the key "out-of-band," and not at the time you were waiting at the door to gain entry. Modern cryptography solves this age-old challenge of key exchange. Exchanging keys in many applications happens securely "in band" during the need to establish a secure session. Any type of out-of-band key exchange will rely on having been shared in advance. That is, the key is delivered outside of the network or process from which it will actually be used.

> **ExamAlert**
>
> Elliptic curve cryptography is an example of an asymmetric public-key cryptosystem.

Session Keys

Session keys, sometimes called *symmetric keys*, are a randomly generated key to perform both encryption and decryption during the communications of a session between two parties. They are known as being symmetric because the key is used for both encryption and decryption. When a session key is generated, they key is only valid during that one communication session. As a result, you can think of a session key as being temporary or for one time use.

Session keys are deleted after the communication ends, but the key exchange mechanism (most notably RSA) used to establish these keys often relies on a private key. This may be the web server's private key, which is used to establish a secure session with the client. Although this is efficient, the challenge is that gaining access to the server's private key would allow an adversary to decrypt the communications. The benefit of this, however, is that organizations can use this private key so that security systems (for example, IDS and web application firewalls) have visibility into the traffic.

Perfect Forward Secrecy

The Diffie-Hellman key exchange deals with session keys differently. Diffie-Hellman uses an ephemeral algorithm, and it is not as efficient as what was previously discussed. The session keys are still created, but someone with access to the server's private key could not uncover the session key. After the session is complete, both sides in the communication process destroy the keys. This process is known as *perfect forward secrecy* or just *forward secrecy*.

> **Note**
>
> *Ephemeral* by definition describes something that is temporary or lasting for a very short time.

The following two schemes support of perfect forward secrecy:

- ▶ **Diffie-Hellman (DHE):** The Diffie-Hellman key agreement protocol in an ephemeral mode of operation

- ▶ **Elliptic Curve Diffie-Hellman (ECDH):** A variant of the Diffie-Hellman key agreement protocol for ECC using an ephemeral mode of operation

This method gained popularity in 2013, as revelations about government monitoring became public, and made mainstream news when Twitter announced that they would adopt forward secrecy to protect recorded traffic from potentially being decrypted later.

> **ExamAlert**
>
> DHE and ECDH are ephemeral key agreement protocols that, although computationally slower, provide perfect forward secrecy.

Transport Encryption

In addition to securing identities and data, encryption is widely used to secure the links between two points. These two points are often referred to as the *client* and the *server*. Without an effective means to protect the transport layer, communications can be exposed. Transport encryption protects communication between the client and the server, preventing the disclosure of sensitive data as well as the manipulation of the data. Another advantage provided by transport encryption is to prevent redirection in which the communication is no longer taking place between the two expected parties. Instead, the client might be communicating with an attacker that otherwise appears to be trusted. Various types of technologies are used to provide transport encryption. These technologies rely on algorithms previously discussed in this chapter. The next section covers the more common uses and applications of transport encryption.

Nonrepudiation and Digital Signatures

Nonrepudiation is intended to provide, through encryption, a method of accountability that makes it impossible to refute the origin of data. It guarantees that the sender cannot later deny being the sender and that the recipient cannot deny receiving the data. This definition, however, does not factor in the possible compromise of the workstation or system used to create the private key and the encrypted digital signature. The following list outlines four of the key elements that nonrepudiation services provide on a typical client/server connection:

▶ **Proof of origin:** The host gets proof that the client is the originator of particular data or authentication request from a particular time and location.

▶ **Proof of submission:** The client gets proof that the data (or authentication in this case) has been sent.

▶ **Proof of delivery:** The client gets proof that the data (or authentication in this case) has been received.

▶ **Proof of receipt:** The client gets proof that the data (or authentication in this case) has been received correctly.

Digital signatures provide integrity and authentication. In addition, digital signatures provide nonrepudiation with proof of origin. Although authentication and nonrepudiation might appear to be similar, the difference is that with nonrepudiation proof can be demonstrated to a third party.

A sender of a message signs a message using his or her private key. This provides unforgeable proof that the sender did indeed generate the message. Nonrepudiation is unique to asymmetric systems because the private (secret) key is not shared. Remember that in a symmetric system both parties involved share the secret key, and therefore any party can deny sending a message by claiming the other party originated the message.

Digital signatures attempt to guarantee the identity of the person sending the data from one point to another. The digital signature acts as an electronic signature used to authenticate the identity of the sender and to ensure the integrity of the original content (that it has not been changed).

> **Note**
>
> Do not confuse a digital signature with a digital certificate (discussed in the next chapter). In addition, do not confuse digital signatures with encryption. Although digital signatures and encryption use related concepts, their intentions and operations differ significantly. Finally, do not confuse a digital signature with the block of identification information, such as the sender's name and telephone number or digitally created image, often appended to the end of an email.

Digital signatures can easily be transported and are designed so that they cannot be copied by anyone else. This ensures that something signed cannot be repudiated.

A digital signature does not have to accompany an encrypted message. It can simply be used to assure the receiver of the sender's identity and that the message's integrity was maintained. The digital signature contains the digital signature of the certificate authority (CA) that issued the certificate for verification.

The point of this verification is to prevent or alert the recipient to any data tampering. Ideally, if a packet of data is digitally signed, it can only bear the original mark of the sender. If this mark differs, the receiver knows that the packet differs from what it is supposed to be, and either the packet is not unencrypted or is dropped altogether. This works based on the encryption algorithm principles discussed previously. If you cannot determine what the original data was in the encrypted data (in this case, the signature), it becomes much harder to fake the data and actually get it past the receiver as legitimate data.

Suppose, for example, that you need to digitally sign a document sent to your stockbroker. You need to ensure the integrity of the message and assure the stockbroker that the message is really from you. The exchange looks like this:

1. You type the email.

2. Using software built in to your email client, you obtain a hash (which you can think of as digital fingerprint) of the message.

3. You use your private key to encrypt the hash. This encrypted hash is your digital signature for the message.

4. You send the message to your stockbroker.

5. Your stockbroker receives the message. Using his software, he makes a hash of the received message.

6. The stockbroker uses your public key to decrypt the message hash.

7. A match of the hashes proves that the message is valid.

Hashing

A *hash* is a generated summary from a mathematical rule or algorithm and is used commonly as a "digital fingerprint" to verify the integrity of files and messages and to ensure message integrity and provide authentication verification. In other words, hashing algorithms are not encryption methods but offer additional system security via a "signature" for data confirming the original content.

Hash functions work by taking a string (for example, a password or email) of any length and producing a fixed-length string for output. Keep in mind that hashing is one way. Although you can create a hash from a document, you cannot re-create the document from the hash. If this all sounds confusing, the following example should help clear things up. Suppose that you want to send an email to a friend, and you also want to ensure that during transit it cannot be read or altered. You would first use software that generates a hash value of the message to accompany the email and then encrypt both the hash and the message. After receiving the email, the recipient's software decrypts the message and the hash and then produces another hash from the received email. The two hashes are then compared, and a match indicates that the message was not tampered with. (Any change in the original message produces a change in the hash.) A message authentication code (MAC) is similar to a hash function, but is able to resist forgery and is not open to man-in-the-middle attacks. A MAC can be thought of as an encrypted hash—combining an encryption key and a hashing algorithm. The MAC is a small piece of data known as an *authentication tag*, which is derived by applying a message or file combined with a secret key to a cryptographic algorithm. The resulting MAC value can ensure the integrity of the data as well as its authenticity, as one in possession of the secret key can subsequently detect whether there are any changes from the original. Specific cryptographic hash functions are covered later in this chapter.

> **ExamAlert**
>
> A message authentication code (MAC) is a bit of a misnomer. Remember that in addition to providing authentication services, as the name suggests, a MAC also provides for data integrity.

Key Escrow

Escrow refers to a trusted third party or broker. A deposit on a new home and a third-party account used to fulfill property tax obligations are examples of escrow. A *key escrow* is similar, but is specifically used to mitigate key loss or protect entities to ensure agreed on obligations are fulfilled. Typically, the key in escrow should not be released to anybody other than the involved parties without appropriate authorization. Key escrow is a controversial topic given that additional concerns are introduced about the process of the escrow's access to the key and abuse by third parties.

Steganography

Steganography is a word of Greek origin meaning "hidden writing." Steganography is a method for hiding messages so that unintended recipients are not even aware of any message. Compare this to cryptography, which does not seek to hide the fact a message exists, but rather to just make it unreadable by anyone other than the intended recipients. For example, writing a letter using plain text but in invisible ink is an example of the use of steganography. The content is not scrambled in any way; it is just hidden. Another interesting example, albeit a bit cumbersome, is the historical use of writing a secret message on the scalp of one's bald head, and then allowing the hair to grow back, ultimately to be shaved again upon arrival at the intended recipient.

ExamAlert

Steganography is not cryptography, but the two are related and often used in conjunction with one another. Steganography seeks to hide the presence of a message, whereas the purpose of cryptography is to transform a message from its readable plain text into an unreadable form known as cipher text.

Of course, steganography is useless if someone other than the intended recipient knows where to look. Therefore, steganography is best used when combined with encryption. This adds an additional layer of security by not even allowing attackers to attempt to crack encryption into a readable form because they do not even know the message exists in the first place. As a result, steganography is not just the stuff of child's play or far-fetched spy movies. In fact, steganography entered into mainstream media with various reports since the terrorist attacks of 9/11—that terrorists may have been and are using this practice to secretly hide messages. Modern uses are various, including hiding messages in digital media and digital watermarking. In addition, steganography has been used by many printers, using tiny dots that reveal serial numbers and time stamps.

Use of Proven Technologies

Because of the sensitive nature behind the uses of cryptography, the use of well-known, proven technologies is crucial. Backdoors and flaws, for example, can undermine any encryption algorithm, which is why proven algorithms such as those discussed in this chapter should always be considered. Although various vendors might have their own encryption solutions, most of these depend on well-known, time-tested algorithms, and generally speaking you should be skeptical of any vendor using a proprietary unproven algorithm.

Kerckhoff's principle (from the nineteenth century) states that a cryptosystem should be secure even if everything about the system is known except for the key. Proven technologies are well-designed cryptosystems. Systems that require the algorithms to be kept secret not only introduce additional measures related to what needs to be protected, but they are often referred to as "security by obscurity."

Cram Quiz

Answer these questions. The answers follow the last question. If you cannot answer these questions correctly, consider reading this section again until you can.

1. In encryption, when data is broken into a single unit of varying sizes (depending on the algorithm) and the encryption is applied to those chunks of data, what type of algorithm is this?

   ○ **A.** Symmetric encryption algorithm

   ○ **B.** Elliptic curve

   ○ **C.** Block cipher

   ○ **D.** All of these

2. Which type of algorithm generates a key pair (a public key and a private key) that is then used to encrypt and decrypt data and messages sent and received?

   ○ **A.** Elliptic curve

   ○ **B.** Symmetric encryption algorithms

   ○ **C.** Asymmetric encryption algorithms

   ○ **D.** Paired algorithms

3. When encrypting and decrypting an email using an asymmetric encryption algorithm, you _____.

   ○ **A.** Use the private key to encrypt and only the public key to decrypt

   ○ **B.** Use a secret key to perform both encrypt and decrypt operations

   ○ **C.** Can use the public key to either encrypt or decrypt

   ○ **D.** Can use the public key to encrypt, and the private key to decrypt

Cram Quiz Answers

1. **C.** When data that is going to be encrypted is broken into chunks of data and then encrypted, the type of encryption is called a block cipher. Although many symmetric algorithms use a block cipher, answer A is incorrect because a block cipher is a more precise and accurate term for the given question. Answer B is incorrect because this describes a public key encryption algorithm. Answer D is incorrect.

2. **C**. Although many different types of algorithms use public and private keys to apply their encryption algorithms in their own various ways, algorithms that perform this way are called asymmetric encryption algorithms (or public key encryption). Answer A is incorrect because this is only a type of asymmetric encryption algorithm. Answer B is incorrect because symmetric algorithms use a single key. Answer D is not a type of algorithm, and so it is incorrect.

3. **D**. Answer D provides the only valid statement to complete the sentence. Answer A is incorrect because the public key would be used to encrypt and the private key to decrypt. Answer B is incorrect because this describes symmetric encryption. Answer C is incorrect because the public key cannot decrypt the same data it encrypted.

Given a Scenario, Use Appropriate Cryptographic Methods

▶ **WEP versus WPA/WPA2 and preshared keys**

▶ **MD5**

▶ **SHA**

▶ **RIPEMD**

▶ **AES**

▶ **DES**

▶ **3DES**

▶ **HMAC**

▶ **RSA**

▶ **Diffie-Hellman**

▶ **RC4**

▶ **One-time pads**

▶ **NTLM**

▶ **NTLMv2**

▶ **Blowfish**

▶ **PGP/GPG**

▶ **Twofish**

▶ **DHE**

▶ **ECDHE**

▶ **CHAP**

▶ **PAP**

▶ **Comparative strengths and performance of algorithms**

▶ **Use of algorithms with transport encryption**

▶ **Cipher suites**

▶ **Key stretching**

CramSaver

If you can correctly answer these questions before going through this section, save time by skimming the Exam Alerts in this section and then completing the Cram Quiz at the end of the section.

1. What are examples of symmetric algorithms?

2. SHA-1 and MD5 are examples of what type of cryptographic function?

Answers

1. Examples of common symmetric algorithms include AES, 3DES, Blowfish, Twofish, and RC4.
2. SHA-1 and MD5 are hashing algorithms.

Wireless Encryption Functions

In recent years, there has been the proliferation of wireless local-area networks (WLAN) based on the standards defined in IEEE 802.11. One of the earlier algorithms used to secure 802.11 wireless networks is Wired Equivalent Privacy (WEP), which uses the RC4 cipher for confidentiality. However, the WEP algorithm, although still widely used, is no longer considered secure and has been replaced. Temporal Key Integrity Protocol (TKIP) is the security protocol designed to replace WEP and is also known by its later iterations of Wi-Fi Protected Access (WPA) or even WPA2. Similar to WEP, TKIP uses the RC4 algorithm and does not require an upgrade to existing hardware, whereas more recent protocols, such as Counter Mode with Cipher Block Chaining Message Authentication Code Protocol (CCMP), which use the Advanced Encryption Standard (AES) algorithm, do require an upgrade.

WPA can either use an authentication server from which keys are distributed or it can use pre-shared keys. The use of pre-shared keys with WPA is also known as *WPA-Personal*. This implementation is more ideally suited for smaller environments, where key management is not necessary. The pre-shared key method requires that all devices on the network use the same shared passphrase.

The following are three wireless encryption functions with which you should be familiar:

▶ **WEP:** This is the original wireless encryption standard, which is still commonly seen. It was, however, superseded in 2003 by WPA.

▶ **WPA:** The successor to WEP (to provide increased security).

▶ **WPA2:** This further improved upon WPA and, since 2006, is required for Wi-Fi–certified devices.

In addition, WPA-Personal and WPA-Enterprise target different users and are applicable to both WPA and WPA2. WPA-Personal is designed for home and small office use, in that it uses a pre-shared key and does not require a separate authentication server. WPA-Enterprise, in contrast, is more ideal for larger organizations, in that it provides for increased security. This comes with a tradeoff, of course. WPA-Enterprise requires a RADIUS server and is more complicated to set up and maintain.

> ### ExamAlert
>
> Remember that WPA2 provides a greater level of protection over WPA and over WEP. Furthermore, WEP has since been deprecated and is not considered secure.

Cryptographic Hash Functions

Numerous hash functions exist, and many published algorithms are known to be unsecure; however, you should be familiar with the following three hash algorithms:

▶ **Secure Hash Algorithm (SHA, SHA-1, SHA-2, SHA-3):** Hash algorithms pioneered by the National Security Agency and widely used in the U.S. government. SHA-1 can generate a 160-bit hash from any variable-length string of data, making it very secure, but also resource intensive. Subsequently, four additional hash functions were introduced. These were named after their digest lengths: SHA-224, SHA-256, SHA-384, and SHA-512. Together, these four hash functions are known as *SHA-2*. In 2007, a contest was announced to design a hash function (SHA-3) to replace the aging SHA-1 and SHA-2 hash functions.

▶ **Message digest series algorithm (MD2, MD4, MD5):** A series of encryption algorithms created by Ronald Rivest (founder of RSA Data Security, Inc.) designed to be fast, simple, and secure. The MD series generates a hash of up to 128-bit strength out of any length of data.

  ▶ **RACE Integrity Primitives Evaluation Message Digest (RIPEMD):** RIPEMD was developed within academia and is based on the design of MD4. The more commonly used 160-bit version of the algorithm, RIPEMD-160, performs comparably to SHA-1, although it is less used.

Both SHA and the MD series are similar in design; however, keep in mind that because of the higher bit strength of the SHA algorithm, it will be in the range of 20% to 30% slower to process than the MD family of algorithms.

ExamAlert

Hashing within security systems is used to ensure the integrity of transmitted messages (that is, to be certain they have not been altered) and for password verification. Be able to identify both the SHA and MD series as hashing algorithms.

The message digest algorithm has been refined over the years (and hence the version numbers). The most commonly used is MD5, which is faster than the others. Both MD4 and MD5 produce a 128-bit hash; however, the hash used in MD4 has been successfully broken. This security breach spurred the development of MD5, which features a redeveloped cipher that makes it stronger than the MD4 algorithm while still featuring a 128-bit hash. Since the mid-2000s, several advances on breaking MD5 have occurred. Although MD5 is still commonly used, U.S. government agencies have stated that MD5 should be considered compromised. Meanwhile, the recommendation is to use the SHA-2 family of hash functions, at least until its successor is formally announced.

In addition to the hashing algorithms just mentioned, you also should be aware of the LAN Manager hash (LM hash or LANMan hash) and the NT LAN Manager hash (NTLM hash, also called the *Unicode hash*). Both are commonly known as authentication protocols.

LM hash is based on DES encryption (discussed in the next section), but it is not considered effective (and is technically not truly a hashing algorithm) because of design implementation weaknesses. (It is quite easy to crack an LM hash using your average computer system and one of the many cracking tools available.) The two primary weaknesses of LM hash are as follows:

▶ All passwords longer than seven characters are broken down into two chunks, from which each piece is hashed separately.

▶ Before the password is hashed, all lowercase characters are converted to uppercase characters. As a result, the scope of the characters set is greatly reduced, and each half of the password can be cracked separately.

As a result of weaknesses within the LM hash, Microsoft later introduced the NTLM hashing method in early versions of Windows NT. However, the LM hash algorithm was still commonly used by Microsoft operating systems before Windows Vista.

The NTLM hash is an improvement over the LM hash. NTLM hashing makes use of the MD series hashing algorithms and is used on more recent versions of the Windows operating system. NTLM, however, was replaced by NTLMv2, which is more secure. Specifically, NTLMv2 protects against spoofing attacks and adds the ability for a server to authenticate to the client as well.

The Challenge Handshake Authentication Protocol (CHAP) is another authentication protocol that can be used to provide on-demand authentication within an ongoing data transmission. CHAP is an improvement over Password Authentication Protocol (PAP). PAP is a basic form of authentication during which the username and password are transmitted unencrypted. CHAP uses a one-way hashing function that first involves a service requesting a CHAP response from the client. The client creates a hashed value that is derived using the message digest (MD5) hashing algorithm and sends this value to the service, which also calculates the expected value itself. The server, referred to as the *authenticator*, compares these two values. If they match, the transmission continues. This process is repeated at random intervals during a session of data transaction. CHAP functions over Point-to-Point Protocol (PPP) connections. PPP is a protocol for communicating between two points using a serial interface, providing service at the second layer of the OSI model: the data link layer. PPP can handle both synchronous and asynchronous connections.

Occasionally, you might find Shiva Password Authentication Protocol (SPAP) implemented. SPAP was designed by Shiva and is an older, two-way reversible encryption protocol that encrypts the password data sent between client and server. Systems such as Windows Vista and older no longer support SPAP.

HMAC

MACs that are based on cryptographic hash functions are known as *hash-based message authentication code* (HMAC). The sender of a message uses an HMAC function to produce the MAC. This is a result of using both the message input along with a secret key.

Thus, MACs and HMACs are similar, but an HMAC provides additional security by adding an additional integrity check to the data being transmitted. For example, SHA-1 can be used to calculate an HMAC, which results in what is called *HMAC-SHA1*. Or if MD5 is used, it is called *HMAC-MD5*. Despite the fact MD5 is vulnerable to collision attacks, this should not impede its use with HMAC. Unlike MD5 alone, HMACs are not as affected by collisions.

Symmetric Encryption Algorithms

Earlier in this chapter, you were introduced to the concept of symmetric key encryption, in which a common shared key or identical key is used between the sender and the receiver. Symmetric algorithms can be classified as either block ciphers or stream ciphers. A stream cipher, as the name implies, encrypts the message bit by bit, one at a time. A block cipher encrypts the message in chunks.

A number of symmetric key algorithms are in use today. The more commonly used algorithms include the following:

▶ **Data Encryption Standard (DES):** DES was adopted for use by the National Institute of Standards and Technology (NIST) in 1977. DES is a block cipher that uses a 56-bit key and 8 bits of parity on each 64-bit chunk of data. Although it is considered a strong algorithm, it is limited in use because of its relatively short key-length limit.

▶ **Triple Data Encryption Standard (3DES):** 3DES, also known as Triple DES, dramatically improves on the DES by using the DES algorithm three times with three distinct keys. This provides total bit strength of 168 bits. 3DES superseded DES in the late 1990s.

▶ **Advanced Encryption Standard (AES):** AES is also known as Rinjdael, which is the name originally given to the cipher upon which AES is based. NIST chose this block cipher to be the successor to DES. AES is similar to DES in that it can create keys from 128 bits to 256 bits in length and can perform the encryption and decryption of up to 128-bit chunks of data (in comparison to the 64-bit chunks of the original DES). Similar to 3DES, the data is passed through three layers, each with a specific task, such as generating random keys based on the data and the bit strength being used. The data is then encrypted with the keys through multiple encryption rounds, like DES, and then the final key is applied to the data.

▶ **Blowfish Encryption Algorithm:** Blowfish is a block cipher that can encrypt using any size chunk of data; in addition, Blowfish can also perform encryption with any length encryption key up to 448 bits, making it a flexible and secure symmetric encryption algorithm.

▶ **Rivest Cipher (RC2, RC4, RC5, RC6):** As far as widely available commercial applications go, the Rivest Cipher (RC) encryption algorithms are the most commonly implemented ciphers for encryption security. The RC series (RC2, RC4, RC5, and RC6) are all similarly designed, yet each version has its own take on cipher design, as well as its own capabilities. RC2, RC5, and RC6 are block ciphers, whereas RC4 is a stream cipher.

Table 12.1 compares the algorithms just mentioned (and some lesser-known ones). In addition, notice the differences between the various types of RC algorithms.

TABLE 12.1 **A Comparison of Symmetric Key Algorithms**

Algorithm	Cipher Type	Key Length
DES	Block	56 bits
Triple-DES (3DES)	Block	168 bits
AES (Rinjdael)	Block	128–256 bits
Blowfish	Block	1–448 bits
RC2	Block	1–2048 bits
RC4	Stream	1–2048 bits
RC5	Block	128–256 bits
RC6	Block	128–256 bits
Twofish	Block	128–256 bits

ExamAlert

Be sure that you understand the differences between various symmetric key algorithms. Note that these are symmetric, and not asymmetric, and be sure to differentiate between stream ciphers and block ciphers. Specifically note that RC4 is the only stream cipher of those mentioned.

Asymmetric Encryption Algorithms

Various asymmetric algorithms have been designed, but few have gained the widespread acceptance of symmetric algorithms. While reading this section about the asymmetric algorithms, keep in mind that some have unique features, including built-in digital signatures (which you learn more about later). Also because of the additional overhead generated by using two keys for encryption and decryption, asymmetric algorithms require more resources than symmetric algorithms.

Popular asymmetric encryption algorithms include the following:

▶ **Rivest, Shamir, and Adleman encryption algorithm (RSA):**
RSA, named after the three men who developed it, is a well-known cryptography system used for encryption and digital signatures. In fact, the RSA algorithm is considered by many the standard for encryption and the core technology that secures most business conducted on the Internet. The RSA key length may be of any length, and the algorithm works by multiplying two large prime numbers. In addition, through other operations in the algorithm, it derives a set of numbers: one for the public key and the other for the private key.

▶ **Diffie-Hellman key exchange (D-H):** The Diffie-Hellman key exchange (also called *exponential key agreement*) is an early key exchange design whereby two parties, without prior arrangement, can agree on a secret key that is known only to them. The keys are passed in a way that they are not compromised, using encryption algorithms to verify that the data is arriving at its intended recipient.

▶ **El Gamal encryption algorithm:** As an extension to the Diffie-Hellman design, in 1985 Dr. El Gamal took to task the design requirements of using encryption to develop digital signatures. Instead of focusing just on the key design, El Gamal designed a complete public key encryption algorithm using some of the key exchange elements from Diffie-Hellman and incorporating encryption on those keys. The resultant encrypted keys reinforced the security and authenticity of public key encryption design and helped lead to later advances in asymmetric encryption technology.

▶ **Elliptic curve cryptography (ECC):** Elliptic curve techniques use a method in which elliptic curves are used to calculate simple but very difficult-to-break encryption keys for use in general-purpose encryption. One of the key benefits of ECC encryption algorithms is that they have a compact design because of the advanced mathematics involved in ECC. For instance, an ECC encryption key of 160-bit strength is, in actuality, equal in strength to a 1024-bit RSA encryption key.

Note

In 2000, RSA Security released the RSA algorithm into the public domain. This release allows anyone to create products incorporating their own implementation of the algorithm without being subject to license and patent enforcement.

Throughout this section on different encryption algorithms, you have learned how each type of symmetric and asymmetric algorithm performs. One thing you have not seen yet is how bit strengths compare to each other when looking at asymmetric and symmetric algorithms in general. The following list reveals why symmetric algorithms are favored for most applications and why asymmetric algorithms are widely considered very secure but often too complex and resource-intensive for every environment. The following examples provide a comparison between a symmetric key and an RSA or Diffie-Hellman asymmetric key:

- ▶ 64-bit symmetric key strength = 512-bit asymmetric key strength
- ▶ 112-bit symmetric key strength = 1792-bit asymmetric key strength
- ▶ 128-bit symmetric key strength = 2304-bit asymmetric key strength
- ▶ 256-bit symmetric key strength = 15360-bit asymmetric key strength

As you can see, a dramatic difference exists in the strength and consequently the overall size of asymmetric encryption keys. For many environments today, 128-bit strength is considered adequate; therefore, symmetric encryption might often suffice. If you want to simplify how you distribute keys, however, asymmetric encryption might be the better choice.

One-Time Pads

Throughout history, the common theme among "unbreakable" algorithms is that through practice or theory, they are all breakable. However, one type of cipher has perhaps earned the distinction of being completely unbreakable: one-time pad (OTP). Unfortunately, the OTP currently has the tradeoff of requiring a key as long as the message, thus creating significant storage and transmission costs. Within an OTP, there are as many bits in the key as in the plain text to be encrypted, and this key is to be random and, as the name suggests, used only once, with no portion of the key ever being reused. Without the key, an attacker cannot crack the ciphertext, even via a brute-force attack in search of the entire key space.

PGP

PGP derives from the Pretty Good Privacy application developed by Phillip R. Zimmerman in 1991 and is an alternative to S/MIME. Basically, it encrypts and decrypts email messages using asymmetric encryptions schemes such as RSA. Another useful feature of the PGP program is that it can include a digital signature that validates that the email has not been tampered with (thus assuring the recipient of the email's integrity).

> **Note**
>
> In the early 1990s, the U.S. government tried to suppress the use of PGP, which was gaining popularity and exposure in the media. The government tried to force the software to be taken down and made unavailable to public consumption. (PGP is the email program that uses encryption and is available to anyone who wants to download it within North America.)
>
> Part of the government's argument against PGP was that it could not control the information people were sending. For example, criminals could use encryption and seemingly be able to hide their online activities and data from the prying eyes of the government. Eventually, the public's right to use encryption (and PGP in particular) won out.

Some systems incorporate a mixed approach, using both asymmetric and symmetric encryption to take advantage of the benefits that each provides. For example, asymmetric algorithms are used at the beginning of a process to securely distribute symmetric keys. From that point on, after the private keys have been securely exchanged, they can be used for encryption and decryption (thus solving the issue of key distribution). PGP is an example of such a system. PGP was originally designed to provide for the encryption and decryption of email and for digitally signing emails. PGP and other similar hybrid encryption systems such as the GNU Privacy Guard (GnuPG or GPG) program follow the OpenPGP format and use a combination of public key and private key encryption. GPG provides an alternative to PGP, under a free software license.

Use of Algorithms with Transport Encryption

Secure Sockets Layer (SSL) and Transport Layer Security (TLS) are the most widely used cryptographic protocols for managing secure communication between a client and server over the Web. Both essentially serve the same purpose (with TLS being the successor to SSL). Both provide for client- and server-side authentication and for encrypted connection between the two. TLS consists of two additional protocols: the TLS Record Protocol and the TLS Handshake Protocol. The Handshake Protocol allows the client and server to authenticate to one another, and the Record Protocol provides connection security.

The three basic phases of SSL and TLS are as follows:

1. Peer negotiation to decide which public key algorithm and key exchange to use. Usually, the decision is based on the strongest cipher and hash function supported by both systems.

2. Key exchange and authentication occurs. A digital certificate is exchanged, which includes the public encryption key, which is used to generate a session key.

3. Symmetric cipher encryption and message authentication occur. Both parties can generate keys for encryption and decryption during the session as a result of the asymmetric cryptography transaction that occurred in Step 2.

SSL and TLS are best known for protecting HTTP (Hypertext Transfer Protocol) web traffic and transactions, commonly known as *Hypertext Transfer Protocol over SSL* (HTTPS), which is a secure HTTP connection. HTTPS, like HTTP, is used as part of the uniform resource locator (URL) specified in the address bar of web browsers (https://). When you use HTTPS rather than just plain HTTP, an additional layer is provided for encryption and authentication. HTTP traffic is usually over port 80, and HTTPS traffic typically occurs over port 443.

> **ExamAlert**
>
> HTTPS simply combines HTTP with SSL or TLS. The default port for unencrypted HTTP traffic is port 80. The secure version, HTTPS, runs by default over port 443.

Web servers are generally ready to begin accepting HTTP traffic to serve up web pages, but to deploy HTTPS the web server must have a certificate signed by a certificate authority (CA). When a web server is serving content outside of the organization (that is, public-facing sites), the certificate is usually signed by a trusted third-party CA. If the site is used internally only (that is, an intranet), however, a certificate signed by an in-house CA generally suffices. In most cases, the use of SSL and TLS is single sided—that is, only the server is being authenticated as valid with a verifiable certificate. For example, when conducting an online banking transaction, you can be certain that you are at the legitimate site by verifying the server-side certificate, whereas the client is verified perhaps by only a username and password. Certificates, however, can also be deployed in a dual-sided scenario in which not only is the server authenticated using a certificate but the client side is as well. Although this certainly can provide for a more secure environment, additional overhead is created, which also includes the fact that a unique client-side certificate now needs to be created and managed for every client rather than just a single server.

Aside from its use with HTTP for web servers, TLS can provide security to many other protocols. It can, for instance, provide the capability to tunnel the connection forming a virtual private network (VPN), providing for easier firewall traversal compared to traditional IPsec VPNs, for example, which we discuss shortly.

Secure Shell

Secure Shell (SSH) provides an authenticated and encrypted session between the client and host computers using public key cryptography. SSH provides a more secure replacement for the common command-line terminal utility Telnet. SSH uses the asymmetric RSA cryptography algorithm to provide both connection and authentication. In addition, data encryption is accomplished using one of several available symmetric encryption algorithms.

The SSH suite encapsulates three secure utilities—slogin, ssh, and scp— derived from the earlier nonsecure Unix utilities rlogin, rsh, and rcp. Like Telnet, SSH provides a command-line connection through which an administrator can input commands on a remote server. SSH provides an authenticated and encrypted data stream, as opposed to the clear-text communications of a Telnet session. The three utilities within the SSH suite provide the following functionalities:

▶ **Secure Login (slogin):** A secure version of the Unix Remote Login (rlogin) service, which allows a user to connect to a remote server and interact with the system as if directly connected

▶ **Secure Shell (ssh):** A secure version of the Unix Remote Shell (rsh) environment interface protocol

▶ **Secure Copy (scp):** A secure version of the Unix Remote Copy (rcp) utility, which allows for the transfer of files in a manner similar to FTP

IP Security

Layer 2 Tunneling Protocol (L2TP) is an encapsulated tunneling protocol often used to support the creation of VPNs. It is important to understand that L2TP typically provides support along with other protocols. For example, L2TP by itself does not provide for authentication or strong authentication.

To meet these needs, L2TP is often combined with Internet Protocol Security (IPsec).

IPsec is a set of protocols widely implemented to support VPNs. It provides for the secure exchange of packets at the IP layer. Therefore, organizations have been able to leverage IPsec to exchange private information over public networks such as the Internet. IPsec can achieve this higher level of assurance for data transport through the use of multiple protocols, including Authentication Header (AH), Encapsulating Security Payload (ESP), and Internet Key Exchange (IKE). The AH protocol provides data integrity, authentication, and (optionally) antireplay capabilities for packets. ESP provides for confidentiality of the data being transmitted and also includes authentication capabilities. IKE provides for additional features and ease of configuration. IKE specifically provides authentication for IPsec peers and negotiates IPsec keys and security associations.

Cipher Suites

A *cipher suite* is a combination of several algorithms. SSL/TLS, for example, can support many of the algorithms already discussed. Different algorithms would be combined for example to support symmetric encryption, asymmetric encryption and message integrity. These cipher suites are based on a human readable identifier. Each cipher suite is made up of identifiers strung together in the following order:

1. The protocol such as TLS or SSL

2. The key establishment algorithm

3. The digital signature algorithm

4. The word *with*

5. The confidentiality algorithm

6. The hash function

Federal Information Processing Standards (FIPS) help take some of the guesswork out of what suites use. They provide suggestions for cipher suites appropriate for secure transport. An example of a cipher suite is the following:

TLS_DHE_DSS_WITH_3DES-EDE-CBC_SHA

The previous example defines a cipher suite that negotiate with Transport Layer Security (TLS), The Ephemeral Diffie-Hellman key agreement (DHE), the Digital Signature Standards (DSS), the Triple Data Encryption Standard

(3DES) set with the Encrypt-Decrypt-Encrypt (EDE) option in Cipher Block Chaining Mode (CBC), and the Secure Hash Algorithm (SHA-1).

Keep in mind, that when selecting cipher suites, you are only as strong as the weakest cipher suite chosen. For interoperability with clients, this is a tradeoff that needs to be considered.

To be considered a strong cipher suite, servers should be configured with the following, at a minimum:

▶ TLS_RSA_WITH_3DES_EDE_CBC_SHA

▶ TLS_RSA_WITH_AES_128_CBC_SHA

In addition, the server should also be configured to support additional suites that provide stronger encryption, such as AES 256, in addition to suites that use more modern public key agreement protocols (for instance, ECDH) and digital signature algorithms based on elliptic curves. On such algorithm is Elliptic Curve Digital Signature Algorithm (ECDSA). ECDSA provides an algorithm for digital signatures that relies on elliptic curves.

▶ TLS_RSA_WITH_AES_256_CBC_SHA

▶ TLS_ECDHE_ECDSA_WITH_3DES_EDE_CBC_SHA

▶ TLS_ECDHE_ECDSA_WITH_AES_128_CBC_SHA

▶ TLS_ECDHE_RSA_WITH_3DES_EDE_CBC_SHA

Meanwhile, following are some guidelines to eliminate weakness from your cipher suite section:

▶ Do not use any ciphers less than 128 bits, and do not use null ciphers.

▶ Do not use anonymous Diffie-Hellman (ADH) because of its lack of authentication.

▶ RC4 should not be used because of crypto analytical attacks.

▶ Disable all weak protocols, such as SSLv2, because of known weaknesses.

▶ RSA or DSA key length should be strong. They should at least be 1024, but 2048 is recommended.

▶ MD5 hashing algorithm should not be used for signatures because of known collision attacks on the hash.

▶ Server should support forward secrecy.

To provide for forward secrecy, DHE and ECDH should be configured and prioritized. Keep in mind, however, that both DHE and ECDH are significantly slower than traditional methods, and client support is another challenge because not all browsers provide such support. However, as of 2014, most of the popular and updated versions of browsers are designed to work with DHE and ECDH. To configure forward secrecy on a server, take the following actions:

1. Configure the server to use the appropriate cipher suites.

2. Configure how the server will select what cipher suite to use.

Key Stretching

Key stretching provides a means to "stretch" a key or password. That is, it makes an existing key or password stronger. Consider the user that uses a weak password. The use of key stretching can take that week password, and perform a function to increase the time it might otherwise take to crack the password via a brute-force attack. Operationally, key stretching takes the original key, and feeds it through an algorithm, which results in a stronger, more secure key. Two of the most widely used key stretching algorithms are as follows:

▶ **PBKDF2 (Password-Based Key Derivation Function 2):** Applies a pseudorandom function to the password, combined with a salt of at least 64 bits, and then repeats the process at least 1,000 times.

▶ **Bcrypt:** Based on the Blowfish cipher, Bcrypt provides an adaptive hash function. This function, based on what Bcrypt calls a "key factor," compensates for increasing compute power used for brute-force attacks.

Cram Quiz

Answer these questions. The answers follow the last question. If you cannot answer these questions correctly, consider reading this section again until you can.

1. What part of the IPsec protocol provides authentication and integrity but not privacy?

   ○ **A.** Encapsulating security payload

   ○ **B.** Sans-privacy protocol

   ○ **C.** Authentication header

   ○ **D.** Virtual private network

2. Which of the following protocols are used to manage secure communication between a client and a server over the Web? (Choose two correct answers.)

   ○ **A.** SSL

   ○ **B.** ISAKMP

   ○ **C.** PGP

   ○ **D.** TLS

3. Which of the following algorithms are examples of a symmetric encryption algorithm? (Choose three correct answers.)

   ○ **A.** Rijndael

   ○ **B.** Diffie-Hellman

   ○ **C.** RC6

   ○ **D.** AES

4. Which of the following algorithms are examples of an asymmetric encryption algorithm? (Choose two correct answers.)

   ○ **A.** Elliptical curve

   ○ **B.** 3DES

   ○ **C.** AES

   ○ **D.** RSA

5. Which of the following is a type of cipher that has earned the distinction of being unbreakable?

   ○ **A.** RSA

   ○ **B.** One-time pad

   ○ **C.** 3DES

   ○ **D.** WPA

6. You are tasked with configuring your web server with strong cipher suites. Which of the following would you choose as part of your cipher suite? (Choose three correct answers.)

   ○ **A.** RSA

   ○ **B.** RC4

   ○ **C.** AES

   ○ **D.** SHA

Cram Quiz Answers

1. **C**. The AH provides authentication so that the receiver can be confident of the source the data. It does not use encryption to scramble the data, so it cannot provide privacy. ESP provides for confidentiality of the data being transmitted and also includes authentication capabilities; therefore, answer A is incorrect. Answer B does not exist, and so it is incorrect. A virtual private network makes use of the IPsec protocol and is used to secure communications over public networks; therefore, answer D is incorrect.

2. **A and D**. SSL is the most widely used protocol for managing secure communication between clients and servers on the Web; TLS is similar, and it is considered the successor to SSL. Answer B is incorrect because ISAKMP is a protocol common to virtual private networks. Answer C is incorrect because PGP is used for the encryption of email.

3. **A, C**, and **D**. Because Rijndael and AES are now one in the same, they both can be called symmetric encryption algorithms. RC6 is symmetric, too. Answer B is incorrect because Diffie-Hellman uses public and private keys, and so it is considered an asymmetric encryption algorithm.

4. **A and D**. In this case, both elliptic curve and RSA are types of asymmetric encryption algorithms. Although the elliptic curve algorithm is typically a type of algorithm incorporated into other algorithms, it falls into the asymmetric family of algorithms because of its use of public and private keys, just like the RSA algorithm. Answers B and C are incorrect because 3DES and AES are symmetric encryption algorithms.

5. **B**. The one type of cipher that has earned the distinction of being completely unbreakable is the one-time pad (OTP). This assumes, however, that the key is truly random, is used only once, and is kept secret. Unfortunately, the OTP currently has the tradeoff of requiring a key as long as the message (and thus creates significant storage and transmission costs). Answers A, C, and D are all incorrect choices.

6. **A, C**, and **D**. RSA, AES, and SHA comprise a suite for strong key exchange, authentication, bulk cipher, and message authentication. Answer B is incorrect. RC4 is a bulk cipher that is considered weak. Other options include AES or 3DES.

What Next?

If you want more practice on this chapter's exam objectives before you move on, remember that you can access all the Cram Quiz questions on the CD. You can also create a custom exam by objective with the practice exam software. Note any objective that you struggle with and go to the material that covers that objective in this chapter.

CHAPTER 13

Public Key Infrastructure

This chapter covers the following official CompTIA Security+ SY0-401 exam objectives:

▶ Given a scenario, use appropriate PKI, certificate management, and associated components

(For more information on the official CompTIA Security+ exam topics, see the "About the CompTIA Security+ SY0-401 Exam" section in the Introduction.)

In Chapter 12, "Cryptography Tools and Techniques," you learned the basic concepts of public and private keys. A public key infrastructure (PKI) makes use of both types of keys and provides the foundation for binding keys to an identity via a certificate authority (CA), thus providing the system for the secure exchange of data over a network through the use of an asymmetric key system. This system for the most part consists of digital certificates and the CAs that issue the certificates. These certificates identify individuals, systems, and organizations that have been verified as authentic and trustworthy.

Recall that symmetric key cryptography requires a key to be shared. For example, suppose the password to get into the clubhouse is "open sesame." At some point in time, this key or password needs to be communicated to other participating parties before it can be implemented. PKI provides confidentiality, integrity, and authentication by overcoming this challenge. With PKI, it is not necessary to exchange the password, key, or secret information in advance. This is useful where involved parties have no prior contact or where it is neither feasible nor secure to exchange a secure key.

PKI is widely used to provide the secure infrastructure for applications and networks, including access control, resources from web browsers, secure email, and much more. PKI protects information by providing the following:

▶ Identity authentication
▶ Integrity verification
▶ Privacy assurance
▶ Access authorization
▶ Transaction authorization
▶ Nonrepudiation support

ExamAlert

A public key infrastructure is a vast collection of varying technologies and policies for the creation and use of digital certificates. PKI encompasses certificate authorities; digital certificates; and the tools, systems, and processes to bring it all together.

Given a Scenario, Use Appropriate PKI, Certificate Management, and Associated Components

▶ **Certificate authorities and digital certificates**

▶ **PKI**

▶ **Recovery agent**

▶ **Public key**

▶ **Private keys**

▶ **Registration**

▶ **Key escrow**

▶ **Trust models**

CramSaver

If you can correctly answer these questions before going through this section, save time by skimming the Exam Alerts in this section and then completing the Cram Quiz at the end of the section.

1. What are the components required to implement PKI?

2. What is the purpose of a certificate authority?

3. Why is it best to take a root certificate authority offline?

4. When implementing PKI, why is it important to consider how private keys are stored?

Answers

1. PKI consists of an infrastructure, as the name implies, of hardware, software, policies, and process. All of these components provide for the management and use of digital certificates. Core components include certificate authorities, certificate policies, digital certificates, certificate policies, and certificate practice statements.

2. A certificate authority is a key component of PKI. The primary purpose of a certificate authority is to verify the holder of a digital certificate, issue certificates, and ensure that the holder of a certificate is who they claim to be.

3. Certificate authorities operate on a hierarchical trust model. So, if the root certificate authority is compromised, the entire architecture is compromised. If the root certificate authority is offline and a subordinate certificate authority is compromised, however, the root certificate authority can be used to revoke the subordinate.

4. The storage of private keys needs to be carefully considered. The private key needs to be protected to ensure the validity of certificate authorities and the certificates they issue.

Public Key Infrastructure Standards

PKI consists of several standards and protocols. These standards and protocols are necessary to allow for interoperability among security products offered by different vendors. Keep in mind, for instance, that digital certificates may be issued by different trusted authorities; therefore, a common language or protocol must exist.

Next, we look at some specific PKI standards. Figure 13.1 illustrates this relationship between standards that apply to PKI at the foundation to the standards that rely on PKI and finally to the applications supported by those standards.

Email	Secure Electronic Commerce	VPN
S/MIME	SSL TLS	IPsec PPTP
PKIX	PKCS	X.509

FIGURE 13.1 **Standards that define PKI up to the applications supported by standards that may rely on PKI**

The PKIX working group of the Internet Engineering Task Force (IETF) is developing Internet standards for PKI based on X.509 certificates with the following focus:

▶ Profiles of X.509 Version 3 public key certificates and X.509 Version 2 certificate revocation lists (CRL)

▶ PKI management protocols

▶ Operational protocols

▶ Certificate policies and certificate practice statements (CPS)

▶ Time-stamping, data-certification, and validation services

Whereas PKIX describes the development of Internet standards for X.509-based PKI, the Public Key Cryptography Standards (PKCS) are the de facto cryptographic message standards developed and published by RSA Laboratories, the research arm of RSA Security. PKCS provides a basic and widely accepted framework for the development of PKI solutions. There were recently 15 documents in the PKCS specification library; however, 2 of the documents have been incorporated into another. These documents are as follows:

▶ PKCS #1 RSA Cryptography Standard provides recommendations for the implementation of public key cryptography based on the RSA algorithm.

▶ PKCS #2 no longer exists and has been integrated into PKCS #1.

▶ PKCS #3 Diffie-Hellman Key Agreement Standard describes a method for using the Diffie-Hellman key agreement.

▶ PKCS #4 no longer exists and has been integrated into PKCS #1.

▶ PKCS #5 Password-Based Cryptography Standard provides recommendations for encrypting a data string, such as a private key, with a secret key that has been derived from a password.

▶ PKCS #6 Extended-Certificate Syntax Standard provides a method for certifying additional information about a given entity beyond just the public key by describing the syntax of a certificate's attributes.

▶ PKCS #7 Cryptographic Message Syntax Standard describes the syntax for data streams such as digital signatures that may have cryptography applied to them.

▶ PKCS #8 Private-Key Information Syntax Standard describes syntax for private key information. This includes the private key of a public key cryptographic algorithm.

▶ PKCS #9 Selected Attribute Types defines certain attribute types of use in PKCS #6, PKCS #7, PKCS #9, and PKCS #10.

▶ PKCS #10 Certification Request Syntax Standard describes the syntax for a certification request to include a distinguished name, a public key, and an optional set of attributes.

▶ PKCS #11 Cryptographic Token Interface Standard defines an application programming interface (API) named Cryptoki for devices holding cryptographic information.

▶ PKCS #12 Personal Information Exchange Syntax Standard specifies a format for storing and transporting a user's private key, digital certificate, and attribute information.

▶ PKCS #13 Elliptic Curve Cryptography Standard addresses elliptic curve cryptography as related to PKI. As of this writing, PKCS #13 is still under development.

▶ PKCS #14 Pseudo Random Number Generation addresses pseudo random number generation (PRNG), which produces a sequence of bits that has a random-looking distribution. As of this writing, PKCS #14 is still under development.

▶ PKCS #15 Cryptographic Token Information Format Standard establishes a standard for the format of cryptographic information on cryptographic tokens.

Each of the preceding standards documents may be revised and amended periodically, as changes in cryptography occur, and they are always accessible from RSA's website. In addition, some have started to move within the control of standards organizations (for example, IETF).

It was stated earlier that PKIX is an IETF working group established to create standards for X.509 PKI. X.509 is an International Telecommunications Union (ITU) recommendation and is implemented as a de facto standard. X.509 defines a framework for authentication services by a directory.

Identity-Based Encryption

It is not uncommon to find many who struggle with PKI. The common complaint is that PKI is too costly and too much of a management challenge. PKI requires that end users manage keys, as well as be able to locate the recipient's public key to send encrypted communications. In a 1984 paper, Adi Shamir proposed a new method for encrypting data based on identity: "An identity-based scheme resembles an ideal mail system: If you know somebody's name and address you can send him messages that only he can read." He continued, "It makes the cryptographic aspects of the communication almost transparent to the user, and it can be used effectively even by laymen who know nothing about keys and protocols." This idea, ahead of its time, finally came to fruition in 2001 with a proposal by Dan Boneh and Matt Franklin. With identity-based encryption (IBE), a third-party server uses something as simple as an email address to identify the user, from which a public key is generated, which can be used for encrypting and decrypting email. Complexity is greatly reduced, and the recipient is not required to do anything to read the message. Voltage Security was later formed to commercialize IBE and now provides the technology to more than 1,000 organizations worldwide. IBE is also now standardized as IEEE 1363.3, in the same family as other public key techniques such as Elliptic Curve, RSA Signatures, and Discrete Logarithm–based crypto systems.

PKI

A public key infrastructure is a vast collection of varying technologies and policies for the creation and use of digital certificates. PKI encompasses certificate authorities; digital certificates; and the tools, systems, and processes to bring it all together.

To begin to understand the applications and deployment of PKI, you should understand the various pieces that make up a PKI.

Digital Certificates

A digital certificate is a digitally signed block of data that allows public key cryptography to be used for identification purposes. CAs issue these certificates, which are signed using the CA's private key. Most certificates are based on the X.509 standard. Although most certificates follow the X.509 Version 3 hierarchical PKI standard, the PGP key system uses its own certificate format. X.509 certificates contain the following information:

▶ Name of the CA

▶ CA's digital signature

▶ Serial number

▶ Issued date

▶ Period of validity

▶ Version

▶ Subject or owner

▶ Subject or owner's public key

The most common application of digital certificates that you have likely used involves websites. Websites that ask for personal information, especially credit card information, use digital certificates. (Not necessarily all do; however, they should.) The traffic from your computer to the website is secured via a protocol called Secure Sockets Layer (SSL), and the web server uses a digital certificate for the secure exchange of information. This is easily identified by a small padlock located in the bottom status bar of most browsers. By clicking this icon, you can view the digital certificate and its details.

ExamAlert

Remember the aforementioned components of an X.509 certificate. You may be required to recognize the contents of a certificate.

The X.509 standard additionally defines the format of required data for digital certificates. The preceding chapter briefly introduced you to the contents of a digital certificate; however, it is worth reiterating some of these fields in more detail, which include those required to be compliant to the X.509 standard (see Figure 13.2). These include the following:

▶ **Version:** This identifies the version of the X.509 standard for which the certificate is compliant.

▶ **Serial number:** The CA that creates the certificate is responsible for assigning a unique serial number.

▶ **Signature algorithm identifier:** This identifies the cryptographic algorithm used by the CA to sign the certificate.

▶ **Issuer:** This identifies the directory name of the entity signing the certificate, which is typically a CA.

▶ **Validity period:** This identifies the time frame for which the private key is valid, if the private key has not been compromised. This period is indicated with both a start and an end time and may be of any duration, but it is often set to 1 year.

▶ **Subject name:** This is the name of the entity that is identified in the public key associated with the certificate. This name uses the X.500 standard for globally unique naming and is often called the distinguished name (DN) (for example, CN=Maria Nardia, OU=Events Division, O=CompTIA, C=US).

▶ **Subject public key information:** This includes the public key of the entity named in the certificate, in addition to a cryptographic algorithm identifier and optional key parameters associated with the key.

FIGURE 13.2 **Details of a digital certificate.**

Certificate Authority

Certificate authorities are trusted entities and are an important concept within PKI. Aside from the third-party CAs, such as VeriSign (now part of Symantec Corp.), an organization may establish its own CA, typically to be used only within the organization. The CA's job is to issue certificates, to verify the holder of a digital certificate, and to ensure that holders of certificates are who they claim to be. A common analogy used is to compare a CA to a passport-issuing authority. To obtain a passport, you need the assistance of another (for example, a customs office) to verify your identity. Passports are trusted because the issuing authority is trusted.

Registration Authority

Registration authorities (RA) provide authentication to the CA as to the validity of a client's certificate request; in addition, the RA serves as an aggregator of information. A user, for example, contacts an RA, which in turn verifies the user's identity before issuing the request of the CA to go ahead with issuance of a digital certificate.

> **ExamAlert**
>
> A CA is responsible for issuing certificates. Remember that an RA would initially verify a user's identity, and then pass the request to issue a certificate to the user on to the CA.

Certificate Policies

A *certificate policy* indicates specific uses applied to a digital certificate and other technical details. Not all certificates are created equal. Digital certificates are issued often following different practices and procedures and are issued for different purposes. Therefore, the certificate policy provides the rules that indicate the purpose and use of an assigned digital certificate. For example, one certificate may have a policy indicating its use for electronic data interchange to conduct e-commerce, whereas another may be issued to only digitally sign documents.

You need to remember that a certificate policy identifies the purpose for which the certificate can be used, but you should also be able to identify the other types of information that can be included within a certificate policy, including the following:

- ► Legal issues often used to protect the CA
- ► Mechanisms for how users will be authenticated by the CA
- ► Key management requirements
- ► Instructions for what to do if the private key is compromised
- ► Lifetime of the certificate
- ► Certificate enrollment and renewal

▶ Rules regarding exporting the private key

▶ Private and public key minimum lengths

Certificate Practice Statement

A *certificate practice statement* (CPS) is a legal document created and published by a CA for the purpose of conveying information to those depending on the CA's issued certificates. The information within a CPS provides for the general practices followed by the CA in issuing certificates and customer-related information about certificates, responsibilities, and problem management. It is important to understand that these statements are described in the context of operating procedures and systems architecture, as opposed to certificate policies, discussed previously, which indicate the rules that apply to an issued certificate. A CPS includes the following items:

▶ Identification of the CA

▶ Types of certificates issued and applicable certificate policies

▶ Operating procedures for issuing, renewing, and revoking certificates

▶ Technical and physical security controls used by the CA

ExamAlert

The focus of a certificate policy is on the certificate, whereas the focus of a CPS is on the CA and the way that the CA issues certificates.

Certificate Signing Request

To install a digital certificate, a specific request needs to be generated and submitted. This request to apply for a digital certificate is known as a *certificate signing request* (CSR), and is requested from the applicant to the CA. Included within the request is the applicant's public key along with information about the applicant. Typical information includes the following:

▶ Fully qualified domain name

▶ Legally incorporated name of the company

▶ Department name

▶ City, state, and country

▶ An email address

The CSR is most commonly based on the PKCS #10 standard mentioned earlier. Before submitting a CSR, the applicant generates a key pair, consisting of a public and private key. The public key is provided with the request, and the applicant signs the request with the private key. If all is successful, the CA returns a digital certificate that is signed with the CA's private key.

Public and Private Key Usage

Digital certificates and key pairs can be used for various purposes, including privacy and authentication. The security policy of the organization that is using the key or the CA will define the purposes and capabilities for the certificates issued.

To achieve privacy, a user will require the public key of the individual or entity he or she wants to communicate with securely. This public key is used to encrypt the data that is transmitted, and the corresponding private key is used on the other end to decrypt the message.

ExamAlert

Keep this in mind: You obtain one's public key (freely available to anyone), which you use to encrypt a message to that person. As a result, that individual can use his private key, which only he or she has to decrypt the message. The public and private keys are mathematically related.

Authentication is achieved by digitally signing the message being transmitted. To digitally sign a message, the signing entity requires access to the private key.

In short, the key usage extension of the certificate specifies how the private key can be used—either to enable the exchange of sensitive information or to create digital signatures. In addition, the key usage extension can specify that an entity can use the key for both the exchange of sensitive information and for signature purposes.

In some circumstances, dual or multiple key pairs might be used to support distinct and separate services. For example, an individual in a corporate environment may require one key pair just for signing and another just for encrypting messages. Another example is the reorder associate who has one key pair to be used for signing and sending encrypted messages and might have another restricted to ordering equipment worth no more than a specific dollar amount. Multiple key pairs require multiple certificates because the X.509 certificate format does not support multiple keys.

Recovery

Key recovery is the process of using a recovery agent to restore a key pair from a backup and re-create a digital certificate using the recovered keys. Unlike in the case of a key compromise, this should be done only if the key pair becomes corrupted but are still considered valid and trusted. Although it is beneficial to back up an individual user's key pair, it is even more important to back up the CA's keys in a secure location for business continuity and recovery purposes.

> ### ExamAlert
> After deploying a CA, you should back up the CA's key for recovery purposes.

M of N Control

M of N control as it relates to PKI refers to the concept of backing up the public and private keys across multiple systems. This multiple backup provides a protective measure to ensure that no one individual can re-create his or her key pair from the backup. The backup process involves a mathematical function to distribute that data across a number of systems. A typical setup includes multiple personnel with unique job functions, and from different parts of the organization, to discourage collusion for the purpose of recovering keys without proper authority.

Centralized Versus Decentralized

There are alternative methods for creating and managing cryptographic keys and digital certificates. These operations may either be centralized or decentralized depending on the organization's security policy.

Centralized key management allows the issuing authority to have complete control over the process. Although this provides for a high level of control, many do not like the idea of a centralized system having a copy of the private key. Whereas the benefit of central control may be seen as an advantage, a centralized system also has disadvantages (for instance, additional required infrastructure, a need to positively authenticate the end entity before transmitting the private key, and the need for a secure channel to transmit the private key).

Decentralized key management allows the requesting entity to generate the key pair and only submit the public key to the CA. Although the CA can still take on the role of distributing and publishing the digital certificate, it can no longer store the private key. Therefore, the entity must maintain

complete control over the private key, which is considered one of the most
sensitive aspects of a PKI solution. In this scenario, the CA has the additional
burden of ensuring that the keys were generated properly and that all key-pair
generation policies were followed.

Storage

After the key pairs are generated and a digital certificate has been issued by
the CA, both keys must be stored appropriately to ensure that their integrity
is maintained. However, the key use must still be easy and efficient. The
methods used to store the keys may be hardware or software based.

Hardware storage is typically associated with higher levels of security and
assurance than software because hardware can have specialized components
and physical encasements to protect the integrity of the data stored within. In
addition to being more secure, hardware devices are more efficient because
they provide dedicated resources to PKI functions. Naturally, however,
hardware solutions often have a higher cost than software solutions.

Although software solutions do not have the same level of security as their
hardware counterparts, the ability to easily distribute the storage solutions
provides for easier administration, transportability, and lower costs.

Because the private key is so sensitive, it requires a higher level of protection
than the public key. As a result, you need to take special care to protect private
keys, especially the root key for a CA. Remember that if the private key is
compromised, the public key and associated certificate are also compromised
and should no longer be valid. If the CA's root key becomes compromised, all
active keys generated using the CA are compromised and should therefore be
revoked and reissued. As a result of this need for increased security over the
private keys, hardware solutions are often used to protect private keys.

ExamAlert

Certificates rely on a hierarchical chain of trust. If the CA's root key is compromised,
any keys issued by that CA are compromised as well.

Even a private key in the possession of an end user should be carefully
guarded. At a minimum, this key is protected via a password. An additional
safeguard is to provide an additional layer of security by storing the private key
on a portable device such as a smart card (thus requiring both possession of
the card and knowledge of the password).

Key Escrow

Key escrow occurs when a CA or other entity maintains a copy of the private key associated with the public key signed by the CA. This scenario allows the CA or escrow agent to have access to all information encrypted using the public key from a user's certificate and to create digital signatures on behalf of the user. Therefore, key escrow is a sensitive topic within the PKI community because harmful results might occur if the private key is misused. Because of this issue, key escrow is not a favored PKI solution.

Despite the concerns of the general public about escrow for private use, key escrow is often considered a good idea in corporate PKI environments. In most cases, an employee of an organization is bound by the information security policies of that organization (which usually mandate that the organization has a right to access all intellectual property generated by a user and to any data that an employee generates). In addition, key escrow enables an organization to overcome the large problem of forgotten passwords. Rather than revoke and reissue new keys, an organization can generate a new certificate using the private key stored in escrow.

Destruction

Destruction of a key pair and certificate typically occurs when the materials are no longer valid. Care should be taken when destroying a key pair. If the key pair to be destroyed is used for digital signatures, the private key portion should be destroyed first to prevent future signing activities with the key. If the materials were used for privacy purposes only, however, it might be necessary to archive a copy of the private key. You might need it later to decrypt archived data that was encrypted using the key.

Revocation

Just as digital certificates are issued, they can also be revoked. Revoking a certificate invalidates a certificate before its expiration date. Digital certificates contain a field indicating the date to which the certificate is valid. This date is mandatory, and the validity period can vary from a short period of time up to a number of years. Revocation occurs for several reasons. This might occur for example if a private key becomes compromised, the private key is lost, or the identifying credentials are no longer valid. Other reasons for revocation include fraudulently obtained certificates or a change in the holder's status, which may indicate less trustworthiness. Revoking a certificate is just not enough, however. The community that trusts these certificates must be notified that the certificates are no longer valid. This is accomplished via a

certificate revocation list (CRL) or the Online Certificate Status Protocol
(OCSP), as follows:

▶ **CRL:** A mechanism for distributing certificate revocation information. A
CRL is used when verification of digital certificate takes place to ensure
the validity of a digital certificate. A limitation of CRLs is that they must
be constantly updated; otherwise, certificates might be accepted despite
the fact they were recently revoked.

▶ **OCSP:** A newer mechanism for identifying revoked certificates. OCSP
checks certificate status in real time instead of relying on the end user to
have a current copy of the CRL.

Both OCSP and CRLs are used to verify the status of a certificate. Three
basic status levels exist in most PKI solutions: valid, suspended, and revoked.
The status of a certificate can be checked by going to the CA that issued
the certificate or to an agreed on directory server that maintains a database
indicating the status level for the set of certificates. In most cases, however, the
application (such as a web browser) will have a function available that initiates
a check for certificates.

> **ExamAlert**
>
> Within a PKI, the CRl and OSCP are methods to identify certificates that can longer
> be trusted.

Prior to revocation, a certificate may be suspended. Certificate suspension
occurs when a certificate is under investigation to determine whether it should
be revoked. This mechanism allows a certificate to stay in place, but it is not
valid for any type of use. Like the status checking that occurs with revoked
certificates, users and systems are notified of suspended certificates in the
same way. The primary difference is that new credentials will not need to be
retrieved; it is only necessary to be notified that current credentials have had a
change in status and are temporarily not valid for use.

Trust Models

Certificate authorities within a PKI follow several models or architectures.
The simplest model consists of a single CA. In the single-CA architecture,
only one CA exists to issue and maintain certificates. Although this model
might benefit smaller organizations because of its administrative simplicity,

it has the potential to present many problems. For example, if the CA fails, no other CA can quickly take its place. Another problem can arise if the private key of the CA becomes compromised; in this scenario, all the issued certificates from that CA would then be invalid. A new CA would have to be created, which, in turn, would need to reissue all the certificates.

A more common model, and one that reduces the risks inherent with a single CA, is the hierarchical CA model. In this model, an initial root CA exists at the top of the hierarchy and subordinate CAs reside beneath the root. The subordinate CAs provide redundancy and load balancing should any of the other CAs fail or be taken offline. As a result of this model, you may hear PKI referred to as a trust hierarchy.

A root CA differs from subordinate CAs in that the root CA is usually offline. Remember, if the root CA is compromised, the entire architecture is compromised. If a subordinate CA is compromised, however, the root CA can revoke the subordinate CA.

An alternative to this hierarchical model is the cross-certification model, often referred to as a *web of trust*. In this model, CAs are considered peers to each other. Such configuration, for example, may exist at a small company that started with a single CA. Then, as the company grew, it continued to implement other single-CA models and then decided that each division of the company needed to communicate with the others and ensure secure exchange of information across the company. To enable this, each of the CAs established a peer-to-peer trust relationship with the others. As you might imagine, such a configuration could become difficult to manage over time.

> **ExamAlert**
>
> The root CA should be taken offline to reduce the risk of key compromise, and the root CA should be made available only to create and revoke certificates for subordinate CAs. A compromised root CA compromises the entire system.

A solution to the complexity of a large cross-certification model is to implement what is known as a *bridge CA model*. Remember that in the cross-certification model each CA must trust the others. By implementing bridging, however, you can have a single CA, known as the *bridge CA*, be the central point of trust.

Cram Quiz

Answer these questions. The answers follow the last question. If you cannot answer these questions correctly, consider reading this section again until you can.

1. To check the validity of a digital certificate, which one of the following would be used?

   - ○ **A.** Corporate security policy
   - ○ **B.** Certificate policy
   - ○ **C.** Certificate revocation list
   - ○ **D.** Expired domain names

2. Which of the following is not a certificate trust model for the arranging of certificate authorities?

   - ○ **A.** Bridge CA architecture
   - ○ **B.** Sub-CA architecture
   - ○ **C.** Single-CA architecture
   - ○ **D.** Hierarchical CA Architecture

3. Which of the following are included within a digital certificate? (Choose all the correct answers.)

   - ○ **A.** User's public key
   - ○ **B.** User's private key
   - ○ **C.** Information about the user
   - ○ **D.** Digital signature of the issuing CA

4. Which of the following is not true about the expiration dates of certificates?

   - ○ **A.** Certificates may be issued for a week.
   - ○ **B.** Certificates are issued only at 1-year intervals.
   - ○ **C.** Certificates may be issued for 20 years.
   - ○ **D.** Certificates must always have an expiration date.

5. In a decentralized key management system, the user is responsible for which one of the following functions?

   - ○ **A.** Creation of the private and public key
   - ○ **B.** Creation of the digital certificate
   - ○ **C.** Creation of the CRL
   - ○ **D.** Revocation of the digital certificate

Cram Quiz Answers

1. **C**. A CRL provides a detailed list of certificates that are no longer valid. A corporate security policy would not provide current information on the validity of issued certificates; therefore, answer A is incorrect. A certificate policy does not provide information on the validity of issued certificates either; therefore, answer B is incorrect. Finally, an expired domain name has no bearing on the validity of a digital certificate; therefore, answer D is incorrect.

2. **B**. Sub-CA architecture does not represent a valid trust model. Answers A, C, and D, however, all represent legitimate trust models. Another common model also exists, called cross-certification; however, it usually makes more sense to implement a bridge architecture over this type of model.

3. **A, C**, and **D**. Information about the user, the user's public key, and the digital signature of the issuing CA are all included within a digital certificate. A user's private key should never be contained within the digital certificate and should remain under tight control; therefore, answer B is incorrect.

4. **B**. Digital certificates contain a field indicating the date until which the certificate is valid. This date is mandatory, and the validity period can vary from a short period of time up to a number of years; therefore, answers A, C, and D are true statements.

5. **A**. In a decentralized key system, the end user generates his or her own key pair. The other functions, such as the creation of the certificate, CRL, and the revocation of the certificate, are still handled by the certificate authority; therefore, answers B, C, and D are incorrect.

What Next?

If you want more practice on this chapter's exam objectives before you move on, remember that you can access all the Cram Quiz questions on the CD. You can also create a custom exam by objective with the practice exam software. Note any objective that you struggle with and go to the material that covers that objective in this chapter.

Practice Exam 1

CompTIA Security+ SY0-401

The multiple-choice questions provided here help you determine how prepared you are for the actual exam and which topics you need to review further. Write down your answers on a separate sheet of paper so that you can take this exam again if necessary. Compare your answers against the answers and explanations that follow.

Exam Questions

1. An organization is looking for a filtering solution that will help eliminate some of the recent problems it has had with viruses and worms. Which of the following best meets this requirement?

    ○ **A.** Intrusion detection

    ○ **B.** Malware inspection

    ○ **C.** Load balancing

    ○ **D.** Internet content filtering

2. Which risk management response is being implemented when a company purchases insurance to protect against service outage?

    ○ **A.** Acceptance

    ○ **B.** Avoidance

    ○ **C.** Mitigation

    ○ **D.** Transference

3. A collection of compromised computers running software installed by a Trojan horse or a worm is referred to as which of the following?

    ○ **A.** Zombie

    ○ **B.** Botnet

    ○ **C.** Herder

    ○ **D.** Virus

4. Adding a token for every POST or GET request that is initiated from the browser to the server can be used to mitigate which of the following attacks?

    ○ **A.** Buffer overflow

    ○ **B.** Cross-site request forgery (XSRF)

    ○ **C.** Cross-Site Scripting (XSS)

    ○ **D.** Input validation error

5. Which of the following is one of the biggest challenges associated with database encryption?

    ○ **A.** Multitenancy

    ○ **B.** Key management

    ○ **C.** Weak authentication components

    ○ **D.** Platform support

6. Which form of access control enables data owners to extend access rights to other logons?

○   **A.** MAC

○   **B.** DAC

○   **C.** Role-based (RBAC)

○   **D.** Rule-based (RBAC)

7. In a decentralized key management system, the user is responsible for which one of the following functions?

○   **A.** Creation of the private and public key

○   **B.** Creation of the digital certificate

○   **C.** Creation of the CRL

○   **D.** Revocation of the digital certificate

8. What is the name given to the system of digital certificates and certificate authorities used for public key cryptography over networks?

○   **A.** Protocol key instructions (PKI)

○   **B.** Public key extranet (PKE)

○   **C.** Protocol key infrastructure (PKI)

○   **D.** Public key infrastructure (PKI)

9. If Sally wants to send a secure message to Mark using public key encryption but is not worried about sender verification, what does she need in addition to her original message text?

○   **A.** Sally's private key

○   **B.** Sally's public key

○   **C.** Mark's private key

○   **D.** Mark's public key

10. Which of the following methods is the most effective way to physically secure laptops that are used in an environment such as an office?

○   **A.** Security cables

○   **B.** Server cages

○   **C.** Locked cabinet

○   **D.** Hardware dongle

11. Which of the following serves the purpose of trying to lure a malicious attacker into a system?

   ○ **A.** Honeypot

   ○ **B.** Pot of gold

   ○ **C.** DMZ

   ○ **D.** Bear trap

12. What is the recommended range of humidity level according to the ASHRAE?

   ○ **A.** 10% to 20%

   ○ **B.** 30% to 40%

   ○ **C.** 40% to 55%

   ○ **D.** 55% to 65%

13. Which of the following is a network protocol that supports file transfers and is a combination of RCP and SSH?

   ○ **A.** HTTPS

   ○ **B.** FTPS

   ○ **C.** SFTP

   ○ **D.** SCP

14. You want to implement a technology solution for a small organization that can function as a single point of policy control and management for access to Internet content. Which of the following should you choose?

   ○ **A.** Proxy gateway

   ○ **B.** Circuit-level gateway

   ○ **C.** Application-level gateway

   ○ **D.** Web security gateway

15. You have recently had security breaches in the network. You suspect they might be coming from a telecommuter's home network. Which of the following devices would you use to require a secure method for employees to access corporate resources while working from home?

   ○ **A.** A router

   ○ **B.** A VPN concentrator

   ○ **C.** A firewall

   ○ **D.** A network-based IDS

16. At which layer of the OSI model does the Internet Protocol Security protocol function?

- ○ **A.** Network layer
- ○ **B.** Presentation layer
- ○ **C.** Session layer
- ○ **D.** Application layer

17. When troubleshooting SSL, which two layers of the OSI model are of most value?

- ○ **A.** Application layer and presentation layer
- ○ **B.** Presentation layer and session layer
- ○ **C.** Application layer and transport layer
- ○ **D.** Physical layer and data link layer

18. Which of the three principles of security is supported by an iris biometric system?

- ○ **A.** Confidentiality
- ○ **B.** Integrity
- ○ **C.** Availability
- ○ **D.** Vulnerability

19. _____ describes the potential that a weakness in hardware, software, process, or people will be identified and taken advantage of.

- ○ **A.** Vulnerability
- ○ **B.** Exploit
- ○ **C.** Threat
- ○ **D.** Risk

20. Which of the following is not a principal concern for first responders to a hacking incident within a corporation operating in the United States?

- ○ **A.** Whether EMI shielding is intact
- ○ **B.** Whether data is gathered properly
- ○ **C.** Whether data is protected from modification
- ○ **D.** Whether collected data is complete

21. Which rule of evidence within the United States involves Fourth Amendment protections?

- ○ **A.** Admissible
- ○ **B.** Complete
- ○ **C.** Reliable
- ○ **D.** Believable

22. A user has downloaded trial software and subsequently downloads a key gener-
    ator in order to unlock the trial software. The user's antivirus detection software
    now alerts the user that the system is infected. Which one of the following best
    describes the type of malware infecting the system?

    ○ **A.** Logic bomb

    ○ **B.** Trojan

    ○ **C.** Adware

    ○ **D.** Worm

23. Which of the following is a coordinated effort in which multiple machines attack
    a single victim or host with the intent to prevent legitimate service?

    ○ **A.** DoS

    ○ **B.** Masquerading

    ○ **C.** DDoS

    ○ **D.** Trojan horse

24. What is the name given to the activity that consists of collecting information that
    will be later used for monitoring and review purposes?

    ○ **A.** Logging

    ○ **B.** Auditing

    ○ **C.** Inspecting

    ○ **D.** Vetting

25. Which of the following are not methods for minimizing a threat to a web server?
    (Choose the two best answers.)

    ○ **A.** Disable all nonweb services

    ○ **B.** Ensure Telnet is running

    ○ **C.** Disable nonessential services

    ○ **D.** Enable logging

26. The organization is concerned about vulnerabilities in commercial off-the-shelf
    (COTS) software. Which of the following might be the only means of reviewing
    the security quality of the program?

    ○ **A.** Fuzzing

    ○ **B.** Cross-Site Scripting

    ○ **C.** Input validation

    ○ **D.** Cross-site request forgery

27. Which of the following is an attack in which the end user executes unwanted actions on a web application while he is currently authenticated?

   ○ **A.** Buffer overflow

   ○ **B.** Input validation error

   ○ **C.** Cross-site scripting

   ○ **D.** Cross-site request forgery

28. Which of the following methods would be the most effective method to physically secure computers that are used in a lab environment that operates on a part-time basis?

   ○ **A.** Security cables

   ○ **B.** Server cages

   ○ **C.** Locked cabinet

   ○ **D.** Hardware dongle

29. An organization is looking to add a layer of security and maintain strict control over the apps employees are approved to use. Which of the following fulfills this requirement?

   ○ **A.** Blacklisting

   ○ **B.** Encryption

   ○ **C.** Lockout

   ○ **D.** Whitelisting

30. Your organization is exploring endpoint data-loss prevention (DLP) solutions. This solution is targeting which of the following data states?

   ○ **A.** In-transit

   ○ **B.** At-rest

   ○ **C.** In-use

   ○ **D.** In-flux

31. Which of the following uses a secure crypto-processor to authenticate hardware devices such as a PC or laptop?

   ○ **A.** Public key infrastructure

   ○ **B.** Full disk encryption

   ○ **C.** File-level encryption

   ○ **D.** Trusted Platform Module

32. Which process involves verifying keys as being authentic?

    ○ **A.** Authorization

    ○ **B.** Authentication

    ○ **C.** Access control

    ○ **D.** Verification

33. Which category of authentication includes smart cards?

    ○ **A.** Something you know

    ○ **B.** Something you have

    ○ **C.** Something you are

    ○ **D.** Something you do

    ○ **E.** Somewhere you are

34. Which of the following will help track changes to the environment when an organization needs to keep legacy machines?

    ○ **A.** Virtualization

    ○ **B.** Network storage policies

    ○ **C.** Host software baselining

    ○ **D.** Roaming profiles

35. Which of the following is information that is unlikely to result in a high-level financial loss or serious damage to the organization but still should be protected?

    ○ **A.** Public data

    ○ **B.** Confidential data

    ○ **C.** Sensitive data

    ○ **D.** Private data

36. Which of the following is a hybrid cryptosystem?

    ○ **A.** PAP

    ○ **B.** MD5

    ○ **C.** RSA

    ○ **D.** GPG

37. Which of the following is the type of algorithm used by MD5?

    ○ **A.** Block cipher algorithm

    ○ **B.** Hashing algorithm

    ○ **C.** Asymmetric encryption algorithm

    ○ **D.** Cryptographic algorithm

38. To check the validity of a digital certificate, which one of the following would be used?

   ◯ **A.** Corporate security policy

   ◯ **B.** Certificate policy

   ◯ **C.** Certificate revocation list

   ◯ **D.** Expired domain names

39. What is the acronym for the de facto cryptographic message standards developed by RSA Laboratories?

   ◯ **A.** PKIX

   ◯ **B.** X.509

   ◯ **C.** PKCS

   ◯ **D.** Both A and C

40. Which of the following is true of digital signatures? (Choose the two best answers.)

   ◯ **A.** They are the same as a hash function.

   ◯ **B.** They can be automatically time-stamped.

   ◯ **C.** They allow the sender to repudiate that the message was sent.

   ◯ **D.** They cannot be imitated by someone else.

41. Which of the following designates the amount of data loss that is sustainable and up to what point in time data recovery could happen before business is disrupted?

   ◯ **A.** RTO

   ◯ **B.** MTBF

   ◯ **C.** RPO

   ◯ **D.** MTTF

42. Which authorization protocol is generally compatible with TACACS?

   ◯ **A.** LDAP

   ◯ **B.** RADIUS

   ◯ **C.** TACACS+

   ◯ **D.** XTACACS

43. Your organization is exploring data-loss prevention (DLP) solutions. The proposed solution is a software storage solution that monitors how confidential data is stored. This solution is targeting which of the following data states?

   ○ **A.** In-transit
   ○ **B.** At-rest
   ○ **C.** In-use
   ○ **D.** In-service

44. Which of the following is needed to establish effective security baselines for host systems? (Select two correct answers.)

   ○ **A.** Cable locks
   ○ **B.** Mandatory settings
   ○ **C.** Standard application suites
   ○ **D.** Decentralized administration

45. Which of the following types of attacks is executed by placing malicious executable code on a website?

   ○ **A.** Buffer overflow
   ○ **B.** Cross-site request forgery (XSRF)
   ○ **C.** Cross-Site Scripting (XSS)
   ○ **D.** Input validation error

46. Which of the following are examples of protocol analyzers? (Check all correct answers.)

   ○ **A.** Metasploit
   ○ **B.** Wireshark
   ○ **C.** OVAL
   ○ **D.** Microsoft Message Analyzer

47. An executive from ABC Corp receives an email from a vice president of XYZ Corp, which is a prestigious partner organization of ABC Corp. This email was formatted using XYZ's corporate logo, images, and text from their website (checked by the executive before opening the included form). After clicking the provided link, the executive was asked to verify his credentials for access to a confidential report about ABC Corp, but after he filled out the form, the executive received only a referral to XYZ's site. What type of attack was used in this scenario?

   ○ **A.** Phishing
   ○ **B.** Smishing
   ○ **C.** Vishing
   ○ **D.** Spear phishing

48. Which form of cabling is least susceptible to EM interference?

    ○ **A.** STP

    ○ **B.** UTP

    ○ **C.** Coaxial

    ○ **D.** Fiber optic

49. An organization is partnering with another organization which requires shared systems. Which of the following documents would outline how the shared systems interface?

    ○ **A.** SLA

    ○ **B.** BPA

    ○ **C.** MOU

    ○ **D.** ISA

50. It is suspected that some recent network compromises are originating from the use of RDP. Which of the following TCP port traffic should be monitored?

    ○ **A.** 3389

    ○ **B.** 139

    ○ **C.** 138

    ○ **D.** 443

51. You are implementing network access for several internal business units that work with sensitive information on a small organizational network. Which of the following would best mitigate risk associated with users improperly accessing other segments of the network without adding additional switches?

    ○ **A.** Log analysis

    ○ **B.** Access control lists

    ○ **C.** Network segmentation

    ○ **D.** Proper VLAN management

52. Your organization is exploring data-loss prevention (DLP) solutions. The proposed solution is a software network solution that would be installed near the network perimeter to monitor for and flag policy violations. This solution is targeting which of the following data states?

    ○ **A.** In-transit

    ○ **B.** At-rest

    ○ **C.** In-use

    ○ **D.** In-arrival

53. What is the first step in performing a basic forensic analysis?

- ○ **A.** Ensure that the evidence is acceptable in a court of law
- ○ **B.** Identify the evidence
- ○ **C.** Extract, process, and interpret the evidence
- ○ **D.** Determine how to preserve the evidence

54. Which of the following is not true regarding expiration dates of certificates?

- ○ **A.** Certificates may be issued for a week.
- ○ **B.** Certificates are issued only at yearly intervals.
- ○ **C.** Certificates may be issued for 20 years.
- ○ **D.** Certificates must always have an expiration date.

55. Which of the following statements are true when discussing physical security? (Select all correct answers.)

- ○ **A.** Physical security attempts to control access to data from Internet users.
- ○ **B.** Physical security attempts to control unwanted access to specified areas of a building.
- ○ **C.** Physical security attempts to control the effect of natural disasters on facilities and equipment.
- ○ **D.** Physical security attempts to control internal employee access into secure areas.

56. Which type of authorization provides no mechanism for unique logon identification?

- ○ **A.** Anonymous
- ○ **B.** Kerberos
- ○ **C.** TACACS
- ○ **D.** TACACS+

57. Which is the best rule-based access control constraint to protect against unauthorized access when admins are off-duty?

- ○ **A.** Least privilege
- ○ **B.** Separation of duties
- ○ **C.** Account expiration
- ○ **D.** Time of day

58. Which of the following protocols supports DES, 3DES, RC2, and RSA2 encryption along with CHAP authentication, but was not widely adopted?

- ○ **A.** S-HTTP
- ○ **B.** S/MIME
- ○ **C.** HTTP
- ○ **D.** PPTP

59. A new switch has been implemented in areas where there is very little physical access control. Which of the following would the organization implement as a method for additional checks to prevent unauthorized access?

- ○ **A.** Loop protection
- ○ **B.** Flood guard
- ○ **C.** Implicit deny
- ○ **D.** Port security

60. There have been some sporadic connectivity issues on the network. Which of the following is the best choice to investigate these issues?

- ○ **A.** Protocol analyzer
- ○ **B.** Circuit-level gateway logs
- ○ **C.** Spam filter appliance
- ○ **D.** Web application firewall logs

61. Which of the following types of attacks can be done by either convincing the users to click on an HTML page the attacker has constructed or insert arbitrary HTML in a target website that the users visit?

- ○ **A.** Buffer overflow
- ○ **B.** Cross-site request forgery (XSRF)
- ○ **C.** Cross-Site Scripting (XSS)
- ○ **D.** Input validation error

62. Which of the following is most likely to use network segmentation as an alternate security method?

- ○ **A.** SCADA systems
- ○ **B.** Mainframes
- ○ **C.** Android
- ○ **D.** Gaming consoles

63. Which of the following algorithms is not an example of a symmetric encryption algorithm?

- ○ **A.** Rijndael
- ○ **B.** Diffie-Hellman
- ○ **C.** RC6
- ○ **D.** AES

64. Which of the following best describes the process of encrypting and decrypting data using an asymmetric encryption algorithm?

- ○ **A.** Only the public key is used to encrypt, and only the private key is used to decrypt.
- ○ **B.** The public key is used to either encrypt or decrypt.
- ○ **C.** Only the private key is used to encrypt, and only the public key is used to decrypt.
- ○ **D.** The private key is used to decrypt data encrypted with the public key.

65. Which one of the following defines APIs for devices such as smart cards that contain cryptographic information?

- ○ **A.** PKCS #11
- ○ **B.** PKCS #13
- ○ **C.** PKCS #4
- ○ **D.** PKCS #2

66. Which of the following are steps that can be taken to harden FTP services?

- ○ **A.** Anonymous access to shared files of questionable or undesirable content should be limited.
- ○ **B.** Regular review of networks for unauthorized or rogue servers.
- ○ **C.** Technologies that allow dynamic updates must also include access control and authentication.
- ○ **D.** Unauthorized zone transfers should also be restricted.

67. A situation in which a program or process attempts to store more data in a temporary data storage area than it was intended to hold is known as which of the following?

- ○ **A.** Buffer overflow
- ○ **B.** Denial of service
- ○ **C.** Distributed denial of service
- ○ **D.** Storage overrun

68. TEMPEST deals with which of the following forms of environmental control?

◯   **A.** HVAC

◯   **B.** EMI shielding

◯   **C.** Humidity

◯   **D.** Cold-aisle

69. Which of the following is included in hardening a host operating system?

◯   **A.** A policy for antivirus updates

◯   **B.** A policy for remote wipe

◯   **C.** An efficient method to connect to remote sites

◯   **D.** An effective system for file-level security

70. Which of the following is the preferred type of encryption used in SaaS platforms?

◯   **A.** Application level

◯   **B.** Database level

◯   **C.** Media level

◯   **D.** HSM level

71. Several organizational users are experiencing network and Internet connectivity issues. Which of the following would be most helpful in troubleshooting where the connectivity problems might exist?

◯   **A.** SSL

◯   **B.** IPsec

◯   **C.** SNMP

◯   **D.** Traceroute

72. An organization has an access control list implemented on the border router, but it appears that unauthorized traffic is still being accepted. Which of the following would the organization implement to improve the blocking of unauthorized traffic?

◯   **A.** Loop protection

◯   **B.** Flood guard

◯   **C.** Implicit deny

◯   **D.** Port security

73. An asset is valued at $12,000, the threat exposure factor of a risk affecting that asset is 25%, and the annualized rate of occurrence is 50%. What is the SLE?

- ○ **A.** $1,500
- ○ **B.** $3,000
- ○ **C.** $4,000
- ○ **D.** $6,000

74. Which form of fire suppression functions best in an Alaskan fire of burning metals?

- ○ **A.** Dry-pipe sprinkler
- ○ **B.** Wet-pipe sprinkler
- ○ **C.** Carbon dioxide
- ○ **D.** Dry powder

75. While performing regular security audits, you suspect that your company is under attack and someone is attempting to use resources on your network. The IP addresses in the log files belong to a trusted partner company, however. Assuming an attack, which of the following might be occurring?

- ○ **A.** Replay
- ○ **B.** Authorization
- ○ **C.** Social engineering
- ○ **D.** Spoofing

76. Due to organizational requirements, strong encryption cannot be used. Which of the following is the most basic form of encryption that can be used on 802.11-based wireless networks to provide privacy of data sent between a wireless client and its access point?

- ○ **A.** Wireless Application Environment (WAE)
- ○ **B.** Wireless Session Layer (WSL)
- ○ **C.** Wired Equivalent Privacy (WEP)
- ○ **D.** Wireless Transport Layer Security (WTLS)

77. After a new switch was implemented, some sporadic connectivity issues on the network have occurred. The issues are suspected to be device related. Which of the following would the organization implement as a method for additional checks in order to prevent issues?

- ○ **A.** Loop protection
- ○ **B.** Flood guard
- ○ **C.** Implicit deny
- ○ **D.** Port security

78. Which of the following is an example of a false negative result?

- ○ **A.** An authorized user is granted access to a resource.
- ○ **B.** An unauthorized user is granted access to a resource.
- ○ **C.** An authorized user is refused access to a resource.
- ○ **D.** An unauthorized user is refused access to a resource.

79. Which of the following is the best choice for encrypting large amounts of data?

- ○ **A.** Asymmetric encryption
- ○ **B.** Symmetric encryption
- ○ **C.** Elliptical curve encryption
- ○ **D.** RSA encryption

80. You want to be sure that the FTP ports that are required for a contract worker's functionality have been properly secured. Which of the following ports would you check?

- ○ **A.** 25/110/143
- ○ **B.** 20/21
- ○ **C.** 137/138/139
- ○ **D.** 53

81. Security guards are a form of which specific type of control?

- ○ **A.** Management
- ○ **B.** Technical
- ○ **C.** Physical
- ○ **D.** Access

82. You have been tasked with mitigating the risk of password-based attacks. Which of the following should you consider to provide a control beyond just what someone knows?

- ○ **A.** Enforce complex passwords
- ○ **B.** Prevent the user from entering more than three incorrect passwords
- ○ **C.** Implement use of a one-time use token
- ○ **D.** A and B

83. Which one of the following is not considered a physical security component?

- ○ **A.** VPN tunnel
- ○ **B.** Mantrap
- ○ **C.** Fence
- ○ **D.** CCTV

84. A physical security plan should include which of the following? (Select all correct answers.)

    ○ **A.** Description of the physical assets being protected

    ○ **B.** The threats from which you are protecting against and their likelihood

    ○ **C.** Location of a hard disk's physical blocks

    ○ **D.** Description of the physical areas where assets are located

85. Never inserting untrusted data except in allowed locations can be used to mitigate which of the following attacks? (Select two answers.)

    ○ **A.** Buffer overflow

    ○ **B.** Cross-site request forgery (XSRF)

    ○ **C.** Cross-Site Scripting (XSS)

    ○ **D.** Input validation error

86. Which of the following is included in a BYOD policy?

    ○ **A.** Key management

    ○ **B.** Data ownership

    ○ **C.** Credential management

    ○ **D.** Transitive trusts

87. Which of the following is a common storage networking standard chosen by businesses for ease of installation, cost, and utilization of current Ethernet networks?

    ○ **A.** Fibre Channel

    ○ **B.** FTP

    ○ **C.** iSCSI

    ○ **D.** HTTPS

88. Which one of the following best describes the type of attack designed to bring a network to a halt by flooding the systems with useless traffic?

    ○ **A.** DoS

    ○ **B.** Ping of death

    ○ **C.** Teardrop

    ○ **D.** Social engineering

89. The process of making an operating system more secure by closing known vulnerabilities and addressing security issues is known as which of the following?

- ○ **A.** Handshaking
- ○ **B.** Hardening
- ○ **C.** Hotfixing
- ○ **D.** All of the above

90. An organization is looking for a mobile solution that allows both executives and employees to discuss sensitive information without having to travel to secure company locations. Which of the following fulfills this requirement?

- ○ **A.** GPS tracking
- ○ **B.** Voice encryption
- ○ **C.** Remote wipe
- ○ **D.** Passcode policy

91. Users received a spam email from an unknown source and chose the option in the email to unsubscribe and are now getting more spam as a result. Which one of the following is most likely the reason?

- ○ **A.** The unsubscribe option does not actually do anything.
- ○ **B.** The unsubscribe request was never received.
- ○ **C.** Spam filters were automatically turned off when making the selection to unsubscribe.
- ○ **D.** They confirmed that their addresses are "live."

92. Which of the following provides a clear record of the path evidence takes from acquisition to disposal?

- ○ **A.** Video capture
- ○ **B.** Chain of custody
- ○ **C.** Hashes
- ○ **D.** Witness statements

93. Which of the following is not an example of multifactor authentication?

- ○ **A.** Logon and password
- ○ **B.** Smart card and PIN
- ○ **C.** RFID chip and thumbprint
- ○ **D.** Gait and iris recognition
- ○ **E.** Location and CAC

94. Which of the following is an example of role-based access control criteria?

- ○ **A.** GPS coordinates
- ○ **B.** Trusted OS
- ○ **C.** Members of the Administrators group
- ○ **D.** Time of day

95. The sender of data is provided with proof of delivery, and neither the sender nor receiver can deny either having sent or received the data. What is this called?

- ○ **A.** Nonrepudiation
- ○ **B.** Repetition
- ○ **C.** Nonrepetition
- ○ **D.** Repudiation

96. Which of the following are steps that can be taken to harden DHCP services?

- ○ **A.** Anonymous access to share files of questionable or undesirable content should be limited.
- ○ **B.** Regular review of networks for unauthorized or rogue servers.
- ○ **C.** Technologies that allow dynamic updates must also include access control and authentication.
- ○ **D.** Unauthorized zone transfers should also be restricted.

97. Which of the fields included within a digital certificate identifies the directory name of the entity signing the certificate?

- ○ **A.** Signature algorithm identifier
- ○ **B.** Issuer
- ○ **C.** Subject name
- ○ **D.** Subject public key information

98. Which type of authorization provides a mechanism for validation of both sender and receiver?

- ○ **A.** Anonymous
- ○ **B.** Kerberos
- ○ **C.** TACACS
- ○ **D.** RADIUS

99. Which type of biometric authentication involves identification of the unique patterns of blood-vessels at the back of the eye?

- ○ **A.** Facial recognition
- ○ **B.** Iris
- ○ **C.** Retina
- ○ **D.** Signature

100. An organization that relies heavily on cloud and SaaS service providers, such as Salesforce.com, WebEx, and Google, would have security concerns when implementing which of the following?

- ○ **A.** TACACS+
- ○ **B.** Secure LDAP
- ○ **C.** SAML
- ○ **D.** XTACACS

Answers at a Glance

1.	B	35.	D	69.	D
2.	D	36.	D	70.	A
3.	B	37.	B	71.	D
4.	B	38.	C	72.	C
5.	B	39.	C	73.	B
6.	B	40.	B and D	74.	D
7.	A	41.	C	75.	D
8.	D	42.	D	76.	C
9.	D	43.	B	77.	A
10.	A	44.	B and C	78.	C
11.	A	45.	C	79.	B
12.	C	46.	B and D	80.	B
13.	D	47.	D	81.	C
14.	D	48.	D	82.	C
15.	B	49.	D	83.	A
16.	A	50.	A	84.	A, B, and D
17.	C	51.	D	85.	A and D
18.	A	52.	A	86.	B
19.	C	53.	B	87.	C
20.	A	54.	B	88.	A
21.	A	55.	B, C and D	89.	B
22.	B	56.	A	90.	B
23.	C	57.	D	91.	D
24.	A	58.	A	92.	B
25.	B and D	59.	D	93.	A
26.	A	60.	A	94.	C
27.	D	61.	B	95.	A
28.	C	62.	A	96.	B
29.	D	63.	B	97.	B
30.	C	64.	D	98.	B
31.	D	65.	A	99.	C
32.	B	66.	A	100.	C
33.	B	67.	A		
34.	C	68.	B		

Answers with Explanations

1. Answer B is correct. A malware inspection filter is basically a web filter applied to traffic that uses HTTP. The body of all HTTP requests and responses is inspected. Malicious content is blocked, but legitimate content passes through unaltered. Answer A is incorrect because intrusion-detection systems are designed to analyze data, identify attacks, and respond to the intrusion. Answer C is incorrect because load balancers are servers configured in a cluster to provide scalability and high availability. Answer D is incorrect because Internet content filters use a collection of terms, words, and phrases that are compared to content from browsers and applications.

2. Answer D is correct. The liability of risk is transferred through insurance policies. Answer A is incorrect because accepting a risk is to do nothing in response. Risk avoidance involves simply terminating the operation that produces the risk, making answer B incorrect. Answer C is not correct because mitigation applies a solution that results in a reduced level of risk or exposure.

3. Answer B is correct. Answers A and C are incorrect but are related to a botnet in that a zombie is one of many computer systems that make up a botnet, whereas a bot herder is the controller of the botnet. Answer D is incorrect. A virus is a program that infects a computer without the knowledge of the user.

4. Answer B is correct. To mitigate cross-site request forgery (XSRF) attacks, the most common solution is to add a token for every POST or GET request that is initiated from the browser to the server. Answer A is incorrect because buffer overflows are associated with input validation. Answer C is incorrect because setting the HTTPOnly flag on the session cookie is used to mitigate XSS attacks. Answer D is incorrect because input validation tests whether an application properly handles input from a source outside the application destined for internal processing.

5. Answer B is correct. One of the biggest challenges associated with database encryption is key management. Answer A is incorrect because multitenancy is a security issue related to cloud computing implementations. Answer C is incorrect because lack of management software and weak authentication components are associated with hardware hard drive encryption. Answer D is incorrect because cost and platform support are concerns with smartphone encryption products.

6. Answer B is correct. Discretionary access control (DAC) systems enable data owners to extend access rights to other logons. Mandatory access control (MAC) systems require assignment of labels to extend access, making answer A incorrect. Answers C and D are incorrect because both RBAC access control forms rely on conditional assignment of access rules either inherited (role-based) or by environmental factors such as time of day or secured terminal location (rule-based).

7. Answer A is correct. In a decentralized key system, the end user generates his or her own key pair. The other functions, such as creation of the certificate, CRL, and the revocation of the certificate, are still handled by the certificate authority; therefore, answers B, C, and D are incorrect.

8. Answer D is correct. Public key infrastructure describes the trust hierarchy system for implementing a secure public key cryptography system over TCP/IP networks. Answers A, B, and C are incorrect because these are bogus terms.

9. Answer D is correct. Sally needs Mark's public key to encrypt her original message in a form that only Mark can decrypt. Neither of Sally's keys is needed because the originator does not need to be validated, making answers A and B incorrect. Answer C is incorrect because Mark's private key is used for decrypting the encrypted message to reveal Sally's original message.

10. Answer A is correct. Security cables with combination locks can provide such security and are easy to use. They are used mostly to secure laptops and leave the equipment exposed. Answer B is incorrect because PC Safe tower and server cages are designed to bolt to the floor and are meant to be in an environment that is static. Answer C is incorrect because a locked cabinet is an alternative for equipment that is not used or does not have to be physically accessed on a regular, daily basis. Vendors provide solutions such as a security cabinet locker that secures CPU towers. The housing is made of durable, heavy-duty steel for strength. Answer D is incorrect because a hardware dongle is used for license enforcement.

11. Answer A is correct. A honeypot is used to serve as a decoy and lure a malicious attacker. Answers B and D are incorrect answers and are not legitimate terms for testing purposes. Answer C is incorrect because a demilitarized zone (DMZ) is an area between the Internet and the internal network.

12. Answer C is correct. The American Society of Heating, Refrigerating and Air-Conditioning Engineers (ASHRAE) recommends optimal humidity levels in the 40% to 55% range, making answers A, B, and D incorrect. Very low levels of humidity can promote the buildup of electrostatic charges that can harm sensitive electronic components. Very high levels of humidity can promote condensation on chilled surfaces and introduce liquid into operating equipment.

13. Answer D is correct. The Secure Copy Protocol (SCP) is a network protocol that supports file transfers. SCP is a combination of RCP and SSH. It uses the BSD RCP protocol tunneled through the Secure Shell (SSH) protocol to provide encryption and authentication. Answer A is incorrect because HTTPS is used for secured web-based communications. Answer B is incorrect. FTPS, also known as FTP Secure and FTP-SSL, is an FTP extension that adds support for TLS and SSL. Answer C is incorrect because SFTP, or secure FTP, is a program that uses SSH to transfer files. Unlike standard FTP, it encrypts both commands and data, preventing passwords and sensitive information from being transmitted in the clear over the network.

14. Answer D is correct. Web security gateways offer a single point of policy control and management for web-based content access. Answer A is too generic to be a proper answer. Answer B is incorrect because a circuit-level gateway's decisions are based on source and destination addresses. Answer C is incorrect because an application-level gateway understands services and protocols.

15. Answer B is correct. A VPN concentrator is used to allow multiple users to access network resources using secure features that are built in to the device and are deployed where the requirement is for a single device to handle a very large number of VPN tunnels. Answer A is incorrect because a router forwards information to its destination on the network or the Internet. A firewall protects computers and networks from undesired access by the outside world; therefore, answer C is incorrect. Answer D is incorrect because network-based intrusion-detection systems monitor the packet flow and try to locate packets that are not allowed for one reason or another and might have gotten through the firewall.

16. Answer A is correct. IPsec validation and encryption function at the network layer of the OSI model. Answers B, C, and D are incorrect because IPsec functions at a lower level of the OSI model.

17. Answer C is correct. SSL connections occur between the application and transport layers. Answer A is incorrect because SSL operates at a deeper level. Answer B is incorrect because the Secure Sockets Layer transport effectively fills the same role as these OSI model layers. Answer D is incorrect because the data has been abstracted beyond the level at which SSL operates.

18. Answer A is correct. Confidentiality involves protecting against unauthorized access, which biometric authentication systems support. Integrity is concerned with preventing unauthorized modification, making answer B incorrect. Answer C is not correct because availability is concerned with ensuring that access to services and data is protected against disruption. Answer D is incorrect because a vulnerability is a failure in one or more of the C-I-A principles.

19. Answer C is correct. A threat is the potential that a vulnerability will be identified and exploited. Answer A is incorrect because a vulnerability is the weakness itself and not the likelihood that it will be identified and exploited. Answer B is incorrect because an exploit is the mechanism of taking advantage of a vulnerability rather than its likelihood of occurrence. Answer D is incorrect because risk is the likelihood that a threat will occur and the measure of its effect.

20. Answer A is correct. EMI shielding is important to protecting data and services against unauthorized interception as well as interference but is not a principal concern for first responders following an incident. First responders must ensure that data is collected correctly and protect it from modification using proper controls ensuring a clear chain of evidence, making answers B and C incorrect. Answer D is incorrect because a first responder might be the only agent able to ensure that all data is collected before being lost due to volatility of storage.

21. Answer A is correct. Admissibility involves collecting data in a manner that ensures its viability in court, including legal requirements such as the Fourth Amendment protections against unlawful search and seizure. Answers B and C are incorrect because data must be collected completely and protected against modification to ensure reliability, but these are not concerns of the Fourth Amendment. Answer D is incorrect because believability focuses on evidence being understandable, documented, and not subject to modification during transition.

22. Answer B is correct. Trojans are programs disguised as something useful. In this instance, the user was likely illegally trying to crack software, and in the process infected the system with malware. Although answers A, C, and D are types of malware, they are not the best choices.

23. Answer C is correct. A distributed denial of service (DDoS) attack is similar to a denial-of-service (DoS) attack in that they both try to prevent legitimate access to services. However, a DDoS attack is a coordinated effort among many computer systems; therefore, answer A is incorrect. Masquerading involves using someone else's identity to access resources; therefore, answer B is incorrect. A Trojan horse is a program used to perform hidden functions; therefore, answer D is incorrect.

24. Answer A is correct. Logging is the process of collecting data to be used for monitoring and auditing purposes. Auditing is the process of verification that normally involves going through log files; therefore, answer B is incorrect. Typically, the log files are frequently inspected, and inspection is not the process of collecting the data; therefore, answer C is incorrect. Vetting is the process of thorough examination or evaluation; therefore, answer D is incorrect.

25. Answers B and D are correct. Having Telnet enabled presents security issues and is not a primary method for minimizing threat. Logging is important for secure operations and is invaluable when recovering from a security incident. However, it is not a primary method for reducing threat. Answer A is incorrect because disabling all nonweb services might provide a secure solution for minimizing threats. Answer C is incorrect because each network service carries its own risks; therefore, it is important to disable all nonessential services.

26. Answer A is correct. In some closed application instances, fuzzing might be the only means of reviewing the security quality of the program. Answer B is incorrect because Cross-Site Scripting (XSS) vulnerabilities can be used to hijack the user's session or to cause the user accessing malware-tainted Site A to unknowingly attack Site B on behalf of the attacker who planted code on Site A. Answer C is incorrect because input validation tests whether an application properly handles input from a source outside the application destined for internal processing. Answer D, Cross-site request forgery (XSRF), is an attack in which the end user executes unwanted actions on a web application while she is currently authenticated.

27. Answer D is correct. Cross-site request forgery (XSRF) is an attack in which the end user executes unwanted actions on a web application while he is currently authenticated. Answer A is incorrect because a buffer overflow is a direct result of poor or incorrect input validation or mishandled exceptions. Answer B is incorrect because input validation errors are a result of improper field checking in the code. Answer C is incorrect because Cross-Site Scripting (XSS) vulnerabilities can be used to hijack the user's session or to cause the user accessing malware-tainted Site A to unknowingly attack Site B on behalf of the attacker who planted code on Site A.

28. Answer C is correct. A locked cabinet is an alternative for equipment that is not used or does not have to be physically accessed on a regular, daily basis. Vendors provide solutions such as a security cabinet locker that secures CPU towers. The housing is made of durable, heavy-duty steel for strength. Answer A is incorrect because security cables with combination locks can provide such security and are easy to use but are used mostly to secure laptops and leave the equipment exposed. Answer B is incorrect because PC Safe tower and server cages are designed to bolt to the floor and are meant to be in an environment that is static. Answer D is incorrect because a hardware dongle is used for license enforcement.

29. Answer D is correct. Application whitelisting only permits known good apps. When security is a concern, whitelisting applications is a better option because it allows organizations to maintain strict control over the apps employees are approved to use. Answer A is incorrect because although blacklisting is an option, it is not as effective as whitelisting. Answer B is incorrect because encryption has nothing to do with restricting application usage. Answer C is incorrect because lockout has to do with number of times a user can enter a passcode.

30. Answer C is correct. Protection of data in-use is considered to be an endpoint solution and the application is run on end user workstations or servers in the organization. Answer A is incorrect because protection of data in-transit is considered to be a network solution and either a hardware or software solution is installed near the network perimeter to monitor for and flag policy violations. Answer B is incorrect because protection of data at-rest is considered to be a storage solution and is generally a software solution that monitors how confidential data is stored. Answer D is incorrect because there is no such data state.

31. Answer D is correct. Trusted Platform Module (TPM) refers to a secure crypto-processor used to authenticate hardware devices such as a PC or laptop. The idea behind TPM is to allow any encryption-enabled application to take advantage of the chip. Answer A is incorrect because public key infrastructure (PKI) is a set of hardware, software, people, policies, and procedures needed to create, manage, distribute, use, store, and revoke digital certificates. Answer B is incorrect because full-disk encryption involves encrypting the operating system partition on a computer and then booting and running with the system drive encrypted at all times. Answer C is incorrect because in file- or folder-level encryption, individual files or folders are encrypted by the file system itself.

32. Answer B is correct. Authentication involves the presentation and verification of credentials of keys as being authentic. Answer A is incorrect because authorization involves checking authenticated credentials against a list of authorized security principles. Once checked, resource access is allowed or limited based on access control constraints, making Answer C incorrect. Answer D is incorrect because verification of credentials occurs during authentication (as being authentic) and authorization (as being authorized to request resource access) and is not a recognized access control process.

33. Answer B is correct. Something you have includes smart cards, tokens, and keys. Something you know includes account logons, passwords, and PINs, making answer A incorrect. Answers C and D are incorrect because both something you are and something you do involve measures of personal biological qualities and do not require an external device such as a smart card or key. Answer E is incorrect because somewhere you are is generally associated with either being in a trusted or less trusted location which could be based on GPS coordinates or IP address.

34. Answer C is correct. Host software baselining can be done for a variety of reasons including malware monitoring and creating system images. Generally, the environment needs of an organization will fall into a legacy, enterprise, or high-security client. Answer A is incorrect because virtualization adds a layer of security as well as improves enterprise desktop management and control with faster deployment of desktops and fewer support calls due to application conflicts. Answer B is incorrect because network storage policies have nothing to do with desktop management. Answer D is incorrect because roaming profiles do not add a layer of security.

35. Answer D is correct. Private data is information that is unlikely to result in a high-level financial loss or serious damage to the organization but still should be protected. Answer A is incorrect because the unauthorized disclosure, alteration, or destruction of public data would result in little or no risk to the organization. Answer B is incorrect because confidential data is internal information that defines the way in which the organization operates. Security should be high. Answer C is incorrect because sensitive data is considered confidential data.

36. Answer D is correct. Privacy Guard (GnuPG or GPG) is a hybrid cryptosystem that uses combination of public key and private key encryption. The incorrect choices are A, B, and C: PAP is a basic form of authentication during which the username and password are transmitted unencrypted, RSA is an asymmetric cipher, and MD5 is a hash.

37. Answer B is correct. Although the message digest (MD) series of algorithms is classified globally as a symmetric key encryption algorithm, the correct answer is hashing algorithm, which is the method that the algorithm uses to encrypt data. Answer A in incorrect because a block cipher divides the message into blocks of bits. Answer C is incorrect because MD5 is a symmetric key algorithm, not an asymmetric encryption algorithm (examples of this include RC6, Twofish, and Rijndael). Answer D is incorrect because cryptographic algorithm is a bogus term.

38. Answer C is correct. A certificate revocation list (CRL) provides a detailed list of certificates that are no longer valid. A corporate security policy would not provide current information on the validity of issued certificates; therefore, answer A is incorrect. A certificate policy does not provide information on invalid issued certificates, either; therefore, answer B is incorrect. Finally, an expired domain name has no bearing on the validity of a digital certificate; therefore, answer D is incorrect.

39. Answer C is correct. The Public Key Cryptography Standards (PKCS) are the de facto cryptographic message standards developed and maintained by RSA Laboratories, the Security Division of EMC. PKIX describes the development of Internet standards for X.509-based digital certificates; therefore, answers A, B, and D are incorrect.

40. Answers B and D are correct. Digital signatures offer several features and capabilities. This includes being able to ensure the sender cannot repudiate that he or she used the signature. In addition, nonrepudiation schemes are capable of offering time stamps for the digital signature. Answer A is incorrect. Hashing algorithms are only used for integrity purposes and only confirm original content. Answer C is incorrect because a key feature of digital signatures is to provide for nonrepudiation.

41. Answer C is correct. Recovery point objective (RPO) is the amount of time that can elapse during a disruption before the quantity of data lost during that period exceeds the BCP's maximum allowable threshold. Simply put, RPO specifies the allowable data loss. It determines up to what point in time data recovery could happen before business is disrupted. Answer A is incorrect because recovery time objective (RTO) is the amount of time within which a process must be restored after a disaster to meet business continuity. It defines how much time it takes to recover after notification of process disruption. Answer B is incorrect because mean time between failures (MTBF) is the average amount of time that passes between hardware component failures excluding time spent waiting for or being repaired. Answer D is incorrect because

mean time to failure (MTTF) is the length of time a device or product is expected to last in operation.

42. Answer D is correct. The Extended Terminal Access Controller Access Control System (XTACACS) protocol is a proprietary form of the TACACS protocol developed by Cisco and is compatible in many cases. Neither LDAP nor RADIUS is affiliated with the TACACS protocol, making answers A and B incorrect. Answer C is incorrect because the newer TACACS+ is not backward compatible with its legacy equivalent.

43. Answer B is correct. Protection of data at-rest is considered to be a storage solution and is generally a software solution that monitors how confidential data is stored. Answer A is incorrect because protection of data in-transit is considered to be a network solution and either a hardware or software solution is installed near the network perimeter to monitor for and flag policy violations. Answer C is incorrect because protection of data in-use is considered to be an endpoint solution and the application is run on end-user workstations or servers in the organization. Answer D is incorrect because there is no such data state.

44. Answers B and C are correct. To establish effective security baselines, enterprise network security management requires a measure of commonality between the systems. Mandatory settings, standard application suites, and initial setup configuration details all factor into the security stance of an enterprise network. Answer A is incorrect because cable locks have nothing to do with effective security baselines. Answer D is incorrect because decentralized management does not have anything to do with security baselines.

45. Answer C is correct. Cross-Site Scripting (XSS) vulnerabilities can be used to hijack the user's session or to cause the user accessing malware-tainted Site A to unknowingly attack Site B on behalf of the attacker who planted code on Site A. Answer A is incorrect because a buffer overflow is a direct result of poor or incorrect input validation or mishandled exceptions. Answer B is incorrect. The key element to understanding XSRF is that attackers are betting that users have a validated login cookie for the website already stored in their browsers. Answer D is incorrect because input validation errors are a result of improper field checking in the code.

46. Answers B and D are correct. Windows Server operating systems come with a protocol analyzer called by Microsoft Message Analyzer. Third-party programs such as Wireshark can also be used for network monitoring. Metasploit is a framework used for penetration testing, and OVAL

is intended as an international language for representing vulnerability information using an XML schema for expression; therefore, answers A and C are incorrect.

47. Answer D is correct. This is an example of a spear phishing attack, which uses fraudulent email to obtain access to data of value (here, the executive's credentials) from a targeted organization. Answer A is incorrect because while phishing attacks involve email, spear phishing attacks are targeted and customized to a selected target. The question's description of the images, links, and report all indicate a very targeted attack. Answer B is incorrect because smishing attacks are conducted using SMS messages. Answer C is similarly incorrect because vishing attacks employ telephone or VoIP audio communications.

48. Answer D is correct. Fiber-optic cabling is least subject to electromagnetic interference because its communications are conducted by transmitting pulses of light over glass, plastic, or sapphire transmission fibers. Twisted-pair (shielded STP as well as unshielded UTP) copper cables provide minimal shielding against interference but can function as antenna picking up nearby EM sources when extended over long cable runs, making answers A and B incorrect. Answer C is incorrect because although coaxial cables limit EM interference by encasing one conductor in a sheath of conductive material, they are still conductive and not as resistant as purely optical forms of communication.

49. Answer D is correct. An interconnection security agreement (ISA) is an agreement between organizations that have connected IT systems. Answer A is incorrect because a service level agreement (SLA) is a contract between a service provider and a customer that specifies the nature of the service to be provided and the level of service that the provider will offer to the customer. Answer B is incorrect because a business partners agreement (BPA) is a contract that establishes partner profit percentages, partner responsibilities, and exit strategies for partners. Answer C is incorrect because a memorandum of understanding (MOU) is a document that outlines the terms and details of an agreement between parties, including each party's requirements and responsibilities.

50. Answer A is correct. TCP port 3389 is used by RDP. Answer B is incorrect because UDP uses port 139 for network sharing. Answer C is incorrect because port 138 is used to allow NetBIOS traffic for name resolution. Answer D is incorrect because port 443 is used for HTTPS.

51. Answer D is correct. VLANs provide a way to limit broadcast traffic in a switched network. This creates a boundary and, in essence, creates

multiple, isolated LANs on one switch. Answer A is incorrect because logging is the process of collecting data to be used for monitoring and auditing purposes. Answer B is incorrect because access control generally refers to the process of making resources available to accounts that should have access while limiting that access to only what is required. Answer C is incorrect because network segmentation is used for interconnected networks where a compromised system on one network can easily threaten machines on other network segments.

52. Answer A is correct. Protection of data in-transit is considered to be a network solution and either a hardware or software solution is installed near the network perimeter to monitor for and flag policy violations. Answer B is incorrect because protection of data at-rest is considered to be a storage solution and is generally a software solution that monitors how confidential data is stored. Answer C is incorrect because protection of data in-use is considered to be an endpoint solution and the application is run on end-user workstations or servers in the organization. Answer D is incorrect because there is no such data state.

53. Answer B is correct. It is necessary to first identify the evidence that is available to be collected. Answer A is incorrect because protecting data's value as evidence must come after the type and form of evidence is known. Extraction, preservation, processing, and interpretation of evidence also follow the identification of data types and storage that must be collected, making answers C and D incorrect.

54. Answer B is correct. Digital certificates contain a field indicating the date to which the certificate is valid. This date is mandatory, and the validity period can vary from a short period of time up to a number of years; therefore, answers A, C, and D are incorrect.

55. Answers B, C, and D are correct. Natural disasters, unwanted access, and user restrictions are all physical security issues. Preventing Internet users from getting to data is data security, not physical security; therefore, answer A is incorrect.

56. Answer A is correct. During anonymous access, such as requests to a public FTP server, unique identify of the requester is not determined and so cannot be used for personalized logon identification. Answers B, C, and D are incorrect because authorization services such as Kerberos, TACACS, and its replacement TACACS+ all verify access requests against a list of authorized credentials and so can log individual visits and identify access request logons.

57. Answer D is correct. Time-of-day rules prevent administrative access requests during off-hours when local admins and security professionals are not on duty. Answer A is incorrect because least privilege is a principle of assigning only those rights necessary to perform assigned tasks. Answer B is incorrect because separation of duties aids in identification of fraudulent or incorrect processes by ensuring that action and validation practices are performed separately. Answer C is incorrect because account expiration policies ensure that individual accounts do not remain active past their designated lifespan but do nothing to ensure protections are enabled during admin downtime.

58. Answer A is correct. An alternative to HTTPS is the Secure Hypertext Transport Protocol (S-HTTP), which was developed to support connectivity for banking transactions and other secure web communications. S-HTTP was not adopted by the early web browser developers (for example, Netscape and Microsoft) and so remains less common than the HTTPS standard. Additionally, S-HTTP encrypts individual messages so it cannot be used for VPN security. Answer B is incorrect. S/MIME is used to encrypt electronic mail transmissions over public networks. Answer C is incorrect because HTTP is used for unsecured web-based communications. Answer D is incorrect because Point-to-Point Tunneling Protocol (PPTP) is a network protocol that enables the secure transfer of data from a remote client to a private enterprise server by creating a virtual private network (VPN) across TCP/IP-based data networks.

59. Answer D is correct. Port security is a Layer 2 traffic control feature on Cisco Catalyst switches. It enables individual switch ports to be configured to allow only a specified number of source MAC addresses coming in through the port. Answer A is incorrect because the loop guard feature makes additional checks in Layer 2 switched networks. Answer B is incorrect because a flood guard is a firewall feature used to control network activity associated with denial-of-service (DoS) attacks. Answer C is incorrect because implicit deny is an access control practice wherein resource availability is restricted to only those logons explicitly granted access.

60. Answer A is correct. Protocol analyzers help you troubleshoot network issues by gathering packet-level information across the network. These applications capture packets and can conduct protocol decoding, putting the information into readable data for analysis. Answer B is incorrect because a circuit-level gateway filters based on source and destination addresses. Answer C is incorrect because all-in-one spam filter appliances

allow for checksum technology, which tracks the number of times a particular message has appeared, and message authenticity checking, which uses multiple algorithms to verify authenticity of a message. Answer D is incorrect because a web application firewall is software or a hardware appliance used to protect the organization's web server from attack.

61. Answer B is correct. The key element to understanding XSRF is that attackers are betting that users have a validated login cookie for the website already stored in their browsers. All they need to do is get the browsers to make a request to the website on their behalf. This can be done by either convincing the users to click on an HTML page the attacker has constructed or inserting arbitrary HTML in a target website that the users visit. Answer A is incorrect because a buffer overflow is a direct result of poor or incorrect input validation or mishandled exceptions. Answer C is incorrect because Cross-Site Scripting (XSS) vulnerabilities can be used to hijack the user's session or to cause the user accessing malware-tainted Site A to unknowingly attack Site B on behalf of the attacker who planted code on Site A. Answer D is incorrect because input validation errors are a result of improper field checking in the code.

62. Answer A is correct. Network segmentation is one of the most effective controls an organization can implement in order to mitigate the effect of a network intrusion. Due to the sensitive nature of supervisory control and data acquisition (SCADA) systems, they would most likely use network segmentation. Answer B is incorrect because mainframes would most likely use security layers. Answer C is incorrect because Android would most likely use security layers. Answer D is incorrect. Most gaming consoles use firmware version control as an alternative security method.

63. Answer B is correct. Diffie-Hellman uses public and private keys, so it is considered an asymmetric encryption algorithm. Because Rijndael and Advanced Encryption Standard (AES) are now one in the same, they both can be called symmetric encryption algorithms; therefore, answers A and D are incorrect. Answer C is incorrect because RC6 is symmetric, too.

64. Answer D is correct. When encrypting and decrypting data using an asymmetric encryption algorithm, you use only the private key to decrypt data encrypted with the public key. Answers A and B are both incorrect because in public key encryption, if one key is used to encrypt, you can use the other to decrypt the data. Answer C is incorrect because the public key is not used to decrypt the same data it encrypted.

65. Answer A is correct. PKCS #11, the Cryptographic Token Interface Standards, defines an API named Cryptoki for devices holding cryptographic information. Answer B is incorrect because PKCS #13 is the Elliptic Curve Cryptography (ECC) standard. Both answers C and D are incorrect because PKCS #4 and PKCS #2 no longer exist and have been integrated into PKCS #1, RSA Cryptography Standard.

66. Answer A is correct. Anonymous access to shared files of questionable or undesirable content should be limited for proper FTP server security. Answer B is incorrect because it is a hardening practice for DHCP services. Answers C and D are incorrect because they are associated with hardening DNS service.

67. Answer A is correct. A buffer overflow occurs when a program or process attempts to store more data in a buffer than the buffer was intended to hold. The overflow of data can flow over into other buffers, overwriting or deleting data. A denial of service is a type of attack in which too much traffic is sent to a host, preventing it from responding to legitimate traffic. A distributed denial of service is similar, but it is initiated through multiple hosts; therefore, answers B and C are incorrect. Although answer D sounds correct, it is not.

68. Answer B is correct. TEMPEST protections involve the hardening of equipment against EMI broadcast and sensitivity. Answers A and C are incorrect because HVAC controls include temperature and humidity management techniques to manage evolved heat in the data center and to minimize static charge buildup. Answer D is incorrect because hot-aisle/cold-aisle schemes provide thermal management for data centers by grouping air intakes on cold aisles and air exhausts on designated hot aisles, making HVAC more effective.

69. Answer D is correct. Hardening of the operating system includes planning against both accidental and directed attacks, such as the use of fault-tolerant hardware and software solutions. In addition, it is important to implement an effective system for file-level security, including encrypted file support and secured file system selection that allows the proper level of access control. Answer A is incorrect because it is a host protection measure, not an OS hardening measure. Answer B is incorrect because this is a feature associated with data security, not host hardening. Answer C is incorrect because this is a secure communication measure.

70. Answer A is correct. In a software-as-a-service (SaaS) environment, application-level encryption is preferred because the data is encrypted by the application before being stored in the database or file system. The advantage is that it protects the data from the user all the way to storage. Answer B is incorrect because in cloud implementations data should be encrypted at the application layer rather than within a database due to the complexity involved, and media encryption is managed at the storage layer. Answer C is incorrect because encryption of a complete virtual machine on infrastructure-as-a-service (IaaS) could be considered media encryption. Answer D is incorrect because a hardware security module (HSM) solution is mainly found in private datacenters that manage and offload cryptography with dedicated hardware appliances.

71. Answer D is correct. Traceroute uses an ICMP echo request packet to find the path between two addresses. Answer A is incorrect because SSL is a public key-based security protocol that is used by Internet services and clients for authentication, message integrity, and confidentiality. Answer B is incorrect because the Internet Protocol Security (IPsec) authentication and encapsulation standard is widely used to establish secure VPN communications. Answer C is incorrect because SNMP is an application layer protocol whose purpose is to collect statistics from TCP/IP devices. SNMP is used for monitoring the health of network equipment, computer equipment, and devices such as uninterruptible power supplies (UPSs).

72. Answer C is correct. Implicit deny is an access control practice wherein resource availability is restricted to only those logons explicitly granted access. Answer A is incorrect because the loop protection feature makes additional checks in Layer 2 switched networks. Answer B is incorrect because a flood guard is a firewall feature to control network activity associated with denial-of-service (DoS) attacks. Answer D is incorrect because port security is a Layer 2 traffic control feature on Cisco Catalyst switches. It enables individual switch ports to be configured to allow only a specified number of source MAC addresses coming in through the port.

73. Answer B is correct. The single loss expectancy (SLE) is the product of the value ($12,000) and the threat exposure (.25), or $3,000. Answer A is incorrect because $1,500 represents the annualized loss expectancy (ALE), which is the product of the SLE and the annualized rate of occurrence (ARO). Answers C and D are incorrect calculated values.

74. Answer D is correct. Combustible metal fires (Class D) require sodium chloride and copper-based dry powder extinguishers. Although dry-pipe would be preferable to wet-pipe sprinklers in regions that experience very low temperatures such as Alaska, water is only appropriate for wood,

paper, and trash fires (Class A), making answers A and B incorrect. Answer C is incorrect because carbon dioxide and Halon extinguishers are useful for fires involving live electric wiring (Class C) and would not be used for burning metals.

75. Answer D is correct. The most likely answer is spoofing because this enables an attacker to misrepresent the source of the requests. Answer A is incorrect because this type of attack records and replays previously sent valid messages. Answer B is incorrect because this is not a type of attack but is instead the granting of access rights based on authentication. Answer C is incorrect because social engineering involves nontechnical means of gaining information.

76. Answer C is correct. WEP is the most basic form of encryption that can be used on 802.11-based wireless networks to provide privacy of data sent between a wireless client and its access point. Answer A is incorrect. Wireless Application Environment (WAE) specifies the framework used to develop applications for mobile devices, including cell phones, data pagers, tablets, and laptops. Answers B and D are incorrect. Wireless Session Layer (WSL), Wireless Transport Layer (WTL), and Wireless Transport Layer Security (WTLS) are the specifications that are included in the WAP standard.

77. Answer A is correct. The loop protection feature makes additional checks in Layer 2 switched networks. Answer B is incorrect because a flood guard is a firewall feature to control network activity associated with denial-of-service (DoS) attacks. Answer C is incorrect because implicit deny is an access control practice wherein resource availability is restricted to only those logons explicitly granted access. Answer D is incorrect because port security is a Layer 2 traffic control feature on Cisco Catalyst switches. It enables individual switch ports to be configured to allow only a specified number of source MAC addresses coming in through the port.

78. Answer C is correct. A false negative result involves access refusal for an authorized user, which makes answer D incorrect. Answers A and B are incorrect because they represent granted resource access.

79. Answer B is correct. Public key encryption is not usually used to encrypt large amounts of data, but it is does provide an effective and efficient means of sending a secret key from which to do symmetric encryption thereafter, which provides the best method for efficiently encrypting large amounts of data. Therefore, answers A, C, and D are incorrect.

80. Answer B is correct. Ports 20 and 21 are used for FTP. Answer A is incorrect because these ports are used for email. Answer C is incorrect because these NetBIOS ports are required for certain Windows network functions such as file sharing. Answer D is incorrect because this port is used for DNS.

81. Answer C is correct. Physical controls include facility design details such as layout, door, locks, guards, and surveillance systems. Management controls include policies and procedures, whereas technical controls include access control systems, encryption, and data classification solutions, making answers A and B incorrect. Access controls include all three classifications (management, technical, and physical), making Answer D incorrect because the question asks for a specific type.

82. Answer C is correct. Although both A and B provide controls for passwords, they are still both based on something the user knows: a password. A one-time use token can be a dedicated hardware token or may be a software token or text message on a mobile device. This would be an example of something the user has (for example, a hardware token or registered mobile device). Answer D is incorrect.

83. Answer A is correct. A VPN tunnel is an example of data security, not physical security. Mantrap, fence, and CCTV are all components of physical security; therefore, answers B, C, and D are incorrect.

84. Answers A, B, and D are correct. A physical security plan should be a written plan that addresses your current physical security needs and future direction. With the exception of answer C, all the answers are correct and should be addressed in a physical security plan. A hard disk's physical blocks pertain to the file system.

85. Answers A and D are correct. A buffer overflow is a direct result of poor or incorrect input validation or mishandled exceptions, and input validation errors are a result of improper field checking in the code. Answer B is incorrect because Cross-site request forgery (XSRF) is an attack in which the end user executes unwanted actions on a web application while they are currently authenticated. Answer C is incorrect because Cross-Site Scripting (XSS) vulnerabilities can be used to hijack the user's session or to cause the user accessing malware-tainted Site A to unknowingly attack Site B on behalf of the attacker who planted code on Site A.

86. Answer B is correct. When formulating a bring-your-own-device (BYOD) policy, the organization should clearly state who owns the data stored on the device, specifically addressing what data belongs to the organization. Answer A is incorrect because key management is intended to provide a single point of management for keys, enable users to manage the lifecycle of keys and to store them securely, and make key distribution easier. Answer C is incorrect because the use of credentials is to validate the identities of users, applications, and devices. Answer D is incorrect because transitive trusts enable decentralized authentication through trusted agents.

87. Answer C is correct. Businesses choose Internet Small Computer System Interface (iSCSI) due to ease of installation, cost, and utilization of current Ethernet networks. Answer A is incorrect. Fibre Channel infrastructure generally is more costly and complex to manage due to the separate network switching infrastructure. Answer B is incorrect. FTP servers provide user access to upload or download files between client systems and a networked FTP server. Answer D is incorrect because HTTPS is used for secured web-based communications.

88. Answer A is correct. A DoS attack is designed to bring down a network by flooding the system with an overabundance of useless traffic. Although answers B and C are both types of DoS attacks, they are incorrect because DoS more accurately describes "a type of attack." Answer D is incorrect because social engineering describes the non-technical means of obtaining information.

89. Answer B is correct. Hardening refers to the process of securing an operating system. Handshaking relates the agreement process before communication takes place; therefore, answer A is incorrect. A hotfix is just a security patch that gets applied to an operating system; therefore, answer C is incorrect. Hardening is the only correct answer; therefore, answer D is incorrect.

90. Answer B is correct. Mobile voice encryption can allow executives and employees alike to discuss sensitive information without having to travel to secure company locations. Answer A is incorrect because in the event a mobile device is lost, GPS tracking can be used to find the location. answer C is incorrect because remote wipe allows a handheld's data to be remotely deleted in the event the device is lost or stolen. Answer D is incorrect because a screen lock or passcode is used to prevent access to the phone.

91. Answer D is correct. Often an option to opt out of further email does not unsubscribe users; instead it means, "send me more spam" because it has been confirmed that the email address is not dormant. This is less likely to occur with email a user receives that he or she opted into in the first place, however. Answers A, B, and C are incorrect because these are less likely and not the best choices.

92. Answer B is correct. The chain of custody provides a clear record of the path evidence takes from acquisition to disposal. Answer A is incorrect because videotaping the actual entrance of a forensics team into the area helps refute claims that evidence was planted at the scene. Answer C is incorrect because hashes allow validation that the forensic analysis itself has not produced unexpected modifications of evidentiary data. Answer D is incorrect because witnesses provide statements about what they saw, when, where, and how.

93. Answer A is correct. Both logon and password represent a form of "what you know" authentication. Answers B, C, D, and E are all incorrect because they represent paired multifactor forms of authentication. A smart card and PIN represent what you have and know, and an RFID chip and thumbprint link what you have with what you are. Gait is a measure of what you do, and iris details are an example of what you are. Somewhere you are is a location, which could be based on GPS coordinates or IP address, and a common access card (CAC) is something you have.

94. Answer C is correct. Role-based access control involves assignment of access rights to groups associated with specific roles, with accounts inheriting rights based on group membership. Answers A and B are incorrect, as requirements for access only from specific locations or only from systems running a trusted OS are examples of rule-based access controls. Time of day restrictions are also rule-based access controls, making answer D incorrect.

95. Answer A is correct. Nonrepudiation means that neither party can deny either having sent or received the data in question. Both answers B and C are incorrect. And repudiation is defined as the act of refusal; therefore, answer D is incorrect.

96. Answer B is correct. Regular review of networks for unauthorized or rogue servers is a practice used to harden DHCP services. Answer A is incorrect because anonymous access to share files of questionable or undesirable content should be limited for proper FTP server security. Answers C and D are incorrect because they are associated with hardening DNS servers.

97. Answer B is correct. The Issuer field identifies the name of the entity signing the certificate, which is usually a certificate authority. The Signature Algorithm Identifier identifies the cryptographic algorithm used by the CA to sign the certificate; therefore, answer A is incorrect. The Subject Name is the name of the end entity identified in the public key associated with the certificate; therefore, answer C is incorrect. The

Subject Public Key Information field includes the public key of the entity named in the certificate, including a cryptographic algorithm identifier; therefore, answer D is incorrect.

98. Answer B is correct. Kerberos authentication enables validation of both endpoints and can help protect against interception attacks such as the "man-in-the-middle." Anonymous connections do not even allow verification of the access requestor, making answer A incorrect. Answers C and D are incorrect because neither TACACS or RADIUS services provide mutual endpoint validation.

99. Answer C is correct. Retinal biometric systems identify unique patterns of blood vessels in the back of the eye. Facial recognition systems identify fixed spacing of key features of the face such as bones, eyes, and chin shape, making answer A incorrect. Answer B is incorrect because iris scanning involves identification of unique patterns in the outer colored part of the eye. Answer D is incorrect because signature analysis is a form of what you do biometric authentication recording the speed, shape, and unique kinematics of a personal written signature.

100. Answer C is correct. SAML (Security Assertion Markup Language) is an Extensible Markup Language (XML) framework for creating and exchanging security information between online partners. The weakness in the SAML identity chain is the integrity of users. To mitigate risk, SAML systems need to use timed sessions, HTTPS, and SSL/TLS. Answer A is incorrect because TACACS+ protocol provides authentication and authorization in addition to accounting of access requests against a centralized service for authorization of access requests. Answer B is incorrect because secure LDAP is a way to make LDAP traffic confidential and secure by using Secure Sockets Layer (SSL) / Transport Layer Security (TLS) technology. Answer D is incorrect because XTACACS is a proprietary version of the original TACACS protocol that was developed by Cisco.

Index

Symbols

J-K

O